SOCIOLOGY AND ITS PUBLICS

THE HERITAGE OF SOCIOLOGY
A Series Edited by Donald N. Levine
Morris Janowitz, *Founding Editor*

SOCIOLOGY AND ITS PUBLICS

The Forms and Fates of
Disciplinary Organization

Edited by
TERENCE C. HALLIDAY
and MORRIS JANOWITZ

THE UNIVERSITY OF CHICAGO PRESS
Chicago and London

Terence C. Halliday is research fellow at the American Bar Foundation and visiting associate professor of sociology at the University of Chicago. He is the author of *Beyond Monopoly: Lawyers, State Crises, and Professional Empowerment,* published by the University of Chicago Press in 1987.

Morris Janowitz (1919–1988) taught sociology at the University of Chicago for twenty-six years. He was founder and general editor of the Heritage of Sociology series. Among his books published by the University of Chicago Press are *The Last Half-Century* (1978) and *The Reconstruction of Patriotism* (1983).

The University of Chicago Press, Chicago 60637
The University of Chicago Press, Ltd., London
© 1992 by The University of Chicago
All rights reserved. Published 1992
Printed in the United States of America

00 99 98 97 96 95 94 93 92   5 4 3 2 1

ISBN (cloth): 0-226-31379-4
ISBN (paper): 0-226-31380-8

Library of Congress Cataloging-in-Publication Data

Sociology and its publics : the forms and fates of disciplinary
   organization / edited by Terence C. Halliday and Morris Janowitz.
        p.   cm. —(The Heritage of sociology)
     Includes bibliographical references and index.
        1. Sociology—United States.   I. Halliday, Terence C. (Terence
Charles).   II. Janowitz, Morris.   III. Series.
HM22.U5S574   1992
301′.0973—dc20   91–38024
                                                                          CIP

Contents

Series Editor's Foreword

This volume, as a multiauthored work focused on a common theme, deviates from the standard format of Heritage of Sociology productions; a word of explanation from the series editor is therefore in order.

I begin with a natural history. In 1985, Morris Janowitz secured a grant from the Spencer Foundation for a project on "the organization and utilization of sociological knowledge." He designed this project to assess "the strength and weakness of social science capabilities" and to appraise "the consequences of sociology for American society." The book he envisioned had two components. First, it would examine the sociological profession. By considering the postwar transformation of the discipline, the recruitment of sociologists, their teaching and training, the tensions of sociological research in the academic setting, the development of university research centers, and the growth of sociology as "big science," it would identify those elements in the recent history and organization of the discipline that affect sociology's capacity to contribute to the work of social institutions. The second component was to be an institution-by-institution evaluation of sociology's influence. By moving from education to medicine to the local community to the military, Janowitz then wanted to track the form and extent of sociology's impact and trace the effects of disciplinary organization on that impact.

In sum, Janowitz aspired to see how effective sociology had been "in contributing to institution building or successful collective problem solving"—though he expected the answer to be: not very. By focusing on this issue and sorting out the conditions of sociology's potential civic contributions, he intended to confront the discipline with a ringing challenge.

The project evolved out of Janowitz's longstanding commitment to what he considered the central disposition of prewar Chicago sociology—a mission to understand and enhance the process of social control, defined as the capacity of a society to regulate itself according to desired principles and values. As James Burk's companion volume in this series, *Morris Janowitz on Social Institutions and Social Control*, makes clear, that commitment animated his earlier studies on the community press and the military profession as well as the studies in which he went on to write forcefully—and to a growing public audience—on institution building in education and in society at large.

For what he surmised would be his final testament, Janowitz turned to sociology itself. Having challenged other institutional domains, he wanted his final legacy to be a searching and provocative appraisal of the enterprise to which he had committed most of his life and to the discipline in whose capacity to enlighten liberal democratic societies he believed passionately. To sociology he would throw down the gauntlet of public service.

Janowitz's progressive incapacitation from Parkinson's disease overtook this task. When it became clear that he could no longer manage the project by himself, he invited Terence Halliday to join him in a collaborative effort. The choice was felicitous. Halliday's interest in civic professionalism, centered on the legal profession's potential for making civic contributions, complemented Janowitz's shift of focus from the obligations of citizens-at-large to the civic responsibilities of the sociological profession, while Janowitz's attention to the internal organization of the field paralleled Halliday's longstanding interest in the conditions of professional mobilization.

The collaborators proceeded to make two changes in the project. They dropped the institution-by-institution evaluation in favor of more sustained analysis of the internal dynamics of sociology. Regarding those dynamics, they articulated three questions that came to structure the papers assembled in this volume: (1) how susceptible are the intellectual agenda and social organization of the discipline to the external influences of state interests, market forces, philanthropic impulses, cultural currents, and political preferences? (2) how do disciplinary, professional, or academic structures affect the theoretical orientations, methodologies, and intellectual coherence of sociology? and (3) how does sociology relate to its diverse audiences?

The second change was to widen the sphere of debate by including sociologists eager to engage these issues but who did not necessarily subscribe to the normative stance embodied in Janowitz's commitment to social control and institution building. The upshot was a conference in November 1988; most of the papers presented at that gathering constitute the present volume. Thanks to the conference's widened compass, the contributors to this volume embrace a refreshing variety of perspectives. Unfortunately, some time before the conference, Morris Janowitz entered a period of worsening health, leading to his untimely death in September 1988.

While I believe it would have been the intention of the founder of this series to include this volume under the imprint of The Heritage of Sociology, I have now chosen to include it on substantive grounds as well. For the effort to attain a critical synoptic view of the present state of the sociological enterprise serves a purpose akin to that represented by the systematic effort to recover the seminal works with which sociology has been endowed by its forebears. In a paper, "On the Heritage of Sociology," published in the volume of essays honoring Morris Janowitz edited by Gerald Suttles and Mayer Zald (*The Challenge of Social Control,* Ablex, 1985), I expressed this point in the following words, which I hope bear repeating:

> Heightened awareness of this complex common heritage of contemporary sociologists may help us to overcome the parochial isolation of our divided specialties and to temper the exorbitant and sterile polemics of many of our scholarly exchanges. In that sense, our rich legacy stands to be drawn on to contribute a mode of self-regulation for the disciplines—to function, in terms featured in other papers in [the festschrift] volume, as a form of social control.

I share the hope of the editors of this volume that its arguments may rekindle a sense of responsibility to the collective purposes of sociology and to the greater society which nourishes it and which it has been deemed to serve.

DONALD N. LEVINE

Acknowledgments

Like the wanderings of Odysseus, this book has had a circuitous route to its final destination. Along the way, I have enjoyed many lively exchanges on the well-being of sociology, been the recipient of generous financial support, profited from thoughtful advice, and enriched my understanding of sociological professionalism and its disciplinary core.

My principal thanks go to Morris Janowitz. This book grew out of many hours of conversation in Morris's living room, lubricated by innumerable cups of coffee, as Morris ranged freely back and forth across the history and geography of the profession, sometimes bemoaning its pretensions, at other times applauding its aspirations, at all times probing for its vulnerabilities. From discontent over methodological individualism to distress over departmental fragmentation, from reservations about excessive specialization to proposals for humanistic encounters, Morris talked trenchantly, ironically, but always perceptively, about sociology and its futures. Many of the questions he raised were subsequently debated, in his absence, at the Arizona conference "Sociology and Institution Building" in November 1988. This volume is not a festschrift, but it is a testimony to disciplinary self-reflection of very much the sort Morris welcomed, if not always to the point he might have made.

Morris had an uncanny ability to put his finger on the pulse of institutional strains. When I invited contributors to reflect sociologically on sociology, their positive, even enthusiastic, responses confirmed Morris's prescience that there were matters troubling to many leaders of the profession that needed a fresh airing, though not all agreed where the trouble lay or how it should be remedied. This book profits enormously from the breadth of perspectives presented by the contributors. Most have had extensive experience in leading public and private universities; several have directed research centers or chaired departments; and a number have been scholarly commentators on the development of the discipline. A few bring some comparative and historical points of view. All view sociology from expansive and illuminating vantage points.

For all this, we make no claim that the contributors represent every shade on the sociological spectrum. There are no advocates of applied or instrumental sociology, and there are no radicals from the poles of the ideological continuum, but to each contributor we are indebted. Both the discussions at the conference and the substance of individual papers owe much to the critical commentaries of James Davis, Joseph Galaskiewicz, Jerome Karabel, Paul Starr, and Stanton Wheeler, some of whose observations have informed my introduction. I am especially grateful to all the contributors to this volume who provided critical comments on the introductory essay.

This project has been made possible by a grant from the Spencer Foundation, which provided generous financial report, and by the flexibility of its vice president, Marion Faldet. The American Bar Foundation, which itself has done much to stimulate scholarly research on professions, provided me with leave and supplementary support. I am grateful to Edward Laumann for his good judgment and periodic lunchtime advice during each stage of the project. Thanks are also due for the research and administrative assistance capably provided by Roya Stern and Scott Parrott and for the highly competent secretarial assistance of Susie Allen and Brenda Smith. Finally, I express my appreciation to Gayle Janowitz, who exemplified patience and courage during the long illness of her husband and whose encouragement helped bring this volume to fruition.

TERENCE C. HALLIDAY

Contributors

TERENCE C. HALLIDAY is a research fellow at the American Bar Foundation and visiting associate professor in the Department of Sociology, University of Chicago. He is editor of the journal *Law and Social Inquiry,* published by the University of Chicago Press, and the author of *Beyond Monopoly: Lawyers, State Crises, and Professional Empowerment* (1987). He is chair of the Working Group on Comparative Studies of Legal Professions (International Sociological Association), and a board member of the ISA Research Committee on the Sociology of Law and the International Institute for the Sociology of Law (Oñati, Spain).

MORRIS JANOWITZ (1919–1988) taught sociology at the University of Chicago for twenty-six years. He served as chairman of the department, directed the Center for Social Organization Studies, helped establish the Committee for the Comparative Study of New Nations, and was the founder and general editor of the Heritage of Sociology series published by the University of Chicago Press. Among his extensive publications are *The Professional Soldier* (1960), *The Last Half-Century* (1978), and *The Reconstruction of Patriotism* (1983). He wrote widely on the profession of sociology and institution building.

* * *

MARTIN BULMER is reader in Social Administration at the London School of Economics and Political Science, where he teaches social research methods, applied sociology, and the sociology of race and ethnic relations. He has also worked as a statistician in British central government, and served on committees of the U.K. Economic and Social Research Council. His publications include *The Chicago School of Sociology* (1984) and *The Social Basis of Community Care* (1987). He has also edited *Essays on the History of British Sociological Research* (1985) and *Social Science Research and Government* (1987), and he has jointly edited *The Goals of Social Policy* (1989) and *The Social Survey in Historical Perspective* (1992).

WILLIAM J. BUXTON is associate professor of Communication Studies at Concordia University in Montréal. He is a former Rhodes Scholar who holds degrees from the University of Alberta, Oxford University, London University, and Die Freie Universität Berlin. Author of *Talcott Parsons and the Capitalist Nation-State: Political Sociology as a Strategic Vocation* (1985), he is currently editing a collection of Parsons's unpublished writings for Princeton University Press and doing research on the professionalization of social science and the humanities in the interwar period.

CRAIG CALHOUN is professor of Sociology, director of International Programs, and director of the Program in Social Theory and Cross-Cultural Studies at the University of North Carolina at Chapel Hill. He is currently chair of the ASA's Committee on International Sociology and chair-elect of the Section on Theoretical Sociology. He is a past chair of the Section on Comparative Historical Sociology. Calhoun is consulting editor for sociology to McGraw-Hill Publishers, coauthor (with Donald Light and Suzanne Keller) of a widely used introductory textbook, and coeditor (with George Ritzer) of sociology's first electronically published customized textbook project, a Social Problems offering. His scholarly publications include *The Question of Class Struggle: Popular Radicalism in Industrializing England* (1982), *Habermas and the Public Sphere* (1991), and a wide variety of articles.

DIANA CRANE is professor and graduate chair of the Department of Sociology at the University of Pennsylvania. She has been a Guggenheim Fellow and a member of the Institute for Advanced Study at Princeton. She is currently chair-elect of the Sociology of Culture Section of the American Sociological Association. Her specialties are the sociology of science, the arts, and culture. She is the author of *Invisible Colleges: Diffusion of Knowledge in Scientific Communities* (1972); *The Sanctity of Social Life: Physicians' Treatment of Critically Ill Patients* (1975); and *The Transformation of the Avant-Garde: The New York Art Market, 1940–1985* (1987).

WILLIAM V. D'ANTONIO is executive officer of the American Sociological Association, 1982–91. He was formerly chair of the sociology departments in Notre Dame and the University of Connecticut and has served as president of AAUP chapters at both universities. He has also served as editor of *Contemporary Sociology* (1980–82), president of the Society for the Scientific Study of Religion, president of the

North Central Sociological Association, vice president of the International Institute of Sociology, and president-elect of the District of Columbia Sociological Society. He is coauthor and coeditor of seven books, including a text, *Sociology: Human Society*, that has been through four editions.

SAMUEL Z. KLAUSNER holds doctorates in psychology and sociology from Columbia University. He has taught at Columbia, Union Theological Seminary, the Hebrew University in Jerusalem, AlMansoura University in Egypt, and Mohammad V University in Rabat. He is now professor of Sociology at the University of Pennsylvania. During the 1970s and 1980s he was director of the Center for Research on the Acts of Man in Philadelphia. He is an author and editor (along with Victor Lidz) of *The Nationalization of the Social Sciences* (1986), an analysis of government support of the social sciences and of a post–World War II effort to persuade Congress to include social science in the National Science Foundation.

LESTER R. KURTZ is associate professor of Sociology at the University of Texas at Austin. He is the author of three books, including *The Nuclear Cage: A Sociology of the Arms Race* (1988), and edits the Peace and War Section newsletter for the American Sociological Association. Kurtz was awarded Indo-U.S. and Fulbright Fellowships for research in India in 1990. He is now writing a monograph on the impact of Gandhian thought on Indian political culture and editing the books *Gods and Bombs: Religious Legitimation of War and Peace* and *The Geography of Nonviolence*.

ALBERT J. REISS, Jr., is the William Graham Sumner Professor of Sociology at Yale University. He has directed research centers at the Universities of Iowa, Wisconsin, and Michigan and chaired departments of sociology at Vanderbilt, Iowa, Michigan, and Yale. As a methodologist, he contributed to survey methodology and is one of the developers of the National Crime Survey. He also developed systematic social observation of natural social phenomena. His article on sociology in the *International Encyclopaedia of the Social Sciences* is a history of the social organization of the discipline.

ALAN SICA has served as associate editor of *Contemporary Sociology* and the *American Journal of Sociology*, was editor and publisher of *History of Sociology: An International Review* for several years, and is currently editor of *Sociological Theory*. Professor of sociology at the

University of Kansas, he has also taught at Amherst College, the University of Chicago, and the University of California/Riverside. He co-edited *Hermeneutics* (1984) and is the author of *Weber, Irrationality, and Social Order* (1988).

HENRY SMALL, who holds a doctorate in the history of science, is director of Corporate Research at the Institute for Scientific Information (ISI) in Philadelphia, Pennsylvania. After three years at the American Institute of Physics' Center for History of Physics, he joined ISI in 1972. His research interest is the use of bibliographic data, and especially citations, to monitor the output of science and study the relations among scientific fields. A long-term goal is to develop clustering and network analysis methods for mapping science through its literature and for tracking the evolution of scientific fields. He is also working on applying these methods to information retrieval problems.

NEIL J. SMELSER is University Professor of Sociology at the University of California, Berkeley, where he has taught since 1958. He has been elected vice president of the American Sociological Association (1973) and vice president of the International Sociological Association. He is also a member of the American Academy of Arts and Sciences and the American Philosophical Society. Among his publications are *Social Change in the Industrial Revolution* (1959), *Theory of Collective Behavior* (1962), *Comparative Methods in the Social Sciences* (1976), and *Social Paralysis and Social Change: British Working-Class Education in the Nineteenth Century* (1991).

STEPHEN P. TURNER is Distinguished Research Professor of Philosophy at the University of South Florida. He has been visiting professor at Virginia Tech., Notre Dame, and Boston University, and he has been elected to positions in various sociological societies, including, most recently, chair of the Theory Section of the American Sociological Association. His books include *Sociological Explanation as Translation* (1980) and *The Impossible Science* (1990) with Jon Turner.

HALLIMAN H. WINSBOROUGH is Emma Welch Conway-Bascom Professor in Sociology at the University of Wisconsin, Madison, and chair of the Social Sciences Computing Cooperative. From 1985 to 1988 Winsborough was chair of Sociology at Wisconsin. From 1967 to 1972 he was director of the Center for Demography at Wisconsin. In 1963 he cofounded the Population Studies Program at Duke University. Winsborough is a demographer who studies demographic change in the United States. From 1978 to 1983 he codirected (with Karl Taeuber and Robert M. Hauser) a project to make machine-readable, public use, sample files from the U.S. Censuses of 1940 and 1950. Those files are now available from the Bureau of the Census and ICPSR.

SOCIOLOGY AND ITS PUBLICS

Introduction: Sociology's Fragile Professionalism

Terence C. Halliday

It is time for a fresh look at the sociological enterprise. Although sociology appears to be comfortably ensconced in academic life, enjoying robust professional associations and an attentive public, the discipline faces troubling developments. Various essays in this book propose that the quality of sociology's graduate student recruits has dropped radically since the late 1960s, that sociology lags well behind history, anthropology, and economics in its appeal to outstanding future scholars, and that the intellectual integrity of sociology is threatened by external financial and managerial pressures. Subspecialties in the discipline have become vulnerable to raids or even annexation by adjacent disciplines. Contributors also assert that the organization of sociology within the university faces powerful centrifugal and sometimes disintegrative forces. They suggest that the substantive core of the discipline may have dissolved. Its public voice has grown dimmer, its prestige in governmental circles has sunk. Whether these developments constitute a crisis is a matter of definition. At the very least, they warrant careful reflection.

It is my purpose in this introductory essay to set these varied claims in context, to bring a disparate set of viewpoints onto a common terrain, and to advance an argument about the complex status of sociology as a profession. This volume calls for renewed attention to sociology's core institutions and activities. By reexamining some of the perennials of professional organization, we seek to stimulate renewed debate about the consequences of the ways in which sociology conducts its affairs. The book makes no claim to be exhaustive and completely systematic in its point of view. It does offer a set of perspectives on issues that have an impact not only on the quality of disciplinary scholarship but, more importantly, on sociology's public presence.

I wish to thank for their comments Neil Smelser, Bill Buxton, Sam Klausner, Bill D'Antonio, Joe Galaskiewicz, Craig Calhoun, Jim Burk, Martin Bulmer, Michael Powell, and Don Levine.

Sociological Professionalism and Institution Building

Self-reflective studies on sociology have addressed a number of themes over the past several decades. A number of scholars in the late 1950s and early 1960s celebrated sociology's coming of age (Lipset and Smelser 1961; Madge 1962) as a scientific and scholarly discipline. Recognition of its enlarged capabilities for the solution of social problems and the attainment of social goals penetrated to the highest levels of national scientific policymaking. A series of reports on the maximal utilization of social science and sociological research were sponsored in the 1960s by the Social Science Research Council (1969), the National Research Council of the National Academy of Sciences (1968), and the Special Commission on the Social Sciences that was set up by the National Science Board (1969). All registered differing prescriptions to the same end—the effective public deployment of advances in social science analysis and methods. This upbeat and optimistic self-appreciation by social scientists was sharply contested in very short order. Friedrichs (1970), Gouldner (1970), Birnbaum (1971), and Colfax and Roach (1971), among others, all challenged what they saw to be naive conceptions of sociology either as a science or as a politically neutral enterprise placing the fruits of its empirical analysis at the service of the public good. This skeptical counterpoint did not deter leaders in the academic profession from continuing to explore more pragmatic contributions of sociology to work settings, evaluation research, and public policy (Demerath, Larson, and Schuessler 1975; Komarovsky 1975; Lazarsfeld, Sewell, and Wilensky 1967; Scott and Shore 1979). Throughout the entire period, institutional and historical appraisals of sociology continued to appear (see Oberschall 1972, Bramson 1961, Carey 1975, and the volumes on the Chicago School by Faris 1967, Bulmer 1984, and Kurtz 1984 in the Heritage of Sociology series), although, for the most part, these concentrated on sociology's childhood and adolescence rather than its mature postwar years.

Although this volume revives questions broached in these earlier self-reflective studies, it differs from them in three respects. In the first place, its subject matter has changed: the state of sociology in the early 1990s has altered perceptibly from what it was fifteen or thirty years ago (see D'Antonio, chap. 3, and Crane and Small, chap. 5, this volume). In addition, the current climate within the discipline allows issues to be debated in a less ideologically charged atmosphere than existed even a decade ago. Finally, its authors are in a position to apply to the sociological profession the more sophisticated range of conceptual resources and substantive insights that have emerged from intervening work on other professions such as medicine and law.

It is instructive in this context to compare the analyses of the sociological enterprise advanced by Talcott Parsons and Morris Janowitz.[1] Both made significant contributions to contemporary understanding of particular professions; both had encompassing visions of professionalism in modern societies. In sharp contrast to the dominant note of criticism that has constituted theoretical discourse over the last two decades, they both envisaged a cooperative relationship between sociology and the larger society. Yet they differed markedly in the ways their views were articulated, and each proceeded almost entirely independently of the other, despite considerable underlying consonance in their views. Most important for our purposes, both turned their formidable analytic powers onto aspects of their own profession's development, organization, and civic vocation. Capsules of their self-reflective understandings can be found in two prominent essays published in 1959 by Parsons and in 1972 by Janowitz, although I will elaborate Janowitz's views with reference to his later writings. Their points of convergence set an intellectual and programmatic point of embarkation for this volume. Their points of divergence emphasize alternative visions of sociology's professionalism.

Intimations of Parsons's later expansive conception of modern professions (Parsons 1968) can be found in the essay on the "problems confronting sociology as a profession," prepared for the 1959 American Sociological Association (ASA) annual meeting. For Parsons, a profession was more than a cluster of roles occupying a privileged niche in the division of labor. It was an occupation with distinctive societal responsibilities. On the one hand, it had "a fiduciary responsibility for any important segment[s] of a society's cultural tradition" as it is perpetuated within the university; on the other hand, sociology also had "responsibility for the application of its knowledge in practical situations" (Parsons 1959:547). This conjunction of fiduciary and practical obligations fused sociology's twin elements: it was at once a discipline and a profession.

The *discipline* of sociology was embedded in the university, which effectively sponsored sociology's full citizenship in the republic of sci-

---

1. Of course, these are not the only two representatives of what might be called a constructivist approach to sociology's professionalism. Perhaps the most notable spokesman in this vein has been Edward Shils, whose "Calling of Sociology" (Shils 1961) was widely influential in the heyday of functionalist orthodoxy. For further discussion of Shils, Parsons, and Janowitz, see the chapters by Buxton and Turner, and Sica.

ence. From this "secure locus," painstakingly institutionalized over the preceding half-century, sociology's research enterprise generated new knowledge according to the canons of science. Sociologists were obliged to regenerate their own enterprise by advancing and transmitting their knowledge to successive generations of scholars. Moreover, the discipline was expected to carry its weight in the general scientific enterprise, in part, it can be assumed, by providing its theory and findings to other scholarly enterprises and in part by scrutinizing the academy itself as a social process.

Nevertheless, the responsibilities of sociology as a *profession* demanded that the knowledge developed by the discipline be carried outside the university.[2] In his ASA report, Parsons briefly encapsulated his views on the need for "good citizenship . . . in the general society" (Parsons 1959:559). One set of commitments would take an applied turn: sociological knowledge would be made available to government departments, corporations, social agencies, and professions such as education, law, public administration, business, and divinity. Another set of obligations would go to clarification of "society's general 'definition of the situation'" (1959:548). By deploying its analytic insight, its empirical knowledge, and a worldview in counterpoint to psychology, sociology might play an ideological role by framing general public discourse and "intellectual preoccupations" in its own distinctive terms.

Nevertheless, for Parsons there is a sharp disjunction between sociology's disciplinary commitments within the academy and its civic obligations to wider publics. The critical function of the discipline lies in the development of an intellectual tradition within the scientific community. As a scientific discipline, sociology "is clearly primarily dedicated to the advancement and transmission of empirical knowledge" and only "secondarily to the communication of such knowledge to non-members and its utilization in practical affairs" (Parsons 1959:547). Indeed, the historical development of the discipline must be seen as a process of differentiation of the sociological enterprise from the practical concerns that preoccupied its formative years in the United States. In this sense, Parsons's disjunction of pure and applied sociology has a sequential logic: the latter is a by-product of the former, an application of empirical research driven by intellectual agendas in the inner logic of scientific development. While Parsons shares with Janowitz a recognition of sociology's civic potentialities, for the

2. A more elaborate account of Parsons's earlier efforts as a prophet of sociological professionalism is provided by Buxton and Turner in chapter 11.

former they are secondary and derivative but for the latter they are inseparable and, indeed, constitutive of each other.

This critical difference may account for Janowitz's almost willful neglect of Parsons in his plowing of the same field some thirteen years later. Yet the differences should not detract from fundamental points of consensus in their common assumptions that the secure institutionalization of sociology in the academy has repercussions for sociology's professional responsibilities to publics outside the university. It is in his 1972 essay that reflections on the professionalization of sociology presaged Janowitz's provocative thesis in *The Reconstruction of Patriotism* (1983), which in turn laid the groundwork for an even more expansive conception of sociological professionalism. The argument in *Patriotism* drew moral force from T. H. Marshall's contention that the "balance between rights and obligations," in British society, "had moved too far towards rights." In Janowitz's view, over the preceding half-century the American preoccupation with "an expansion in the substance or procedure of citizen rights" had not been adequately balanced with the "clarification of citizen obligations" (Janowitz 1983:x). Citizenship, he contended, was integral to political freedom. For every entitlement there should be a commensurate duty. Hence the behavior of individuals in a democratic polity was more than an expression of narrow self-interest; it was—and should be—motivated "by a sense of moral responsibility for the collective well-being" (Janowitz 1983:xii).

While the thrust of *Patriotism* was directed to the inculcation of civic consciousness in the young, much of the impetus behind that volume found expression in an elaborated conception of sociological professionalism. Just as it was the responsibility of the individual citizen to develop a civic consciousness that complemented rights with duties, so too it was the obligation of a profession to engage in civic action. In Janowitz's thought, professionalism thus became fused with a civic comportment to be expressed through institution building. "When I speak of institution building," he wrote, "I mean those conscious efforts to direct societal change and to search for more effective social control which are grounded in rationality and in turn are supported by social science efforts" (Janowitz 1978:400). Political elites, in tandem with "enlarged citizen participation," were charged with the creation, adaptation, and maintenance of the central social organizations of liberal democratic societies. Sociology's role is to bring the "application of the scientific method to social and political reality" to decision makers and the public-at-large (1978:401). It employs data and theory to analyze organizational performance and measures

the adequacy of internal decision making and the processes of delib-
eration. Sociology reveals gaps between expected and actual outcomes, and it elaborates theories to account for both. Armed with
data and theory, sociology can provide a basis—and recognize it as
incomplete at best—for organizational or institutional adaptation.

Janowitz sharpened his views on sociology's corporate responsibility by contrasting two sociological orientations towards social institutions, namely, the engineering and enlightenment models (1970;
1972). They differ in their objectives, clients, and approach to research. In the engineering model, sociology is "concerned with definitive answers to specific questions and particular hypotheses in order
to make concrete suggestions" on matters of the moment (1970:252).
Engineering sociology's reach is constrained and its conclusions are
self-consciously particular. It responds directly to the precise requests
of particular clients, whether government agencies or corporations. Its
methodology is usually individualistic and, by necessity (for convenience and scienticity), leans toward cross-sectional surveys. This type
of sociology was personified in the applied sociology of Paul Lazarsfeld and found its capital at the Bureau of Applied Social Research.

Enlightenment sociology, by contrast, directs its research to long-
term trends of major social institutions. It explores major policy and
institutional alternatives, bringing data and analysis to bear on each.
Hence its findings provide resources for decision making rather than
explicit recommendations for action. For enlightenment sociologists,
"sociology produces knowledge which increases one's understanding
of the social process. . . . It assists elected officials, policy makers, administrators, and the citizenry to make more effective decisions, to
think more effectively, both by sharpening their conceptual outlook
and by supplying basic information" (Janowitz 1978:404). Its findings are not directed to particular clients "under license" but to a
variety of publics. It is didactic rather than programmatic. As its objectives and auspices differ, so too do its forms of research. Because
enlightenment sociology reaches to broader theory and longer-term
processes and problems, it has a greater degree of methodological
eclecticism. Its units of analysis are more institutional than individual,
and its reach is systemic.

A critical difference between the two perspectives turns on the issue
of autonomy. The merits of the enlightenment approach, argued Janowitz, inhere exactly in its greater autonomy from the opportunities of the market, the expectations of government, or the current concerns of foundations. By diversifying its methods, by treating issues
that transcend limited study, and by broadening its auspices, sociology

can demonstrate its worth by addressing the fundamental questions of society in a holistic manner. Moreover, the varieties of its theory, the multiple levels of analysis, and the complementarity of its several methods allow the discipline to provide less specific but more broadly informed contributions to public debate and awareness. Sociology in this mode offers thoughtful reflection and social intelligence on issues without arrogating to itself a false certitude expressed through specific recommendations.

Janowitz maintains a sober realism about the promise of sociology's professional responsibilities. He observed the excessive promises and ultimate inadequacy of many explicit policy recommendations made during the War on Poverty in the 1960s. Consequently, it would be imprudent of sociology to "supply specific answers to 'social problems'" (1978:404). It was a false expectation that sociological knowledge could "produce definitive answers on which professional practice can automatically be based" (1972:108). Moreover, sociology's contributions were necessarily incomplete without either the insights of the other social sciences or the value-analysis of the humanities. An acute awareness of the discipline's own "intellectual limits and defects" (1976:403), combined with the complex political barriers to change, convinced Janowitz that sociology should temper the boldness of its claims without abdicating the responsibility of its civic obligations.[3]

Sociology's own exemplary displays of civic comportment in the enlightenment mode were represented by its participation in several major public commissions before and after World War II. Robert Park, his black graduate student Charles Johnson, and several other members of the University of Chicago sociology department played a notable role in the inquiries of the Chicago Commission on Race Relations, which was established in 1919 following race riots. The natural history of the riot contained in the commission report explored both its causes and the adequacy of the response by social control agencies. Ten years later, William Ogburn of Chicago and Howard Odum of the University of North Carolina sociology department

---

3. Compare Janowitz's (1970:263–64) stinging critique of professional psychologists who, at once, he charges, were unable to distance themselves from "the anti-philosophical, anti-historical, narrowly means-oriented, and optimistic character of much American thought and culture," and who proffered "a fantastic exaggeration of the potentialities of social science." These reservations about the social sciences may be contrasted with the more expansive expectations of applied social science expressed in the recently published essay by Talcott Parsons (1986), which was submitted to the Social Science Research Council in 1948.

headed the research team that produced extensive statistical indicators for Herbert Hoover's Research Committee on Recent Social Trends. Even Gunnar Myrdal's searching inquiry on "the Negro problem" in American society, published as *An American Dilemma* (1962), made extensive use of sociologists in its compilation of extensive data and its conceptual and theoretical analysis.

Janowitz found less compelling instances of enlightenment sociology in post–World War II commissions, although he applauded the contributions of sociologists to the National Commission on the Causes and Prevention of Violence and aspects of the Coleman Report on racial segregation in schools. Yet his reservations about these commissions usefully display the obverse of the enlightenment concept of professionalism. In the case of the Kerner Commission, for instance, he faulted the breadth of documentation and the incomplete assessment of what valuable data were collected. While he praised the mass of data collected by sociologists, among others, for the Eisenhower Commission on Violence, he had reservations about how effectively the findings were integrated or how adequately connections were made with policy issues. He criticized the failure of the Coleman Report to explore fully enough the policy alternatives to busing that might have effected school integration. In part, that lapse followed from the limits of the survey data on which the report primarily relied, a recurring methodological motif in much of Janowitz's writing on sociological professionalism.

These examples clarify Janowitz's concept of a civic sociology. It is a discipline-cum-profession where there is a disposition towards the public good. That disposition is vindicated by a pattern of professional activity that includes the following elements. First, sociologists orient much of their research and thinking towards major social problems, recurring institutional strains, or tears in the social fabric that may threaten the liberal political and social order. Identification of problems rests not only on the definitions of situations provided by public officials or particular interest groups, but also on the trained perceptions of social scientists themselves. That is, the scholar bears some responsibility for perceiving institutional breakdown or human misery that may not be apparent to others. Second, sociologists gather extensive data on issues of institutional failure or breakdown. These data may include but cannot be restricted to cross-sectional survey data. Indeed, adequate understanding usually always demands historical or natural history approaches together with a research style that obtains understanding of social processes from close observation of institutional processes through field work. Third, the eclectic forms of data that are collected by the researcher will be analyzed in "fundamental sociological terms" by making use of the concepts and theories of sociology. Such analysis should produce an accounting of current or prospective policies with a careful weighing of the likely consequences of alternatives. Their strengths and weaknesses should be appraised within the limits of the empirical findings and conceptual formulations. Fourth, both the data and its interpretation will be conveyed to political leaders, the media, and the public at large without compromising sociology's "dual responsibility" to the academy and society at large. Janowitz repudiated a sociology whose products were limited to unconstructive critique. Enlightenment sociology entailed a moral obligation for institutional adaptation.

As Burk has pointed out, Janowitz echoed John Dewey's conviction that "social science research was part of a larger social process of public discussion." The ultimate validation of sociology "depended on its contribution to public enlightenment" about social problems. Within the pragmatic framework, "sociological practice involve[d] a commitment to social reconstruction" (Burk 1991:43, 68). Furthermore, sociology should act as something of a public pedagogue (Janowitz 1970:251). Dennis Smith (1988) observes that Chicago sociologists had two broad approaches to moral issues: some, such as W. I. Thomas, were activists, and others, including Small, Park, and Janowitz, were "persuaders." Thus Janowitz's expectations of the profession were consistent with a long-standing Chicago commitment to the "educability of American public opinion" and hence the enlightenment of American civic culture (Smith 1988:8). It was sociology's duty, therefore, to instruct the citizenry-at-large about the conditions of key social institutions and to combine social intelligence with measured analysis. Janowitz conceived of a service profession from which a stream of empirical findings, data, analysis, and insight would constantly flow into the public arena.

Why, then, Janowitz's ambitious project on the worth of sociology? In the 1980s, sitting at the University of Chicago almost a century after the founding of its department of sociology, Janowitz quite plausibly may have been seeking to reformulate or revivify a professional identity he associated with the department from its inception (Hobsbawm and Ranger 1983). Indeed, he portrayed Chicago sociology as an early model of enlightenment sociology with periodic skirmishes, of varying severity, with the engineering approach as it was exemplified by the Bureau of Applied Social Research.

However, Janowitz's work through the early 1980s did not systematically deal with two critical issues. In the first place, while he could point to the occasional public inquiry in which the discipline had made a perceptible impact, there existed no adequate evaluation of the actual impact sociology had made upon institutions such as education, law, the military, the community, or the health system. His own magisterial appraisals of several institutions in *The Last Half-Century* began this process without completing it. In the second place, and most salient for this volume, at no point did Janowitz systematically canvass the conditions under which sociology could adequately acquit itself of the technical and moral calling that civic professionalism demanded. It was this second concern, which emanated from a lifetime of reflection on the institution of sociology itself, that led to the evaluative project from which this volume developed.

An Equivocal Status

By the standards of the medical and military professions, which had engaged the respective minds of both Parsons and Janowitz, there was and is a certain peculiarity about the character of sociology's professionalism that appears at odds with the expansive expectations expressed in their work. Compared to most professions that have informed these theoretical formulations, sociology has an equivocal status. As a "profession," sociology has no generally accepted authority or "knowledge mandate" over a particular set of problems that it can legitimately claim as its own. It has no discernible clientele outside the academy. It has no monopoly over an area of work. Admission to its ranks has a de facto credential—of a doctoral degree in sociology itself—determined by the labor market, but it has no legal force, it is administered in an entirely decentralized manner, and it is not infrequently honored in the breech, often by its most prestigious institutions, who may appoint scholars to sociology departments whose disciplinary training is in history, political science, or some other cognate field. Its professional associations are relatively weak and its codes of ethics weaker still.[4] As a profession, therefore, sociology fits uneasily with the lofty aspirations envisaged by Parsons and Janowitz.

Of course, it may be objected that a comparison between sociology and the stereotypes of standard professionalism is fundamentally misconceived. If sociology has any claim to professionalism, it can only

4. The comparison is most sharply drawn with law and medicine. Nonetheless, the ASA executive director, William D'Antonio, believes that among academic disciplines the ASA Code is probably the strongest of the social sciences, and quite possibly of the humanities as well.

be in the sheltered niche it occupies in the academic profession. As Ben-David (1972:87, 91) argued, in postwar America the academic profession has been thoroughly institutionalized around the pursuit of research and the training of professional researchers in the university. Professional authority has drawn heavily on the prestige of science, in the first instance, through the accepted value of fundamental research and, in the second instance, through its application of research to industry and government. Research, therefore, became "a professional service like law or medicine" (Ben-David 1972:102). The doctorate was its primary credential, the university its guarantor. At once, therefore, universities provided a professional service to prospective private and public clients as, concomitantly, their professional schools prepared doctors, lawyers, teaches, nurses, architects, and engineers, among others, for admission to restricted occupations, which are based on knowledge and expertise authenticated by academic qualifications. So important has this function become in the latter part of the twentieth century that one social historian has labelled academics the "key profession" (Perkin 1969).

Sociology has a fairly secure niche within the academic profession and the university. Most major American universities consider it necessary to have a sociology department, and the discipline appears fairly well institutionalized by the standard criteria of disciplinary identity. Sociology has its national association, its journals, its scholarly networks, its line item at the National Science Foundation, its annual meetings. Even so, its identity is a little peculiar, if not completely exceptional. As an occupation, sociology has no clear image or demarcated terrain of work outside the university. In contrast to psychology, no clinical occupation has emerged.[5] In contrast to economics, no distinctive role has been institutionalized in private industry or public administration. In contrast with history, no curricular slot has been reserved for sociology in the standard secondary school curriculum. And in contrast with political science, there is no obvious institution where graduates would seem to have an immediate affinity. Somewhat more akin to anthropology, the principal educational product of sociology departments in the university system is therefore absorbed by the university itself. Sociologists who are graduated with first or terminal degrees and who do not embark on careers in higher education are dispersed imperceptibly throughout the labor market.

---

5. In a private communication, Albert Reiss noted that sociology in the United States began with an applied profession—that of social work. Although many departments of sociology, including Chicago, did their best to divest themselves of their social work wings, had they failed to do so, sociology might well be the largest professional-cum-academic society in the social sciences.

The only discernible professional career in sociology is located in the academy.[6]

Sociology's only reasonable claim to a recognizably conventional professionalism, therefore, is inseparable from its standing in the university. Having established the inextricability of sociology and the academy, however, merely pushes the question of its societal responsibilities back one step without resolving it. The vulnerability of sociology's professional standing independent of the university means its capacity to exercise professionalism through institution building will turn, in the first place, on the general robustness of the academic profession and its host institution, the university, and, in the second place, on sociology's standing within that profession and, most notably, within the university itself. This book makes problematic what Parsons and Janowitz largely took for granted—the secure institutionalization of sociology as a discipline-cum-profession within the university.

Contingencies of Professionalism

Like many other disciplines, sociology experiences an enduring tension between its intellectual integrity as a scholarly discipline and its civic obligations as a public profession. Its social organization is highly implicated in its capacity to resolve this tension. But in contrast to other disciplines, such a tension may be experienced more acutely in sociology and its resolution managed less adeptly. The remainder of this essay, and the chapters that follow, reflect on several facets of this tension: intellectual autonomy, disciplinary identity, academic organizations, and alternative audiences or publics.

Vulnerabilities to Exogenous Influences

Sociology's reflections on other professions point to pervasive problems of control and legitimacy. On the one hand, it is a defining characteristic of professionalism that an occupation obtain some control over its domain of work, though the types and extent of that control vary widely over professions and time. On the other hand, the special sorts of control to which most professions aspire are founded on a

---

6. This observation does not conflict with data on the extensive employment of sociologists [with first or doctoral degrees] outside higher education, in such practices as the civil service, research organizations, and industry. It proposes that the only *clear image* of a career as a sociologist lies in the academy.

particular claim to legitimacy. This special authority may be sought for priority over certain areas of work, for the distinctiveness of a profession's knowledge and expertise, for a particular style of career, or for certain regulatory mechanisms. It is a central conundrum of professionalism that the value of autonomy from clients must frequently be legitimated and institutionalized by the very parties that periodically may have an interest in curtailing that autonomy.

As Johnson (1972) brought clearly into focus, much of what professionalism is about must be understood by the relationships a profession has with its clients. When that "client" happens to be the state, a profession risks complete absorption within the bureaucratic apparatus of public administration. Of course, the gamut of relationships between professions and state runs widely. If professions are not completely absorbed within the state, as is the case with the military or the British civil service, the state may still be a heavy consumer of professional services; it may be a direct employer of significant numbers of professionals; it may subsidize professional work by providing a variety of monetary supplements (as in subsidized medicine) or tax concessions (as in tax preparation fees), and it may use professions as instruments of public control. Yet it is this same client that can extend or withhold legitimation through its legal capacity to protect occupations from competition or incursion.

Something of this same tension between professions and clients carries over into the private sector. Individuals and corporations may recognize, at least in principle, the value of professional autonomy and the benefits of professional independence. They may be aware that excessive encroachment on professional autonomy can work against their own interests in obtaining expert advice that is not compromised by excessive defensiveness. Furthermore, they may legitimate that autonomy through lip service and political restraint. Yet powerful clients also shop for the accounting firms that will be accommodating to a self-serving social construction of the company accounts, and they look for law firms that will tell them what they want to hear—in other words, they use their economic leverage or political influence to buy a particular result at the expense of professional detachment.

We should not expect that sociology will be immune from such pressures. In the United Kingdom, where the academic profession of sociology is resident almost completely within the state education system, various structural arrangements and cultural understandings have provided degrees of freedom from direct political or administrative interference. Yet, as events in recent years have shown, a hostile government can substantially erode the economic resources and structural defenses that universities, university grants committees, committees of vice-chancellors, and research councils, among others, had erected around the academic profession (Westergaard and Pahl 1989). In the United States, the academic profession of sociology is institutionally lodged in a much more variegated system where various levels of government and private resources sustain a bewildering array of educational institutions. In one respect, this very diversity provides a classic American constitutional solution to the problem of state control. In another respect, however, it multiplies the forces that can exert control over the functions and structure of the academy.

Sociology may be exceptionally vulnerable to external influences that impinge only slightly on other branches of the academic profession, in part because it appears unusually implicated in the object of its inquiry and in part because the mantle of the university cannot entirely protect it from subtle incursions or even frontal assault. The contributors to this volume, and particularly some of the early chapters, draw attention to both incursions and assaults that might threaten sociology's intellectual integrity. Some of these emerge from national values, public policy, and popular culture; some from the patronage influence of government and private foundations; and others from the impact of labor markets. How sociology copes with these forces substantially determines its independent capacity for civic responsibility. Sociology's capacity to bring a detached perspective to civic issues is constricted by too little legitimacy and too much external control. These factors may compromise its focus, hinder it from identifying problems that are not high on the public agenda of the moment, distort its findings and interpretations. Too little control or too much autonomy may contribute to isolation, irrelevance, and ultimately an alternative sort of delegitimation.

Smelser (chap. 1) makes the case that generic American values, such as individualism, voluntary cooperation, moral consensus as a basis of social order, and incremental approaches to social change serve not only to distinguish American sociology from much sociology elsewhere, but from other disciplines, such as economics. A good deal of the internal dynamism of the discipline arises from the friction between concepts and theories that draw deeply from American culture, such as role theory, functionalism, and social exchange theory, and those that owe their provenance to European scholarship, with its sometime focus on domination, coercion, and class conflict.[7] Indeed, it is in the spirit of just such a European counterpoint that Sica (chap.

---

7. For two very recent European commentaries on American sociology, see the contributions by Alain Touraine and Niklas Luhman in Gans (1990).

10) attacks Janowitz's notion of institution building as a concept that reflects an outmoded, and quintessentially American, epistemology. Cultural orientations may equally well take issues off sociology's substantive agenda. Kurtz (chap. 2) indicates that the aversion of mass popular culture to thinking about nuclear annihilation has been reflected in the marginal importance the discipline has given to war and peace. As a result, military sociology has a peripheral status in the discipline, despite the consumption of more public resources by the military than any other American institution.

Although sociology appears deeply permeated by ascendant cultural values, it scarcely responds in a united chorus. But its enduring search for legitimacy, and its need for financial resources, may lead the profession to harness its research interests to prevailing cultural moods. Hence the health of the discipline may ebb and flow with its adeptness at presenting a public image concordant with the values of its audiences and clients. When the cultural mood resonates with core values of the discipline, it will flourish—perhaps through improved recruitment, a faster flow of resources, and more sympathetic audiences. When the tide of affinity begins to ebb, the discipline may resist and become relatively impoverished, or it may feel incumbent to reconstruct itself in the image of disciplines that are favored by the new ascendant values—which may amount to a different kind of impoverishment. This interpretation might help explain, at once, Crane and Small's finding (chap. 5) that over the last fifteen years centrifugal forces have decentered sociology, that economics currently exerts a magnetic attraction for the sociological imagination, and D'Antonio's (chap. 3) statistics on the decline in the quality of sociology's recruits since the mid-1960s.

Even if the degree of mutual entailment between the sociological observer and the observed exceeds those of most other disciplines, there are clear exceptions to sociology's permeability by ambient milieus. One need only to point to sociology's general aversion to law and religion, and to its marked neglect of banking, the insurance industry, and much else in the business and financial sectors. Sociology has passed by not only the military, as Kurtz convincingly argues in chapter 2, but many of the key institutions in advanced capitalist societies.

While the influence of cultural values may be diffuse, the impact of the state and private foundations in their various manifestations represent at once a prime source of sociology's legitimation and a keen threat to its autonomy. Smelser believes that while the university has sheltered the discipline from ideological political pressure, there nevertheless remains a deep ambivalence in government toward sociology. The demands of the welfare state require reliable information on the populations that benefit from it and the institutions that administer it. Yet sociology is criticized for the softness of its methods, the trivial issues it addresses, and the critical tone in much of its discourse. Government exerts a powerful influence on what gets research funding and therefore what gets researched. Moreover, because government officials are disposed to quantitative empirical data, they encourage a positivistic, empirical science model of sociology. To the extent sociology covets the legitimacy of the state, it must clothe itself in scientific garb.

This legitimation strategy carries its own risks. As long as sociology can persuade influential publics that it owes allegiance to the republic of science, it may borrow the charisma of the scientific establishment. Quite apart from the instability of that republic, however, the manifest gap between sociology's claims of scientific precision and the adequacy of predictions and explanations it can deliver may lead to the unmasking of sociology as an impostor and delegitimate it even further. It was precisely this overreaching that drew Janowitz's urging that sociology retreat to defensible ground, to enlightenment and illumination rather than to the pretensions of social engineering.

If the state helps legitimate a particular conception of sociological knowledge, its enormous resources should also enable it to influence sociology's substantive agenda. However, the evidence presented in this volume is mixed. The pivotal events in the growth of the American state during this century left various imprints on the discipline. The social reconstruction surrounding Roosevelt's New Deal would seem to have offered a great step forward for sociology. But Bulmer (chap. 9:338) believes that social scientists failed to make any major inroads into national planning and that the New Deal brought only years of disappointment for social scientists in general. Greater opportunities opened up in World War II. Sociologists like Janowitz and Shils served with other social scientists in the Psychological Warfare Division of the Supreme Headquarters Allied Expeditionary Force. Government funding for scientific research contracts grew markedly. *The American Soldier* exemplified the promise of large surveys. Other sociologists found their way into programs training officers for military occupation as the victorious Allies advanced across Europe and Asia (Buxton and Turner, chap. 11). For Klausner (chap. 6), one of the principal legacies of wartime support for social science was the promise of "large scale and large budget" research—big science, in other words.

Wartime notwithstanding, Kurtz is unconvinced that massive government funding has the capacity to mold sociology's substantive agenda at will. The experience of military sociology presents a limiting case. While enormous investments have been made in social science research by the military—the Army Research Institute for the Behavioral and Social Sciences had a 1988 budget that exceeded the combined research budgets of NSF, NIMH, and the Department of Education—most of these resources are absorbed within the military. Other government granting agencies maintain a hands-off policy. In any event, the ideological dispositions of sociologists are generally resistant to research on war and the war-machine, underlining Janowitz's more general view that "the development of a topic of special interest only partially reflects budgetary support" (Kurtz, chap. 2:82). The contrary relationship between funding and subdisciplinary development is exemplified by the growth of Marxist sociology since the 1960s. As Crane and Small demonstrate, Marxism has emerged as an important subspecialty in the discipline. Yet we can assume that unless suitably disguised, its prominence will have owed little to the infusion of government research moneys. In short, the vulnerability of sociology to state influence partly depends on the costs of research and support for certain topics and styles of research. Where scholarship does not depend on the collection of vast data sets, with their demands for major investments in labor and capital, then disciplinary specialties may be less susceptible to manipulation by the state, however well intended.

Private foundations present a similar problem, but on a narrower front. Bulmer and Klausner agree on the extensiveness of external influence, but they focus on different points of impact. Bulmer argues that major foundations, such as Rockefeller, Carnegie, and Russell Sage "had a disproportionate influence upon the early expansion of empirical social science." Rockefeller, for instance, made an extraordinary impact through its huge block grants on the institutionalization of sociological research in such centers as Chicago, North Carolina, and the London School of Economics. It also laid the groundwork for the large-scale grant-aided research that became so prominent after WWII. Moreover, Rockefeller affected the development of social science disciplines through its emphasis on interdisciplinarity in the 1920s and early 1930s (cf. also Buxton and Turner on Harvard), and a move back towards disciplinarity in the later 1930s as a result of its shift from block to project grants. But Bulmer rejects hegemonic or class explanations of philanthropic influence. He is clearly uncomfortable about generalizing from Coser's notion that foundations acted as gatekeepers "and that an elective affinity developed between foundation officials and large-scale research entrepreneurs." While foundation support was a necessary condition for sociology's development, it was scarcely sufficient. In any event, some foundation initiatives did not come to fruition. In others there were unintended consequences. Indeed, it is not altogether clear that the flow of influence did not work in reverse—that foundations were the servants of academics, and depended on their ideas for philanthropic direction, rather than vice versa.

Klausner is less sanguine about the patronage of either foundations or the state when it takes the form of contract research. "Sponsorship . . . is the exercise of power" and "research sponsors wield a big stick, a stick given them by the research community in its hunger for support" (Klausner chap. 6:236). As in other sciences, he argues, the practice of contract research in sociology has an adverse effect on hiring practices, alters the internal distribution of power within the department and university, and changes the curriculum to conform to current contract research topics. It produces conflict within the department and the university. It may also distort the methodological orientations of the discipline in ways that impoverish sociological explanation (see Reiss, chap. 8). As an alternative he proposes that contract research be lodged outside the university in a research corporation, with an independent governance structure—a form of administration tailored to the needs of research enterprises and with an attenuated relationship to the core functions of the university, such as basic research and teaching.

Sociology's legitimacy and control over its focus and theory, methods and discourse, also stems from its market for educational consumers. Buxton and Turner point out that sociology has failed to sustain itself either through support from the general public for its writings or from support by government and private foundations for its research. It has no products that can support more than a fraction of its practitioners on the open market. Consequently, it depends on its teaching function to maintain academic professional work and to ensure the continuity of the profession as an institution. The public legitimacy accorded the profession therefore comes not only from the state, but also from who chooses to study sociology and to pursue careers in the field. Furthermore, the quality of the profession's research for any of its patrons or publics rests heavily on its recruits. Conceivably, so too do its substantive emphases, methodological styles, and theoretical leanings.

The evidence on recruitment presented by D'Antonio (chap. 3) leaves little room for self-congratulation on this account. It raises vexing questions about legitimacy, and it allows the interpretation that much of the intellectual direction of the discipline enters with its students. D'Antonio reports that the scores of *prospective* sociology graduate students on the Graduate Record Examination rank below all other social science disciplines, with the exception of education. On both the verbal and quantitative scales, sociology falls well below anthropology and history, and it is radically lower on the quantitative scale than economics. Indeed, on average, *humanities* graduate students in general have perceptibly higher scores on qualitative *and* quantitative scales than sociologists. Moreover, on the GRE subject test scores, there has been a radical drop in average scores of prospective sociology graduate students from 535 in 1966 to 427 in 1986. By contrast, economics scores fluctuated around 600, with a low of 581 in 1970–71 and a high of 623 in 1984–85.[8]

Quite apart from these admittedly narrow indicators of recruitment quality, sociology has also experienced a massive loss of students. The 35,491 majors in 1974 had declined by two-thirds to approximately 12,000 by 1985 before beginning a slow rise in the late 1980s. Between 1976 and 1985 the number of Ph.D.'s graduated from sociology departments fell from 729 to 480. Proportionately, sociology's loss of undergraduates was not so radical as that of history, but then neither did it fare so well as economics or psychology. Its loss of doctoral graduates kept roughly in step with anthropology and political science. Undoubtedly, however, the most unsettling of these statistics concern the decline in quality. The contribution of sociology to institution building must ultimately depend on the intellectual worth of its practitioners. The lower the quality of sociologist, the more limited the capacity of the discipline to fulfill the sorts of civic responsibilities articulated by Janowitz. And if the absolute decline in quality were not enough, the relative decline within the university erodes the standing of sociology in its host institution and subverts the authority of its public pronouncements.

How are these declines in numbers and quality to be explained? Why is it that sociology graduate students on average underperform most other social sciences? Why does the standardized test score pro-

---

8. Considerable caution should be exercised in the interpretation of these figures. They are the scores of *prospective*, not actual, enrollees in graduate department. The subject scores presumably count against a discipline that draws many graduate students from undergraduate majors in other disciplines. And, of course, there are also the proper reservations about the adequacy of multiple choice questions as indicators of academic achievement and promise.

file of the sociology graduate student contrast so strikingly with that of the anthropology student, despite the close intellectual affinity of the two fields? Tantalizing speculations are offered in several of the papers and the conference proceedings. It is noticeable, for instance, that the radical slide in graduate GRE scores coincides remarkably closely with the right turn of American politics and the muting of campus and social protest. The high point was in 1968. Then came the fall. Other disciplines fell, too, but they bottomed out quickly. Sociology continued to fall for twelve to thirteen years. One speculative reading might be that sociology attracted its best students precisely when it was most radicalized. A critical orientation attracted good students who otherwise would not have found sociology to be substantively appealing or intellectually demanding. As sociology moved away from social criticism, its best recruits moved from sociology. Curiously enough, then, these data prompt the speculation that while a scientific commitment may garner support from government, it is a reform commitment that stimulates the interest of students. Should this be correct, it places sociology in a double bind: to gain the respect from one constituency demands it compromise its reputation with another.

The comparison with anthropology is particularly intriguing because, as Calhoun (chap. 4) observes, they are very close cousins. One view has it that anthropologists have historically been recruited from higher social classes and are therefore better prepared educationally. It may be that anthropology's focus on ancient or primitive sites captures the imagination of more intellectually inquiring minds. Calhoun has proposed that another part of the answer may lie in the teaching of the two disciplines. Whereas anthropology introduces new students to the classic works of fieldworkers who have attempted to embrace holistic understandings of small societies, sociology most often treats its first-year students to abstracted generalizations in bland textbooks that do not ignite first-rate minds.

During the late eighties, sociology's graduate student body had also begun to shift in composition. According to D'Antonio, women now make up 53–59 percent of the students enrolled in graduate departments. Foreign students now make up a quarter to a third of all enrollments in sociology graduate departments. What are the implications of these figures for the future of the discipline? Sociology seems to be especially permeable by the background experiences and attributes of its new recruits. It has been variously proposed that sociology's coloration has had special appeal for classes, ethnic, religious, and other status groups which lie on the periphery of American society. That observation goes some considerable distance to explaining the specialty clusters identified by Crane and Small. It makes sense of the emphasis on stratification, social mobility, ethnic and race relations, and social movements. It is also consistent with sociology's neglect of the institutions at the center of American society, such as law and banking.

There is a temporal dimension to the development of specializations. D'Antonio notes that the founding of ASA groupings on Marxism, the Environment, World Systems, Collective Behavior, and Racial/Ethnic Minorities coincided with the protest movements of the 1960s and 1970s. As the public came to register increasing concern with aging and gender equality, the emerging specialities in sociology were reflected in the new ASA sections in both areas. As women and minorities move into sociology in greater proportions, we can expect their impact on the curriculum and quite possibly as well on theories and methods.

But "keeping up with society," as Smelser puts it, has characterized sociology for decades. From Progressivism, the Depression, and the New Deal through to the civil rights era, sociology has drawn much of its substantive direction from the public agenda, as subspecialties rise and (do not always) fall with transitory policy priorities. Quite apart from its impact on recruitment, "keeping up" can have uncertain consequences for the organizational coherence of the discipline. Not only does the accretion of discrete problem-related topics of inquiry tend to detract from the broad cumulative growth of sociological knowledge (Crane and Small, chap. 5), but the problem-driven organization of research is reflected in the proliferation of university structures to house problem- or area-oriented, multidisciplinary research centers (Winsborough, chap. 7). While these have their benefits, they do little to forestall the disarticulation of an already loosely integrated discipline.

The chapters in this volume do nothing to allay the sense that sociology appears unusually vulnerable to exogenous influences, whether they be diffuse cultural understandings, state and private institutions, shifts in popular moods or public policy, or recruitment of new professionals. Yet those external pressures may be given sharply divergent readings. On the one hand, they suggest that the discipline-cum-academic profession has a limited capacity to set its own course with any reasonable detachment from exogenous constraint. When sociology does attempt to secure its legitimacy and exert control over its own fate, it must satisfy publics that may have conflicting standards. Incomplete adherence to the canons of science in service of the state may disaffect other audiences in the classrooms and university.

Yet the very permeability of sociology may be an index of its re-

sponsiveness to the calling of an engaged professionalism. Sociology
has no monopoly over any important market. In has no unchallenged
jurisdiction over an area of work in or out of the academy, and its
cultural authority is ambiguous at best. Nevertheless, from this perspective, the porous quality of sociology, susceptible particularly to
substantive agendas, represents an uneasy compromise between the
detachment provided by the university and the immersion threatened
by the ambient environment. A satisficing resolution of these countervailing pressures depends substantially on academic organization.

The Fragility of Disciplinary Identity

The forms of organization that house the discipline of sociology mediate external influences. They also have an independent impact.
Many potential and real conflicts arise out of the sociology community's organization within the university that have repercussions for
the character of sociology's intellectual coherence, for the quality of
its explanatory and interpretive powers, and for its contributions to
other disciplines, social problems, and sociology's heterogeneous publics.

The concept of community has occupied a central position in sociological reflections on professions. Goode's (1957) evocative paper on
professional "communities within communities" signaled, in midcentury, the collegial essence of the professional ideal. But this notion
had long been a hallmark of thinking about professions. From Weber's
treatment of guilds and Durkheim's notions of occupational corporations to the social historians' account of the "distended society"
(Wiebe 1967; Bledstein 1976), it has been supposed that the expert
occupations found part of their cultural identity in a tight community
of equals. The functionalists sanctified this as a necessity for self-
regulation of dangerous knowledge. Critical theorists who followed
turned the collegiality of self-regulating communities into a conspir-
acy of self-interested monopolists (Halliday 1983). In either case, the
meaning of professionals for contemporary society rested heavily on
the cohesion of their occupational associations.

Fifteen years of research has burst any easy assumptions that a
tightly integrated, consensually oriented, homogeneous community
anchors the professional "project." Nevertheless, the literature has not
yet closed the circle on the treatment of professional communities. The
process of equilibration remains poorly understood. No accounts sat-
isfactorily appraise the new integrative mechanisms developed by pro-

fessional elites to combat excessive disarticulation. Meanwhile, professionals and their observers recognize the negative consequences of unreconstructed differentiation. The commonality of professional education, agreed standards of admission, consensually enacted codes of ethics, binding modes of regulation, effective capacities for political mobilization, and cultural authority rest on adequate structural integration and the construction of a persuasive occupational image.

Chapters in the middle of this volume underline the immediacy of professional community and differentiation for sociology. Crane and Small, Calhoun, and Winsborough canvass several aspects of the tension between occupational community, as it is expressed in the form of a discipline locally integrated in departments, and professional disarticulation, as it is reflected in extradepartmental centers of gravity within the university.

The problem of disciplinarity has been a central conundrum of the social sciences since the 1920s and 1930s. As the chapters by Buxton and Turner and by Bulmer demonstrate, the impact of the Rockefeller Foundation on the development of sociology at the University of Chicago and Harvard must be partly understood in terms of its shifting support for disciplinary identification. The issue is hardly antiquarian. Sociology's intellectual integrity and its survival as an academic community are issues at stake in several of the essays. Crane and Small make the provocative argument that the academic profession is losing its substantive core. Calhoun contests the claim that sociology has any valid intrinsic reason to distinguish its theory or focus or methods or discourse from the other social sciences (cf. Klausner). Both point to an uncertain cognitive center.

Through the use of co-citation analysis to build a changing map of sociology's specialties, Crane and Small conclude that the discipline appears to be "losing a clearcut identity." The core areas of sociology have virtually disappeared. The discipline appears more as an archipelago of poorly connected islands of specialization. At the same time, sociology has become increasingly imbedded in the literatures of other disciplines. Crane and Small do not necessarily consider this a bad thing. In one sense, sociology has been especially successful in exporting some of its most interesting developments to other parts of the university, where, like organization theory, they may take up residence in a professional school. But in contrast to economics, sociology has grown more slowly, its center has lost its resilience, and the traffic of ideas back and forth between the two disciplines has been asymmetrical, to the disadvantage of sociology.

In his conference commentary, Starr (1988) also observed in sociology a loss of internal connectedness and a willingness to ignore disciplinary lines. He argued that the disciplinary involvement of sociologists has attenuated and that rival involvements have provided alternative bases of intellectual focus and community. Some alternatives arise in the multidisciplinary affiliations that arise from "problem-centered involvements." Institutional and geographical networks or centers (such as law, medicine, communications, and the military, and East Asian studies, respectively) that cut across disciplines often provide more congenial scholarly communities, with greater prestige and resources, than can be offered by sociology. Schismatic involvements, such as Marxism or feminism, provide potentially oppositional centers of activity and publication. And proprietary involvements, of the kind exemplified by Lazarsfeld, can distract sociologists from the discipline in favor of clients outside the university. All exert centrifugal force on departments.

The magnetism of sociology's neighbors does not trouble Calhoun. He asserts that "the disciplinary division of labor in the social sciences is essentially arbitrary and largely the result of academic politics." Attempts to justify this division of labor are not intellectually cogent. Even worse, they are "pernicious" (Calhoun, chap. 4:139). After repudiating the conventional defenses of sociology's distinctiveness from anthropology, history, psychology, and economics, he proposes that the division of academic labor owes more to affinities of style and ideology rather than any defensible principles of identity.

Whatever the merit of the intrinsic case against a strong view of sociology's disciplinarity, it is clear that disciplinary identification is impelled by factors other than internal intellectual logic. In addition to university politics, Calhoun (chap. 4:138) observes that textbook publishers demand that their authors provide a justification for the singularity of a sociological perspective. Academic employers have proved impatient with sociologists whose qualifications have been obtained in unconventional programs or interdisciplinary committees. Funding agencies and university authorities lean heavily on disciplinary reference groups and clearly identifiable disciplinary indicators, such as departmental rankings, to determine the allocation of resources.[9]

9. At the same time, there are countermovements in the academic establishment as represented, for instance, by the highly interdisciplinary character of the volume on new directions in the social sciences produced by the Committee on Basic Research in the Behavioral and Social Sciences of the Commission on Behavioral Sciences and Education (Gerstein et al. 1988). The Committee purposefully eschewed disciplinary definitions of social science and organized its "report on scientific frontiers" in terms of problem-oriented topics, in part because the fields of inquiry were doing the same thing themselves.

Nevertheless, a rigid disciplinarity can be pernicious, according to Calhoun, because it discourages undergraduates from adopting a richer view of sociological inquiry, it diverts the best and brightest from going on to advanced work, and it contributes to overspecialization. More fundamentally, however, disciplinary rigidity detracts from the general understanding of life. It removes the excitement that is sparked along the boundaries of interdisciplinary collaboration, and it presents tendentious and incomplete understandings of phenomena under study. Ultimately, it "weakens the usefulness of social science in providing for practically relevant public discourse." Starr (1988:2) concurs: "The willingness to ignore disciplinary lines is a wholesome counter-tendency" to the academic "world of excessive specialization." Starr (1988:7) is doubtful that "it would be best to try to recenter sociologists within the discipline. Sociology provides a home for much valuable scholarship and intellectual work of public importance. It provides a base for resisting excessive specialization. Its variety stands as a positive contrast to the more structured world of economics."

Nevertheless, an abandonment of disciplinarity brings its own risks. Several of the authors note that the loss of a substantive core inhibits the generation of new knowledge, reduces the likelihood of cumulative theoretical development over anything broader than isolated specialities, and breaks down the intellectual consensus necessary to obtain competitive funding. During the conference, D'Antonio and Karabel (conference proceedings) pointed out that in interdisciplinary funding panels, sociologists frequently subverted claims for funds by their colleagues through a lack of agreement on the merits of their research proposals, something that was much less evident in other scientific disciplines.[10]

The intellectual heartland of a discipline, as well as its border areas, are housed in different kinds of organizations within the university. These express and sustain the intellectual differences. They may also exacerbate the tendencies to disarticulation that are fostered by sociology's environs. The vitality of the academic profession, therefore, owes much to its interior organization. And therein lies the rub. As Winsborough (chap. 7) suggests, there is a sort of functional division of labor among the research centers and departments. Yet this structural expression of differing aspects of the academic life can debilitate both. Janowitz believed that the tension between centers and departments represented one of the most basic threats to sociology's capacity

10. For a discussion of crossdisciplinary relations and the vulnerability of sociology's core in British universities, see Westergaard and Pahl (1989).

for institution building. In times of proliferating research groups, the department center risks becoming a hollow core.

Winsborough points out that there are good reasons for the development of both sorts of structures. Departments, after all, are the administrative components of the university. Their primary calling is teaching. Research centers arise for more complicated reasons. Sometimes they share a "round-of-life" that can more efficiently be organized in a separate place. Sometimes they are an adaptation to the interests of external donors. They may be a strategy to keep star faculty members. Or they may be a defensive strategy for incorporating faculty members excluded from other centers. Often they grow up around crossdisciplinary clusters of scholars concerned with particular problems such as poverty or the family, particular areas such as South Asian Studies, or certain institutions such as law or medicine. Winsborough canvasses the affinities between assorted branches of sociology and the existence of centers. Survey researchers and demographers invariably find their homes in research centers. Historical sociologists, social psychologists, critical sociologists, and organizational scholars do not. Winsborough proposes that the difference has to do with the round-of-life. Historical sociologists lead solitary research lives and do not need expensive technology or unusual administrative arrangements. Demographers may need both.

The results of all these complex organizational arrangements in and around disciplines bear on sociology and its publics. Clearly, centers offer a great deal that relates directly to institution building. Interdisciplinary arrangements ensure more satisfactory general understandings of social life. The specialization that is nurtured in many research centers facilitates the accumulation of knowledge, the advancement of techniques, and the visibility of substantive interests. But if at once centers are structural manifestations of all that is best about interdisciplinarity and specialization, several of the chapters point to costs they exact on the discipline. Klausner's forceful indictment of research centers inside the university that sacrifice intellectual autonomy for the straitjacket of contract research has already been noted. Janowitz maintained that research centers segregated the more scientific from humanistic sociologists and inhibited the lively exchange of perspectives that can provide an inner dynamism to disciplinary development. And although he clearly is a veteran of research centers, Winsborough, too, acknowledges the complaints that they "consume the time and energy of faculty," provide "hideouts" where the researchers can desert the department, and allow the "rich" to abandon the poor. Conflicts between departments and centers can become acute over faculty hiring. Even in the best of circumstances, the density of interaction among members of a department becomes attenuated as they are dispersed into other corners of the campus.

Despite these criticisms, Winsborough creates a virtue out of the vice. Departments and centers, he asserts, are rather different sorts of things. Activity in departments is synthetic because courses in the curriculum teach what is "known." [11] Teaching is centripetal, because it points to the disciplinary core. In research centers, research is analytic because it breaks phenomena apart. It is also centrifugal because it extends the bounds of knowledge. The inherent strains between these divergent processes constitute an essential tension. They are to be celebrated rather than abolished.

Winsborough's essay sounds a note registered in several chapters. The methods of sociology, in part reflected by differing rounds-of-life, are an important organizing principle of its community and its intellectual core. It has already been recognized that much of sociology's methodological profile stems from external influences. Most reinforce positivism, big science, and the survey method (see Bulmer, Klausner, and Smelser). Other methods have arisen from such diverse points of the compass as the social movements of the 1960s, the growth of historical sociology, and literary theory. Whatever the source, science of some sort dominates. Methods associated with survey research occupied a central position in the loose disciplinary core of 1972–74 (Crane and Small). They are institutionalized in survey and demography research centers that are defined more by method than substance. Consequently, the polarities represented by differing methods have alternative structural expressions within the university—one in research centers, the other, residually, in the department.

The method associated with survey centers permeates the curriculum. This is not to say that it is ubiquitous, but quantitative analysis, most often of survey data, forms the core of regular training in sociological methods found in most departments. This prominence disturbs Reiss (chap. 8). He is not surprised that *some* sort of method should form the centerpiece of graduate instruction. After all, the discipline is more concerned with methods than theory and the character of its

---

11. How much this is true depends as much on pedagogical style as on the level of instruction. In introductory courses for undergraduates, surveys of knowledge may predominate, although more creative faculty members will often strive to synthesize "what is known" in innovative ways. In advanced graduate seminars in research universities, however, especially where courses parallel closely the research agendas of faculty members, the emphasis is likely to shift towards what is *not* known, and hence warrants inquiry.

theorizing about individuals, organizations, and society is distorted by the limits of conventional data collection and analysis. Reiss's principal critique is directed to the primacy of *indirect* over *direct* observation in sociological research. Why the concern? Because indirect observation leads to a focus more on population aggregates than natural social units. Survey methods offer a limited means of understanding social processes. They produce too little description and classification, which Reiss takes to be the core of any science. Finally, they place excessive reliance on external validity, on generalization rather than a better understanding of internal variability.

However, this assault on a methodological proclivity does not amount to an attack on either research centers or quantitative analysis. Reiss has no quarrel with quantification per se. He only wishes that it were better grounded in observational methods, some of which might equally well be located in research centers. But his vision of sociological inquiry encompasses much more than quantification, even in the service of direct observation. He calls for renewed attention to participant observation, field experiments, and other less conventional methods of research. Failure to do so "trains incapacities into each generation of sociologists." By so arguing, Reiss makes explicit a number of intimations underlying many of the chapters that touch on social organization. He senses, as does Calhoun, an intimate connection between teaching and curriculum on the one hand, and sociology's appeal to primary audiences on the other.

In short, there is much argument in these essays that sociology faces threats to its disciplinary integrity. It struggles to establish and maintain a satisfactory balance between countervailing centripetal and centrifugal tendencies. The centripetal pull is centered on disciplinarity and is expressed by the department. The centrifugal tendencies include specialization, interdisciplinarity, research centers, contract research, and the intellectual fracturing of the discipline's core. The resolution of these tensions has important repercussions for the character of sociology's professionalism, and its ability and desire to engage assorted publics.

Private Conversations and Public Audiences

In Janowitz's mind, the capacity of sociology to become a publicly engaged profession, true to academic norms and faithful to civic obligations, depended heavily on professional organization, most especially in the university. An excessive disciplinarity becomes provincial and remote from the central issues within society. A dissolved disciplinary identity loses the distinctive systemic insight at the core of the sociological enterprise. In either case, the range of audiences for the sociological profession is sharply constricted and, whatever the audience, the quality of its insight is compromised. The calling of sociology, therefore, demands attention to the fit between the publics it can—and should—address and the organizational bases of sociological professionalism.

Janowitz's view of sociology as a vocation drew heavily on pragmatist thought (Burk 1991). It also resonated with a longer tradition of reflection on professions that reaches back into the nineteenth century and finds its grounding in quite different philosophical soil. Janowitz signaled his familiarity with some of the British writings on professions in his sympathetic appraisal of T. H. Marshall, who wrote not only on citizenship, but on the special responsibilities of professions in class societies. Where nineteenth-century utilitarians saw the potential of professional expertise to improve social efficiency, English socialists such as Marshall envisaged a society where professions might vindicate their service ideology by placing their resources at the disposal of both the needy and the mighty. In this view, professions would ensure the robustness of welfare society by placing expertise at the service of power to the end of the public good (Perkin 1989).

This moral image of professionalism, with its attendant empirical presuppositions—that professions had expertise, that states were committed to the public good, that both might coincide—has fared badly in the decades since Janowitz wrote *The Professional Soldier* and Parsons celebrated the virtues of professions as the occupational vanguard—the secular priesthood—of modern societies (Parsons 1968). A literature within sociology, variously styled as realist or critical, finds little virtue in professional collective action except for a grudging admiration of their monopolistic single-mindedness and success at status mobility. Yet a careful examination of the inner life of professional groups reveals that there are perceptible, if not always dominant, strains of a civic professionalism, which expresses itself in ostensible commitments by professional elites to a conception of the public good that cannot simply be reduced to a pursuit of narrow professional interests by a more acceptable means (Halliday 1987). There are intimations in some contemporary writing on professions of renewed, if more wary, attention to the moral and empirical conditions of an expansive professionalism that holds professionals accountable to their ideologies of service.

Thus, just as sociology confronts a tension between its disciplinarity identity and interdisciplinary associations, so too its vocation as a

profession reflects its negotiation of another set of potentially conflicting claims—those of collegial and public audiences. And in parallel
fashion to conflicting priorities within the academy, a concern with
broader civic obligations necessarily broaches the questions of which
nonacademic publics sociology is best suited and morally compelled
to serve.

There are dangers either in a narrow vocationalism in which sociologists engage in private conversations with each other or in a civic
professionalism of the sort exemplified by Janowitz's enlightenment
sociology. What success sociology has realized as an academic discipline reinforces an inward turn. With the massive size of the national,
and now international, scholarly audiences, the opportunities for academic speech to be contained within academic institutions have never
been greater. Indeed, the inner logic of publishing, whether by individuals impelled by career imperatives, by universities and departments
for reasons of institutional prestige, or by commercial publishers for
profit motives, extends the boundaries around the garden of high
learning to contain entire careers without ever needing a passport to
the wider world.

Facilitated by ease of communications, and pressured by publication productivity standards, scholars in general have also been drawn
into specialist networks that concomitantly weaken their attachment
to their home universities and insulate their writing from publics outside the world of scholarship. Such splendid isolation merely reinforces the linguistic and conceptual inaccessibility usually attendant
on specialization. This is not to deny the value in specialization, technical advances, or theoretical reflection. Every profession has an intellectual core, usually presided over by an academic elite, around which
swirl abstract and technical debates that are not readily accessible to
general practitioners, let alone the general public. But when the part
becomes mistaken for the whole, civic professionalism is stillborn.

For all of sociology's impulsion into private scholastic worlds, the
sociological profession confronts multiple publics that draw it away
from disciplinary preoccupations. The million or so sociology students who enroll in college classes each year present the most immediate counterclaim to rights as an audience. Their claims have the persuasive incentive that, if unsatisfied, they take their custom elsewhere,
thereby ultimately turning an intellectual judgment into an economic
sanction. Outside the university, sociology's potential publics extend
from policy-making elites to curious general readerships. Here, again,
pragmatic and moral questions are replayed about sociology's vocation; this time, however, they concern the capacities and responsi-

bilities of sociology to diverse constituencies found within the wider public.

Much of the reflective writing on sociology has concentrated on its potential services to clients or its contributions to public policy making. In the volumes edited by Gouldner and Miller (1965) on *Applied Sociology,* and by Lazarsfeld, Sewell, and Wilensky (1967) on *The Uses of Sociology,* for instance, many contributors were optimistic about sociology's potential contributions to a variety of clients, who are broadly construed to include the professions, management, and various government institutions. A concern that sociology be taken seriously in public policy making runs through both volumes and is dealt with directly by Komarovsky's (1975) edited volume, which appraises the uses of sociology in presidential commissions, such as those on pornography, population growth, violence, and law enforcement. These edited collections, which are by no means exhaustive, grew out of the thematic focus of annual meetings held by the American Sociological Association and the Society for the Study of Social Problems. The institutional sponsorship signalled the continuing aspirations of associational leaders for a professionalism that would break out of a narrow academic straitjacket. That recurring hope stirred again in the 1990 ASA annual meeting, which canvassed sociology's relevance for issues on the public agenda.

Consistent with Janowitz's high view of a professional civic responsibility, several chapters and much conference discussion grappled with sociology's putative public roles. Bulmer (chap. 9), for example, makes the case that an applied sociology, directed to political leaders, government officials, practicing professionals, and interest group elites, has become "explicit and integral to the self-conception of the discipline." Yet he affirms Janowitz's enlightenment model of sociological comportment as the preferred means of expressing an effective public voice. Institutional elites and community and business leaders all constitute intelligent audiences with an ability to comprehend relatively sophisticated presentations of expert opinion and knowledge. For this public, the mission of sociology is to shape opinion and thus to exercise a diffuse and somewhat indirect influence on general public culture. The sociologist in this guise becomes a catalyst of public discourse.

The idea that sociology's calling to address an educated public runs deep through its history is a theme developed by Buxton and Turner. Early sociology, they argue, was committed to public edification. As diverse a group as Ward, Giddings, Ross, and Ellwood directed themselves variously to reformist circles, the consumers of public lectures, or Chautauqua-like audiences. The public often provided financial support through purchase of books, lecture fees, and even the funding of community surveys. But from the 1920s and 1930s, sociology began to shift its emphasis. Whereas its calling was once primarily to "public teaching" and only secondarily to build a body of knowledge, from the 1920s sociology became more a body of knowledge that only incidentally was to be taught. In a word, the audiences shifted from outside a neophyte profession to inside an institutionalizing discipline. Public intellectuals, such as Ellwood and Harry Elmer Barnes, lost their battle for the future direction of the profession. The attacks on popular sociological writing led to its substantial abandonment in favor of technical sociology addressed preponderantly to a "professional" audience within an academic discipline.

The earlier "edifying" model has not altogether been lost. One can point to notable works that have shaped public discourse. The Lynds' *Middletown* (1929), Sutherland's *White Collar Crime* (1949), Riesman's *Lonely Crowd* (1953), and Whyte's *Organization Man* (1956) were all notable for their accessibility to an educated lay public. More recently, a lot of play has been given to Bellah et al.'s *Habits of the Heart* (1985), Starr's history of American medicine (1982), and William Wilson's (1978) writings on the black underclass. Rosabeth Kanter's (1977) work on corporations, and Lenore Weitzman's *The Divorce Revolution* (1985) fall into this category. Nevertheless, this list is circumscribed at best.

In part, this may have to do with the size of the audience. Conference discussions led to wildly differing estimates of how many educated consumers were in sociology's potential market. Estimates ranged from some fraction of the 23–25 percent of Americans who obtain a bachelor's degree from college to the occasional 100,000 best-seller, down to the 10,000 or so people who regularly buy and read serious nonfiction. More likely, sociology's limited impact has to do with another sort of "trained incapacity." In the view of Buxton and Turner, contemporary sociologists are simply not taught *how* to write for an educated or mass public. To do so risks marginality within the academic profession—the specter of being labeled a "popularizer" for which there is little collegial recognition and virtually no academic reward. Sociology's prevailing reward system favors those whose principal audience is their narrowly trained colleagues and their "disencultured undergraduate and graduate students" (404).

Trained incapacity reaches also to moral reasoning. As Paul Starr indicated at the conference, the public involvements of sociologists inevitably entail a larger moral dimension than is customary in the model of standard science. Thus, the publicly involved intellectual has a greater willingness than the normal scientist "to make explicit normative judgments about culture and politics, the sort of judgments that the disciplinary professional often regards as a violation of professionalism" (1988:6). This incapacity in moral reasoning is consistent with Calhoun's assertion that an excessive specialization in sociology biases and constricts the understanding of social processes and institutions. The partiality of sociology's disciplinary vision of the world can defeat its purpose of appealing to an intellectually alert public that has not been inculcated with the special language and concepts of the cognoscenti. Indeed, unlike history or anthropology, Calhoun states, sociology seems to have retreated from either a general or a richly textured understanding of social life. In its place it too often offers vacuous generalizations, dry analysis, or scientifically veiled findings whose presentation to the layperson is incomprehensible. As a result, "sociology does a poor job in producing general, synthetic works which present research and theory to the educated public in an attractive form" (ch. 4:188). In similar vein, Karabel (1988:9) recommended "that sociologists try to extend the great classical tradition and, in so doing, speak not to themselves . . . or to decisionmakers . . . but to what remains of an increasingly fragmented educated public."

Those general senses of incapacity evoke the argument pressed by Reiss. After all, one corollary of a sociological method founded more firmly on direct observation would be to pay closer attention to institutions and processes easily recognizable by their participants and observers. Focus on family breakdown, church expansion, company failures, or party resurgence has an immediacy that the abstracted principles of status attainment or labor market segregation do not. In short, sociology's ability to address an educated public turns heavily on what methods it employs to study which institutions and how it couches and conveys its insights. There is considerable sentiment in these papers, as in the conference commentaries, that sociology's disciplinary introversion subverts its ability to reclaim the edifying role effectively played by many of its earlier leaders.

Even if the sociology profession agreed on the merits of public edification, Karabel maintains that all edifying roles are not morally equivalent. Sociology should not be preoccupied with elites, however consequential their power, precisely because they already have ample resources to satisfy their decision-making needs. A more morally justifiable case can be made on behalf of subordinate groups that have fewer resources to sponsor their own research and therefore have a greater need for the knowledge and public legitimation that sociology can supply. It is possible that recruitment patterns identified by D'Antonio may already be contributing to this cause. To the extent that sociology's agenda is driven by recruitment, the swelling numbers of women and minorities may ensure that subordinate groups receive attention in much the same way that research on social movements has been fueled by sociologists whose experience has been charged by their association or identification with insurgency.

Perhaps the most expansive expression of sociology's calling to address wider publics came from Paul Starr's conference commentary (1988:7–8):

> Living for sociology has never struck me as an attractive proposition. The wider world offers more to live for; if in the course of doing sociology for those other purposes, we add to the discipline, so much the better. But disciplinary involvement is not the only legitimate kind. What concerns me is the effort by some to make disciplinary involvement the final test of value of a sociologist's work and, in particular, to drive out the more publicly involved from the field because they are not really sociologists. But if to build a discipline you must create a desert, that will be no victory.

Nevertheless, criticism of a civic sociology comes not only from those committed to a disciplinary professionalism, but from postmodern skepticism about the possibility of public enlightenment by sociological observers. In his chapter, Sica mounts a spirited attack on the false hopes and faulty epistemology he finds in the enlightenment cause championed by Janowitz and Shils. Sica deconstructs Janowitz's texts on institution building by arguing that the position Janowitz shares with Shils is a somewhat quaint and innocent reminiscence by a generation of scholars whose formative years antedated the scholarship that elevated the critical potential of sociology. While Janowitz's aspirations for sociology were high-minded and redolent of liberal enthusiasm, Janowitz had a misplaced confidence in the capabilities and responsiveness of elites. In any event, it was doubtful that a sociology undermined by postmodern criticism could have much to say beyond offering an analysis of the deformations in language that underlie contemporary institutions. Since the optimism in Janowitz's thought was based on an antiquated understanding of the sociological enterprise, for Sica the contribution of sociology to power was more rhetorical than real—although, *après* the "linguistic turn," rhetoric takes on a reality of its own.

Despite Sica's concession that the power of rhetoric in Janowitz and Shils forced people to think carefully about institution building—even if sociology itself had limited constructive capacities—Karabel warned against any sociology that became unduly enamored of the linguistic turn. If, according to Sica, Janowitz and Shils were guilty of "poignant moralism" or a vain effort to make sociology out to be "intellectually rock-solid and eminently powerful as a tool for political and cultural analysis" (Sica, chap. 10:360), Karabel cautioned that a linguistic approach could turn sociology in on itself. The great risk was that "those who have access to specific linguistic codes and forms of cultural capital would talk alone to one another, leaving the public (and the great issues of the day) unaddressed (1988:8–9).

In other words, Sica's proposal for more rhetorical analysis may reinforce the pathology that several observers identified with excessive disciplinarity. A sociology unduly detached from publics outside the academy becomes less appealing to patrons, less magnetic for students, and less engaging for other disciplines. A myopic preoccupation with narrowly construed subdisciplinary issues threatens both the integrity of sociology as a discipline and the utility of sociology as a profession. At the other extreme, a professionalism that has been covertly coopted by its financial clients and political patrons loses its detachment. It sacrifices an autonomy that can be directed to a public good for a mess of potage consumed by particular publics for limited, and often ephemeral, purposes.

Into the Second Century

This volume has its origins in Morris Janowitz's conviction that sociology should adopt a professionalism that takes civic obligations every bit as seriously as its academic calling. Following some of its most notable early citizens, he proposed that sociology should vindicate the vocation of professionalism by contributing its knowledge and understanding, deploying its methods and techniques, and offering its insights and analyses to political elites and educated publics. It should reflect soberly on its responsibilities for civic professionalism. In this capacity, it should help underwrite the humane and participatory values constitutive of a liberal democratic society. Sociology fails as a profession if it abnegates institution building in favor of interminable private conversations with itself.

The contributors to this volume canvass impediments that would abort an expansive sociological professionalism. They identify aspects of the current sociological enterprise that are more or less conducive to civic professionalism. Some of these emanate from outside the discipline. Contributors present contemporary and historical evidence that should alert sociology to the countervailing necessities of external reliance and sponsorship while maintaining a modicum of self-determination. The possibilities of cultural capture, the patronage constraints of funding agencies, the organizational responses to public and private clients, the unstable quality and composition of recruits, the potential client control of agendas and methods—all foster cautions that sociology's peculiar vulnerability should be the object of continuous vigilance.

Clearly, sociology is not simply at the mercy of its diverse sponsors, even when they enter into the minds and souls of its students and faculty. The various pressures discussed in this volume are neither stable over time nor evenly spread over academic institutions. Not infrequently, they check each other. An ideology of antimilitarism drawn into sociology with its recruits of the past two decades significantly nullifies the warping effects of massive government funding for sociological research on the military. Regulatory standards propounded by government can inhibit the intrusiveness of private interests into the academy, just as responsiveness to private clients can balance political agendas that are translated into research budgets. But it is equally plain that American sociology is readily permeated by the moods and moneys of the moment, that it may not have the same resilience and detachment enjoyed by some of its sister disciplines. In short, it must struggle constantly to ensure a degree of independent scholarly control over its own internal ordering in ways that will enable a responsive professionalism to bring independent points of view on significant public issues of our time.

Sociology's vulnerability to external influences might not be so vexing if its internal condition were more resilient. The contributors point to an internal fragility in sociology's academic organizations that subverts the confident protestations of secure institutionalization. It is true that relatively few departments have been closed down. However, signs of fragmentation, unstable centrifugal and centripetal crosscurrents, and internal biases in the organization of the research enterprise and the content of education add up to structural and substantive strains that are likely to inhibit an engaged public professionalism. Some of the impediments to institution building are methodological in the broadest sense. By narrowing or confining the sociological methods of research to one or two dominant styles, the power of explanation is eroded. Some problems are presentational. Sociologists are trained to talk to each other, not to informed publics. Other difficulties arise from the internal architecture of the discipline, from the places where sociologists do their work. When these reinforce specialty attachments scattered around the campus, they can undermine the organizational core centered on the department. By the same token, departments that become insular and self-contained lose the rich possibilities of understanding that are developed by alternative intellectual centers in the university. Sociology must therefore negotiate its way between the Scylla of crossdisciplinary assimilation and the Charybdis of disciplinary aloofness. To err in either direction will impoverish the character of the discipline's civic professionalism by constricting the range of influential publics it can address, not to mention diluting the persuasiveness of its enlightenment.

Sociology is a fragile and uncertain discipline. It must therefore pay special attention to the conditions of its existence, especially those that have bearing on its capacity to retain and enrich its collective citizenship. To the extent that the essays in this volume stimulate debate about the obligations of scholarly and civic professionalism, and to the degree they refocus attention on points of vulnerability, this book will keep alive the self-examination that Morris Janowitz sought to provoke at the beginning of his project on the worth of sociology and at the close of his career as a champion of institution building. It will also help ensure the vitality and vindicate the promise of sociology as it enters its second century in North America.

References

Bellah, Robert N., et al. 1985. *Habits of the Heart: Individualism and Commitment in American Life*. Berkeley: University of California Press.

Ben-David, Joseph. [1972] 1981. *Trends in American Higher Education*. Chicago: University of Chicago Press.

Birnbaum, Norman. 1971. *Toward a Critical Sociology*. New York: Oxford University Press.

Bledstein, Burton J. 1976. *The Culture of Professionalism: The Middle Class and the Development of Higher Education in America*. New York: Norton.

Bramson, Leon. 1961. *The Political Context of Sociology*. Princeton: Princeton University Press.

Bulmer, Martin. 1984. *The Chicago School of Sociology: Institutionalization, Diversity, and the Rise of Sociological Research*. Chicago: University of Chicago Press.

Burk, James. Forthcoming. "Introduction: A Pragmatic Sociology." In *Morris Janowitz on Social Organization and Social Control*, ed. James Burk. Chicago: University of Chicago Press.

Carey, James T. 1975. *Sociology and Public Affairs*. Beverly Hills: Sage.

Colfax, J. David, and Jack L. Roach, eds. 1971. *Radical Sociology*. New York: Basic Books.

Demerath, N. J., Otto Larson, and Karl F. Schuessler, eds. 1975. *Social Policy and Sociology*. New York: Academic Press.

Faris, Robert E. L. 1967. *Chicago Sociology, 1920–1932*. Chicago: University of Chicago Press.

Friedrichs, Robert W. 1970. *A Sociology of Sociology*. New York: Free Press.

Gans, Herbert, ed. 1990. *Sociology in America*. Beverly Hills: Sage.

Gerstein, Dean R., R. Duncan Luce, Neil J. Smelser, Sonja Sperlich, eds. Committee on Basic Research in the Behavioral and Social Sciences. Commission on Behavioral Sciences and Education. National Research Council. 1988. *The Behavioral and Social Sciences: Achievements and Opportunities*. Washington, D.C.: National Academy Press.

Goode, W. J. 1957. "Community within a Community: The Professions." *American Sociological Review* 22:194–200.

Gouldner, Alvin W. 1970. *The Coming Crisis of Western Sociology*. New York: Basic Books.

Gouldner, Alvin W., and S. M. Miller, eds. 1965. *Applied Sociology: Opportunities and Problems*. New York: Free Press.

Halliday, Terence C. 1983. "Professions, Class and Capitalism." *Archives Européennes de Sociologie*.

———. 1987. *Beyond Monopoly: Lawyers, State Crises, and Professional Empowerment*. Chicago: University of Chicago Press.

Hobsbawm, Eric, and Terence Ranger, eds. 1983. *The Invention of Tradition*. Cambridge: Cambridge University Press.

Janowitz, Morris. 1969. *Institution Building in Urban Education*. Chicago: University of Chicago Press.

———. 1970. "The Ideology of Professional Psychologists." In *Political Conflict: Essays in Political Sociology*, ed. Morris Janowitz. Chicago: Quadrangle.

———. 1972. "Professionalization of Sociology." *American Journal of Sociology* 78:105–135.

———. 1976. *Social Control of the Welfare State*. New York: Elsevier.

———. 1978. *The Last Half-Century: Societal Change and Politics in America*. Chicago: University of Chicago Press.

———. 1983. *The Reconstruction of Patriotism: Education for Civic Consciousness*. Chicago: University of Chicago Press.

Johnson, Terence. 1972. *Professions and Power*. London: Macmillan.

Kanter, Rosabeth M. 1977. *Men and Women of the Corporation*. New York: Basic Books.

Karabel, Jerome. 1988. Commentary on Bulmer and Sica, presented at conference on "Sociology and Institution-Building." Arizona, Nov. 16–17.

Klausner, Samuel Z., and Victor M. Lidz, eds. 1986. *The Nationalization of the Social Sciences*. Philadelphia: University of Pennsylvania Press.

Komarovsky, Mirra, ed. 1975. *Sociology and Public Policy: The Case of Presidential Commissions*. New York: Elsevier.

Kurtz, Lester R. 1984. *Evaluating Chicago Sociology*. Chicago: University of Chicago Press.

Lazarsfeld, Paul F., William H. Sewell, and Harold L. Wilensky, eds. 1967. *The Uses of Sociology.* New York: Basic Books.

Lipset, Seymour Martin, and Neil J. Smelser, eds. 1961. *Sociology: The Progress of a Decade.* Englewood Cliffs, N.J.: Prentice-Hall, 1961.

Lynd, Helen, and Robert S. 1919. *Middletown, A Study in American Culture.* New York: Harcourt-Brace and Co.

Madge, John. 1962. *The Origins of Scientific Sociology.* Glencoe: Free Press.

Myrdal, Gunnar. 1962. *An American Dilemma: The Negro Problem and Modern Democracy.* New York: Harper and Row.

National Academy of Sciences. 1968. *The Behavioral Sciences and the Federal Government.* Washington, D.C.: Government Printing Office.

National Science Foundation. National Science Board, Special Commission on the Social Sciences. 1969. *Knowledge into Action: Improving the Nation's Use of the Social Sciences.* Washington D.C.: National Science Foundation.

Parsons, Talcott. 1959. "Some Problems Confronting Sociology as a Profession." *American Sociological Review* 24:547–59.

———. 1968. "Professions." In *International Encyclopedia of Social Sciences,* ed. David Sills. New York: Macmillan-Free Press.

———. 1986. "Social Science: A Basic National Resource." In *The Nationalization of the Social Sciences,* ed. Samuel Z. Klausner and Victor M. Lidz. Philadelphia: University of Pennsylvania Press.

Perkin, Harold J. 1969. *The Key Profession: The History of the Association of University Teachers.* London: Routledge & Kegan Paul.

———. 1989. *The Rise of Professional Society: England Since 1880.* New York: Routledge.

Riesman, David. 1953. *The Lonely Crowd: A Study of the Changing American Character.* New York: Doubleday.

Scott, Robert A., and Arnold R. Shore. 1979. *Why Sociology Does Not Apply: A Study of the Use of Sociology in Public Policy.* New York: Elsevier.

Shils, Edward. 1961. "The Calling of Sociology." In *Theories of Society,* ed. Talcott Parsons, 1403–48. New York: Macmillan.

Smith, Dennis. 1988. *The Chicago School: A Liberal Critique of Capitalism.* New York: St. Martins.

Social Science Research Council & National Research Council. 1969. *The Behavioral and Social Sciences: Outlook and Needs.* Englewood Cliffs, N.J.: Prentice-Hall.

Starr, Paul. 1982. *The Social Transformation of American Medicine.* New York: Basic Books.

———. 1988. "Drifting Involvements: The Diffusion and Decentering of Sociology." Commentary presented at conference on "Sociology and Institution-Building." Arizona, Nov. 16–17.

Sutherland, Edwin H. 1949. *White Collar Crime.* New York: Holt, Rinehart & Winston.

Weitzman, Lenore. 1985. *The Divorce Revolution.* New York: Free Press.

Westergaard, John, and Ray Pahl. 1989. "Looking Backwards and Forwards: The UGC's Review of Sociology." *British Journal of Sociology* 40:374–92.

Whyte, William H. 1956. *Organization Man*. New York: Simon & Schuster.

Wiebe, Robert H. 1967. *The Search for Order, 1877–1920*. New York: Hill & Wang.

Wilson, William. 1978. *The Declining Significance of Race: Blacks and Changing American Institutions*. Chicago: University of Chicago Press.

1

External Influences on Sociology

It is common—and helpful—to distinguish between internal or autonomous forces that shape the development of scientific inquiry on
the one hand and those that arise externally in the cultural and social
milieus of that scientific enterprise on the other. By the former we refer
to the power of unsolved paradigmatic puzzles and implications to
drive scientific thought. The readiest examples come from the "pure"
sciences of mathematics, logic, and philosophy: efforts to solve Xeno's
paradox, to fathom the nature of infinity and the logic of negative
numbers, and (perhaps) to divine the existential characteristics of an
omnipresent God come to mind. By the latter forces we refer to those
factors that are subsumed under the heading of the sociology of
knowledge; these include the influences found in the larger cultural
and linguistic contexts within which scientists work, the influences
imparted by the social origins and positions of scientists, the hostility
or receptivity of the political environment, and the organizational setting (e.g., university, research academy, industry, government) in
which scientific work is executed.

It is not always easy to observe this distinction in practice. For example, it is apparent that the main "forces" that have shaped neo-
Marxist sociological thought have been scholars' efforts to come to
terms with the fact that many of the predictions that Marx derived
from his theoretical diagnosis of capitalism have apparently not come
to pass historically—the failure of the major capitalist classes to po-
larize because of the internal differentiation of each (Dahrendorf
1956), the failure of the proletariat to develop into a world-
revolutionary force (Marcuse 1964), and the emergence of a large and
autonomous state apparatus that is not subordinated to the dynamics
of class domination and conflict (Habermas 1975). That is to say, new
theoretical work has arisen as the original Marxian paradigm has
been adapted or elaborated to account for these evident predictive
failures. But are those forces internal or external to Marxian thought?

Another version of this chapter appeared in *International Sociology* 4, no. 4 (1989),
© 1989 by The University of Chicago.

They are internal in that they are logical parts of the organized corpus of that theory, and any change in their validity status ramifies and presses for change in its theoretical foundations. They could be considered external, however, in the sense that they are the products of subsequently generated historical processes that were beyond the range of early capitalist societies encompassed by Marx's theoretical formulations.

This apparent ambiguity complicates any neat effort to identify the precise status of the factors that have influenced the historical development of a field like sociology. In this paper I will allude to the ambiguity from time to time, but I will make an effort to identify factors that appear to be primarily external.

Accumulated research in the history and sociology of science has established no scientific line of inquiry—not even physics, chemistry, and mathematics—that escapes external influences. At the very least, every line of scientific inquiry recruits its practitioners selectively from different groups in society. Academic sociology in the United States, for example, was, for the most of its early history, populated mainly by white Protestant males; most recently, it has been somewhat "cosmopolized" by an increased entry of women and minorities. In addition, every science is housed in a distinctive kind of organizational structure (academy, university, government, etc.). Both factors—personnel and organization—shape its style of research and its conditions of inquiry. In addition, commercial and industrial needs constitute factors that drive scientific questions and technological applications in the natural sciences.

The presence of external influences on the behavioral and social sciences is more nearly self-evident. The reason for this is that these sciences deal with the very subject matter from which many of those external influences arise, namely, the polity, the economy, social institutions, and culture. In the nature of the case, they are more likely to be responsive to changes in this subject matter. It can be speculated, but surely not demonstrated, that sociology itself occupies the questionable honor of being the most likely to be influenced by these kinds of external forces. Its origins are in normative areas—philosophy, law, and some branches of historical inquiry in Europe, and religious impulses and social reform in the United States. In addition, sociology deals with a range of subjects that are morally, politically, and ideologically highly charged. Among these subjects are inequality, family, education, and religious and ideological beliefs themselves. It is evident that the questions posed and findings reported in these areas can never be isolated from strong reactions in the larger society, which subsequently may influence the directions of inquiry in those areas.

In any event, it should come as no surprise that there is a certain tradition of inquiry in the sociology of sociology with respect to these external factors. We have the early industrial sociology of Mayo (1949) and Roethisberger and Dickson (1944) being interpreted as "managerial sociology" (e.g., Burawoy 1979), suggesting either a direct or indirect domination of the subfield by the ideology and interests of the business classes; we have Gouldner's critique (1970) of Parsons's sociological theory as directed toward fending off, if not denying, the crisis-revolutionary forces in America associated with the Great Depression and subsequent developments; we have a general book on Western sociology (Reynolds 1977), which is also critical in tone, suggesting the domination of the field by establishment forces; we have the critique by Habermas (1973) and other critical theorists, who regard mainline (i.e., positivist) sociology as kind of handmaiden of the instrumental/rational/technological interests of the postindustrial state apparatus; and we have at least one example of an analysis that regards sociological developments mainly as a result of sociometric and generational dynamics (Mullins 1973). Most of these treatments—and my illustrations are not exhaustive—are critical in character, and focus on the business establishment or political establishment, or both, as the main determining forces in question. As such, they tend to be one-dimensional and can in turn be criticized for this. The research traditions of the sociology of science and the sociology of knowledge should tell us that there is a multiplicity of cultural, economic, political, and organizational influences involved in the evolution of a field of knowledge as large and complex as sociology.

In keeping with this critical remark, I will develop not one line of analysis but several, and these will fall under the headings of cultural and personal, social, scientific, and political influences on the development and status of principally American sociology.

Cultural and Personal Influences

To speak of cultural influences is to recognize that major motifs and emphases in any national sociological tradition will reflect the implications of the major values and ideological components of the larger culture that harbors it. Several examples come readily to mind. In Latin American sociology, there is a special emphasis on the political and class dimensions. It has been declared that even though the starting point of inquiry may be work, health, or social protest, all sociological analysis in Latin America ends up as political analysis. This is clearly an exaggeration, but any review of theoretical writings and empirical research in these countries reveals the salience of that theme. In Great Britain a special scholarly fascination with social stratification and social classes is found, along with the manifestation of these in all other areas of social life, such as education, culture, and family.

Sociological theory in the Soviet Union and the socialist countries of Eastern Europe was for a long time under the ideological shadow of often orthodox Marxist-Leninist doctrines that prescribed official interpretations of capitalist and socialist societies, which left little room for the development of alternative lines of thought. As that shadow has lifted and as other "cultures" are infusing those societies, Soviet (or Eastern) bloc sociological theory is becoming increasingly variegated.

American research on social stratification has stressed individual mobility more than collective mobility, and upward mobility more than downward mobility. These emphases can be seen as manifesting a special preoccupation with the American cultural value of individual achievement. That research also has focused on rates of individual mobility over time and, above all, with blockages to mobility (e.g., racial discrimination), which no doubt reveals a sensitivity to the degree to which the American cultural value of equality of opportunity is or is not being realized (Blau and Duncan 1967).

Turning to the American value system even more generally, it is possible to cull from the insights of various observers and analysts (Tocqueville 1841; Parsons 1951; Williams 1963) a number of recurrent themes: individualism, with an assumption of responsibility for one's conduct; mastery of nature and of one's fate; voluntary cooperation as the basis of interaction; a social order based on moral consensus in contrast with hierarchical ordering, class, or authority, consistent with the early Republican rejection of European patterns of monarchy and aristocracy; pragmatism, incrementalism, and reform as principles of social changes; and a resultant optimism.

It would be a serious oversimplification to argue that these themes have dominated American sociology and, more broadly, the behavioral and social sciences in general, but it would also be a mistake to ignore them. Perhaps the case could be better made for two of our sister disciplines of economics and psychology, with the former's emphasis on voluntary exchange, freedom from constraint, entrepreneurship, and survival through success, and the latter's emphasis on individual adjustment, competence, and coping. (Psychology's "individualism" may be traced to its focus on the individual as the basic unit of analysis; see Calhoun, chap. 4.) It might also be remembered that one of the distinctively American adaptations of Freudian psychoanalytic theory (largely pessimistic in character) was ego psychology, which stressed individual adaptation and flexibility above all.

Similar continuities might be observed in many schools of thought that have had indigenous American origins. It can be argued, for example, that role theory is based on the assumption of more or less voluntary compliance with and socialization into the "expectations" of others, and the mechanisms of social control associated with role theory stress conformity rather than obedience to authority or submission to coercion. The school of symbolic interaction, rooted in the pragmatic philosophies of Dewey, Mead, and Blumer, conceives of the actor as an agent, an active user and manipulator of his or her symbolic environment who is not in any way enslaved by instinct, by the structural forces of society, or by mechanical principles such as behavioral conditioning. In this sense, the tenets of symbolic interactionism can be regarded as a kind of celebration of individual mastery and freedom, in contrast with the more deterministic theories against which it is counterpoised. Furthermore, much of exchange theory has its origins in economic theories of competition and shares with these the underlying assumption that exchange is a matter of freely supplying and demanding resources and rewards to and from others. Finally, the central features of Parsonsian sociology and functionalism in general are voluntarism and consensus around a moral order.

To point out these continuities, of course, is to simplify matters greatly. American sociology has been characterized also by theoretical formulations that stand in critical dialogue with these strands and that stress themes of inequality, domination, and coercion. Many of these theories are of European origin, and have found their way into American sociology through the works of those who came from Europe (e.g., Sorokin 1928), or studied in Europe (e.g., Parsons 1937), or who were otherwise inspired by the European masters (e.g., Mills 1956).

Such system/collectivist/critical/radical perspectives have themselves come to constitute a major part of sociology in this country, and continue to be nourished by the more contemporary contributions of European scholars such as Habermas, Touraine, Bourdieu, Giddens, and others. The field of sociology can be regarded as a kind of continuous dialogue and ferment among these perspectives, some consonant with and some in critical opposition to the dominant themes of the American cultural tradition. American sociology, in short, stands divided by the distinctively cultural emphases supplied by American culture and those supplied by European culture, and in this way it is less a purely "American" subject than that of economics, psychology, and political science, despite the latter's emphasis on power and authority.

It might be argued, finally, that sociology has experienced cyclical movements between dominant cultural themes and their counter-emphases. Perhaps more accurately, there is a cultural differentiation between those leaning in the direction of the dominant cultural themes and those leaning toward their opposites, making for a more or less enduring cultural division within the discipline. An example of this is the recurring tension between the "consensus" and "conflict" approaches in American sociology.

This notion of a continuous cultural dialogue within the discipline is closely connected with an observable but not very well understood phenomenon of the periodic rise and fall of the great historic figures of the field in sociological research and explanation. In the 1950s, Durkheim and Freud held great sway in American sociology and social science generally, but the fortunes of both, especially Freud, have now faded somewhat and the neo-Marxian and neo-Weberian themes have risen in salience. European sociology has witnessed an ebbing of Marxian sociology as such, but continues to generate and nurture theories that cannot be described as Marxian but which retain some distinctive thread of Marxian thought, such as the ideas of domination and protest (e.g., the new critical theory (Habermas 1975) and the new social movements school (Melucci 1980)). As indicated, we do not understand the vicissitudes of the great figures very well. Some of these might be a generational matter; one cohort of sociologists may embrace and make productive use of the insights of a Tocqueville or a Freud, while the next, facing new intellectual problems and perhaps eager to distance itself from the work of its teachers, will forsake those figures and resurrect others; still another cohort will call up the heroes of their teacher's teachers. The current interest in "neofunctionalism" (Alexander 1985) may be an example of the revival of Talcott Parsons and other functionalists after a period of twenty years of discrediting of those works.

These observations raise explicitly the topic of generational effects in any field of scientific inquiry. Such effects are multiple and mixed in their import. On the one hand, influential figures in a discipline "place" their students in important places around the academy as they are trained. In general, this makes for a continuity in the ideas of the "fathers" or "mothers" of those trained, as the students carry forward the traditions and styles of their "parent" in their teaching and research. The influences of Paul Lazarsfeld on the work of his students—Charles Glock, Allen Barton, Martin Trow, and others—is an example. On the other hand, students of influential scholars commonly feel the need to set up their own shop, as it were, to carve out a certain terrain or approach that is different from or perhaps opposed to that of their mentors. This has the contrary effect of dispersing or even diminishing the influence of the progenitors.

Mention might also be made of the "grandparent" effect, that is, the intellectual impact of a major figure on the students of his or her students. Perhaps the third generation can come to terms more comfortably with the traditions and themes of their teachers' teachers than can the immediate offspring, who are likely to be more deeply involved in the dynamics of conformity and rebellion with the original figure. Anecdotal possibilities of this effect can be considered—for example, Jeffrey Alexander as the intellectual grandson of Talcott Parsons, with Robert Bellah and me as a kind of middle generation—but little is known or even thought about the grandparent effect in general.

In this section I have mentioned a range of cultural and personal dialogues that influence the direction of an academic discipline like sociology. These dialogues may be regarded as simultaneously reflecting larger cultural tendencies and constituting an important set of internal dynamics in the discipline. As such, they illustrate the difficulty of drawing a clear and distinct line between external and internal influences on the evolution of a field of inquiry.

Keeping up with Society

One of the key influences in the development of sociology—if not the social and behavioral sciences generally—is the fact that much of its subject matter is dictated by real and perceived social trends in the larger society. If one examines the rise of new areas of interest in the past several decades, one will find the family and unemployment emerging in the years of the Great Depression; propaganda, public opinion, and rumor in World War II; a burst of new interests in the sociology of poverty, sociology of education, sociology of youth, and feminist sociology in the 1960s and immediately thereafter; and environmental sociology, the sociology of energy, and the sociology of occupational risk in chemical and other dangerous industries more recently. All these are evident reactions to social problems, and a quantitative study might reveal a quite real correspondence between the appearance of these problems and a flurry in the literature, if the appropriate time lags for funding, research, execution, and publication delays are taken into account.

The tendency for sociology to develop new subfields around newly emerging social phenomena and social problems evidently contributes to the increasing proliferation of specialized areas of inquiry in the discipline, and in this way to its intellectual fragmentation. The same tendency may have certain organizational consequences. For example, academic departments of sociology, slow as they are to grow and shrink because of the tenure process for faculty, and prone as they are to develop vested intellectual interests that strive to perpetuate themselves, are likely to resist incorporating new intellectual developments in the field. One of the ways that new areas of interest and importance are incorporated into the academy is that development of problem- or area-oriented, multidisciplinary research centers, such as institutes of industrial relations and international studies, and centers for the study of important countries and areas of the world—the Soviet Union, China, and Africa, for example (see Winsborough chap. 7). These research units themselves may develop their own forms of organizational inertia, but the main point to be stressed here is that, for better or for worse, they confuse any correspondence between disciplinary boundaries and organizational realities (which is already confused in any event—see Calhoun, chap. 4), because they are established on problem-oriented, multidisciplinary bases.

The rise and fall of major figures might also be explained in part by the changing historical circumstances of any given society. The evident rise of interest in Marx and Weber in American society in the 1960s and 1970s can be regarded as a kind of intellectual mirror of the group conflict and political turmoil of those decades. It also makes sense that as colonial countries are struggling under the yoke of the colonial powers and subsequently are fighting to consolidate their own independence, they may turn to the Marxian notions of exploitation and dominance to enlighten their understanding; when they move actively into the phase of building institutions and promoting economic growth, the theories of a Joseph Schumpeter might appear more attractive.

Another observable tendency is for our subject matter to run ahead of the conceptual frameworks under which we study it. The most important illustration of this concerns the study of international relations and international interdependencies. If we examine our major sociological heritage, it is apparent that the majority of our theories are based on the postulate that most of what transpires in social life does so *within* single societies and, indeed, intrasocietal forces are the main operative determinants. Put another way, sociologists have tended to regard the single society, nation, or culture as the principal unit of analysis for their studies. When we look around the contemporary world, however, it is apparent that the relevance of this kind of approach grows less and less. Nations grow more dependent on one another; the major forces affecting the decisions of national governments are not within the hands of national decision makers but lie outside their control; in short, it is systems of societies, not single societies, that constitute the most important level of analysis. Accordingly, analyses built on the idea of single societies, states, nation-based ideologies, and the like are less powerful. But with few exceptions the corpus of our inherited traditions does not provide very many theories and frameworks for moving to the higher systemic levels.

Those few exceptions include, of course, early general theories of "civilizations" and colonialism, by figures such as Sorokin (1937), Lenin (1939), and Kroeber (1944), and, more recently, dependency theory and world-systems analysis. Both of these latter formulations, which crystallized in the 1960s and 1970s, can be interpreted in part as reactions to the "external" factors contained in that complex of changes we refer to as the increasing internationalization of the world. (The rise of the latter theoretical approaches reflects an "internal" dialogue as well, namely, who can lay the more legitimate theoretical claim to the area of development theory: functionalist-minded "modernization" theorists or neo-Marxist, conflict-minded "internationalist" theorists.) In addition, a 1979 international survey of scholars in the "economy and society" area also showed a growing preoccupation with the international dimensions of economic life (Makler, Sales, and Smelser 1982). That the particular dependency and world-system emphases have themselves waned in the 1980s should provide no particular embarrassment to the general point; both of these perspectives have proved to be limited in their capacity to account for certain empirical phenomena (e.g., the rise of Asian economies such as Taiwan and South Korea (Gold, 1986)) and vulnerable to theoretical and methodological criticisms. These kinds of theoretical ups and downs can occur—in this case for primarily "internal" reasons—in the context of a gradually increasing emphasis on international factors.

Influences from Science

One of the remarkable features of the past several hundred years is the extent to which science as a culture has come to be such a dominant feature of Western culture in general. Its conquest has been selective with the early strides being made in astronomy and physics, with subsequent developments being made in chemistry and the life sciences, and, finally, beginning in the late eighteenth and nineteenth centuries, in economics and psychology, then in political science, anthropology, and sociology. In all instances the scientific impulse displaced a preexisting religious or philosophical one, and in no case was that transition an easy one, involving as it did a threat to established claims to legitimacy and to individuals and groups who represented those claims.

It is important to recognize, moreover, that as the scientific impulse emerged in one intellectual area after another, it arose in a unique historical context, and its character was influenced by that context. Here the contrast between the histories of European and American sociology are instructive. The emergence of the field in continental Europe—associated above all with the efforts of Karl Marx, Emile Durkheim, Ferdinand Toennies, Georg Simmel, and Max Weber—occurred in two principal contexts: first, in the distinctive emphases in European social thought and, second, in the simultaneous emergence of the scientific impulse in economics and psychology. With respect to the first, European sociology oriented itself above all to the intellectual traditions of European thought as represented in the study of history, philosophy, law, and the classics in the academy and in the critical intellectual traditions focusing on the state, social classes, and the economy, to be found both in the academy and in the more general intellectual life of those countries. It also oriented itself to the emerging social-scientific emphases of the day, as Durkheim's negative polemic toward psychology and Weber's suspicion of the assumptions of formal economics attest. The current preoccupation of European sociology with macroscopic and critical issues—phenomenology excepted—of the state, classes, and the economy, and the critical treatment of each, bears witness to the power of these traditions.

England is something of an exception here. While not totally disconnected from continental traditions, English sociology developed in the context of the rise of liberal politics and then labor reformist politics in the mid- to late-nineteenth century and in the peculiar context of English empiricism, manifested in the early "survey" techniques of Booth (1892) and Rowntree (1922). This put a permanent imprint of a somewhat left-wing but simultaneously fact-oriented stamp on British sociology.

The United States also exhibits individual characteristics. Just as its nation arose without the necessity to fight off the burdens of European feudalism, so its sociology arose in a context that did not include (with exceptions to be noted presently) the peculiar intellectual history of European nations. Our sociology grew up in two major intellectual and social contexts. First, it made its appearance in the public institutions of higher education in this country several decades after the passage of the Morrill Act of 1862, which solidly established the scientific and applied impulses (mechanical and agricultural) in American higher education. A related part of this development was that economics and psychology preceded sociology, and had fully adopted the scientific "definition" of their own fields. These pressures to strive for scientific legitimacy were probably manifested more in the new land grant universities than in the older, private universities where that drive was blunted by the prestigious humanistic traditions in those institutions. The origins of what is inexactly but meaningfully entitled "Midwestern positivism"—which includes an emphasis on quantitative analysis of empirical "facts," a stress on induction as the main avenue to scientific truths, and aspiration to some kind of natural science model—may be found in the same historical forces. Second, in the 1890s, sociology picked up the reform theme from both the Social Gospel and the Progressive movements. It is not surprising that sociology, struggling to establish its legitimacy in those days, picked up the twin themes of scientific respectability and social reform as its motifs to broadcast to the academy and to the larger society. Those themes persist to the present day. They also fit comfortably into American cultural emphases on pragmatism, reform, and optimism identified in the previous section. American sociology appears to have had an odd preoccupation with how scientific it is or is not.

Within the confines of this preoccupation is an additional concern with and debate over what kind of science sociology should be modeled after. Durkheim's early preoccupation with social facts as "things" and fixed scientific laws ([1893] 1958) suggests that he had the model of the physical sciences mainly in mind. His functionalist sociology, however, invokes biological analogies like that of the structural-functionalists in general. The positivists of the first half of the twentieth century, especially Ogburn (1930) and Lundberg (1947), build on a positivistic, inductive model of scientific accumulation, with theory occupying only a modest role and emerging only as a result of that process. Parsons and his associates (1951) erected a hypothetical-deductive image of scientific sociology, which gives theoretical structure and logical derivation a more independent role in the generation of empirical knowledge. Still others tend to stress scientific method or procedure as a model, taking the experimental methods, with its stress on the analysis of controlled variation, as the model. Accordingly, they regard other methods, such as statistical analysis of aggregated survey data and systematic comparative illustrations, as approximations of the experimental method, that is, as accommodations to the fact that sociology is built largely on an empirical base of historical data that are not experimentally generated (Smelser 1976).

Political Influences

Sociology's general relations with national governments and its many publics are always fraught with uncertainty and ambivalence. These relations may be likened to a troubled marriage. The two partners may constantly irritate one another, as governments and publics raise ideological concerns and pressures that threaten to compromise the freedom of thinkers and researchers in the discipline, and sociologists forever generate information and ways to describe social events and situations that have an unsettling, needling, and even debunking effect. At the same time the two may find that they cannot live without one another, as governments and publics are dependent on data, information, and perspectives for their policies and their interpretations of the social world, and sociology requires financial and institutional support as well as autonomy. This inevitable ambivalence can be resolved in a variety of ways. Sociology may be afforded a free and happy welcome as part of the academy; it may be given only low status and a bad press in the public eye; or it may be constantly hounded to be something that it is not or driven underground altogether by oppressive measures.

One of the remarkable features of American sociology is that it has been housed in academic departments in universities, which have as a matter of historical fact been institutionally removed from the political winds, despite periodic forays of interested legislators and usually right-wing political groups that have imperiled academic freedom in the universities. This is a relative statement, of course, but if one compares the American case with many others—especially those of Eastern European societies—the field has emerged as one that is, by and large, nonpoliticized from the standpoint of its environment. The field is in another sense a very political one, since it sometimes manifests skeptical if not critical views of its subject matter, the institutions and social problems of the country, views that perforce trigger political reactions. For example, the empirical research of Morris Rosenberg on the self-esteem of black children in racially-integrated schools (1971), while ideologically neutral in intent and execution, touches politically explosive sentiments about race relations and education.

As the functions of the state have grown, sociology and the other social sciences have taken on a different kind of political significance. Government agencies, pursuing their various missions, are inevitably called upon to justify both their concerns with societal problems and their policies relating to these problems in terms of some kind of factual base. (For example, in order to define teenage pregnancy as a "problem" it is necessary to establish some kind of empirical scope of its incidence, and presumably to hold this scope up to some kind of standard that would make it a "nonproblem.") In establishing this kind of empirical scope, political agencies have borrowed both methods (mainly survey) and findings from sociology and the other social sciences, giving them applied or political significance. In many respects the research carried out by agencies is very similar to social science research in general.

Where sociology has come under greater political influences is not in its significance as an academic discipline in the university setting, but in its significance as a science based on research, with the support for that research coming from the science establishment (and ultimately from the Congress and the executive branch). It is the case, furthermore, that the phenomenon of research has a political dimension.

From the vantage point of government sponsorship, the behavioral and social sciences are organizationally a part of the National Science Foundation, and are supported by the same general budget that is appropriated for the Foundation annually by Congress. Yet it is apparent that these disciplines occupy a minor place in that agency; the Science Board (its policy-making board of trustees) has virtually no behavioral or social sciences as a subpart of a division known as the Biological, Behavioral, and Social Sciences, the director of which is invariably a biological scientist. Furthermore, the sums available to the behavioral and social sciences within the Foundation are minuscule in comparison with the total budget for scientific research. Perhaps most decisive, however, and perhaps the ultimate reason for all of the above, is the fact that much of the "hard-science" leadership of the National Science Foundation and the science establishment in Washington, while they grant a place for the behavioral and social sciences, still regard these enterprises as basically "soft" and not really "scientific."

In addition, the National Science Foundation, and all other government granting agencies, are publicly visible, and come under annual review at budget time by the Office of Management and Budget in the executive branch and both Houses of Congress. The view of the behavioral and social sciences in the halls of government, moreover, is fraught with ambivalence. On the one hand, government officials are forever faced with and must deal with pressing social problems of poverty, unemployment, crime, mental health, economic instability, and so on, all of which are most directly related to and informed by behavioral and social science research. This concern tends to generate a positive attitude toward the behavioral and social sciences, and to incline government officials to support research in those areas out of the conviction that increased knowledge about those problems will be enlightening and will lead to more effective attacks on them.

On the other hand, there are pockets of hostility (emanating mainly from the right) toward the behavioral and social sciences on the part of politicians and government officials. While these vary in importance and salience over time, they are identifiable and their arguments have taken a number of forms:

1. Research in the behavioral and social sciences produces trivial, obvious, and unimportant results, and expenditures on that kind of research are wasteful of public funds. This attitude is symbolized in the annual "Golden Fleece" awards named by Senator William Proxmire, the intent of which is to show that the federal government has been fleeced of its gold by studies funded to study the sex life of goats, the sociology of love, and other such subjects.

2. Research in the behavioral and social sciences is of no use to the government, and therefore should not be funded; this opinion is associated with public statements by David Stockman, President Reagan's former budget adviser, made during Congressional budgetary hearings in the early 1980s.

3. Research in the behavioral and social sciences is basically unscientific—according to the canons of "hard" science—and is therefore undeserving of study. This is a kind of spillover of the above-mentioned attitude on the part of many physical and life scientists.

4. Research in some branches of the behavioral and social sciences (such as the study of race relations, fundamentalist religious beliefs, family life, and other areas) is ideologically dangerous, because it is likely to generate criticism of institutions and practices that are either considered too sacred or uneasily taken for granted to suggest changes in such areas. This kind of hostility is difficult to document, because it is often shrouded in one of the less frank forms just listed; nevertheless, it exists, and reflects both right-wing political sentiments and the fact that social scientists, especially sociologists, themselves are more politically liberal and critical than other groups in the political spectrum. From time to time this ideological hostility breaks into the open and results in direct assaults on certain kinds of social science research; in the early Reagan years, for example, budget cuts in the National Science Foundation, National Institute of Mental Health, and elsewhere were directed toward discouraging research that focused on systemic accounts and explanations of social problems (e.g., class, race), but left alone or encouraged research that involved genetic and psychogenic understandings of them.

It is difficult to conceive how the behavioral and social sciences could be simultaneously trivial, useless, unscientific, and yet threatening. Be that as it may, these attacks surface sporadically, and as such they constitute a source of embarrassment and difficulty for the leadership of the National Science Foundation and other funding agencies. To them the behavioral and social sciences appear as a minor part of their operation from an organizational and budgetary point of view, but as a major source of criticism and trouble from quarters that matter.

It follows from this account that the main temptations generated by these pressures on the behavioral and social sciences are two: first, to maintain as low a profile as possible, to avoid political notice and to thereby survive; and second, to present themselves as respectably and undangerously as possible and thereby to curry political and budgetary support. The main response to these temptations, according to my observations, is for the spokespeople of the behavioral and social sciences to represent themselves as adhering to the model of positive science, as methodologically sound, and as therefore supportable on the grounds that they are legitimately scientific. This strategy emerges— whether it is, in the end, effective or self-defeating—as the one that is most likely to blunt criticism both within the donor agencies and on the part of other government officials. Ultimately, of course, this response emerges as a victory of the positive-science emphasis, and as a kind of marriage of convenience between the behavioral and social scientific investigators in the academy on the one hand and the Washington social-science establishment on the other—a marriage that encourages those in the academy to support "hard" behavioral and social scientific investigators because such a policy encourages funding agencies to give research grants to such investigators because it provides evidence that their own standards are strictly "scientific." The only cautionary qualification to this diagnosis is to note that if the liberal voice in the Democratic Congress presses, and the accommodative voice of the Bush administration responds, a more supportive stance toward a greater diversity of social science research—including research that has politically more critical implications—may resurface.

This "sociology of knowledge" diagnosis has clear implications. Unless we witness major changes in the structure and prestige systems of universities, or major changes in the politics affecting the behavioral and social sciences, the model of the social sciences—including, of course, sociology—as sciences will be the dominant voice of the future. Empirical-science models of social study and explanation will be center stage, and will call the tune, as it were, for those voices that will continue to reassert the concern with philosophical, moral, and social problems that has occupied a salient past in sociology. The content and tone of the dominant voice in counterpoint with subordinate protesting voices will change with changing times, but I would predict that it will be the main melody of the sociological future in substantial part in response to forces outside sociology.

References

Alexander, Jeffrey, ed. 1985. *Neofunctionalism*. Beverly Hills, Ca.: Sage.

Blau, Peter, and Otis D. Duncan. 1967. *The American Occupational Structure*. New York: John Wiley and Sons.

Booth, Charles. [1892] 1902. *Life and Labour of the People of London*. New York and London: Macmillan.

Burawoy, Michael. 1979. *Manufacturing Consent*. Chicago: University of Chicago Press.

Dahrendorf, Ralf. 1956. *Class and Class Conflict in Industrial Society*. Stanford: Stanford University Press.

Durkheim, Emile. [1893] 1958. *The Rules of Sociological Method*. Glencoe, Ill.: The Free Press.

Gold, Tom. 1986. *State and Society in the Taiwan Miracle*. New York: M. E. Sharpe.

Gouldner, Alvin Ward. 1970. *The Coming Crisis in Western Sociology*. New York: Basic Books.

Habermas, Jurgen. 1973. *Theory and Practice*. Boston: Beacon Press.

———. 1975. *Legitimation Crisis*. Boston: Beacon Press.

Kroeber, Alfred L. 1944. *Configurations of Culture Growth*. Berkeley and Los Angeles: University of California Press.

Lenin, Vladimir I. 1939. *Imperialism: The Highest Stage of Capitalism*. New York: International Publishers.

Lundberg, George. 1947. *Can Science Save Ills?* New York: Longmans, Green.

Makler, Harry, Arnaud Sales, and Neil J. Smelser. 1982. "Recent Trends in the Theory and Methodology in the Study of Economy and Society." In *Sociology: The State of the Art*, ed. Tom Bottomore, Stefan Novak, and M. Sokolowska. London: Sage, 147–71.

Marcuse, Herbert. 1964. *One-Dimensional Man*. Boston: Beacon Press.

Mayo, Elton. 1949. *The Social Problems of Industrial Civilization*. London: Routledge and Kegan Paul.

Melucci, Albert. 1980. "The New Social Movements: A Theoretical Approach." *Social Science Information* 19:199–226.

Mills, C. Wright. 1956. *The Power Elite*. New York: Oxford University Press.

Mullins, Nicholas C. 1973. *Theories and Theory Groups in Contemporary American Sociology*. New York: Harper and Row.

Ogburn, William F. 1930. "Presidential Address: The Folkways of a Scientific

Sociology." Papers presented at the Twenty-fourth Annual Meeting of the American Sociological Society. Chicago: University of Chicago Press.

Parsons, Talcott. 1937. *The Structure of Social Action*. New York: Macmillan.

———. 1951. *The Social System*. Glencoe, Ill.: The Free Press.

Parsons, Talcott, and Edward A. Shils, eds. 1951. *Toward a General Theory of Action*. Cambridge: Harvard University Press.

Reynolds, Larry T. 1977. *The Sociology of Sociology*. New York: McKay.

Roethlisberger, Fritz, and William Dickson. 1944. *Management and the Worker*. Cambridge, Mass.: Harvard University Press.

Rosenberg, Morris. 1971. *Black and White Self-Esteem: The Urban School Child*. Washington, D.C.: American Sociological Association.

Rowntree, Benjamin C. 1922. *Poverty, A Study of Town Life*. London: Longmans, Green.

Smelser, Neil J. 1976. *Comparative Methods in the Social Sciences*. Englewood Cliffs, N.J.: Prentice-Hall.

Sorokin, Pitirim. 1928. *Contemporary Sociological Theories*. New York: Harper.

———. 1937. *Social and Cultural Dynamics*. 4 vols. New York: American Book Company.

Tocqueville, Alexis de. 1841. *Democracy in America*. New York: J. and H. G. Langley.

Williams, Robin. 1963. *American Society: A Sociological Interpretation*. New York: Knopf.

2

War and Peace on the Sociological Agenda

No field of inquiry is fully autonomous. Tension between autonomy from and dependence on external environments plays a part in forming every discipline's boundaries. This tension is especially conspicuous in sociology, whose research agenda frequently mirrors society's concern about certain topics. In recent decades, for example, public concern about racial and sexual equity has stimulated a surge of research on race and gender stratification, while the sheer availability of funding in the health area has greatly increased the work devoted to medical sociology.

The sociology of war and peace provides a useful case for examining the interplay between disciplinary autonomy and environmental dependence. I shall argue that, while the state clearly attempts to manipulate the agenda of socology in this area, sociology's autonomy as a professional discipline keeps the state from intervening very effectively. In spite of this autonomy, however, sociology's relative inattention to war and peace issues reflects society's tendency to ignore such issues and to relegate their examination to specialized institutions created to deal with them. Moreover, such work as sociologists do carry out on war and peace reflects the priorities of society more than those of the state.

Sociologists may appear to have considerable autonomy, because matters of war and peace have had remarkably little impact on the sociological agenda, despite the importance attached to these topics

I am indebted to Albert Biderman, Elise Boulding, Martin Bulmer, John S. Butler, Craig Calhoun, Jerome Karabel, Samuel Klausner, Louis Kriesberg, Donald Levine, John Lofland, Sam Marullo, Charles Moskos, David Segal, Neil Smelser, Gideon Sjoberg, Paul Starr, and Paul Wehr for the comments and suggestions on this paper, although the mistakes in it remain mine. There are points at which many of the above will disagree with the analysis that follows. My special thanks go to Terence Halliday and Sarah Beth Asher, who have sheperded this paper through several versions with their insightful comments and criticisms.

by the state. Nations throughout the globe devote major proportions of their resources to war, and their ability to wage it, but sociologists have given it scant attention. Despite the massive funding of social science research by the military, sociological research has received only a very small portion, and that research has had little impact on the intellectual life of the discipline in recent decades. Consequently, sociology appears to be relatively autonomous from its cultural context in its lack of priority on these issues.

This apparent autonomy is misleading, however. Although sociologists as a whole resist the state's emphasis on warmaking, the field is dependent on broader sociocultural trends in four ways. First, the ebb and flow of war and peace research is closely tied to external events. The more the larger society fights wars, talks about them, and prepares for them, the more sociologists study them.

Second, the study of war and peace is organized into two camps reflecting two cultures in the broader society. One camp is drawn toward military institutions and the other toward peace movement organizations. These two cultures differ in terms of worldview and ethos. The researchers pulled toward the military institutions—in a field generally called "military sociology"—focus in large part on the institutional problems of military forces in the twentieth century. Those pulled toward peace movement organizations—often self-defined as "peace researchers"—emphasize a critical analysis of the war system, but also focus on the social institutions that help to set their agenda.

Third, as in the broader culture, sociologists pay more attention to war than to peace. There is more military sociology than peace research, in large part because the funding is distributed unevenly. There is very little funding for either camp, but more for military sociology than for peace research (although the amount of available funds for the latter has increased substantially in recent years). Because of the nature of the work being funded, and the places where the money is going, most social science research on issues of war and peace reinforces mainstream frameworks for analyzing such topics (despite some sharply dissenting views), just as virtually all modern cultures are far more concerned with refining their methods of war-fighting rather than those of peace-making.

Finally, a major reason why sociologists pay so little attention to war and peace is that the topic is too complex to consider adequately within the narrow methodological parameters established by late twentieth-century scientific culture. One of the ironies of scientific methodology is that some of our most important issues are defined as out of bounds, so that we describe the world inadequately by focusing only on those issues about which we have enough certainty to say anything (see Kurtz 1989). Sociologists are more comfortable when studying institutions, which are concrete and measurable. As military institutions are the most well developed, one would expect more attention to that sector; as the peace movement has grown institutionally in recent years, so has the sociology of the peace movement.

One important caveat is in order here: I focus primarily on the sociology of peace and war in the United States, although some of the most significant sociological work on the topic has been done elsewhere, as with the important contributions by Alva Myrdal (1982). Raymond Aron (1973), Johann Galtung (1984), and J. D. Sethi (1980). Indeed, sociology outside of the U.S. is more amenable to such issues, because it is more comfortable with engagement with broader social issues in a less empiricist mode.

Other sociological works on war, like that in Pitirim Sorokin's third volume of *Social and Cultural Dynamics* (1937), Quincy Wright's *A Study of War* (1965), and Stanislav Andreski's *Military Organisation and Society* ([1954] 1962) have received almost no attention. In looking at twenty-five introductory sociology textbooks published between 1945 and 1954, Alvin Gouldner (1962) found that only 275 out of 17,000 pages touched on the causes or effects of war. Charles Tilly (1988) contends that "sociologists have neglected their opportunity and responsibility to explain the rise of military power in the contemporary world."

The Dearth of Sociological Research

> A good case can be made that the contribution of the social sciences to arms control and disarmament has been negligible, or at least trivial. Of course, governmental achievements in arms control and disarmament efforts over the last quarter century are also hardly profound.
>
> MORRIS JANOWITZ

The most striking fact about the sociology of war and peace is how little of it there is, given the significance of the issue. It is true that an enormous amount of social science research on war and peace issues is carried out every year, but little of it finds its way into the sociological journals. It is carried out largely within the military, by people trained in other disciplines, notably psychology. The study of international relations in any form has not historically been part of the province of American sociology; for the most part, such matters have been left to the political scientists (especially in the subfield of international relations). More importantly, most social science investigations of war and peace have not been basic research designed to expand our knowledge of human behavior and institutions, but are highly instrumental works paid for by the military to make the armed forces more efficient and effective (see Janowitz 1974). Consequently, as Diana Crane and Henry Small have shown elsewhere in this volume (chap. 5), military sociology plays a very marginal role in the discipline as a whole.

The Minimal Institutional Base of Peace and War Studies

In mainstream sociology, war and peace have not been major topics on the agenda. There is little research and few research centers or articles published in the area. First, of the research centers that have been created to address these topics, the major institutional focus of military sociology is the Inter-University Seminar on Military Organization (later the Inter-University Seminar on Armed Forces and Society) formed by Morris Janowitz at the University of Michigan in the midfifties. Military sociology has become increasingly internationalized in scope and participation, a trend accelerated by the creation of the Research Committee on Armed Forces and Conflict Resolution of the International Sociological Association, and a European association of military sociologists.

Additional research is carried out within the Army Research Branch, later the Army Research Institute for the Social and Behavioral Sciences, formed in 1941 and initially directed by a sociologist. Its work is not generally considered by military sociologists to be military sociology, however, despite the fact that sociological research is part of the Institute's agenda.

There have been academic centers of military sociology at the Universities of Michigan, Chicago, Maryland, and Northwestern University, which exist primarily because of a few individuals, such as David Segal, Janowitz, C. H. Coates, and Charles C. Moskos. Janowitz also played a key role in organizing the Research Committee on Armed Forces and Society of the International Sociological Association.

Second, a group of sociologists organized around the Peace and War Section of the American Sociological Association (ASA) includes both military sociologists and peace researchers, although the latter tend to dominate. The section remains consistently at or near the bottom of the list of ASA sections in terms of membership, mirroring the broader society's lack of commitment to these topics and thus minimizing its impact on the agenda of the annual ASA meetings. (The number of sessions on a topic at those meetings is determined largely by the size of the section memberships.)

Beyond that, there is little organized activity within the sociological community itself. Some individuals (like Elise Boulding, James Laue, Louis Kriesberg, and James Skelly) have been actively involved in interdisciplinary groups such as the International Peace Research Association (IPRA), the Consortium on Peace Research, Education, and Development (COPRED), the University of California's Institute on Global Conflict and Cooperation, and the recently formed Peace Studies Association. Institutional centers with a sociological focus on peace studies and conflict resolution in which sociologists are heavily involved include the University of California at San Diego, the University of Colorado at Boulder, Syracuse University, and Boston College.

Because peace and war studies are marginal within the discipline, and interdisciplinary groups are organized outside the field, sociologists interested in such matters look for colleagueship outside sociology and seldom publish in sociological journals.

Few Publications

In 1984, Kurt Finsterbusch surveyed the work on nuclear issues in the major sociology journals. What was most striking about his findings is that almost no literature exists. Sociologists have remained independent from the state's obsession with war in the nuclear age. The forty volumes of the three major sociological journals since 1945 (*American Sociological Review (ASR), American Journal of Sociology (AJS)*, and *Social Forces (SF))*, contain about 6,500 articles, of which only *four* deal with war and peace issues.

In the *AJS*, for example, an article by W. F. Ogburn was published in the year after the invention of the bomb, called "Sociology and the Atom" (Ogburn 1946). Only two articles that analyze military expenditures (Cobb 1976; Szymanski 1973) appeared in that journal through the 1984 period included in Finsterbusch's survey; it had nothing else on the arms race.

Similarly, the *ASR* had an article in 1946 on "Technological Acceleration and the Atomic Bomb," written by Harnell Hart. That journal followed up, however, with three additional articles (one per decade): "Some Social Consequences of Atomic Discovery," by Feliks Gross (1950); "Some Factors Associated with Student Acceptance or Rejection of War," by Snell Putney and Russell Middleton (1962); and

"Arms Races: A Test of Two Models," by Robert Hamblin et al. (1977). *Social Forces* had published nothing on the topic.

Even the social problems literature has paid scant attention to the nuclear arms race. The journal *Social Problems* began publishing in 1953; during the next thirty-one years, it contained only fourteen articles dealing with nuclear arms race issues, ten of which were in a special 1963 issue published in the wake of the Cuban missile crisis.

Despite the persistent concern among modern states about the problems of war, sociologists, even most of those who specialize in social problems, have not made this problem a significant element of their research or teaching (see Lauer 1976; Sofios 1983). There has been a substantial increase in the 1980s in the number of articles on the topics of atomic and nuclear war, as shown in the *Social Science Citation Index,* because society at large developed an interest in such issues, but the increase may have been short-lived. Although there were only six articles in the 1976–80 period, there were thirty-five in the next five-year period (1981–85), and an additional ten in 1986 alone.

What is remarkable is not so much how many more articles were published in the later period, but that the total number is so small—a mere forty-one sources compared to the thousands of articles published in the social sciences during that decade.

More War Than Peace

Although sociologists demonstrate autonomy from the state by avoiding studying issues of war and peace, when they do consider these topics, they reflect the same priorities as that culture by looking more to the former than the latter. This pattern can be seen in *Sociological Abstracts* by examining the categories in the subject index of "military," "war," and "peace." The number of publications on the "military" (and related categories, such as militarism, militarists, military-civilian relations, and military sociology) is consistently several times that of articles classified as being about "peace."[1] "War" falls between the two, except toward the end of the last decade (1986), when research on peace movements escalated, pushing the "peace" category above "war" for the first time (see Fig. 1).This publication trend lags

1. The number of articles put in each category may, of course, be an artifact of the compiler's biases when the abstract was constructed, as the classifications are somewhat subjective.

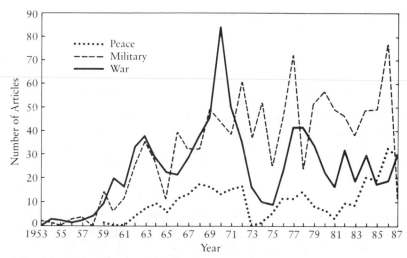

Fig. 1. Index Citations of Sociological Abstracts

three or four years behind the political trend, because of the time involved in conducting and publishing research.

The differential attention to war and peace in the social sciences is
analogous to the two cultures in sociology and in the broader culture.
Despite the lack of an institutional base for sociological war and peace
research, a massive wave of antinuclear protest in Western Europe and
the United States in the 1980s helped to precipitate increased interest
among sociologists. The peace movements themselves were fueled, in
large part, by President Reagan's inflammatory rhetoric at the beginning of the period (see Benford 1988).

The increase in research on peace, rather than war, in recent years
is primarily due to the fact that more sociologists are studying a revitalized peace movement. This suggests an affinity between methods
and topics—sociologists are more at ease when they have an institution to study.

The peace movement provides sociologists with an object of study,
that is, a movement organization. Such study has a widely accepted
methodology and theoretical framework in a central subfield of the
discipline (social movements). Thus, with the peace movement, peace
researchers have a phenomenon observable with a conventional approach, just as the military sociologists have the military to study.

It is, consequently, the interaction between the internal organization
of the discipline and its methodological proclivities, on the one hand,

and the external pull of the two cultures toward war-making and peace-making institutions, on the other hand, which shapes the sociological study of war and peace.

The Two Cultures

One of the most striking aspects of the research on issues of war and peace among sociologists is the presence of two distinct camps, one drawn toward military institutions and the other toward peace movements. These two networks of scholars have different agendas, different sources of funds, and different traditions of research. For the most part, those drawn toward the military have themselves been in the service, and those studying peace organizations have participated in those movements. The way in which those institutions help to shape the sociological agenda is apparent in the review that follows.

There is very little overlap between the networks, they cite each other infrequently, and, with few exceptions (e.g., in the Peace and War Section of the American Sociological Association), they have little in common except a concern about war and peace. There are substantial problems created by the gap between the cultures, such as redundant or missing research, and the myopia caused by influence from and attention to different institutional milieus. There is, however, clearly unanimity on a number of issues, including the desirability of avoiding war.

The existence of two cultures should not be overemphasized or false distinctions drawn between them. Like all analytical distinctions, this one also disappears under the microscope, and some scholars do attempt to bridge the gap. It is not my intention to widen the gap; indeed, continued dialogue and interaction between these two traditions is essential.

Military Sociology

Military sociology has two characteristics (besides an obvious interest) that draw scholars into the field; one is an external influence, and the second is a result of the nature of sociology. First, there is funding available for research and consulting,[2] even if it is minuscule compared to the overall Pentagon budget. Second, there is a concrete phe-

---

2. One military sociologist told me that he made as much consulting with the Pentagon as he makes from his university position.

nomenon to study with traditional sociological frames and methods, that is, the military itself.

Military sociologists trace their roots to earlier speculative work by Adam Ferguson (1767) and Herbert Spencer (1898), as well as the group that formed around political scientists Harold D. Lasswell and Quincy Wright (see Wright 1965). The field did not flourish, however, until after World War II, when many veterans turned their attention to military issues. The field had an existential base: it was founded by ex-soldiers. The July 1946 issue of the *American Journal of Sociology* was entitled "Human Behavior in Military Society." Some wartime military research became part of the sociological literature, which mainly comprised surveys of German prisoners (see Shils 1950), studies of incidents of "poor" combat performance (Marshall 1947), and psychiatric observations (Grinker and Spiegel 1945).

In the immediate post–World War II period, military sociology was closely linked to the military, but has since developed more autonomy. The sociologically most important of the early studies were conducted by the Army Research Branch, and summarized in the two volumes of *The American Soldier* (Stouffer et al. 1949a, 1949b). They provide both a significant contribution to the understanding of the military, and a model of mass production in sociological research that foreshadowed much of postwar U.S. sociology (see Kurtz 1984:79). A considerable discussion of the methodological innovations and implications of the study ensued (see Merton and Lazarsfeld (1950); cf. Shils 1950; Merton and Kitt 1950; Speier 1950; Kendall and Lazarsfeld 1950; Stouffer 1950; Lerner 1950).

Other publications in the immediate postwar period offered insights gained from participant observation by scholars-cum-soldiers (see Lang 1972:20), concerning such issues as the character of military structure (see Page 1946; Turner 1947; Spindler 1948) or military culture (see, e.g., Berger 1946; Elkin 1956; Anonymous 1946; Caplow 1947; White 1946).

The military sociology agenda is constructed out of a combination of sociological concern with institutional issues, on the one hand, and out of matters of concern to the military itself, on the other. The tension between these two concerns is apparent if one reviews the literature, which focuses on (1) civilian-military relations; (2) the extent to which the military has become more convergent with civilian institutions; (3) military occupations and organizations (e.g., the profession of arms, forms of racial, gender, and class stratification, institutionalization of more effective management, decision making, and training); (4) debates about conscription; and (5) the role of military forces in the new nations. In addition, (6) the military sociologists share with the peace researchers a general concern about the nature of war, especially in light of the development of implements of mass destruction and the total war of the twentieth century.

Much of the research in the field is paid for by military organizations, which help to set the agenda for military sociologists despite their efforts to maintain independence.

CIVIL-MILITARY RELATIONS

Research conducted by centers and institutes within the armed forces tends to be somewhat limited to the specific purposes of those institutions (see Lang 1972:20, and summaries in Hall 1956; Bowers 1967; Vial 1959; Chandessais 1959; Solomon 1954; cf. Michaels 1957). One of the most existentially based concerns of early military sociology was the issue of civil-military relations, which remains a central theme of the field.

The relationship between the civilian state and the military was an issue at the founding of the American Republic, when the founding fathers built checks against military power into the structure of the new government. Samuel Adams wrote a letter to the *Boston Gazette* contending that "it is a very improbable supposition, that any people can long remain free, with a strong military in the very heart of their country:—Unless that military power is under the direction of the people, and even then it is dangerous" (Adams [1768] 1904).

Military officers always have some involvement in politics, no matter how powerfully the civilian control over them is institutionalized. Work on this topic is diverse (see Segal et al. 1978), although most of it seems to reflect a general consensus in U.S. culture that at least some control over the military is a good thing to have, but that controlling the military is problematic. Sociologists have reflected that concern in the wider U.S. culture in their research.

C. Wright Mills (1957) argues that for most of history, the military controlled the state, except around the time of the Enlightenment when an effort was made in Western Europe and the United States to bring the military under civilian control. This historically unique event was relatively successful for some time, but since the development of the A-bomb, the military has begun once again to take control. In the middle of the twentieth century, for the first time, the American elite "begin to realize what it means to live in a military neighborhood, what it means to be technically open to catastrophic attack upon the national domain" (1956:183). With the change in the nature of warfare, Mills argues, the nature of civil-military relations shifts dramatically as well: "Peace is no longer serious; only war is serious. Every man and every nation is either friend or foe, and the idea of enmity becomes mechanical, massive, and without genuine passion" (1956:206).

Virtually all of the work on civil-military relations lacks the critical bite that Mills brings in his stinging critique of the "warlords" (see, e.g., Huntington 1957; Hong 1979). That may be because the topic has been left to the military sociologists who, although they maintain some critical edge, are too close to the military establishment to make the kind of indictments provided by Mills. Much of the work is historical and comparative (see, e.g., Skelton 1978), but ignores the so-called military-industrial complex. This avoidance by sociologists includes both military sociologists and peace researchers.

CONVERGENCE WITH CIVILIAN INSTITUTIONS

The apparent transformation of military organizations into structures that increasingly resemble civilian institutions has become one of the mainstays of military sociology. Like people in skilled jobs in virtually every other sector of the labor market, military officers have become more professionalized (see Huntington 1957). Military officers belong to an occupational group with a long, distinguished tradition that is highly valued. Like Simmel's "stranger," they are near to centers of political power and remote from them at the same time. As Lang (1972:29) puts it, "The unique customs, codes, traditions, and lore that are part of the military way of life, the clubs and associations officers belong to, the uniforms and insignia they wear—all of these tend to set them apart from other officials."

Huntington (1957) notes that the professional military has a distinct field of expertise, the management of violence, but that the organization's distinctiveness appears to be waning. In *The Professional Soldier,* Janowitz (1960) traces some of the implications of new forms of management, from the change in recruitment ("from ascription to achievement") to issues of commitment (see Zald and Simon 1964) to career mobility (see Segal 1967) and ideology and self-image (see Vagts 1959; Janowitz 1960). The shift hypothesized by Moskos (1977b; cf. Moskos and Wood 1988) as a change in the character of the military from an "institution" to an "occupation" involves, according to Moskos (1988), a transformation from an emphasis on the value orientation of the institution to a rational calculation of the marketplace (see Faris 1988). A wide range of issues is involved, such as changes in societal regard for the military, role commitments, reference groups, basis or mode of compensation, the legal system, residence, sex roles, and performance evaluation.

In the decade since the publication of Moskos's 1977 article, more than 30 studies have tested the "institutional/organizational" (I/O) hypothesis. This has been a rare example of a single conceptual scheme imposed on a set of cross-national studies (Moskos and Wood 1988:9). Although there is considerable support for the hypothesis in the American military, it is not universal (see Downes 1988; Jans 1988; Smokovitis 1988). In Israel, for example, the military is very "institutional" in character, "almost completely value-driven" (Gal 1988). The hypothesis may reflect a change in the U.S. military as much as a general trend, and underlines a problem with research that is not comparative.

Although the implications of this large set of studies are certainly broader than the question of what manpower choices the military will make, that is the focus of the articulated contribution (see Moskos and Wood 1988). In other words, the literature's major purpose seems to be to develop not sociological theory, but a set of policy recommendations for the military.

MILITARY OCCUPATIONS AND ORGANIZATIONS

Another major item on the military sociologists' agenda concerns specific studies of military occupations and organizations. This research reflects factors both internal and external to the field. A large proportion of the social science research on the military focuses on these matters because funding is available, since it is useful to the military, and it can be examined with empiricist methods highly valued in sociology.

This area concerns such matters as how the military is stratified according to race and gender. Other key topics include: the question of unit cohesion (a fundamental principle of military organization), problems of leadership, and the nature of service and motivations to serve (Segal and Segal forthcoming).

Military occupations and organizations are topics in which there is a strong affinity between traditional sociological concerns and methods and the needs of the subculture toward which military sociologists are drawn. Sociologists have insights and methods of investigation that are helpful to the military, and it is in the interests of both to promote such research. For example, the military is one of the most racially integrated institutions in U.S. society as a result of deliberate policy (and its enforcement); sociologists have offered empirical assessments of the process and have identified ways in which it might be enhanced.

THE DEBATE OVER CONSCRIPTION

The debate over conscripted versus all-volunteer armed forces is another major military sociology issue, one waged consistently throughout U.S. history (see Segal and Segal forthcoming). In recent years, the problem has been exacerbated by what the Segals call "the waning of the principle of the citizen-soldier," which has "deprived the nation of the mobilization base that it is likely to need in the event of a major war." This topic is likely to become even more significant in light of recent geopolitical changes. On the one hand, as the popular sense of a military threat erodes, it may become increasingly difficult to recruit volunteers to the military. In East Germany, for example, morale within the military collapsed along with the Berlin Wall, as soldiers began to question whether they were serving any worthwhile purpose. On the other hand, the military achieved a new stature in many circles because of its activities in the Gulf War.

THE MILITARY IN NEW NATIONS

Some literature on the role of the military in the new nations has been compiled, since military forces have become crucial ingredients in those countries during the period of decolonization following World War II (see Janowitz and Little 1974:10). Sociologists have examined the impact of military control on state and society, and the conditions under which coups occur (see, e.g., Janowitz and van Doorn 1971; Bienen 1968; Zimmerman 1979; Cochran 1974; Fidel 1975; Schmitter 1973; Janowitz 1971; Schmidt and Dorfman 1974; Pitcher, Hamblin, and Miller 1978; Horowitz and Trimberger 1976).

The internationalization of military sociology has increased interest in this issue. Segal and Segal (forthcoming) contend that research interests in this area "have shifted from emphasizing the role of military elites as forces of modernization toward analyses of military regimes and processes of returning politicized military forces to the barracks and reestablishing civilian rule." This issue reflects an independence of military sociology from military institutions, because it is not a topic of central concern within the latter.

Again, the research trend in this field tends to follow what is going on in the broader society. Because of the large number of coups and coup attempts in the 1970s and 1980s around the world, sociologists have developed a keen interest in such matters.

WAR AND WAR PREVENTION

Finally, military sociologists are concerned about the nature of modern war and how to prevent it. A series of research projects on arms control was sponsored in the 1960s by the U.S. Arms Control and Disarmament Agency, although funding was reduced markedly in the 1970s. According to Janowitz (1974:22), the most significant element of studies by the agency staff was the collection of worldwide data on military expenditures (cf. Millet 1974).

A major contribution to this area has been the study of peacekeeping forces, notably Charles Moskos's salient work, *Peace Soldiers: The Sociology of United Nations Military Force* (1976). Another significant area of study is the examination of the Vietnam War (see, e.g., Gibson 1986).

The development of nuclear weapons, and the recent increase in consciousness about them, has resulted in polarization in the broader culture, but it has facilitated shared values between military sociologists and peace researchers. As Janowitz (1974:24) contends, "There is no reason why military strategists cannot and should not build hypothetical models of a 'world without war'—for such models can contribute to the next steps in arms control, international peacekeeping, and a realistic understanding of the positive and negative roles of force in international relations. In the continuing search for such an outlook, the categories of strategy and social science become fused." Janowitz (1974:22) observes further that there is an inherent tension in the study of the military, because "military institutions are organized on the basis of nation-states and coalitions, voluntary and enforced, of nation-states," whereas "scholarship has aspirations for international perspective and international cooperation." The increasing internationalization of the field of military sociology should serve to make the field more independent of military organizations and reduce the distance between military sociologists and peace researchers.

Peace Research

In contrast with the research done under the rubric of military sociology, peace researchers usually focus on broader issues, such as the causes of war and peace. They explore (1) the social structure of the arms race and the military-industrial complex; (2) the nature of discourse about weapons and international relations; (3) the dynamics of conflict and its resolution; (4) global structures; and (5) peace movement organizations and public opinion about war and peace issues. Because it is more difficult to study these broader issues, there has been more peace research at times when there is increased peace movement activity because these activities provide data that allow sociologists to utilize conventional study methods. In that sense, internal and external factors interact—broader cultural preferences lead to the structuring of the sociological enterprise in such a way that it promotes empiricist methods of investigation, and the sociological predisposition to study institutions is stimulated by the growth of movement organizations.

Many of the scholars who do peace research are active in the peace movement, which helps to set their agenda. Like many military sociologists, peace researchers are, or have been, active in the institutions toward which they are pulled; but the financial resources flow in opposite directions, that is, toward the military sociologists from the military and away from the peace researchers toward peace movement organizations. The autonomy of both military sociologists and peace researchers is at least potentially compromised by financial exchanges between them and the institutions they are studying.

If military sociology is a marginal field, peace research is scarcely even hanging onto the margins. Both military sociologists and peace researchers reflect the concerns of a marginalized subculture—people who sustain an interest in peacemaking. Martin Shaw (1984:2) notes:

> It would be nice to think that social science had transcended the limitations of popular consciousness and sustained ongoing theory and research into war in modern civilisation. And yet most of the mainstream academic writing about war dates back to the 1950s and early 1960s, if not before. The great social science boom of the later sixties and seventies almost wholly neglected the issue. The intellectual revolution which produced so much radical and Marxist social theory bypassed this most fundamental of problems. C. Wright Mills' other writings were pivotal to the changes in sociology, but his appeal for a study of war went almost completely unheeded.

It is instructive to compare two major issues identified as significant by scholars outlining sociological contributions to studies of war in peace, one a military sociologist, Morris Janowitz, and the other a peace researcher, Martin Shaw. Janowitz (1974:8–9), on the one hand, emphasizes two historical trends: the shift from conscription to increased reliance upon an all-volunteer force, and "the emergence of military forces as crucial ingredients in the political realities of the new nations." Shaw (1984:4), on the other hand, identifies two main types of problems. The primary issue has been "to produce an account of the causes of war and its significance for society. The secondary one is to explain particular features of war and war preparation in social terms." Whereas the military sociologist (Janowitz) is more concerned about the impact of historical trends on the military, the peace researcher (Shaw) attends to the impact of the military on historical trends.

SOCIAL STRUCTURE OF THE ARMS RACE

Shaw rightly contends that there is very little of the framework required for carrying out a sociology of war. The sociology of war, as Shaw (1984:5) observes, faces the same problems faced by sociology generally: the dilemma of "grand theory" versus "abstracted empiricism." Efforts to bridge this gap by Arthur Marwick (1968, 1977) and Andreski (1968), for example, have been useful, but not entirely successful. There is no easy empirical handle for exploring the broader issues of peace and war, and the empiricist bent of U.S. sociology discourages the undertaking.

The founders of the discipline paid little attention to the issue, because they believed that it was a problem of the past. Auguste Comte thought that industrial society was replacing military society. The towering figure of the field is C. Wright Mills, whose 1958 *The Causes of World War Three* was largely ignored, went out of print, and was only recently reissued as an expensive reprint.

Although sociologists have paid little attention to the structure of the arms race, there are some exceptions, especially efforts to examine the U.S.–U.S.S.R. arms race, subjected to quantitative analysis by Hamblin et al. (1977). Similarly, Louis Kriesberg (1986) has examined trends in U.S.–Soviet relations, looking primarily at efforts to deescalate the conflict. Robert Angell's (1951) American Sociological Association presidential address discussed the emergence of a global social system in which issues of war and peace must be analyzed by sociologists, but few heeded his call (see Boulding et al. 1974).

CULTURAL STUDIES

A second major area of peace research is the use of techniques of discourse analysis recently developed by anthropologists, cultural sociologists, and semioticians to identify the pragmatic and metapragmatic devices used to articulate and sustain political positions and processes (see Mehan and Skelly 1987; Gamson 1984; Gumperz 1982; Molotch and Boden 1985; Verschueren 1985; Chilton 1985; Van Dijk 1985; Chick 1985; Kurtz 1988). In lieu of institutional objects of study, this research focuses on texts, which are easily observable and don't resist examination. Although discourse analysts tend not to be empiricist in a strict sense, textual analysis offers them a semblance of scientific rigor.

These scholars examine the texts as part of the discourse of international relations, which, as Mehan and Skelly (1987) contend, "is similar to the discourse which routinely occurs in face-to-face encounters and literary texts." Written texts are part of an ongoing dialogue in which participants anticipate further responses and actions (Voloshinov; cf. Natanson 1984; Wertsch 1986). A conference on "Nuclear Policy, Culture and History" was held at the University of Chicago, 13–14 March 1987. Another group met for a two-week period to discuss the "Discourse of the Nuclear Arms Debate," Ballyvaughn, Ireland, 9–16 August 1987, sponsored by the Institute on Global Conflict and Cooperation (IGCC) of the University of California.

Finally, some scholars have examined images and perceptions that perpetuate the arms race, and those that might reverse it (see Boudling 1988; Kelman 1965; Lifton 1967; Ziegler 1985). A precursor to contemporary cultural studies is contained in an analysis by Gamson and Modigliani (1966), which explores U.S.–Soviet relations between 1946 and 1963. They contend that official belief systems of each power mirror that of the other, claiming that the purpose of their foreign policy is consolidation, whereas the other nation's goal is expansion (and that the opponent correctly perceives those goals). Similarly, Benford and Kurtz (1988) explore ways in which beliefs and values are related to ritual elements of the arms race.

A more conventional way of studying cultural factors is by examining public opinion, although there has been surprisingly little opinion research (see Gamson and Modigliani 1966; Mills 1956; Kriesberg 1981). It is a convenient empirical handle, albeit sometimes simplistic, that one would expect might be used more often by peace researchers. One project now under way is a "Peace Barometer" survey of university students in the Soviet Union, Finland, France, and the United States. They survey will examine images of the superpowers as developed by students in those countries, and is the result of cooperation by Soviet, U.S., Finnish, and French sociologists.

ALTERNATIVES FOR SECURITY AND CONFLICT RESOLUTION

A third major area of interest is that of conflict and conflict resolution, a well-established interdisciplinary field in which some sociologists have played a pivotal role. A modest but significant literature on social conflict has emerged in recent decades (see, e.g., Coser 1956; Wehr 1979; Deutsch 1973; Oberschall 1973). James Laue has a "conflict clinic" at George Mason University and is organizing an international network of negotiators for solving international conflicts. Louis Kriesberg, the 1990–91 chair of the Peace and War Section of the ASA (see, e.g., Kriesberg 1981, 1982, 1986), directs a program on conflict resolution at Syracuse University. Much of the work in this area, however fruitful, is published outside of the mainstream sociology journals in such publications as the *Journal of Conflict Resolution,* and is often ignored by sociologists outside of the field. This area of investigation has grown in recent years as it has developed techniques that some government officials have found useful (e.g., the Camp David process), and it is the one area of peace studies that is not very politically controversial.

A related effort is the important work on alternative security and nonviolent coercive action, notably that by Gene Sharp, a sociologist who has an Institute on Nonviolent Sanctions at Harvard (see Sharp 1973) and Paul Wehr at the University of Colorado at Boulder (see Wehr 1979; 1988). These studies explore the extent to which popular resistance can affect the ability of a government regarded as illegitimate to impose its rule (see Kriesberg 1981b; Boserup and Mack 1975). Others, such as Ted Gurr, are developing theories of civil conflict that increasingly involve military confrontation.

Included in this sort of research are such concepts as civilian-based, or social, defense, nonviolent collective action, and alternative defense paradigms. Although sometimes dismissed in mainstream political debate, these notions are gaining some credence in circles that are exploring alternatives to war in the contemporary world. Much of it is based upon the theories and practice of Mohandas K. Gandhi and Martin Luther King, Jr. The leader of efforts to translate their theories into practical political strategies has been Sharp (1973), who has developed a set of 198 categories of nonviolent action that can be used as a means for deterrence or as ways of making a subjected population ungovernable, should deterrence fail. Although Sharp is widely known and respected in the peace movement, he is virtually unknown among sociologists and does not publish in sociological journals.

In the early 1970s, an intellectual debate flourished in the American Sociological Association's Section on World Conflicts (now the Peace and War Section) between the integration theorists and the conflict theorists. As Boulding et al. (1974:187) put it:

> The integrationists rely on the "sisterhood of man" principle: we are evolving, however slowly, toward a harmonious world society. The task of the researcher is to identify and strengthen communication networks. The conflict theorists argue that most of the initiatives which have brought people together have been coercive, imperialist, elitist, racist, and must be resisted and destroyed.
>
> Increasingly, scholars examining alternative forms of security are exploring ways in which the concept of peace cannot be limited to the absence of war. Attention to this sort of issue leads to an examination of the continuity of violent conflict from the personal to the global.

GLOBAL STRUCTURES STUDIES

Some sociologists have engaged in the analysis of global structures and transnational networks such as governmental, nongovernmental, and United Nations organizations, in an effort to explore ways in which alternative futures might be developed that facilitate a world without war.

Relatedly, scholars have analyzed cooperative international interactions that might help to mitigate international conflicts, such as student exchanges, trade, and postal services. If such social forms can be understood more clearly, the mechanisms of cooperation and conflict management employed there might be applicable to other spheres.

The study of global structures tends to be, by necessity, broad and somewhat speculative. Consequently, although a number of persons both within and outside the discipline of sociology find it appealing, it remains marginalized within the field. It does not have the same empirical grounding as studies of fertility, morality, and income distributions.

Comparative work is highly labor-intensive, and academia is structured in such a way as to reward those who publish frequently more than those who engage in time-consuming data-gathering that requires spending time traveling in and learning about other cultures. Gathering reliable statistics for a global analysis is extremely difficult, if not impossible, and sociology has no strong tradition of comparative field work like anthropology which would encourage international data-gathering activities. Sociologists are encouraged, instead, to study discernible, manageable institutional objects of investigation, which is why the most frequent sociological studies in peace research are of the peace movement itself.

STUDIES OF THE PEACE MOVEMENT

The fastest growing area of peace research among sociologists is the study of peace movement organizations. They are concrete institutions that can be examined through conventional sociological methods (primarily ethnography). Despite peace movement rhetoric about being international in character—and there are many intellectual currents that flow across national boundaries—the structures of peace movements tend to be national in scope.

The number of articles on peace in the index of the *Sociological Abstracts* remained consistently minute, until a dramatic jump in the late 1980s. The reason was the increase in articles published about the peace movement. In fact, in 1986, those articles were broken out of the general category of "peace" and placed in a new category of their own. A number of individuals, such as Sam Marullo and John Lofland (who are preparing an edited volume on the peace movement), Robert Benford, John MacDougall, and others, are involved in extensive studies of the movement, although much of the work is not yet published (see, e.g., Benford 1988). Before the peace movement studies of the 1980s, sociologists had examined antiwar sentiment (see Schuman 1972).

Funding Peace and War Research

Perhaps the most striking difference between the "peace" and "military" cultures is the flow of resources for research. Military sociologists are often paid by the military, either as consultants or by contract for specific projects. A handful of them have worked within the military, especially with the Army Research Institute for the Behavioral and Social Sciences, which had an annual budget of $59.9 million in 1988. That budget exceeds the total combined social science research budget of the National Science Foundation, the National Institute of Mental Health, and the Department of Education. It is highly unlikely that there is any such source of major funding for any kind of social science research in any field. (It does, however, constitute only about two hours of the Pentagon's annual budget prior to the Gulf War, so must be measured not only against the standards of social science funding, but also military funding.)

There is little systematic evidence that demonstrates what is widely assumed about the effect of funding sources on the agenda-setting process in research activities. Foundations and government agencies operate on the assumption that more research is done on an area when there are ample resources. Similarly, most scholars know the experience of either "adjusting" one's research plans or pursuing an unexpected topic because of the availability of funds.

The largest proportion of research on war and peace issues is military sociology applicable to the institution building of the armed forces. That is the case, in large part, because it is being done by contract with, or under the direct auspices of, a military organization. The funding institution expects some useful work, even when funding basic research. Some of the military's research is scarcely recognized by military sociologists as legitimate social science, despite the fact that it uses social science techniques and is carried out by individuals with training in those disciplines. It is, I think, partly a territorial matter—the agenda is set quite blatantly by the military, so military sociologists do not feel as though they own it, and often do not wish to claim it.

There is a certain irony in the fact that although the largest single funder of social science research in the world is the U.S. military, military sociology remains relatively insignificant. That is largely due to the fact that there is a broad chasm between the discipline at large and military social science research, and also because sociologists have played a less important role in such research than have people from other disciplines, notably psychology. The Army Research Institute, for example, employs 213 scientists, of which 197 are psychologists and 5 are sociologists. The Chief of Plans, Programs and Operations of the Institute, Dr. James Bynam, suggests that it is probably the "country's largest single employer of psychologists." [3]

According to the "dean of the military sociologists," Morris Janowitz:

> The funds expended by the U.S. military to study itself are used to collect a vast array of statistical data, conduct numerous sample surveys, and sponsor social science research by its own personnel and, through contracts and grants, by universities, nonprofit research centers, and commercial groups. Military agencies, on a much more limited basis, support "policy studies" designed to assess alternative U.S. military strategies and plans. These studies are carried out by closely affiliated research institutes, generally on a "crash" basis.

3. Telephone interview, 24 September 1988.

The bulk of their findings receive at best informal distribution; and, although they draw on social science and sociological concepts, their overall contribution to the social sciences is limited. (1974:14)

According to Bynum, about 80 percent of the research carried out by the Army Research Institute in 1988 consisted of basic research contracts by scholars such as Charles Moskos and Fred Fiedler and a group of people at Yale. Most of the reports coming from the Institute's research discuss internal organizational problems of the Army, for example, "Receptiveness of Army Families in USAREUR to Incentives for Extension," and "After Action Review (AAR) Guide for the Army Training Battle Simulation System (ARTBASS)." The tendency by independent military sociologists to reject the military's inhouse research as part of their field suggests that they are more oriented toward what Janowitz calls the enlightenment, rather than the engineering, model of sociology (see Terence Halliday's introduction to this volume).

Outside of the military, resources for military sociology are scarce. As Janowitz (1974) notes, "The National Science Foundation completely avoids involvement and probably rightly so; in part it does not wish to 'elevate' the performance of U.S. military institutions." Similarly, the Social Science Research Council discontinued funding research on military institutions or civil-military relations in 1974 (1974:13), although they do have a program of "Advanced Research Fellowships in Foreign Policy Studies" funded by the Ford Foundation. Perhaps funders do not wish to fund military sociology, either because of the political implications of doing so or because they assume that the military itself is paying for such research. Consequently, the agenda for the field is set, in large part, by the military itself, at least insofar as the military's priorities overlap with those of the scholars.

Military sociologists are sensitive to the problem of their intellectual autonomy and insist that they maintain their independence. Janowitz, for example, contends that "it is necessary . . . to assert that the development of a topic of special interest only partially reflects budgetary support. In the social sciences, the intellectual attraction of a problem is important, and the sheer willingness of scholars to allocate time and effort in the context of their teaching responsibilities is an essential and almost overriding factor" (1974:12).

Military sociologists feel as though they are not well funded and their feelings are accurate when their resources are compared with those for internal research within the military. Of course, military sociology research funding is generous in comparison to funds received by peace researchers. As Janowitz (1974:13) notes, "most of the funds spent on the study of military institutions deal with internal organization, management, and personnel dimensions." The scholars' own agenda is usually *not* met by the military research institutes—such questions as "the impact of U.S. military operations at home and abroad" and "comparative or cross-national" studies of military institutions (ibid). Another problem faced by military sociologists, of course, is the security classification of some materials, which prevents their being part of the ongoing process of public scholarly activity.

For the peace researchers, the resources usually flow from them toward the organization. Peace organizations lack money to fund research and rely upon voluntary donations for their survival so that many peace researchers donate money to peace groups. Some foundations, such as Ploughshares, give money for both activist and research causes, but such funds are exceedingly limited. Like the military, peace movement institutions (and the foundations that promote them) further research that meets institutional needs; they are not always sensitive to the potential long-term benefits of basic research. Funding agencies in the peace arena will sometimes prefer a project that is more activist in its orientation.

A handful of research institutes and organizations are supported primarily by foundations and private donations, such as the Institute for Policy Studies in Washington, D. C., and The Cambridge Institute in Massachusetts. The bulk of funding for peace research, however, comes through academic channels, some of it from the recently established United States Institute of Peace.

The Institute was created by Congress in 1984 and, according to its introductory pamphlet, strives to attain the following goals:

- to help those who are working to resolve international conflicts by expanding the body of knowledge about the origins, nature, and processes of peace and war; and
- to serve as an important source of support for education and training programs and for the dissemination of information to the public about peace, war, and international conflict management.

A total of 103 awards totaling $3,004,430 had been made through 4 October 1988, ranging from $3,000 to the Woodrow Wilson International Center for Scholars (to make available in the United States and Sudan the proceedings of a conference on armed conflict in the Sudan) to $118,656 to the Council for the Advancement of Citizenship (for program activities on the importance of international relations for educational organizations). Although minuscule compared to the Army Institute, the Peace Institute's funding has made a significant difference in the amount of funds available for peace research.

Among all of the Peace Institute's award recipients, I was only able to identify two as sociologists: David Segal, one of the military sociologists, and Louis Kriesberg, a peace researcher who has done extensive research and writing on the issue of conflict. Segal received a $10,000 partial support grant to assist in the writing of "a book on the experience of U.S. military participation in the Multinational Force and Observers in the Sinai subsequent to the Camp David Accords." The project has one foot in each camp; although it is a traditional "military sociology" topic, its focus on international peacekeeping missions places it in the peace research camp as well. Kriesberg's grant was to "support the writing of a collaborative book on deescalating international conflicts between the U.S. and the U.S.S.R."

A more significant source of funding for sociological research per se is the Institute for Global Conflict and Cooperation (IGCC) of the University of California system, which has an annual budget of approximately $1.6 million.[4] The IGCC is "an interdisciplinary Multicampus Research Unit of the University of California," founded in June 1983 to support research and teaching about international peace and conflict. The Institute is, in part, a consequence of dissatisfaction with that University's administration of two national weapons labs: Lawrence Livermore and Los Alamos.

The IGCC's primary source of funds has been the university's regents, who provided approximately $1,144,000 in 1985–86 and 1986–87. The state of California provided an additional $766,000, and the remainder of the budget came from private foundations (including the Alfred P. Sloan Foundation, the John D. and Catherine T. MacArthur Foundation, and the Ploughshares Fund).

According to the IGCC's 1985–1987 *Biennial Report:* "The IGCC focus is two-fold: it is concerned with conflict situations which are so severe that escalation into large-scale war might result and with various forms of international cooperation to meet problems which threaten world peace. The main but not exclusive emphasis is on threats of and avoidance of nuclear war. IGCC's programs focus on the causes of such conflicts as well as the ideas, institutions, policies, and mechanisms relevant for eliminating, reducing, or managing conflict that might lead to global war" (IGCC 1987:1).

4. According to the 1987–88 Annual Report of the Institute.

The Institute works through the various campuses of the University of California system, with its central office in San Diego. James Skelly, a sociologist who was the 1987–88 president of the American Sociological Association's Peace and War Section, was one of the associate directors of the IGCC until the summer of 1989. One of the two most active groups of sociologists doing collaborative work on the arms race is at the University of California at San Diego, with Aaron Cicourel, Hugh Mehan, Charles Nathanson, James Skelly, and James Wertsch working on the discourse of the nuclear arms debate. The other collection of sociologists working on the topic is the Boston Nuclear Study Group.

The IGCC supports a variety of activities within a number of disciplines, including grants for campus programs (seminars, lecture series, etc.), conferences, teaching development, research, dissertation fellowships, science and other fellowship programs (e.g., science and engineering, international, and public policy fellowships). What amounts to a relatively small amount of money going to sociologists has made a substantial impact on the field, in part because so little work is being done in the area. When the Peace and War section of the ASA held a nationwide student paper contest in 1988, three entries came from the University of California at San Diego, including the winning paper.

The IGCC avoids affiliation with any peace groups, and, until 1989, was run by a former director of Livermore, Herbert York (who also worked on the Manhattan Project and was U.S. Ambassador to the Comprehensive Test Ban Negotiations in Geneva, 1979–81). The sociological research supported by the IGCC, however, is of the "peace research" genre, rather than military sociology.

In short, that small amount of money that is available for peace research has made a significant impact in the field in recent years, often as seed money for research and conferences, and should continue to make a difference in the building of peace research institutions. The funding of such research and institution-building activities in the field have helped to stimulate its growth, a trend that was probably initiated by the peace movement of the 1980s. As that movement wanes, pressure for funding peace research will probably decline as well, although the institutional mechanisms established in the 1980s could persist without the external pressure, and the Gulf War may renew interest in the field. These efforts parallel recent advances in the institutionalization of the broader field of peace studies, such as the recent creation of a Peace Studies Association.

The Peace and War Section of the American Sociological Association remains small, but has been active in recent years, building upon the groundswell of interest created by a revived peace movement. In addition to the longtime stalwarts like Elise Boulding, Bill Gamson, Louis Kriesberg, and others, a number of well-known figures in sociology who have not been known for their peace research, such as Kai Erikson,[5] Charles Tilly, John Meyer, and others, have lent their support to the building of that institution and the call for peace research within the discipline. Efforts by John Lofland, president during the 1989–90 year, will probably pay off with a revitalized section.

Much of the peace research enterprise is promoted by interdisciplinary professional associations, notably COPRED, the International Peace Research Association, and the newly formed Association of Peace Studies. Although clearly interdisciplinary, sociologists have played formative roles in all three institutions. A cycle has emerged in recent decades—marginalized in sociology, peace researchers are drawn to interdisciplinary organizations for colleagueship, institutional resources, and publication outlets. Consequently, sociologists discover an institutional base outside their discipline, seldom publish in mainstream sociology journals, and find their work thus further marginalized.

Some of the institutionalization of peace research is quite informal, most notably the Boston Nuclear Study Group, formed in the early 1980s, which met on a regular basis in an effort to apply a sociological perspective to the study of the nuclear arms race. It has resulted in some significant publications, notably Derber's (1990).

War, Peace, and the Sociological Agenda

The attempt by sociologists to address issues of war and peace has been meager indeed. The priority placed on war and peace issues is one accepted by the state, but not the society. Although people are concerned about war if asked, they usually do not think much about it; that concern is left to the state, which is charged with the responsibility in a specialized society. The attention given by the public to the Gulf War was something of an exception, and partly a media phenomenon that considerable segments of the population came to resist long before that short war ended. Most individuals are more concerned about local and family gossip, health, sports, and economic affairs than matters of war and peace. Sociology does not always at-

5. Erikson also used his position as president of the ASA to promote consideration of peace and war issues, primarily by inviting E. P. Thompson to present the major address at the convention on the topic of the Cold War (see also Lifton and Erikson 1982).

tend to what is most important to individuals' lives, of course; the choice of research topics seems to reflect the funding priorities of granting agencies, the methodological constraints of the discipline, and societal concerns indirectly through sociologists' personal biographies.

Sociologists reflect the broader social apathy about these issues rather than succumbing to the seduction of large amounts of resources provided by the military for social research. Furthermore, those sociologists who do concern themselves with such matters reflect not the state's concern so much as the interests of the marginalized subcultures of the military and the peace movement.

What work has been done by sociologists has had relatively little impact on public policy. Its effects have been primarily indirect— through the institutions that have been aided by the two cultures in sociological studies of war and peace. This institution-building role of sociologists has not been central to the development of either set of institutions, but is not altogether meaningless.

Why have war and peace been so far down the priorities list of the sociological agenda? Why has the impact of sociologists on the topic been so meager? Why is it that, despite enormous sums of money available for research on the military, so little of it has been captured by sociologists?

Sociological attitudes and behavior with reference to war and peace in some ways mirror those of the larger culture, and in some ways resist them. On the one hand, sociologists mirror the larger culture by attending more to war than to peace, and by promoting military solutions to international problems. There has been little systematic or concerted effort to solve the dilemma, short of the continued amassing of increasingly sophisticated weapons and delivery systems. Significant alternatives to existing institutional arrangements are not widely supported, and there is the legacy of the McCarthy period, in which many with deviant positions (especially with regard to the Soviet Union) were drummed out of the academy. Sociologists have not provided research fundamental to the growth or maintenance of the military machine (as have its sibling disciplines of economics and political science), but neither has it made a major contribution to its critique.

Some characteristics of the academic community and the structure of scholarly research also contribute to the failure of sociologists to address the issues of war and peace. Institutional arrangements internal to the field of sociology have mitigated against work on these topics, and subfields of the discipline tend to become more or less wealthy in proportion to their networks and resources. For example, until very recently, war and peace were not taught in introductory sociology texts, and have not been featured in general definitions of mainstream sociology. Moreover, academic life in the latter half of the twentieth century, and the field of sociology itself, is not structured so as to promote the solving of the big issues of our time, but toward getting publications and expanding vitas. It is organized around the production of publications, facilitated by the use of a particular kind of empiricist methodology.[6]

Most sociologists, consequently, do not tackle the big issues, unless they happen to be in an area in which there is significant funding (e.g., William Julius Wilson's important work on the black underclass), or where interest is stimulated by increased societal attention. As Tilly (1988:3) observes, "In the discipline's present condition, its best minds do not turn easily to the study of war and military power— untidy phenomena that lend themselves badly to 'clear, brilliant solutions.' " Although the Gulf War turned society's attention to the issue of war in a significant new way, it will be difficult for sociologists to examine the issue, because of the problems with operationalizing the larger issues in concrete, empirical studies beyond attitudinal surveys.

There is no doubt a psychological dimension to the failure of sociologists to address the issue of war, as encapsulated in Robert Jay Lifton's concept of "psychic numbing," which occurs when individuals are incapable of coping with an overwhelming problem. Sociologists are no doubt susceptible to the same defense mechanisms that others use to avoid thinking about modern warfare, especially given the nature of contemporary weapons of mass destruction.

Finally, the failure of sociologists to address issues of war and peace in a meaningful way is related, at least in part, to the structure of war and peace research itself. Despite efforts to maintain a modicum of independence (and certainly a *sense* of independence) from the institutions they are aiding, both military sociologists and peace researchers are allowing the institutions toward which they are respectively drawn to influence the agenda for their work. Because military research is more predominant, that is what gets funded most frequently, and the work tends to be myopic. Most of it remains outside of the disciplinary boundaries of sociology, even when it is carried out by sociologists. Even that peace research and military sociology within the discipline still tends to exist on the margins. Because their numbers are so small, and since there are many outside the discipline who share their substantive interests, peace researchers and military sociologists tend to work in interdisciplinary networks. (It is ironic that the mili-

6. I am indebted to Gideon Sjoberg for a discussion on this issue.

tary sociologists constitute one of the least nationalistic sectors of the discipline, because of the increasingly international organization of their work.)

Unless sociologists begin to change the way in which they address issues of war and peace, it is unlikely that sociologists will play a major role in helping humanity to escape the nuclear cage in which it has entrapped itself. The lack of attention to the issues of war and peace by most of the sociological mainstream has resulted in the failure of the discipline to meet its responsibilities, if one accepts the notion that sociologists have a responsibility to humanity. This idea has gained popularity since the social turmoil of the 1960s, as reflected in the growing interest in applied sociology, although it has been the subject of considerable debate.

Such concerns are often expressed in terms of the tension between the "relevance" of sociological research, on the one hand, and the necessity of carrying out basic research that transcends one's own interests (and those of one's funders), on the other. Recent changes in the Soviet Union and Eastern Europe provide some important challenges to sociologists; they offer an important arena in which relevant social problems combine with opportunities to understand basic processes of social structure and social change. Certainly these changes are of great interest to business people. Perhaps establishing and maintaining peaceful international relationships will become a priority of international capital, and sociologists will be able to contribute to the process, while at the same time pointing out the dangers of an increasingly stratified global order dominated by cooperating superpowers.

Sociologists could make a significant contribution to our understanding of both war and peace, and the social processes, cultural orientations, and institutional configurations that predispose human activities in war- and peace-making. If there is going to be a society left for us to study, sociologists must create an agenda for the study of war and peace, beginning with an application of existing research traditions to those issues (see Kurtz 1988). The sociological and anthropological literature on reciprocity provides insights into personal motivations, interactions, and conflict processes. Much of the vast literature on bureaucracy is relevant to understanding not only the military and governments, but the military-industrial complex and the ways in which predispositions toward military solutions to international conflict dominate interstate relations. Finally, cultural sociology provides rich concepts, such as ritual, which could help us understand the symbolic dimensions of international conflict.

If they are to do so, sociologists must have the means for carrying

out research independent of either the military or the peace movement, and there must be an infrastructure to promote such studies
within the sociological community, even if it means promoting unconventional methods of analysis. Finally, peace researchers and military
sociologists have much to learn from each other, in examining their
common concerns about war and peace, especially as the world continues to change so rapidly as we move into the 1990s.

References

Adams, Samuel. [1768] 1904. "A Letter From Samuel Adams." In *The Writings of Samuel Adams,* ed. H. A. Cushing, 264–68. Boston.

Ahmad, Aqueil, and Arthur S. Wilke. 1973. "Peace and War Themes in Social
Science Periodicals: 1946 to Present." *Journal of Political and Military Sociology* 1:39–56.

Andrews, William G., and Uri Ra'anan, eds. 1969. *The Politics of Coups
d'Etat: Five Case Studies.* New York: Van Nostrand Reinhold.

Angell, Robert. 1979. *The Quest for World Order.* Ann Arbor: University of
Michigan Press.

Aron, Raymond. 1973. *Peace and War: A Theory of International Relations.*
Abridg. ed. Trans. R. Howard and A. B. Fox. Garden City, N.Y.: Anchor.

Baldwin, Robert H., Jr. 1982. "The Decision to End the Draft: Economics vs.
Sociology." *Joint Perspectives* 3:58–68.

Benson, John. 1982. "The Polls: U.S. Military Intervention." *Public Opinion
Quarterly* 46:592–98.

Berger, M. 1946. "Law and Custom in the Army." *Social Forces* 25:82–87.

Bienen, Henry, ed. 1968. *The Military Intervenes: Case Studies in Political
Development.* New York: Russell Sage Foundation.

Boer, Connie de. 1981. "The Polls: Our Commitment to World War III."
Public Opinion Quarterly 45:126–34.

Boserup, Anders, and Andrew Mack. 1975. *War Without Weapons: Nonviolence in National Defense.* New York: Schocken.

Boulding, Elise M., Joseph W. Elder, Ted Goertzel, Ruth Harriet Jacobs, and
Louis Kriesberg. 1974. "Teaching the Sociology of World Conflicts: A Review of the State of the Field." *American Sociologist* 9:187–93.

Bowers, R. V. 1967. "The Military Establishment." In *The Uses of Sociology,*
ed. P. F. Lazarsfeld, W. H. Sewell, and H. L. Wilensky, 234–74. New York:
Basic.

Bowman, Claude C. 1963. "The Family and the Nuclear Arms Race." *Social
Problems* 11:29–34.

Butler, John Sibley. 1980. *Inequality in the Military: The Black Experience.*
Saratoga, Calif.: Century Twenty One.

———. 1988. "Race Relations in the Military." In Moskos and Wood (1988),
115–28.

Caplow, Theodore. 1947. "Rumors in War." Social Forces 25:298–302.

Chandessais, C. 1959. La psychologie dans l'armée. Paris: Presses Universitaires de France.

Chilton, Paul. 1985. Language and the Nuclear Arms Debate: Nukespeak Today. London: Francis Pinter.

Coates, C. H., and R. J. Pellegrin. 1965. Military Sociology. University Park, Md.: Social Sciences Press.

Cobb, Stephen. 1976. "Defense Spending and Defense Voting in the House: An Empirical Study of an Aspect of the Military-Industrial Complex Thesis." American Journal of Sociology 81:163–82.

Cochran, Charles L., ed. 1974. Civil-Military Relations: Changing Concepts in the Seventies. New York: Free Press.

Coles, H. L., ed. 1962. Total War and Cold War: Problems in Civilian Control of the Military. Columbus: Ohio State University Press.

Cooper, Richard V. L. 1977. Military Manpower and the All-Volunteer Force. Santa Monica, Calif.: Rand.

Coser, Lewis A. 1956. The Functions of Social Conflict. New York: Free Press.

———. 1963. "The Dysfunctions of Military Secrecy." Social Problems 11:13–22.

Cotton, Charles A. 1988. "The Institutional Organization Model and the Military." In Moskos and Wood (1988), 3–56.

Crawford, Elizabeth T., and Albert D. Biderman. 1969. Social Scientists and International Affairs. New York: Wiley.

David, R. H. 1966. "International Influence Process: How Relevant Is the Contribution of Psychologists?" American Psychologist 21:236–43.

Dentler, Robert, and Phillips Cutright. 1963. Hostage America: Human Aspects of a Nuclear Attack and a Program of Prevention. Boston: Beacon.

Derber, Charles. 1990. The Nuclear Seduction: Why the Arms Race Doesn't Matter—and What Does. Berkeley: University of California Press.

Deutsch, Morton. 1973. The Resolution of Conflict: Constructive and Destructive Processes. New Haven, Conn.: Yale University Press.

Deutsch, Morton, and Robert M. Krauss. 1960. "The Effects of Threat upon Interpersonal Bargaining." Journal of Abnormal and Social Psychology 61:181–89.

Downes, Cathy. 1988. "Great Britain." In Moskos and Wood (1988), 153–76.

Elkin, F. 1956. "The Soldier's Language." American Journal of Sociology 51:408–13.

Erskine, Hazel Gaudet. 1973. "The Polls: Atomic Weapons and Nuclear Energy." Public Opinion Quarterly 45:126–134.

Etzioni, Amitai. 1962. The Hard Way to Peace. New York: Collier.

———. 1963. "Synopsis of The Hard Way to Peace." Social Problems 11: 22–24.

———. 1967. "Nonconventional Uses of Sociology as Illustrated by Peace

Research." In *The Uses of Sociology,* ed. P. Lazarsfeld, W. H. Sewell, H. L. Wilensky, 806–35. New York: Basic Books.

Faris, John H. 1988. "The Social Psychology of Military Service and the Influence of Bureaucratic Rationalism." In Moskos and Wood (1988), 57–78.

Fidel, Kenneth, ed. 1975. *Militarism in Developing Countries.* Edison, N.J.: Transaction Books.

Finer, Samuel E. 1975. *The Man on Horseback.* 2d ed. Baltimore: Penguin.

Finsterbusch, Kurt. 1984. "The Sociological Literature on Nuclear Issues." Paper delivered at the American Sociological Association, San Antonio.

———. 1985. "Nuclear Issues in Social Research." *Society* 22:2–3.

Foster, Gregory D. 1984. "The Effect of Deterrence on the Fighting Ethic." *Armed Forces and Society* 10:276–92.

Fox, Byron L. 1953. "The Cold War and American Domestic Problems." *Social Problems* 1:10–12.

Fox, W. T. R. 1954. "Civil-Military Relations Research: The SSRC Committee and its Research Survey." *World Politics.* 6:278–88.

Franck, James. 1986. "The Franck Report: A Report to the Secretary of War, June 11, 1945." In Gregory (1986), 43–52.

Gal, Reuven. 1988. "Israel." In Moskos and Wood (1988), 267–75.

Galtung, Johan. 1984. *There Are Alternatives! Four Roads to Peace and Security.* Nottingham, England: Spokesman.

Gamson, William A., and Andrew Modigliani. 1966. "Tensions and Concessions: The Empirical Confirmation of Belief Systems, and Soviet Behavior." *Social Problems* 11:34–48.

———. 1984. "Political Symbolism and Nuclear Arms Policy." Paper presented at the annual meeting of the American Sociological Association, August 1984. San Antonio, Texas.

Gouldner, Alvin. 1962. "Introduction to Durkheim." In *Socialism and Saint-Simon.* London: Collier-Macmillan.

Gregory, Donna Uthus, ed. 1986. *The Nuclear Predicament.* New York: St. Martin's Press.

Gumperz, J. J. 1982. *Discourse Strategies.* Cambridge: Cambridge University Press.

Hall, R. L. 1956. "Military Sociology." In *Sociology in the United States of America,* ed. H. L. Zetterberg, 59–62. Paris: UNESCO.

Hamblin, Robert L., et al. 1977. "Arms Races: A Test of Two Models." *American Sociological Review* 42:338–54.

Handberg, Robert B. 1972. "The Vietnam 'Analogy': Student Attitudes on War." *Public Opinion Quarterly* 36:612–15.

Harries-Jenkins, Gwyn. 1982. *Armed Forces and the Welfare Societies.* London: Macmillan.

Harries-Jenkins, Gwyn, and Charles C. Moskos. 1981. "Armed Forces and Society." *Current Sociology* 29:1–170.

Harries-Jenkins, Gwyn, and Jacques van Doorn, eds. 1976. *The Military and the Problem of Legitimacy.* Beverly Hills, Calif.: Sage.

Hart, Hornell. 1946. "Technological Acceleration and the Atomic Bomb." *American Sociological Review* 11:277–94.

Henderson, William Darryl. 1985. *Cohesion*. Washington, D.C.: National Defense University Press.

Hong, Doo-Seung. 1979. "Retired U.S. Military Elites." *Armed Forces and Society* 5:451–66.

Horowitz, Irving Louis, and Ellen Kay Trimberger. 1976. "State Power and Military Nationalism in Latin America." *Comparative Politics* 8:223–43.

Huntington, Samuel P. 1957. *The Soldier and the State*. Cambridge, Mass.: Harvard University Press.

Huntington, S. P. 1968. "Civil-Military Relations." In *International Encyclopedia of the Social Sciences*. Vol 2, 487–94. New York: Macmillan & Free Press.

IGCC. 1987. *Biennial Report*. San Diego, Calif.: University of California Institute on Global Conflict and Cooperation.

Ikle, Fred. 1967. *How Nations Negotiate*. New York: International Institute for Peace and Conflict Research.

Jacobs, James B. 1986. *Socio-Legal Foundations of Civil-Military Relations*. New Brunswick, N.J.: Transaction.

Janowitz, Morris. 1960. *The Professional Soldier*. New York: Free Press.

———. 1975. *Military Conflict: Essays in the Institutional Analysis of War and Peace*. Beverly Hills, Calif.: Sage.

———. 1977a. "From Institutional to Occupational: The Need for Conceptual Clarity." *Armed Forces and Society* 4:51–54.

———. 1977b. *The Military in the Political Development of New Nations*. Rev. exp. ed. Chicago: University of Chicago Press.

Janowitz, Morris, and R. W. Little. 1974. *Sociology and the Military Establishment*. Beverly Hills, Calif.: Sage.

Janowitz, Morris, and Jacques Van Doorn, eds. 1971. *On Military Intervention*. Rotterdam: Rotterdam University Press.

Janowitz, Morris, and S. D. Wesbrook, eds. 1983. *The Political Education of Soldiers*. Beverly Hills, Calif.: Sage.

Jans, Nicholas A. 1988. "Australia." In Moskos and Wood (1988), 211–26.

Jenkins, Brian Michael. 1980. "Nuclear Terrorism and Its Consequences." *Society* 17:5–15.

Johns, J. H. 1984. *Cohesion in the U.S. Military*. Washington, D.C.: National Defense University.

Johnson, Harry G. 1975. "Egregious Economics as Pacifist Propaganda: Melman's Methodology of Defense Disbursements." *Social Problems* 1:498–504.

Kahn, Herman, and Anthony J. Wiener. 1967. *The Year 2000: A Framework for Speculation on the Next Thirty-Three Years*. New York: Macmillan.

Kelleher, Catherine, ed. 1974. *Political-Military Systems: Comparative Perspectives*. Beverly Hills, Calif.: Sage.

Kelman, H. C., ed. 1965. *International Behavior: A Social-Psychological Analysis*. New York: Holt, Rinehart & Winston.

Kendall, Patricia L., and Paul F. Lazarsfeld. 1950. "Problems of Survey Analysis." In Merton and Lazarsfeld (1950), 133–96.

Kennedy, Gavin. 1974. *The Military in the Third World*. London: Duckworth.

Kriesberg, Louis. 1968. *Social Processes in International Relations*. New York.

———. 1981. "Noncoercive Inducements in U.S.-Soviet Conflicts: Ending the Occupation of Austria and Nuclear Weapons Tests." *Journal of Political and Military Sociology* 9:1–16.

———. 1982. *Social Conflicts*. Englewood Cliffs, N.J.: Prentice-Hall.

———. 1986. "Consequences of Efforts at Deescalating the American-Soviet Conflict." *Journal of Political and Military Sociology* 14:215–34.

Kurtz, Lester R. 1984. *Evaluating Chicago Sociology*. Chicago: University of Chicago Press.

———. 1988. *The Nuclear Cage: A Sociology of the Arms Race*. Englewood Cliffs, N.J.: Prentice-Hall.

———. 1989. "Between Scylla and Charybdis: Sociological Objectivity and Bias." *Sociological Forum* 4:139–49.

Ladd, Everett Carl. 1982. "The Freeze Framework." *Public Opinion* 5: 20, 41.

Larus, John. 1967. *Nuclear Weapons Safety and the Common Defense*. Columbus: Ohio State University Press.

Lasswell, Harold D. 1935. *World Politics and Personal Insecurity*. New York: McGraw-Hill.

Lauer, Robert H. 1976. "Defining Social Problems: Public and Professional Perspectives." *Social Problems* 24:122–30.

Lerner, Daniel. 1950. "The American Soldier and the Public." In Merton and Lazarsfeld 1950, 212–51.

Lifton, Robert Jay. 1967. *Death in Life: Survivors of Hiroshima*. New York: Basic.

Lifton, Robert Jay, and Kai Erikson. 1982. "Nuclear War's Effect on the Mind." In Lifton and Falk (1982), 274–78.

Lifton, Robert Jay, and Richard Falk. 1982. *Indefensible Weapons: The Political and Psychological Case Against Nuclearism*. New York: Basic Books.

Lipset, Seymour Martin, et al. 1956. *Union Democracy*. New York: Free Press.

Luttwak, Edward. 1969. *Coup d'Etat: A Practical Handbook*. Harmondsworth: Penguin.

Madge, John. 1962. *The Origins of Scientific Sociology*. New York: Free Press.

Margiotta, F. D. 1978. *The Changing World of the American Military*. Boulder, Colo.: Westview Press.

Marshall, S. L. A. 1947. *Men Against Fire*. New York: William Morrow & Co.

Mattic, Paul. 1956. "The Economics of War and Peace." *Dissent* 3:376–89.

Mehan, Hugh, and James M. Skelly. 1987. "Reyjkavik: The Breach and Repair of the Pure War Script." Paper presented at a conference on "Discourse of the Nuclear Arms Debate," Ballyvaughn, Ireland, August 9–16, sponsored by the Institute on Global Conflict and Cooperation, University of California.

Melman, Seymour. 1975. "Twelve Propositions on Productivity and War Economy." *Armed Forces and Society* 1:490–98.

Merton, Robert K., and Alice S. Kitt. 1950. "Contributions to the Theory of Reference Group Behavior." In Merton and Lazarsfeld, 40–105.

Merton, Robert K., and Paul F. Lazarsfeld, eds. 1950. *Studies in the Scope and Method of "The American Soldier."* Glencoe, Ill.: Free Press.

Michael, Donald N. 1963. "Charity Begins at Home: Four Domestic Problems for Americans Crucial to International Peace." *Social Problems* 11:24–29.

———. 1957. "Some Factors Tending to Limit the Utility of the Social Scientists in Military Systems Analysis." *Operations Research* 5:90–96.

Michels, Robert. 1962. *Political Parties.* New York: Collier.

Millet, Allan R. 1974. "Arms Control Research on Military Institutions." *Armed Forces and Society* 1:61–78.

Millis, Walter, and James Real. 1963. *The Abolition of War.* New York.

Mills, C. Wright. 1956. *The Power Elite.* New York: Oxford University Press.

———. [1958] 1976. *The Causes of World War III.* Westport, Conn.: Greenwood Press.

Moore, W. 1966. "World Sociology." *American Journal of Sociology* 71:475–82.

Moskos, Charles C. 1970. *The American Enlisted Man: The Rank and File in Today's Military.* New York: Russell Sage Foundation.

———. 1971. "Structured Strain in a United Nations Constabulary Force." In Janowitz and van Doorn (1971), 248–63.

———. 1973. "The Emergent Military: Civil, Traditional, or Plural?" *Pacific Sociological Review* 16:255–79.

———. 1976. *Peace Soldiers: The Sociology of United Nations Military Force.* Chicago: University of Chicago Press.

———. 1977a. "The All-Volunteer Military: Calling, Profession, or Occupation?" *Parameters* 7(1):41–50.

———. 1977b. "From Institution to Occupation: Trends in Military Organization." *Armed Forces & Society* 4:41–50.

———. 1988. "Institutional and Occupational Trends in Armed Forces." In Moskos and Wood, 15–27.

Moskos, Charles C., and Frank R. Wood. 1988. *The Military: More Than Just a Job?* Washington: Pergamon-Brassey.

———. 1988. "Institution Building in an Occupational World." In Moskos and Wood (1988), 279–91.

———. 1988. "Introduction." In Moskos and Wood (1988), 3–14.

Myrdal, Alva. 1982. *The Game of Disarmament.* Rev. ed. New York: Pantheon.

Nordinger, Eric A. 1977. *Soldiers in Politics: Military Coups and Governments.* Englewood Cliffs, N.J.: Prentice Hall.

Oberschall, Anthony. 1973. *Social Conflict and Social Movements*. Englewood Cliffs, N.J.: Prentice-Hall.

Ogburn, William Fielding. 1946. "Sociology and the Atom." *American Journal of Sociology* 51:267–75.

Oppenheimer, Martin. 1964. "The Peace Research Game." *Dissent* 11:444–48.

Osgood, Charles E. 1962. *An Alternative to War or Surrender*. Urbana: University of Illinois Press.

———. "Questioning Some Unquestioned Assumptions About National Security." *Social Problems* 11:6–12.

Page, C. H. 1946. "Bureaucracy's Other Face." *Social Forces* 25:88–94.

Pitcher, Brian L., Robert L. Hamblin, and Jerry L. L. Miller. 1978. "The Diffusion of Collective Violence." *American Sociological Review* 43:23–35.

Putney, Snell, and Russell Middleton. 1962. "Some Factors Associated with Student Acceptance or Rejection of War." *American Sociological Review* 27:655–67.

Raser, John R. 1969. "The Failure of Fail-Safe." *Trans-action* 6:110–19.

Rose, A. M. 1946. "The Social Structure of the Army." *American Journal of Sociology,* 51:361–364.

Russett, Bruce M. 1969. "The Price of War." *Trans-action* 6:28–35.

Scheer, Robert. 1982. *With Enough Shovels: Reagan, Bush and Nuclear War*. New York: Random House.

Schell, Jonathan. 1982. *The Fate of the Earth*. New York: Knopf.

Schmidt, Steffan W., and Gerald A. Dorfman. 1974. *Soldiers in Politics*. Los Altos, Calif.: Geron-X.

Schmitter, Philippe C., ed. 1973. *Military Rule in Latin America*. Beverly Hills, Calif.: Sage.

Schuman, Howard. 1972. "Two Sources of Anti-War Sentiment." *American Journal of Sociology* 78:513–36.

Segal, David R. 1967. "Selective Promotion in Officer Cohorts." *Sociological Quarterly* 8:199–206.

———. 1983. "From Political to Industrial Citizenship." In Janowitz and Wesbrook (1983), 285–306.

———. 1986. "Measuring the Institutional Occupational Change Thesis." *Armed Forces and Society* 12:351–76.

Segal, Mady Wechsler. 1988. "The Military and the Family as Greedy Institutions." In Moskos and Wood (1988), 79–98.

Segal, David R., and Mady Wechsler Segal. Forthcoming. "Military Sociology." *International Military and Defense Encyclopedia*.

Sethi, J. D. 1989. *Gandhian Critique of Western Peace Movements*. Delhi: Chanakya Publications.

Sharp, Gene. 1973. *The Politics of Nonviolent Action*. Vols. 1–3. Boston: Porter Sargent.

Shaw, Martin. 1984a. "Introduction: War and Social Theory." In Shaw (1984b), 1–21.

————. 1984b. *War, State, and Society.* New York: St. Martin's.

Shields, Patricia. 1988. "Sex Roles in the Military." In Moskos and Wood (1988), 9–114.

Shils, Edward A. 1950. "Primary Groups in the American Army." In Merton and Lazarsfeld (1950), 16–39.

Skelton, William B. 1978. "Officers and Politicians: The Orgins of Army Politics in the United States Before the Civil War." *Armed Forces and Society.*

Smith, Tom W. 1983. "The Polls: American Attitudes Toward the Soviet Union and Communism." *Public Opinion Quarterly* 47:277–92.

Smokovitis, Dimitrios. 1988. "Greece." In Moskos and Wood (1988), 24–54.

Sofios, Nicholas. 1983. "The Threat of Nuclear War as a Social Problem: Denial, Disregard or Despair?" Paper presented at the annual meeting of the Society for the Study of Social Problems, Detroit.

Solaun, Mauricio, and Michel A. Quinn. 1973. *Sinners and Heretics: The Politics of Military Intervention in Latin America.* Urbana: University of Illinois Press.

Solomon, D. N. 1954. "Civilian to Soldier: Three Sociological Studies of Infantry Recruit Training." *Canadian Journal of Psychology,* 8:87–94.

Sorokin, Pitirim. 1937. *Social and Cultural Dynamics. Vol. 3: Fluctuation of Social Relationships, War, and Revolution.* London: Allen and Unwin.

Speier, Hans. 1950. "'The American Soldier' and the Sociology of Military Organization." In Merton and Lazarsfeld (1950), 106–32.

Spindler, G. D. 1948. "The Military—a Systematic Analysis." *Social Forces.* 27:83–88.

Stephenson, Carolyn, ed. 1982. *Alternative Methods for International Security.* Washington, D.C.: University Press of America.

Stouffer, S. A. 1950. "Some Afterthoughts of a Contributor to 'The American Soldier.'" In Merton and Lazarsfeld (1950), 192–211.

Stouffer, S. A., E. A. Suchman, L. C. DeVinney, S. A. Star, and R. M. Williams, Jr. 1949a. *The American Soldier,* Vol. 1: *Adjustment During Army Life.* Princeton: Princeton University Press.

Stouffer, S. A., A. A. Lumsdaine, R. M. Williams, Jr. M. B. Smith, I. L. Janis, S. A. Star, and L. S. Cottrell, Jr. 1949b. *The American Soldier,* Vol. 2: *Combat and Its Aftermath.* Princeton: Princeton University Press.

Szymanski, Albert. 1973. "Military Spending and Economic Stagnation." *American Journal of Sociology* 79:1–14.

Teryakian, Edward A. 1958. "Aftermath of a Thermonuclear Attack on the United States: Some Sociological Considerations." *Social Problems* 6: 21–303.

Tilly, Charles. 1988. "Wars, Warmakers, and Sociologists." New York: New School for Social Research. Unpublished Paper.

Turner, R. H. 1947. "The Naval Disbursing Officer as Bureaucrat." *American Sociological Review* 12:342–48.

United States Strategic Bombing Survey. 1945. "Effects of Strategic Bombing on Japanese Morale." *Reports, Pacific War* 14. Washington, D.C.: U.S. Government Printing Office.

————. 1947. "Effects of Strategic Bombing on German Morale." *Reports, European War* 64b. Washington, D.C.

Urban, Van Dijk, T. 1985. *Prejudice in Language.* Amsterdam: John Benjamins.

Vagts, Alfred. 1959. *A History of Militarism.* New York: Free Press.

Verschueren, J. 1985. *International News Reporting.* Amsterdam: John Benjamins.

Vial, J. 1959. "Introduction à la sociologie militaire." *Revue de Défense Nationale (Nouvelle Série)* 15:1225–35.

Vidich, Arthur J. 1980. "Prospects for Peace in the Nuclear World." *Journal of Political and Military Sociology* 8:85–97.

Wehr, Paul. 1979. "Peace and Conflict Processes: A Research Overview." *Armed Forces and Society* 5:467–86.

White, H. B. 1946. "Military Morality." *Social Research* 13:410–40.

White, Ralph K. 1968. *Nobody Wanted War: Misperception in Vietnam and Other Wars.* New York: Doubleday.

Wildavsky, Aaron. 1965. "Practical Consequences of the Theoretical Study of Defense Policy." *Public Administration Review* 25:90–103.

Wood, Frank R. 1988. "At the Cutting Edge of Institutional and Occupational Trends: The U.S. Air Force Officer Corps." In Moskos and Wood (1988), 27–39.

Wright, Quincy. [1942] 1965. *A Study of War.* Chicago: University of Chicago Press.

Wright, Quincy, W. M. Evans, and M. Deutsch, eds. 1962. *Preventing World War III.* New York: Simon and Schuster.

Zald, M. N., and Simon, W. 1964. "Career Opportunities and Commitments among Officers." In *The New Military; Changing Patterns of Organization.* ed. M. Janowitz, 257–85. New York: Russell Sage Foundation.

Zimmerman, Ekkart. 1979. "Toward a Causal Model of Military Coups d'Etat." *Armed Forces and Society* 5:387–413.

————. 1979. *Political Violence, Crises and Revolutions: Theories and Research.* Cambridge, Mass.: Alfred Schenkman.

3

Recruiting Sociologists in a Time of Changing Opportunities

WILLIAM V. D'ANTONIO

In his history of American sociology, Rhoades (1981:42) labeled the period between 1950 and 1970 as sociology's "Golden Era." Some might argue that the Golden Era extended to the mid-1970s. During that period, membership in the American Sociological Association grew more than four times, from 3,500 to more than 14,000. Most observers agree, however, that by the early 1980s sociology was in a period of decline, or in "The Doldrums," as one colleague put it, with ASA membership dropping to less than 12,000. One of the important questions posed by these changes over the course of the past forty years concerns the recruitment of sociologists. What do we know about recruitment patterns from the past, and how, if at all, might they be relevant to the future? What has been the social context within which recruitment has occurred, and how has the context itself changed over time? What forces have spurred and then deterred recruitment into the field? And what may we expect in a time of changing opportunities?

In the first part of the paper I describe patterns of growth and decline in undergraduate majors and in graduate degrees conferred, the changing female-male and foreign student ratios, the quality of students being recruited into sociology, and the jobs available to them. The first part closes with an attempt to explain the changing recruitment and employment patterns. In the second part, I look briefly at the efforts now under way to improve the quality of recruits in the

Special thanks are due the following persons: Ms. Maria Krysan for diligent detective work in searching out the data for and then preparing the tables and figures; Dr. Joseph Conaty for critical help in various stages of this paper; and Drs. Terrance Russell, Joan Huber, Richard Campbell, and Howard Garrison for critical readings of the manuscript. I thank them for their help, but do not hold them responsible for what I did with it. Finally, I want to thank Terence Halliday, coeditor of this volume, for his thoughtful and detailed editorial assistance.

coming years, efforts that include the sociology curriculum from K–12, the undergraduate major, and graduate education.

Patterns of Growth and Decline

Sociology has come through a long dark night of contracting opportunities. During the late 1970s and early 1980s there was a dramatic decrease in numbers of students (undergraduate majors, M.A.'s and Ph.D.'s), loss of regular full-time faculty slots, increased use of part-time lecturers, and a shrinking pool of research funds. Whether in academe, business, or government, we were witness to the growth in numbers of un- and underemployed sociologists. In their essay on "American Sociology since the Seventies" (this volume, chap. 5), Crane and Small document the decline of sociology relative to economics, and conclude that the former may be losing its identity. Other writers also express varying degrees of doubt about sociology's future. My own reading of the data is more optimistic, as my paper will attempt to show. I will place these events in a context going back to the 1950s to gain a better perspective on patterns of growth and decline.

Trends in Majors and Degrees Conferred in Sociology

The following sets of figures summarize the growth and then decline of majors and advanced degree recipients in sociology (Figs. 1, 3, and 4) for the period 1960–89, and then compare sociology and related social sciences (Figs. 2 and 5) for a similar time period.

Figure 1 shows the dramatic growth in sociology majors between 1960 and 1974, a fivefold growth from 7,147 to 35,915. The decline in the curve in the following eleven years between 1974 and 1985 was almost as precipitous as the rise was in the prior period. The data for the period since 1985 suggest an end to the period of decline, and the beginning of another upward trend. These data show that the number of majors increased by almost 20 percent in the four years after 1985. Reports from department chairs in different parts of the country suggest enrollments in undergraduate courses were up by some 15 to 45 percent for the 1989–90 year. There have been no indications of falling enrollments anywhere.

Figure 2 compares the undergraduate major patterns for sociology and four related social sciences. Sociology and history suffered the sharpest declines in majors; economics experienced steady growth throughout most of this twenty-year time period, while the pattern for

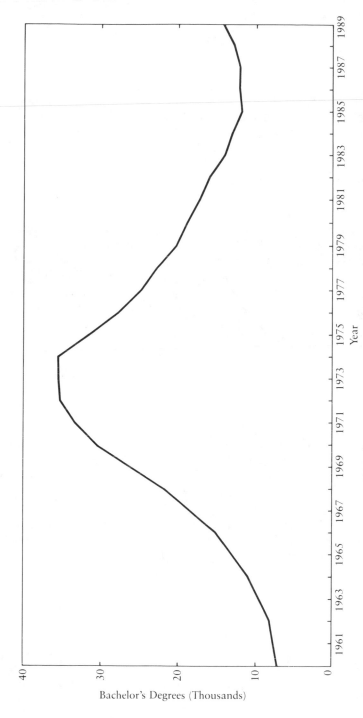

Fig. 1. Bachelor's Degrees Earned in Sociology, 1959/60 to 1988/89. *Sources*: National Center for Education Statistics, U.S. Department of Education, *Digest of Education Statistics 1990* (Washington, D.C.), Table 261; and National Science Foundation, *Science and Engineering Degrees: 1966–1989: A Source Book*, NSF 91–314 (Washington, D.C., 1991), Table 54.

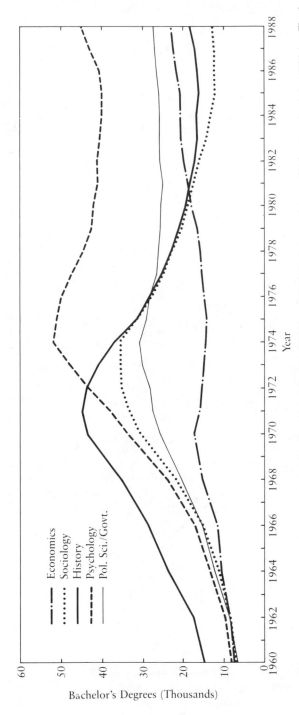

Fig. 2. Bachelor's Degrees Earned in Sociology and Related Disciplines, 1959/60 to 1987/88. *Sources: Digest of Education Statistics 1990* (see Fig. 1 above), Tables 258 and 261; and *Digest of Education Statistics 1987* (Washington, D.C.), Table 177.

political science was one of slow growth and a more gradual decline. Psychology suffered declines after the mid-1970s, but the number of majors leveled off at a much higher level than was the case for sociology or history. Data through 1988 for economics, psychology, and history all showed varying degrees of growth in the most recent years.

The pattern for M.A. graduates in sociology has been similar, growing fivefold from 400 in 1960 to a high of 2,234 in 1974 and then declining rapidly to a low of 970 in 1987. Figures for 1988 and 1989 indicate the beginning of a new upward trend, with an increase of 10 percent to 1,169 (Fig. 3).

The pattern for Ph.D.'s has varied somewhat, with growth more than fourfold, from a modest level of 161 degrees in 1960 to a record of 734 in the peak year of 1976. It is not surprising that the peak for Ph.D.'s should follow the other peaks, since departments recruited heavily during the late 1960s and early 1970s based on the rapidly growing demands from undergraduate programs and research activity. The decline has been much more gradual, finally dropping below 500 in 1985, where it remained through 1989 (Fig. 4).

Figure 5 compares doctorate patterns for the same five social science disciplines compared in Figure 2. Again, the pattern for psychology differs markedly from the rest. The swings for economics have also been more sharply defined, while sociology, history, and political science all followed more or less the same pattern. Current indications are that these disciplines are experiencing upward trends. This may be explained in part by the trends in undergraduate majors, as well as the gradual increase in funding for social research, and the generally more positive climate for the social sciences.

While the total number of Ph.D.'s granted in sociology has been declining from the peak year of 1976, the sex and citizenship composition of those studying for and receiving degrees has also been changing. The pattern has been somewhat uneven; the percentage of doctorates in sociology received by females (Table 1) rose from 33 percent in 1977 to 50 percent in 1985, dropped back to 39 percent in 1987, and has been above 50 percent since. Doctorates to foreign students also have increased, from 13 percent of the total in 1977 to 19 percent in 1987 (Table 2).

Further indicators of the probable direction of change for the next decade are found in the fact that between 1980 and 1990 the percentage of females in sociology graduate student cohorts has grown from 50 percent to 55 percent (Table 3). Since 1980, a majority of graduate students in sociology have been women. During the same time period, the percentage of full-time foreign graduate students has grown from

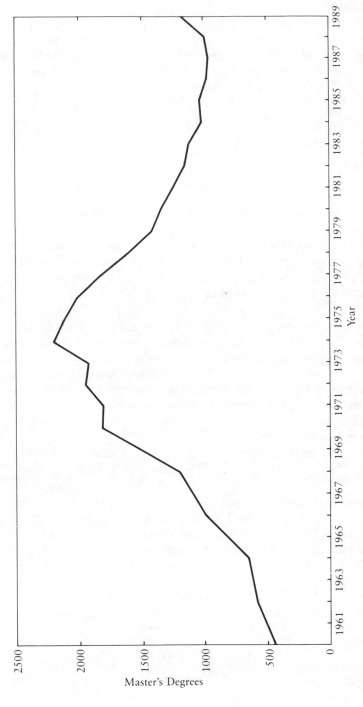

Fig. 3. Master's Degrees Earned in Sociology, 1959/60 to 1988/89. *Sources: Digest of Education Statistics 1990* (see Fig. 1 above), Table 261; and *Science and Engineering Degrees: 1966–1989* (see Fig. 1 above), Table 54.

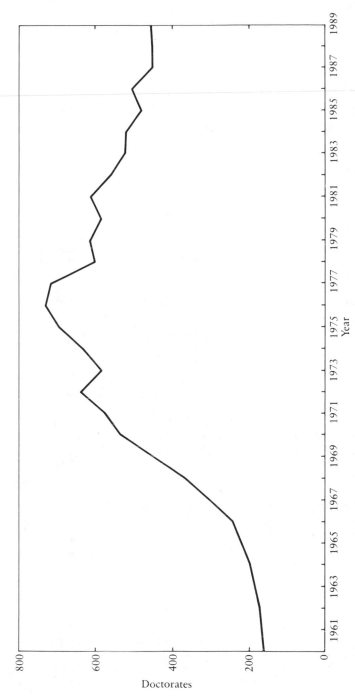

Fig. 4. Doctorates Earned in Sociology, 1959/60 to 1988/89. *Sources: Digest of Education Statistics 1990* (see Fig. 1 above), Table 261; and *Science and Engineering Degrees: 1966–1989* (see Fig. 1 above), Table 54.

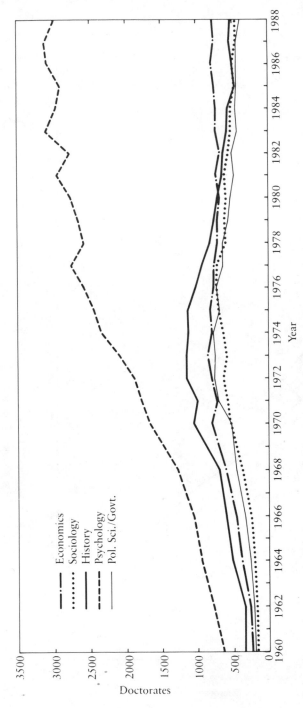

Fig. 5. Doctorates Earned in Sociology and Related Disciplines, 1959/60 to 1987/88. *Sources: Digest of Education Statistics 1990* (see Fig. 1 above), Tables 258 and 261; and *Digest of Education Statistics 1987* (see Fig. 2 above), Table 177.

Table 1.   Sociology Ph.D.'s by Sex, 1977–89

	1977	1978	1979	1980	1981	1982	1983	1984	1985	1986	1987	1988	1989
Male	488	386	400	370	363	354	323	300	243	285	274	219	225
Female	237	224	232	231	242	214	228	234	243	221	175	249	231
Total	725	610	632	601	605	568	551	534	486	506	449	468	456
% Female	33	37	37	38	40	38	41	44	50	44	39	53	51

Source: National Science Foundation, "Science and Engineering Degrees: 1966–1989. A Source Book." NSF 91-314 (Washington, D.C., 1991), Table 54.

Table 2.   Sociology Ph.D.'s by Citizenship, 1977 and 1987

	1977	1987
All students	725	423
Foreign students	95	82
% Foreign	13	19

Source: National Science Foundation, "Profiles—Psychology: Human Resources and Funding" (Washington, D.C., 1988), Table 28.

Table 3.   Sociology Graduate Students in All Institutions by Sex, 1980–87

	1980	1981	1982	1983	1984	1985	1986	1987
Male	3,984	3,780	3,376	3,269	3,190	3,107	2,972	3,146
Female	4,017	4,036	3,870	3,680	3,671	3,485	3,566	3,874
Total	8,001	7,816	7,246	6,949	6,861	6,593	6,537	7,020
% Female	50.2	51.6	53.4	53.0	53.5	52.9	54.6	55.2

Source: "Data on Graduate Science/Engineering Students and Postdoctorates," Science and Engineering Education Sector Studies Group, Division of Science Resource Studies, National Science Foundation, September 1988, Tables B-17, B-18, B-19.

Table 4.   Sociology Full-Time Graduate Students in Doctorate-Granting Institutions by Citizenship, 1980–87

	1980	1981	1982	1983	1984	1985	1986	1987
All student	5,291	5,095	4,643	4,585	4,461	4,367	4,351	4,756
Foreign students	893	1,018	964	1,074	1,038	1,165	1,201	1,282
% Foreign	16.9	20.0	20.8	23.4	23.3	26.7	27.6	27.0

Source: "Selected Data on Graduate Science/Engineering Students and Postdoctorates," Division of Science Resource Studies, National Science Foundation, September 1988, Tables C-8 and C-13.

16.9 to 27 percent (Table 4). We may expect that at least half of the new Ph.D.'s in the early 1990s will be women and a quarter or more will be from places other than the United States.

Women and Minorities

The changing ratio of women to men seems now well established. The only question is, how much will it change? Many of the concerns expressed by Sociologists for Women in Society (SWS) and by ASA about equality of opportunity, and the more equitable distribution of women throughout academe, may be expected to be confronted in new ways in the years ahead. I have already noted (Table 3) the preponderance of female graduate students in sociology today. They will constitute an increasing proportion, most probably a majority, of the Ph.D.'s in the years ahead. The pattern for the discipline as a whole seems to be followed within the top departments. A survey of the top 30 departments (D'Antonio 1988) showed that in the period between 1980 and 1988 women comprised between 53 percent and 59 percent of the total number of enrolled students, paralleling the discipline as a whole.

For almost a decade now, the proportion of minorities receiving Ph.D.'s in sociology has ranged between 9 percent and 12 percent annually (see Table 5). Until 1987, blacks were the largest single category within the minorities, but in 1987 more Asian Americans than blacks received Ph.D.'s. Despite major efforts by the ASA Council, The National Science Foundation, and many graduate departments to promote minority recruitment, budget cutbacks in minority fellowships, coupled with growing interest and opportunities for blacks and Hispanics in business, medicine, and law have made it difficult to do more than maintain past levels. The physical and biological sciences, mathematics, and engineering, as well as the other social sciences, are also making new efforts to recruit a larger number and percentage of minorities. With the number of black males attending college at a new low, attempts to attract them to the several disciplines may be very competitive.

The Quality of Recruits

We have noted the changing sex and citizenship composition of the graduate student cohorts for the most recent decade. What can we learn about the academic quality of sociology graduate students? We

Table 5. Sociology Ph.D.'s by Race/Ethnicity, 1977–88

	1977	1979	1980	1981	1982	1983	1984	1985	1986	1987	1988	Total
Ph.D.'s	725	632	602	603	568	525	555	461	492	423	448	5,310
Nat. Am.	8	5	3	0	2	0	1	0	4	2	2	19
Asian	15	21	14	18	19	10	11	8	11	18	13	143
Black	33	30	24	25	29	26	28	26	25	12	22	247
Minority												
Puerto Rican	—	—	1	2	6	5	4	5	3	2	2	30
Mex. Am.	—	—	4	11	9	4	6	7	4	4	6	55
Other Hisp.	13	15	11	2	5	2	7	5	7	4	8	66
Minority (%)	9.5	11.2	9.4	9.6	11.9	8.9	10.2	11.0	10.9	9.9	11.9	

Sources: National Research Council Summary Reports (1977–88): *Doctorate Recipients from U.S. Universities*. Washington, D.C.: National Academy Press.
Notes: Hispanic data not disaggregated in 1979 and earlier. Consequently, data for all Hispanics (in those years) has been placed in the category "Other Hispanics," for the purposes of this table.
Data are missing for 1978.
Figures do not include degrees in demography and criminology.
There is some discrepancy between these totals and those in Table 1 as NRC updates and corrects its findings.

have available one common measure of academic ability as an indicator of how well sociology students compare with students selecting other disciplines for graduate study. That measure is the Graduate Record Examinations (GREs).

While not precise predictors, the GREs are the most commonly used indicators of ability to perform at a satisfactory level in graduate school. The GRE verbal test measures reading comprehension and other verbal abilities expected of graduate students; the GRE quantitative test measures knowledge of mathematical relationships. GRE subject test scores provide measures of student knowledge and aptitude in the particular subjects being tested. There is general agreement that scores are most predictive for the students scoring in the top 15 or 20 percent and for those scoring in the bottom 15 or 20 percent. A number of studies designed to measure the predictive ability of GRE scores as measures of attainment (in this case the number of publication citations) suggest that GRE scores do correlate in varying degrees with attainment as measured by citations (Schrader 1978, 1980).

Table 6 shows that students who took the sociology subject tests scored dramatically lower than students taking subject tests for other disciplines. A number of factors may help explain this finding. A significant proportion, perhaps even a majority, of students enter gradu-

Table 6. GRE Test Means for Selected Subjects: 1966–67 through 1986–87

	'66–67	'67–68	'68–69	'69–70	'70–71	'71–72	'72–73
Biology	613	614	613	**603**	603	606	619
Economics	619	621	614	600	**581**	581	588
Engineering	603	601	591	**586**	587	594	593
Mathematics	653	655	652	**641**	650	656	661
Physics	**618**	624	624	625	636	643	654
Sociology	535	**539**	518	496	469	459	474

	'73–74	'74–75	'75–76	'76–77	'77–78	'78–79	'79–80
Biology	624	622	**627**	625	622	621	619
Economics	594	596	597	605	609	601	603
Engineering	591	583	594	592	594	592	590
Mathematics	677	680	693	691	692	679	696
Physics	**657**	655	654	656	652	648	650
Sociology	472	461	457	451	450	436	438

	'80–81	'81–82	'82–83	'83–84	'84–85	'85–86	'86–87
Biology	617	616	623	622	619	612	616
Economics	613	614	613	617	**623**	609	612
Engineering	590	593	599	604	615	616	**619**
Mathematics	695	696	700	711	**717**	714	710
Physics	648	647	641	637	640	645	641
Sociology	427	433	434	434	442	430	**427**

Source: Educational Testing Service, Princeton, N.J., 1988.
Note: Low score and high score for each subject test are set in boldface.

ate programs in sociology from other majors. For example, among ASA elected officials and journal editors over a twenty-year period, only 42 percent majored in sociology as undergraduates (D'Antonio 1988). An additional 10 percent reported combining a major in sociology with another major. It should not be surprising, then, that subject test scores were low, given that a significant portion of those taking those tests had rather limited knowledge of sociology. Undergraduate sociology students are also the least likely among students in the six disciplines compared in Table 6 to have followed a structured curriculum as undergraduates in preparation for graduate school. Few, if any, sociology programs are designed to be cumulative or increasingly challenging in nature compared, for example, with chemistry programs. Further, sociology student cohorts are the most likely to include larger proportions of women and minorities than any of the other disciplines listed, both groups that have traditionally scored less well on these kinds of exams.

Educational Testing Service data (June 1988) showed that sociology as the intended field of study was selected by a higher percentage of minorities than was any other discipline. That is, a higher percentage of students listing sociology as their intended major were minorities (14 percent) than was true for any other discipline. Political science and education followed with 11 percent, psychology and economics with 9 percent, anthropology 7 percent, and history 6 percent. For the biological and physical sciences and engineering, 8 percent of the students were minorities. These percentages are consistent with the hypothesis that the higher the percentage of minorities taking the GREs in a discipline, the lower the GRE mean scores, compared with other disciplines.

Verbal and quantitative scores for the disciplines also were available from the Educational Testing Service for separate racial and ethnic groups, as seen in Tables 7 and 8. In these tables, sociology is subsumed as one of the behavioral sciences. Thus, inferences from the data must be read with caution. The gap in scores by race and ethnicity is in the expected direction, and follows a similar pattern for all disciplines. Since sociology had the highest proportion of minorities taking the test, this fact might help explain some of the variance in overall mean scores reported in Table 9.

In addition, Table 9 shows that general test scores (verbal and quantitative) for those planning a doctorate in sociology were the lowest among the social sciences; only students planning to enter the field of education scored lower on the verbal and quantitative tests. Again, it should be noted that the higher scores for the biological and physical sciences on the verbal tests and the biological and physical sciences and engineering on the quantitative test should not be surprising given the differential recruitment patterns. Students in high school with average or marginal grades and SAT test scores are unlikely to consider or be encouraged to consider physics, chemistry, math, or engineering as college majors. Weak or average students are weeded out long before it's time to think about graduate school and the GREs.

Table 7. Verbal GRE Scores by Race/Ethnicity and Intended Graduate Major Field of Study, 1986–87

	Whites	(rank)	Blacks	(rank)	Mexican American	(rank)
Other humanities	566	(1)	433	(1)	473	(3)
Physical sciences	544	(2)	420	(3)	490	(1)
Behavioral science	533	(3)	408	(4)	472	(4)
Biological science	529	(4)	401	(5)	483	(2)
Engineering	527	(5)	433	(2)	452	(5)
Education	472	(6)	358	(6)	395	(6)

Table 8.   Quantitative GRE Scores by Race/Ethnicity and Intended Graduate Major
            Field of Study, 1986–87

	Whites	(rank)	Blacks	(rank)	Mexican American	(rank)
Engineering	685	(1)	571	(1)	621	(1)
Physical science	647	(2)	507	(2)	595	(2)
Biological science	585	(3)	430	(3)	542	(3)
Other humanities	530	(4)	390	(4)	448	(5)
Behavioral science	528	(5)	393	(4)	463	(4)
Education	476	(6)	344	(6)	380	(6)

Source: "A Summary of Data Collected from Graduate Record Examinations Test Takers During 1986–87," *Data Summary Reports* #12, Educational Testing Service, Princeton, N.J., June 1988, Tables 59, 60.

Table 9.   General GRE Test Scores by Intended Graduate Major Field, 1984–87

	Verbal	Quantitative
Social sciences		
Sociology	483	497
Anthropology	553	526
Government/political science	518	524
History	560	523
Clinical psychology	502	512
Experimental/developmental psychology	509	532
Social psychology	494	505
Economics	504	612
Other fields		
Behavioral science	509	526
Education	453	483
Languages and other humanities	542	532
Biological science	507	582
Engineering	477	677
Physical science	518	641

Source: GRE Guide to the Use of the Graduate Record Examinations Program, 1988–89, Educational Testing Service, Princeton, N.J.

Several questions must be asked about these scores and their implications for the quality of students being attracted to graduate study in sociology. It is possible, for example, that a significant proportion of average students who have deep concerns about society take these exams, listing sociology as their intended major. Their limited skills in these kinds of exams then result in lower mean scores for sociology compared with other disciplines (assuming that average students are less likely to take chemistry GREs, for example). Such test scores may obscure the fact that there is a large and healthy cohort of highly talented students also taking the exams. One way to try to measure

Table 10.   GRE Scores of Sociology Enrollees for Selected Departments, 1975–88

	1975 (N=7)	1980 (N=10)	1981 (N=12)	1982 (N=16)	1983 (N=18)	1984 (N=17)	1985 (N=20)	1986 (N=21)	1987 (N=24)	1988 (N=22)
V.	542	554	556	539	524	556	523	556	541	542
Q.	534	535	540	545	530	554	560	562	576	566

Note: N = number of departments reporting GRE scores.

the degree to which this might be the case would be to compare the scores of all those who took the exams with sociology listed as their intended field of study with the scores of students actually admitted and enrolled in graduate programs in sociology. For comparative purposes, one would compare all exam takers with actual enrollees in the other disciplines.

Some data bearing on this question are available from about one-third of the ninety-three top ranked sociology graduate programs (Webster 1983). According to Webster, these ninety-three departments produced about 95 percent of all Ph.D.'s within their respective areas. I conducted a survey of the ninety-three departments in the fall of 1988, requesting information on their application and enrollment patterns. The information requested included numbers of males, females, and minorities applying, accepted, and enrolled each year, and mean GPAs and GREs.

Very few departments had such records beyond the most recent years. Many departments have never kept such records. Most departments were not aware that their graduate schools might actually have some of the information requested. I procured varying amounts of information from twenty-nine departments.

Of the twenty-nine departments reporting GRE data, thirteen were ranked in the top 25 percent of departments, as measured by Webster.[1] The total combined average GRE scores for the period 1975–88 are listed below. The number of departments reporting scores for these years varied from a low of seven in 1975 to a high of twenty-four in 1987. Thus, it would seem most prudent to consider these data as only suggestive of recruit quality as measured by GRE scores.

The verbal means have ranged from a low of 523 to a high of 556. There has been a bit more breadth to the range of the quantitative scores, from a low of 530 to a high of 576. Comparing these data with those in Table 9, for the period 1984–87, verbal scores of actual enrollees in the twenty-nine departments in the study ranged between

1. These thirteen departments are by general consensus of sociologists ranked among the top departments in the country.

41 and 73 points higher than those of the potential applicants. Quantitative scores were between 33 and 79 points higher.

In the sociology departments that have maintained data on GRE scores of actual enrollees over time, sixteen departments had mean scores 50 points or higher than the general applicant pool, while only three departments had scores below the national applicant mean for sociology. On quantitative scores, seventeen departments scored 50 points or higher than the national mean, with four of them scoring above 600 (D'Antonio 1988). In recent years, at least, the verbal and quantitative scores of sociology graduate enrollees in selected departments approached a more competitive academic level.

For the period 1983–86, the mean scores of the thirteen departments reporting GRE data that ranked in the top thirty in the Webster study (1983) were 564 (verbal) and 580 (quantitative).[2] These departments enrolled students whose verbal scores were overall just a bit above the *applicant* scores for anthropology (553) and history (559). On the quantitative side, the combined score of 580 put these department enrollees well above the *general applicant* scores of the above-mentioned social sciences (525), but well below the physical sciences (641) and engineering (677).

In summary, we have presented data that may help explain the low ranking of sociology compared with other social and physical sciences in the mean scores on GRE tests. The fact remains that GREs are only one measure of academic potential. Even as we are concerned about the quality of students we are recruiting, so must we consider recruitment in the light of changing employment patterns.

Employment Patterns in Full- and Part-Time Faculty Positions

The dramatic decline in undergraduate majors and graduate degrees was accompanied by a slow but steady decline in employment of full-time faculty from 1978 through 1985 (Figure 6). Faculty employment held steady at the Ph.D. granting universities until 1980, at which point the percentage of full-time faculty declined by 4 percent; there were slight gains in 1981 and 1982, followed by sharper declines in 1983 and 1984. The 12 percent decline in 1984 from its 1978 high

2. These departments include: Wisconsin-Madison, Indiana, North Carolina-Chapel Hill, Pennsylvania, Duke, California at Santa Barbara, California at San Diego, SUNY-Albany, SUNY-Stony Brook, Cornell, Massachusetts-Amherst, New York University, Minnesota.

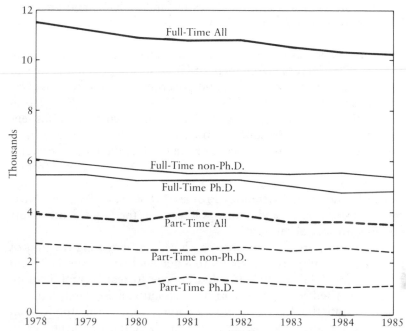

Fig. 6. Sociology Employment Trends at Ph.D., non-Ph.D., and All Universities, Full-Time and Part-Time, 1978 to 1985. *Source:* National Science Foundation, *Academic Science/Engineering: Scientists and Engineers* (Washington, D.C., January 1985), Tables B-4 to B-12.

point represented an absolute loss of 652 full-time faculty positions in sociology in seven years.

The number of part-time faculty at Ph.D. granting institutions actually increased in 1981 and 1982 before declining by 13.1 percent between 1978 and 1984. The data for 1985 suggest that it was the first year of a new recovery, which seems to coincide with the upturn in undergraduate majors, as noted above.

Meanwhile, faculty losses at the non-Ph.D. granting institutions were heavier and more consistent throughout most of the time period. However, for the years 1984 and 1985, full-time faculty losses were slightly lower at the four-year college than at the Ph.D. university level. Judging by the somewhat distinctive patterns evident in the two types of universities and colleges being compared, it would appear that different forces might have been at work. Some further hint of what may be happening is found in two other sets of data: the changes in research funding levels, and the changes in number of graduate students entering sociology. Increases in funding levels and the addition of more graduate students would most probably have an impact on the Ph.D. granting universities more than the others.

With job openings in academe restricted and even shrinking during the late 1970s, increasing numbers of Ph.D. sociologists found jobs in business, nonprofit associations, and government. Data from the National Research Council (NRC) and the National Science Foundation (NSF) (1975, 1981, 1987) showed some dramatic changes in this ten-year time period. The fraction of Ph.D. sociologists employed in business increased from 1 to 5 percent of the total, and then to 9 percent, while the fraction employed in nonprofit organizations ranged from 3 to 6 percent, with 1987 figures at 5 percent. (Huber 1985; National Science Foundation: Psychology-Profiles 1988). For 1987, the NRC combined sociologists and anthropologists, so the latter figures must be read with special caution.[3]

Federal and state governments employed an increasing fraction of Ph.D. sociologists, growing from 5 to 8 percent between the 1975 and 1981 cohorts (Huber 1985:36). During the Reagan administration, the numbers fell to 4 percent in 1987 (National Research Council 1988). Despite the decline in federal employment during the Reagan years, the long-term consequence of the declining opportunities in academe during this period was the growth in the number and percentage of sociologists outside academe, from 8 percent of all Ph.D.'s to almost 18 percent of the total, more than doubling in a decade. This is a phenomenon that many expect to see continue in the years ahead. What began as a necessity for employment seems to have become an attractive alternative source of employment for growing numbers of sociologists.

In trying to determine the significance of the growth of part-time faculty positions during the 1980s, it is important to separate out those part-time faculty who only wanted part-time work from those who were working part-time but wanted full-time employment. National Science Foundation figures for that time period offer some help. The NSF constructed an "Underemployment Rate" that referred to faculty who were working part-time but wanted to work full-time. The data suggest that underemployment reached its highest level in 1984 for both social scientists and sociologists/anthropologists (7.7 percent and 11.1 percent respectively). Their data also suggest that

3. NSF and NAS often combine sociology and anthropology data. In places where we have been able to disaggregate the data we have found no great differences in their patterns. Still, the findings should be judged with caution (National Science Foundation 1986).

the rate of underemployment dropped between 1984 and 1986 (to 7.2 percent and 9.2 percent, respectively), as did the rate of unemployment (to 2.4 percent and 2.2 percent respectively). These findings would be consistent with those reported earlier.

In an effort to ascertain the extent of underemployment and unemployment in sociology, ASA appointed a task force in 1983 to study the problem. It soon became evident that hard data would be difficult to uncover. Estimates of the number of un- and underemployed ranged from 500 to 2,000. In her report on "Employment Patterns in Sociology," Huber (1985) reviewed the data for the 1975 and 1981 periods in two chapters, and concluded that she could find little change in un- and underemployment patterns. ASA Council established a special dues category for un- and underemployed sociologists in 1984, and for the past seven years the number of members selecting that category has remained stable at about 1,000. Until such time as a survey is done of the people in this category, it is not possible to say precisely what this figure means.

Academic Job Opportunities: The Employment Bulletin as a Measure of a Changing Market

The *Employment Bulletin* (*EB*), of the ASA has been appearing since November 1976 (Huber 1985:15). In the period between 1971 and 1976, job vacancies were announced either in *The American Sociologist* or in *Footnotes*. However, for the period before the late 1970s, data on the number of jobs available in any given year must be taken warily. With the rise of affirmative action laws, more and more sociology departments began to use the *EB*, and the "old boy" network of job placements was at least officially reduced in importance. Since the late 1970s, the *EB* has provided a fairly complete reporting of job openings for sociologists within academe.

Table 11 shows the changing trends in employment prospects as listed in *EB* over the past fourteen years. Until the mid-1970s, there seemed to be more jobs available in academe than there were Ph.D.'s to fill them. That may be one reason why such a small percentage of Ph.D.'s held jobs outside of academe. However, this changed in the period between 1977 and 1982. While exact figures are not available, Huber (1985:15–16) reported that the year 1977 was a peak year for advertising jobs in academe. The number of jobs advertised then declined gradually during the ensuing years to a low point in 1983.

The *Employment Bulletin* advertised a total of 444 different jobs in

Table 11.   Jobs Advertised in ASA Employment Bulletins, 1975–91

Academic rank	1975[a]	1982–83	1985–86	1986–87	1987–88	1988–89	1989–90	1990–91
Chair, dir., full prof.	39	44	72	77	100	112	68	59
Full/assoc. prof.	27	—	—	—	—	—	22	28
Assoc. prof.	18	37	68	65	62	59	5	8
Assoc./ asst. prof.	54	—	—	—	—	—	89	95
Asst. prof.	245	224	257	312	337	356	332	331
Asst. prof./ instr./lect.	46[b]	19	16	19	14	16	49	49
Fellows/ applied[c]	—	51	77	103	88	95	85	88
Not specified/ open	168	69	97	126	158	205	194	136
Total	597	444	587	702	759	843	844	794

Source: ASA Employment Bulletins, 1982–1991. Calculations based on an academic calendar year beginning June 1 and ending May 31.

a. Data from 1975 are not verifiable. These figures are from Table 9 in J. Skipper et al., 1978, as reported in B. Huber 1985.

b. Includes category of "Asst. Prof./Instr.," not specified in later data.

c. Disaggregated data for "Fellows/Applied" category are: 20 applied and 31 fellows in 1983 and 53 applied and 42 fellows in 1988–89.

1982–83, with 10 percent directed to persons at the full professor and chair/director level. More than half the jobs (224) were at the level of assistant professor or below. And as Table 12 indicates, less than half (219) were in tenure-track positions. Less than 360 jobs were advertised that would normally be open to new entrants into the job market, while graduate departments produced 522 doctorates that year (see Figure 3 above).

The number of job openings increased steadily in each of the next six years, to a high of 844 for the year 1989–90. The number of jobs at the chair / full professor level increased from 44 in 1982–83 to 112 in 1988–89 (that is, from 10 to 14 percent of the total), before declining in the next two years. The data for 1990–91 suggest the impact of the recession on state budgets.

The number of tenure-track positions (Table 12) also increased, more than doubling from 219 in 1982–83 to 496 in 1990–91. An additional stimulus to the job market was found in the fact that the number of jobs in the applied/practice sector more than doubled from

Table 12.   Tenure-Track Jobs Advertised in ASA Employment Bulletins: 1982–1991

	1982–83	1985–86	1986–87	1987–88	1988–89	1989–90	1990–91
Tenure or tenure track	219	274	350	418	418	481	496
Non-tenure	14	19	13	6	17	25	11
Nonspecific	113	221	232	182	254	176	139
Temporary positions	47	93	93	63	59	74	67

Note: Totals above do not include temporary positions, fellowships, or applied positions.
Source: ASA Employment Bulletins. Calculations based on an academic calendar year beginning June 1 and ending May 31.

20 in 1983 to 53 in 1988–89. Given that most government offices and businesses do not advertise in the *EB,* this is probably a very conservative estimate of the growth in job opportunities in business, government, and nonprofit associations.[4]

The most consistent growth, of course, has been at the assistant professor level, where the figures for the time periods 1982–83 and 1990–91 were, respectively, 224 and 331 (Table 11). Another sign of market expansion was found in the category "academic rank dependent on qualifications and experience, or left open." In the 1982–83 year, the total number of new jobs offered in this category was 69. In 1991 it had leveled off to 136, after a dramatic increase to 205 in 1989. During the period of decline very few jobs were being offered above the assistant professor level. The increase in this "open" category as well as at the senior level suggests a more than minimal increase in funds being made available by administration for new hiring.

The data in Tables 3 and 4 make clear that enrollment trends in graduate departments closely mirrored the degree and employment trends. Graduate enrollments dropped from a high of 8,000 (for all students full- and part-time) in 1980 to a low of 6,537 in 1986. The same pattern held for doctoral students (from a high of 5,291 to a low of 4,351). By 1990 (ASA Guide 1991), the number of full-time doctorate students had grown to 5,631, well surpassing the 1980 high point.

Given the five- to seven-year time period needed to achieve the Ph.D. in sociology, it would appear that it will be three to five years before the next boom in annual production of new Ph.D.'s will occur. If the recession does not do too much damage to employment patterns in the interim, demand may attract a significant proportion of the

4. Given the different employment patterns in business and government, the *Employment Bulletin* has been used very little by them. Employers in those settings want to hire someone within a month or so, and the hiring may take place at any time of the year.

currently underemployed Ph.D.'s who have marketable skills in teaching and/or research.

Explaining the Trends in Growth and Decline: External Factors

Ideology, Demography, and Work

A combination of ideological and demographic factors as well as the gradually changing nature of work in American society are among the important factors that have helped shape the patterns of growth and decline in sociology and the nature of its recruits—and those of most other academic disciplines—since the end of World War II. The G.I. bill made it possible for the ordinary exservice person to get a college education. The college population jumped from half a million in 1945 to several million within three years.

The idea that everyone who was qualified should have a college education caught on as the end of the G.I. bill era was followed by the baby boom, itself a creation of the G.I.s and their siblings. By the time the last of the baby boom generation reached college age in the late 1970s and early 1980s, the number of people in college had reached more than 11 million. Gradually, throughout this same time period, the number and percentage of people in the manufacturing sector of the labor force declined, as did the farm population, while the service sector grew. Within the service sector, information storage, retrieval, and exchange grew in importance with the coming of the computer age. In a variety of ways, these factors stimulated the growth of sociology as a discipline. By 1971 it was estimated that some 900,000 students a year took a course in introductory sociology. Undergraduate courses and majors in sociology flourished first as part of the liberal arts social science requirements, then as sets of courses that purported to tackle the big issues of the times.

Further stimuli for the growth of sociology came with the social protest movements that began with the Berkeley "Free Speech" movement in 1964 and spread into the early 1970s. Sociology courses were seen by students and many faculty as offering a way of understanding the dynamic events that were taking place around them and happening to them. Collins (ASA *Footnotes,* September 1989) pointed out that the social protest movements of the 1960s and 1970s coincided with the growth within the Association of such units as the Marxist, Environmental, Population, World Systems, Collective Behavior and Social Movements, and Racial/Ethnic Minorities sections. The growing public concerns in the late 1970s and early 1980s about aging and equality for women were reflected within the Association by new sections on Aging and on Sex and Gender. Thus, society's interest in social issues helped stimulate sociology's growth in the classroom throughout the forty-year period dating back to the end of World War II.

Funding for Research

Other external forces were also at work helping sociology to grow and prosper. Important among these was the growth of funding for research. Before World War II, most sociological research was funded by such government agencies as the Department of Agriculture (USDA), the WPA Writers' Project, and the Bureau of the Census. It is estimated that about 140 persons were employed in a professional social scientist role in the Division of Farm Population and Rural Life (USDA) between 1935 and 1953. "Most of these were sociologists, but the number also includes some cultural anthropologists, social psychologists, economists and agricultural historians. The maximum level of employment was reached during 1939–42 with about 60 professionals divided between Washington and several regional offices, as many as nine at one point " (Larson 1989). In addition, large numbers of sociologists, including Conrad and Irene Taeuber, Philip Hauser, and Paul Glick were employed in the Census Bureau, contributing greatly to new ways of thinking about marriage, divorce, family, levels of living, fertility patterns, and children.

One of the dramatic changes in college and university life in the post–World War II era was the development of sponsored research and the growth of research labs and centers on university campuses. In land grant colleges, this growth was spurred early on by the Hatch Act, which provided funds for research on rural life projects, such as the diffusion of innovation (corn and cotton, for example), and a wide range of agricultural extension projects. In fact, many of the sociologists who had worked in the USDA during the Depression went forth to establish major programs in sociology and rural sociology during the 1940s and 1950s (Charles P. Loomis to Michigan State University, and Olaf Larson to Cornell, for example).

Funding support for the social sciences also came from foundations such as Russell Sage, Carnegie, Rockefeller, and Ford.[5] Gradually,

5. See also Bulmer (this volume, chap. 9), who concludes that the efforts of social scientists including sociologists to carry out useful research, while never fully supported during the period 1919–1939, did set the stage for post–World War II growth.

Table 13. Federal Obligations for Basic Research in Selected Fields, 1975–89 (in millions)

	1975	1976	1977	1978	1979	1980	1981	1982
Sociology	15.1	16.6	15.9	18.6	18.4	25.4	22.6	18.7
Social science								
(total)	73.8	86.4	95.5	124.3	129.7	147.2	137.0	120.2
Economics	22.1	25.6	29.1	33.6	32.7	40.0	34.1	39.0
Anthropology	7.0	6.4	8.0	12.0	12.5	14.2	13.1	13.1
Psychology	58.6	45.5	55.7	67.5	75.1	84.2	91.0	89.9
Physical science	709.0	721.4	890.0	941.4	1,050.0	1,220.6	1,324.9	1,393.8
Life sciences	1,115.9	1,222.0	1,383.1	1,588.4	1,891.8	2,054.4	2,223.8	2,526.0

	1983	1984	1985	1986	1987	1988[a]	1989[a]
Sociology	32.8	33.9	32.4	30.0	34.3	35.6	34.5
Social science							
(total)	137.7	132.6	140.7	113.5	129.5	133.5	136.1
Economics	41.0	29.7	34.3	26.3	29.0	30.0	31.7
Anthropology	11.2	16.8	15.8	11.2	12.3	12.5	13.4
Psychology	92.9	107.9	132.8	133.0	147.1	151.1	162.2
Physical science	1,587.2	1,728.0	1,815.2	1,914.4	2,096.0	2,284.9	2,547.7
Life sciences	2,891.3	3,287.6	3,786.6	3,858.8	4,363.6	4,674.1	4,859.7

Source. "Federal Funds for Research and Development." Division of Science Resource Studies, National Science Foundation, Tables 2A & 2B.
a. Figures are estimates for 1988 and 1989.

funding from the federal government agencies outstripped private funding. By the 1960s, major social research departments had sprung up in most universities, and even some colleges. The dramatic growth in funding support paralleled closely the growth in student enrollments, as the baby boom generation found its way to college. Much of this funding helped support the new cohorts of graduate students as research and teaching assistants, who quickly moved into the expanding job markets.

Research funding for the social sciences grew steadily during the 1960s and 1970s. Despite the antipathy of the Reagan administration toward the social sciences, funding continued to grow, although at an uneven pace. Table 13 compares the funding for basic research for all the social sciences, as well as the life and physical sciences. While funding for basic research for sociology doubled from $15 million to more than $35 million between 1975 and 1989, funding for psychology more than doubled, from $59 million to more than $162 million. The pattern for economics showed that after a rapid rise from $22 million to more than $41 million in 1983, funding declined to $32 million in 1989.

The big money goes into research in the physical and life sciences. Throughout the fourteen years covered by Table 13, sociology, for example, never received as much as 1 percent of the total funding for basic research. When inflation is taken into account, it can be seen that federal funding for basic research in sociology did not increase in any significant way in this time period.[6]

In addition to the antipathy of the Reagan administration toward sociology and social research in general, there were other forces at work that helped explain the declines in sociology majors, advanced degree recipients, and jobs. These included the rise of the "me" generation, brought on by the aftermath of the protest movements and the disillusionment that set in during and after the Vietnam War. The cutbacks for the social sciences were especially noticeable in 1981 and 1982. Since that time, major efforts to educate the Congress on the importance of the social sciences have led to a reversal of the negative pattern, and a return to slow but steady improvement in funding. This new and more positive level of support for sociology and the other social sciences is exemplified in the statements forthcoming from federal agencies in the past couple of years.

On March 9, 1988, the National Research Council published *The Behavioral and Social Sciences: Achievements and Opportunities* (1988). Dr. Frank Press, the President of the National Academy of Sciences, offered the following introductory remarks: "This report will have the same impact for the social sciences as the Vannevar Bush report had for the physical sciences 40 years ago." It calls for 240 million new dollars for the social sciences.

Sociologist Otto Larsen, then Special Liaison for the Social Sciences to the Director of NSF, and more than anyone else responsible for the idea and for obtaining the funds to support the four-year project that brought forth this report, said that the report's real significance was political; it helped immeasurably within NSF and NRC to bring the social sciences together, and to create a more favorable attitude toward the social sciences among leaders in Congress and in NSF. Whether this will in fact yield significant new dollars in a time of severe budget restraints remains to be seen. Nevertheless, it was influential in stimulating the move for a separate directorate for the social and behavioral sciences, which was formally approved in the Fall of 1991.

6. See Smelser (this volume, chap. 1), who explains the ambivalent attitudes and mixed support from government officials and agencies as a consequence of the perception that sociology is scientifically "soft," and often carries heavy ideological baggage.

Changing Attitudes

We find ourselves in a situation in which attitudes toward sociology are changing ahead of behavior, as manifested in increased budgetary allocations. We need to appreciate how significant the attitude change is, and to seize the opportunity to help bring about a closer relationship between these more positive attitudes and behavioral support for the social sciences, including sociology.

Shortly after his selection as President Bush's Science Advisor, Dr. D. Alan Bromley affirmed his support for the social sciences in a letter (November 1989) to the Executive Committee of the Consortium of Social Science Associations (COSSA). Bromley followed this with the appointment of a social scientist as assistant director for the Social Sciences. In June 1991, he spoke for an hour to an invited audience of some fifty social science leaders, during which he reiterated his belief that such crucial world problems as global warming, health, and education cannot be addressed successfully without the input of the social sciences.

Another sign of the changing attitudes toward the social sciences occurred in the winter and spring of 1991 when the NSF special task force recommended a separate directorate for the behavioral and social sciences, a move strongly supported by sociology and the other social sciences.

In addition to the forces operating outside of sociology, there have been a number of factors operating within the discipline itself that help us understand the patterns that were discussed in the first part of this article.

Factors within Sociology That Help Explain the Patterns

Ideological and Intellectual Orientations

From the very beginning, the substantive areas of interest to sociologists have touched on some of the most intimate and personal aspects of social behavior, including religion, family, sexuality, differential fertility, and suicide. In addition, sociological interest in social and demographic change, crime and delinquency, urbanization, and the growth of the modern corporation have all at one time or another attracted students and the public.

That sociologists were in tune with students during the 1960s and early 1970s is well known and well documented. It is probably the case that sociology was more liberal than other disciplines in the positions its members took on the controversies of the day. A study of academe published by Ladd (1969) illustrates the point. Ladd found that sociologists were the most frequent signers of anti-Vietnam advertisement petitions in the *New York Times* between 1964 and 1968. In fact, they were not only the most likely of the social scientists to sign, but they were three times more likely to sign than were English professors, and four times more than biologists.

Of course, when the mood of the students and public changed, sociologists were hurt badly, as is suggested by the data presented in the tables and figures above. Budgets for teaching were cut, and there was much criticism about the content of undergraduate sociology courses.

Coincident with this development has been the growth of applied sociology and sociological practice. In 1976 there were no departments with such programs. By 1981 there were ninety-three, and the number has continued to grow. The ASA sponsored a special conference on applied sociology in 1981, and in 1984 Rossi and Freeman published "Furthering the Applied Side of Sociology," in the *ASR* (49(4):571–80). Its most important message was that the key to an effective applied program was a challenging curriculum that helped students learn to write, deal with statistics, and express themselves effectively on their feet. Of course, these were and are also key ingredients of a good liberal education.

In a further effort to recognize the changing times, the ASA embarked on a major effort to incorporate the practice of sociology as an integral part of the Association's activities, along with research and the more recently established teaching program. One important feature of ASA's new Professional Development Program is the ASA Committee on Federal Employment of Sociologists. It sponsors special seminars each year for different government agencies. The purpose is to acquaint personnel managers and other officials of those agencies with the work being done by sociologists in and out of government and of its potential relevance to their agencies. The seminars have been well attended and widely acclaimed and, if nothing else, have helped to change attitudes and thinking about the work and recruitment of sociologists.

The Committee also prepared a revised version of the Federal Employment Classification Standard manual to the federal government, and it has now been accepted. As a result, a larger number of federal government jobs than ever before will be open to sociologists. It is difficult to know just what impact such activities have in the short run, but given the growing support for sociology manifested in funding for basic and applied research, and the slow growth in numbers of sociologists now working for the federal government, these moves must be seen as at least supportive of the more positive attitudes and behaviors occurring since 1983.

One of the most important actions taken by the ASA and the other social science associations was the formation of the Consortium of Social Science Associations (COSSA) in 1981. It has been widely credited as being an effective lobbying agent for the social sciences, and as being most responsible for stemming the tide of budget cuts initiated by the Reagan administration in 1981. The ASA has been one of COSSA's strongest supporters.

Whether because of, in spite of, or independent of the ebb and flow of support for sociological research, the fact is that the 1980s have produced a wealth of research and writing that have propelled many sociologists into the forefront of social policy issues. Thus, the *New York Times* throughout this period published feature articles by and about such leading sociologists as William Julius Wilson, Amitai Etzioni, Todd Gitlin, and Rosabeth Moss Kanter. Articles quoting sociologists favorably have become standard fare in the *New York Times,* the *Washington Post,* and other newspapers and newsmagazines.

Sociological research and writing have gained widespread attention in recent years in a number of important areas. Consider such specialized books as the following: Paul Starr's *The Social Transformation of American Medicine;* William Julius Wilson's *The Truly Disadvantaged;* Robert Bellah et al.'s *Habits of the Heart;* Irwin Garfinkel and Sara McLanahan's *Single Mothers and their Children: A New American Dilemma;* Elise Jones's *Teenage Pregnancy in Industrialized Countries;* and Samuel Preston's article in *Demography* on "Children and the Elderly: Divergent Paths for America's Dependents." Dr. William Darrow of the Centers for Disease Control has become widely recognized as one of the nation's leading authorities on the behavioral aspects of AIDS, having provided the critical breakthrough in relating AIDS to certain forms of homosexual behavior.

Also notable has been the work of demographers in helping third-world countries understand the dynamics of population growth; the widespread impact on society of survey research and opinion polling; and William F. Whyte's work in helping to establish legislation in support of employee ownership of companies.

There is a historical government legacy that goes back to William F. Ogburn's "Recent Social Trends"; the pioneering work in the Bureau of the Census by Conrad Taeuber, Paul Glick, Philip Hauser, and others; and the leadership in research provided by Carl Taylor and the scores of sociologists who worked in the Department of Agriculture during his tenure there. These are but a few sociological works that have had important policy implications for significant segments of the society. They remind us not only of major contributions made in earlier decades by sociologists, but of a dynamic and ever-widening range of policy-relevant sociological research going on today. This research is again helping to shape public and student attitudes toward sociology, and to help us further to understand the patterns of growth and decline in our discipline over time.

Where Do We Go from Here?

The evidence presented in this paper makes clear that sociology is emerging from the doldrums that began in the 1970s and continued into the mid-1980s. We seem to be moving into a period of change and growth; whether this growth will lead to a second "golden era" to match that of the post–World War II period is difficult to tell at this point. The discipline is more mature now, significant research is underway in a wide range of specialty areas, and a number of sociologists have gained considerable public recognition for their work. Indeed, the report issued on July 27, 1989, by the National Research Council entitled, "A Common Destiny: Blacks and American Society," is but another example of a major national study chaired by a sociologist, Robin M. Williams, Jr., and including half a dozen other sociologists.

While the work of senior scholars has received national and even international attention, there can be little doubt that the difficult years beginning in the late 1970s have had their impact on academic programs at all levels, including the younger generation of teachers, researchers, and practitioners. The question then arises, how well prepared are we to meet the expanding opportunities that are fast upon us? And what might we do to become more competitive in the market for top quality young students?

I address this question by examining the teaching of sociology at all levels, from K–12 through the undergraduate programs and into the graduate school.

Sociology in K–12

The growing national concerns about elementary and secondary school education in the United States gained focus in 1983 with the

Reagan administration's report "A Nation at Risk." Primary attention was given to the deteriorating quality of science and math education at a time when the nation needed more, not fewer, high school graduates to major in science, math and engineering. A major outgrowth of that report has been "Project 2061," under direction of the American Association for the Advancement of Science (AAAS).

The project title, referring to the year Halley's Comet returns, is meant to suggest the long-range nature of the project, with the goal to bring about a total transformation of what and how we teach science. The social and behavioral sciences are included in the project. The long-term goal is to be able to answer the question, what should a high school graduate know to be literate in matters of science?

The panel recognized that the traditional "social studies" approach used in K–12 has overlooked the significant role of the scientific perspective to the subject matter covered by the social and behavioral sciences. The panel has thus focused on the application of the scientific method to the disciplines comprising the social sciences. It remains for the several social science associations to define how they want to be involved, both individually and collectively.

Another initiative emerging from the "Nation at Risk" study has come from the National Council for Social Studies (NCSS), the major national organization of social studies teachers in K–12. Working independently of Project 2061, NCSS has formed a special commission to carry out a critical review of the content and way that social studies are taught, and to work with teachers and administrators to develop new approaches.

Officials from several of the social sciences, including sociology, have been working with NCSS personnel for more than two years. The NCSS has been gathering and systematizing knowledge about what is being taught, where, when, and by whom. The latter includes sorting out the different state requirements about background qualifications that teachers must have to teach social studies/social sciences courses. The following is clear at this stage:

- something called sociology is taught at almost all grade levels;
- background qualifications for teachers range from "none" to a "minor" concentration in sociology;
- sociology is the second most popular social science elective taught in U.S. high schools;
- many social science/social studies courses are taught by athletic coaches with little or no background in sociology;

° the projects carried out in the 1960s and early 1970s to improve the content and quality of teaching of sociology,
funded especially by NSF, were considered to have been
successful, but have long since fallen into disuse.

The NCSS and COSSA officials have moved slowly toward preparation of a proposal for NSF to fund an experimental project that will
utilize a hands-on approach to social science and, in the process, develop a multidisciplinary scientific approach.

A special task force of sociologists has been appointed to help ASA
coordinate its efforts to be an effective agent for change in K–12 by
working closely with Project 2061 and the NCSS Commission. The
sociologists on the task force have long-standing interests in K–12
education, are highly regarded for their commitment to teaching and
curricular innovation at the undergraduate level, and some of them
have taught or are currently teaching in a secondary school.

Elementary and secondary school officials have made clear that sociology will be taught in K–12; it is in our interest, therefore, to see
that what is taught and how it is taught is of such quality that it will
not only help develop a more informed citizenry, but will also attract
a larger share of the brightest young people to consider the social
sciences and sociology especially as a career possibility. Evidence that
sociology can be taught in a stimulating hands-on fashion in the high
schools comes from the 1989 Westinghouse Science Talent Search,
which awards special prizes for the forty top high school science projects in the country, across all disciplines. For the first time, a student
who did a sociology project took one of the top three prizes.[7]

The Undergraduate Major

Another factor affecting recruitment is the undergraduate major. We
have already alluded to the possible relationship between the major
and GRE scores. The NRC Report on the Behavioral and Social Sciences (1988) provided a brief but important critique of the way the
undergraduate majors in the social sciences are taught in the public
colleges and universities, which enroll about 75 percent of all students. The report made the point that because of the lack of rigorous
social science courses in the secondary schools, the college introduc-

7. See also Calhoun (this volume, chap. 4), who explores efforts to find linkages with
the other social sciences, to be more open to the other sciences, to provide a more
effective understanding of social life, so as "to attract the best students to sociology."

tory courses in the social sciences spent much more time on basics than did the other sciences. Too often the introductory course has been a narrow and limiting experience for students, not one that has drawn them to sociology either as a possible career option, or that stimulated them to see its value as part of a liberal education.

My own experience in three universities, as a coauthor of an introductory text, and with site visits to more than twenty undergraduate programs, plus my work with the Teaching Services Program of the ASA, has made me painfully aware of the dilemmas that many sociologists face and have faced in trying to develop an introductory course in sociology that can satisfy a mix of conflicting needs and demands.

Financial exigencies forced by state governments upon universities and, in turn, upon departments by university administrators have over time fostered the growth of the large introductory course, in sociology and the other social sciences—and in many cases in the physical sciences also. Sections may range as high as a thousand students, with a faculty member who lectures twice a week, and who may have a number of graduate student assistants to handle "quiz" and "discussion" sessions once a week. In these settings, multiple choice tests become the norm, written work disappears as a requirement, and a standard text provides a minimal reading experience. Students see themselves as part of a passive audience before a lecturer whose lectures are important only as they prepare the students for their multiple choice tests.

Long before Bloom (1987) turned his attention to the shortcomings of American undergraduate education, the ASA had become concerned about the quality of undergraduate education in sociology. In the mid-1970s, then executive officer Hans Mauksch, foreseeing troubled times for teaching, received grants from the Fund for the Improvement of Post Secondary Education and from the Lilly Foundation and established the ASA Teaching Services Program. Since 1975, it has served more than 4,000 sociologists, providing opportunities to improve classroom teaching, and to examine a wide range of new materials for almost all sociology courses. In at least some cases, the ASA Teaching Services Program helped departments and faculties to put new life and direction into faltering undergraduate programs.

For several years the Teaching Services Program critically examined the growing body of research (Goldsmid and Wilson 1981) that raised serious questions about the educational value of lecture courses, especially in large class sections. Comparative studies were made of discussion courses and courses built around an individualized system of instruction. *Passing on Sociology,* by Goldsmid and Wilson (1981), summarized the literature and has become the standard text for sociologists seeking to improve the quality of undergraduate education by improving the quality of the classroom environment.

Small liberal arts colleges generally have been able to restrict enrollments to thirty or fewer students per class section, to focus on extensive class discussion, and to create heavy reading and writing expectations. This kind of course has led to successful recruitment of talented majors, a significant portion of whom have gone on to graduate school. In fact, in a recent conference sponsored by NSF and Sigma Xi, the point was made that some fifty liberal arts colleges are responsible for a disproportionate number of doctoral students in almost all fields of study. According to the NSF newsletter, *Directions* (1989:3), "Reed College is among the top five baccalaureate sources [normalized for number of graduates] of U.S. doctorate recipients for all categories of students—total, men, women, and minorities—ranking first among liberal arts colleges."

How is it that the small liberal arts colleges have become the sources for such a large proportion of doctoral students? The president of Reed College, James L. Powell, explained it this way:

> In a nutshell, Reed emulates at the undergraduate level the techniques of graduate institutions. After working closely with faculty in small classes for three years, Reed juniors are required to take a qualifying examination before admission to their senior year. Then each senior—not just a select few—is required to complete an honors thesis, thereby providing students with an opportunity to work closely with faculty, often as near-partners, on significant research projects. In fact, over the last decade, nearly one-third of the papers published by Reed science faculty have listed students as co-authors. (1989:3)

It is time to define more clearly the purposes of the undergraduate program in sociology. On the one hand, it should be designed so that students, who will soon become the next generation of taxpayers, and business, professional, and governmental leaders, will have an appreciation of the contribution that sociology as science and as humanistic interpretation of social life can make to the common good. On the other hand, for the small number among every cohort of students who want to pursue a career in one or another discipline, sociology should be able to offer undergraduates a major that makes sociology as a vocation as intellectually challenging and exciting as any other major. Those of us who know it is have an obligation to work to develop the programs that will enable students to discover the intellectual challenge of sociology. We should not be satisfied to let a few professors at liberal arts colleges carry the burden of preparing the next generation of doctoral students.

A further effort to focus attention on the undergraduate major was fostered by the Association of American Colleges (AAC). A three-year "Study in Depth" of the undergraduate major in sociology was completed in 1991 by a special task force of sociologists commissioned by the AAC. The AAC published this and ten other such studies on a wide range of academic disciplines.[8]

At another level, the Association has continued its efforts to attract more minority scholars to sociology. As Table 5 shows, the percentage of Ph.D.'s who are minorities has remained more or less stable at about 10 percent over the twelve-year time period 1977–88. With funding from the Ford Foundation and other sources, the Minority Opportunity Summer Training (MOST) Program was launched in 1990 and 1991 for undergraduate minority students who applied from all parts of the country. The program, the outgrowth of three years of preparation, was inaugurated on the campuses of the Universities of Delaware and Wisconsin—Madison, with other campuses under consideration for future years. As racial and ethnic minorities become an ever larger percentage of the national population and undergraduate student bodies, we may expect they will be recruited heavily by all sectors of the academic and professional schools. It is important that sociology have a competitive program to offer.

The Graduate Scene: Revitalizing Ph.D. Programs

Finally, a word about graduate education in sociology. Again, we have some of the facts we need with which to evaluate it. The NRC report on the *Behavioral and Social Sciences* (1988:207–12) described the declines in numbers of pre- and post-doctoral fellowships and assistantships going to the social sciences in recent years, and the need to reverse the trend if we hope to develop more research scholars with the tools they need to meet the challenges that are facing us. Within sociology there is also increasing concern about graduate programs themselves, apart from the funding available for the students in them.

A National Science Board report (1985) compared the proportion of doctorates given by the top 25 percent of departments (thirty departments) versus the remaining departments across several disci-

8. Copies of the Sociology Study are available on request from the American Sociological Association Office.

plines. In engineering and the physical and biological sciences, 50 percent or more of the doctorates were given by the top 25 percent of the departments, with the proportions increasing during the period 1973–83. On the other hand, in the social sciences, the top departments gave less than half the degrees, and the proportion given by the lower-ranking departments grew to 68 percent in 1983.

Evidence for this situation in sociology is seen in Figure 7. The number of Ph.D.'s from the top thirty sociology departments, as identified by Webster, declined from a high of 51 percent in 1976 to 41 percent in 1985. Of course, it may well be that faculty changes in the other 75 percent of departments in the past decade have strengthened them, thus lessening concern about the possible implications of this finding. Otherwise, the finding seems consistent with other patterns that need addressing.

In the late 1980s, ASA officials involved in site visits to graduate departments invariably came away dismayed at the state of disarray in which they found graduate programs in leading departments. The question arose about the nature and extent of the problem nationally, and there was enough evidence to suggest that graduate education might benefit from focused attention.

In 1989, the ASA Council formed a Task Group on Graduate Education (TAGGE) that was charged to gather data via a series of meet-

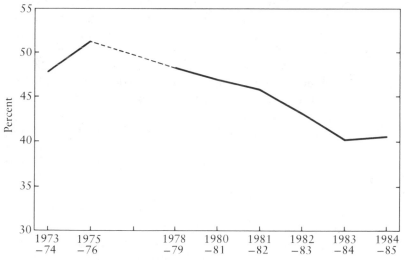

Fig. 7. Proportion of Ph.D.'s Awarded from Top Thirty Sociology Departments, Selected Years, 1973 to 1985. *Source:* American Sociological Association, *Guide to Graduate Departments* (1991).

ings, institutional research, and through correspondence and meetings with department chairs, to see if it is feasible to establish standards for the discipline. The task group examined a number of issues by way of background: the declining GRE scores during the 1970s and 1980s; the lack of standards within distinguished departments, signified by lack of course rigor, and lack of an intellectually coherent curriculum; the laissez-faire stance taken by most departments toward degree requirements; the lack of rigor and sequencing in undergraduate programs; the lack of agreement within the discipline on important problems, standards of adequacy, and shared goals and procedures; and the need to give much more attention to helping prepare graduate students to teach. It soon became clear to the members that a critical examination of graduate education in sociology was an idea whose time had come. At this writing, the task group was preparing a series of meetings and dialogues with department chairs representing the range of graduate departments in the United States.

Sociology has been more successful than other disciplines in attracting women and minorities to its ranks. At the same time, it has been less successful in attracting a full complement of top flight students. Evidence also has revealed that we have been less than rigorous in our education and training programs, which may help explain much of the criticism, both external and self, to which the discipline has been subjected in recent years.

In a personal communication, the late Hubert "Tad" Blalock summed up sociology's shortcomings as he saw them: "My major concern is, and has been, with the quality of students we attract both as majors and as graduate students. Our courses are not sufficiently demanding and do not cumulate or progress from less to more difficult the way they do in math, the sciences, or even economics. We also are often too reluctant to fail students, especially at the graduate level. As a result, we turn out too many underqualified Ph.Ds."

This criticism gets to the heart of the matter. If we are turning out too many underqualified Ph.D.'s, is it not time to expose that fact, and to see what we can do to reverse the pattern? The opportunity is at hand to assert ourselves as a humanistic science, whose methodologies and theories can be exploited by a scholarly generation toward the amelioration of social problems at home and abroad. As this paper is being written, the Association has been awarded a gift of $750,000 to establish the Sydney Spivack Program in Applied Social Research and Social Policy. The gift provides an extraordinary opportunity to increase the public's awareness of sociology's potential to contribute to the common good. The question is whether we have the will and can attract the talent to do so.

References

American Sociological Association. 1991. *Guide to Graduate Departments*. Washington, D.C.

Bellah, R., R. Madsen, W. M. Sullivan, A. Swidler, and S. M. Tipton. 1985. *Habits of the Heart*. Berkeley: University of California Press.

Bloom, A. 1987. *The Closing of the American Mind*. New York: Simon and Schuster.

Bowen, W. G., and J. A. Sosa. 1989. *Prospects for the Faculty in the Arts and Sciences*. Princeton, N.J.: Princeton University Press.

Bromley, D. A. 1989. "White House Science Advisor 'Speaks' to COSSA." *Footnotes,* Dec.:1, 3. Washington, D.C.: American Sociological Association.

Collins, R. 1989. "Future Organizational Trends of the ASA." *Footnotes,* Sept.:1–5, 9. Washington, D.C.: American Sociological Association.

D'Antonio, W. V. 1988. *An American Sociological Association In-House Survey of Association Officials*. Washington, D.C.: American Sociological Association.

Educational Testing Service. 1988. "A Summary of Data Collected from Graduate Record Examinations Test Takers During 1986–87." *Data Summary Report #12*: Table 65. Princeton: New Jersey.

Footnotes. 1989. "MFP Initiates Undergraduate Component." *Footnotes,* Nov.:1–10. Washington, D.C.: American Sociological Association.

Garfinkel, I., and S. McLanahan. 1986. *Single Mothers and Their Children: A New American Dilemma*. Washington, D.C.: Urban Institute Press.

Goldsmid, C., and E. K. Wilson. 1981. *Passing on Sociology*. Washington, D.C.: American Sociological Association.

Huber, B. J. 1985. *Employment Patterns in Sociology: Recent Trends and Future Prospects*. Washington, D.C.: American Sociological Association.

Jones, E. 1986. *Teenage Pregnancy in Industrialized Countries*. New Haven, Conn.: Yale University Press.

Ladd, E. C., Jr. 1969. "Professors and Political Petitions." *Science* 163(28): 1425–29.

Larson, O. F. 1989. Letter to William V. D'Antonio.

National Research Council. 1988. *The Behavioral and Social Sciences: Achievements and Opportunities*. Washington, D.C.: National Academy Press.

———. 1989. *Summary Report: 1989 Doctorate Recipients from United States Universities*. Washington, D.C.: National Academy Press.

National Science Board. 1985. *Science Indicators*. Washington, D.C.: National Science Foundation.

National Science Foundation. 1984. *U.S. Scientists and Engineers.* Washington, D.C.: National Science Foundation.

———. 1985. *U.S. Scientists and Engineers.* Washington, D.C.: National Science Foundation.

———. 1986. *U.S. Scientists and Engineers.* Washington, D.C.: National Science Foundation.

———. 1988. *Profiles—Psychology: Human Resources and Funding.* (NSF 88–325): Table 10. Washington, D.C.: National Science Foundation.

Powell, James L. 1989. "Q and A: James Powell" (with Christine Wise). *Directions,* 2(4):3. Washington, D.C.: National Science Foundation.

Preston, S. 1984. "Children and the Elderly: Divergent Paths for America's Dependents." *Demography* 21(4):435–57.

Rhoades, L. J. 1981. *A History of the American Sociological Association, 1905–80.* Washington, D.C.: American Sociological Association.

Rossi, P. H., and H. Freeman. 1984. "Furthering the Applied Side of Sociology." *American Sociological Review* 49(4):571–80.

Schrader, W. B. 1978. "Admissions Test Scores as Predictors of Career Achievement in Psychology." GRE Board Research Report GREB No. 76–1R. Princeton, New Jersey: Educational Testing Service.

———. 1980. "GRE Scores as Predictors of Career Achievement in History." GRE Board Research Report GREB No. 66–16R. Princeton, New Jersey: Educational Testing Service.

Starr, P. 1982. *The Social Transformation of American Medicine.* New York: Basic Books.

Webster, D. S. 1983. "America's Highest Ranked Graduate Schools, 1925–1982." *Change* 15(4):14–24.

Wilson, W. J. 1987. *The Truly Disadvantaged.* Chicago: University of Chicago Press.

4

Sociology, Other Disciplines, and the Project of a General Understanding of Social Life

CRAIG CALHOUN

No discipline has contributed more to interdisciplinary social science than sociology, and no discipline has suffered more from the poor showing of that enterprise. Sociology, according to August Comte, was to be "queen of the sciences"; more recent sociologists have generally aspired only to be the most synthetically encompassing of the social sciences. Nonetheless, as Rigney and Barnes put it, "for better or worse, contemporary sociology has inherited a dual identity. In principle it has been a *synthetic* discipline; more often in practice it has served as an *interstitial* discipline, filling in gaps among the other social sciences and working along their borders" (1980:116).

Even sociologists who would claim a central and not an interstitial place for their discipline often argue for a discrete division of labor among the social sciences. Durkheim began the tradition with his determination to distinguish sociology from psychology. Though psychology remains the field most cited by sociologists (see Tables 1 and 2), this has not prevented many leading members of the discipline from carrying on Durkheim's argument. Peter Blau, for example, who is perhaps *the* paradigmatic representative of "standard American sociology" over the last forty years (see Mullins 1973; Collins 1979; Calhoun and Scott 1989), has been consistent in arguing against what he sees as the reductionism inherent in any sociological recourse to psychological factors for explanation. He was as explicit in his attempt to define sociology by opposing it to psychology in his incarnation as an exchange theorist (Blau 1964) as in his later structuralist

Participants in the conference on "Sociology and Institution Building" provided useful discussion. Terence M. S. Evens, Lloyd Kramer, and Pamela DeLargy offered helpful readings of various drafts. I am also grateful for research assistance from Rekha Mirchandani, Cynthia Bruss, and Jerome Witschger.

phase, though by the 1970s he argued against the need for macro-sociological arguments to seek even partial foundations in micro-sociology (Blau 1977; 1986). Indeed, Blau has extended his definition of sociology by exclusion of other subject matters to political science and economics; on this view, sociology studies that part of social life that is not politics, economics, or psychology. Blau thus not only distinguishes social from economic exchange (1964), for example, but accepts the conventional definitions of disciplinary boundaries as referring to inherent and substantively significant differences of subject matter (1969). Blau is not atypical in this; he represents a normative position in the discipline. Nearly every introductory sociology textbook on the market carries a paragraph (or several) claiming to distinguish sociology rather sharply from the other social sciences.[1]

Yet sociology retains some claim to be the study of society as a whole or in general. For some, the holistic or generalist claim is simply held in contradiction to the disciplinary division of labor argument. Others disregard the putative division of labor when they go about their own empirical studies, and work, for example, as social psychologists or economic sociologists. Others make reference to the Parsonsian distinction of three systems of action—society, culture, and personality—to justify a claim to deal with all of society while making no more than passing reference to at least some of the other social sciences. This argument is limited, of course, by the presumption that economics, political science, and much of history (not to mention social as distinct from cultural anthropology) must also study the social system, or at least some of its aspects. Most sociologists do not worry about this issue very much (except when teaching introductory sociology, apparently) because they work on such highly specific aspects of social life that any claim to study society in general is something of a religious belief about the eventual cumulative contribution of tens of thousands of separate inquiries, not a description of their own work. Since the demise of functionalist hegemony in social theory, the majority of these empirical specialists have seemed inclined to give up even any frequent ritual homage at the shrine of general sociology. They are content to ignore (or even dismiss as philosophy, not science) those social theories that try to work at that level (and too often general theorists repay the favor by ignoring research).

This paper will argue that the disciplinary division of labor in the

1. The text of which I am coauthor is no exception. The publisher, supported by reviewers at "non-research oriented" schools, in fact insisted in the most recent edition on making stronger distinctions than could be held to correspond to normal disciplinary practice.

social sciences is essentially arbitrary and largely the result of academic politics, but that this has not stopped social scientists from
trying to elevate mere convention to the status of rational principle.[2]
The principles used to describe such disciplinary division of labor are
several: that culture is a matter for anthropologists; that psychologists
study individuals while sociologists study some emergent phenomena;
that historians study (choose one) dead people or people of particular
times and places, while sociologists study (choose the corresponding
one) living people or timeless social laws. None of these principles,
however, is intellectually coherent and justifiable. For the most part,
they are merely the ideological false consciousness of the disciplinarily
self-interested and myopic. And, I shall suggest, they are pernicious.
They are pernicious because they impede fruitful, multifaceted attention to important *sociological* problems. They are pernicious because
they encourage undergraduate students (including future legislators
and members of boards of trustees) to adopt a schematic and impoverished view of social inquiry (and noncoincidentally discourage the
brightest of these from becoming sociologists). They are pernicious
because they discourage adequate attention to the cultural and historical specificity of sociological research and theory. They are pernicious
because they reinforce trends toward overspecialization and undermine efforts to give accounts of the fullness of social life. And perhaps
most of all, these principles are pernicious because they weaken the
usefulness of social science in providing for practically relevant public
discourse.[3]

2. I will not attempt to analyze in any depth the factors that produce the pattern of
disciplinary specialization or its accentuation in postwar America (see Buxton and Turner, this volume, chap. 11). No doubt, the scale of both universities and disciplines
scientism, a turn from "scholarship" (mastery of traditional learning) towards research
(production of "new knowledge"), the growth and bureaucratization of funding
sources, and nonacademic employers all contributed to the compulsion to establish and
enforce boundaries. Disciplines have always been institutionalizations of power (as Foucault has argued); their capacity to organize intellectual discourse has simply been enhanced (relative, for example, to that of the university or the political or literary public).
My concern here, however, is not with the general causes of this process, but with its
specific effects in and on sociology.

3. An aspect of this can be seen in the introductory courses of all the disciplines, but
especially of sociology, where teaching about the discipline sometimes competes with
teaching about its alleged subject matter. This is a major reason why such courses seem
so focused on jargon, abstract conceptual schemes, and discussion of contrasting theory
groups, and why they are currently failing so signally to recruit many of the most talented undergraduates into further study of sociology. Similarly, the discourse of social
theory itself is both impoverished and made less publicly appealing by its constriction
within disciplinary boundaries and its frequent failure to engage issues of general public

Lest this polemical theme turn some readers aside, I shall offer also, and first, an account of the relations of sociologists to other social sciences during the last forty years. I shall look primarily (perhaps unfortunately) from inside sociology out—that is, at the sorts of relationships we have built with members of other disciplines and the use we have made of their work, rather than the use they have made of ours. A key point of departure for this argument will be an analysis of the pattern of citations in the major sociological journals to articles from journals in other disciplines or interdisciplinary fields. Proceeding one by one through the other major social sciences, I shall try to show why the notion of clear and principled disciplinary divisions of labor does not hold, though there are certainly differences of characteristic or statistically preponderant style and substance among fields. I shall focus in more detail on anthropology and history, two disciplines that share with sociology arguable claims to offer a general understanding of social life. Because of these shared claims, sociologists have tried much harder to adduce principles to rationalize the differentiation of their field from anthropology and history. The de-

---

concern, making the connection between those issues as immediately formulated and as embodied in more enduring theoretical problems. Why do Americans look so often to Europeans for great theory? Because Europeans are both less constrained by disciplinary boundaries and more willing to make the link between "scientific" concerns of social theory and public discourse about current social issues. One of the reasons why Parsons is almost alone among postwar American theorists in acquiring international standing and importance in general theoretical discussion is because he too refused to be limited by disciplinary boundaries. Bourdieu noted something of this in an early article on sociology and philosophy in France since 1945. He observed a distinctively high level (by comparison with America) of "intercommunication among French intellectuals in different fields and of different persuasions" (1967:167). This manifested itself, for example, in Simone de Beauvoir's request to see the proofs of Lévi-Strauss's *Elementary Structures of Kinship* while she was writing *The Second Sex;* she wrote an article on Lévi-Strauss's work simultaneous with its publication for the semi-popular but intellectually serious journal *Temps Moderne.* Bourdieu, by the way, is ambivalent about this feature of French intellectual life. While he offers no praise for narrow disciplinary boundaries or the refusal of public engagement, he does see something problematic in the "logic peculiar to the French intellectual field that requires every intellectual to pronounce himself totally on each and every problem" (1967:174). His concern is akin to that of Foucault about theoretical totalism or foundationalism, and is linked to Bourdieu's distaste for abstract, theoretical system-building of the Germanic sort. Bourdieu himself ranges widely across fields, of course, and has not remained disengaged from public discourse (his engagement, moreover, does not involve a sharp distinction between political essays and academic or scientific work). But Bourdieu's rejection of the theoretical and intellectual "totalism" he saw in Sartre, for example, has been deep enough that he has systematically avoided giving a general statement of his theoretical position separable from his various specific investigations.

marcation from psychology has centered on one idea, level of analysis, while economics and political science are generally seen as highly similar enterprises to sociology but focused on specific subject matters that receive their general context from sociology, and that indeed are included within (but not made the focus of) sociology.[4] These accounts will of necessity be brief, undersupported, and schematic; I hope they will be suggestive.

One issue to which I will not do justice is the internal functioning of interdisciplinary fields. Throughout the last forty years there has been a trend towards growth in interdisciplinary social science publications (see Crane and Small, this volume, chap. 5). This is perhaps goods news for interdisciplinary cooperation, though (a) some of them represent quasidisciplines such as urban studies or area studies (see Winsborough, this volume, chap. 7), and (b) the rise of citations to such journals has been offset by declines in citations to the journals of other disciplines.[5] I am particularly sorry not to have been able to take up the issue of the relation of sociology to area studies programs, as these are among the most enduring ventures in interdisciplinary collaboration. The first point at which a significant number of citations to area studies journals turns up in our sample is 1965 (nearly all of that year's large number stemming from a single article by Shmuel Eisenstadt). Such journals are cited with some consistency but not great frequency thereafter. The tendency seems to be for area studies, where they prosper, to be consolidated into a quasidisciplinary field separate from the original disciplines of the practitioners and, correspondingly, to have less influence on sociology or any of the other core disciplines than might be hoped. It is hard to say how much this is due to the ethnocentric insularity of mainstream sociology, and how much to the centrifugal pull of the various area studies programs and fields.[6]

---

4. Given our present-day concern with boundaries, it is worth recalling that early meetings of the American Sociological Association were often held jointly with those of the American Political Science Association and the American Economics Association. Moreover, in the era of Giddings, Small, and Cooley, public figures from Theodore Roosevelt (while President) to Jane Addams addressed the ASA meetings and were engaged in dialogue with its members (Sica, 1989).

5. The same is basically true of interdisciplinary behavioral science journals, distinguished largely by a greater involvement with psychology, but including such fields as marriage and family studies, social work, and aging.

6. This varies with cultural and geopolitical area, and with social science discipline. Soviet and East European studies, and more recently Asian studies, have had relatively greater prominence, for example, than African studies, especially in political science but also in sociology, largely because of their strategic geopolitical significance. Middle East-

There is important work to be done here, exploring, for example, the question of when and why some interdisciplinary fields develop a substantial and enduring identity, and often a quasidisciplinary status, while others never gel in that way. But I have not done this work, nor even fully conceptualized the issues. Certainly interdisciplinary programs fail, or at least fail to achieve their intellectual promise and the ambitions of their creators, for a variety of organizational and political reasons. Universities enter periods of retrenchment. New programs lose political struggles with traditional departments—for example, over assignment of FTEs (full time equivalents = a measure of enrollments and positions), or over who will make tenure and promotion decisions. Ph.D.'s from interdisciplinary programs often have a hard time finding jobs and an especially hard time finding acceptance within traditional disciplinary departments.[7] My contention, however, is that there are deeper reasons lying under these purely political ones, and they have to do with the attempt to base an essentially arbitrary disciplinary division of labor on intellectual principles. Though spurious, these principles are linked in important ways to disciplinary self understanding and undermine more intellectually sound attempts at disciplinary reconstruction. I will return to these issues in the conclusion, asking about the relation of sociology to the project of providing a general understanding of social life. I take this to be central to our intellectual future, to our ability to attract the best students to sociology, and to how well our work serves to nurture public discourse.

---

ern studies have been dominated by political attention to the Arab-Israeli conflicts, with relatively less sociological attention to the societies and cultures of the region. Latin American studies benefit from proximity and the relative accessibility of the relevant linguistic skills (both in the sense that it is easier to learn Spanish or Portuguese—that is, they are less difficult languages and more widely taught—and in the same sense that two languages provide access to the entire continent, unlike polyglot Africa). The presence of relatively well-developed sociological traditions in some areas—notably Eastern Europe and Latin America—serves to boost the involvement of U.S. sociologists in those fields, and also to make it easier for data to be assembled to enable the kinds of studies which can go beyond description to analytic work likely to have a significant impact on mainstream American sociology. African studies has been one of the weakest area studies traditions, though it has gained some support from the interest of African-American students. This has been the area most likely to be seen as deserving anthropological rather than sociological attention, on account of its presumed primitiveness. A variety of other prejudices are also at work to reduce sociological attention to Africa: the low level of economic development, the lesser involvement of American foundations and government funders, and the low level of news media coverage.

7. This has been a problem even for graduates of some of the most distinguished interdisciplinary programs, such as the University of Chicago's Committee on Social Thought and Committee on Human Development, and the University of California at Santa Cruz's Program in the History of Consciousness.

Sociologists and the Other Social Sciences

Sociology is neither the most open nor the most insular of social sciences. In a study of citations in one leading journal per discipline between 1936 and 1975, Rigney and Barnes (1980:117) found sociologists citing articles in sociology journals 58.1 percent of the time, compared to in-citation rates of 41.2 percent for political scientists, 50.7 percent for anthropologists, 73.4 percent for psychologists, and 78.8 percent for economists.[8] The frequency with which sociologists cite articles from outside the discipline declined from the late 1940s to the middle 1950s, remained low throughout the 1960s, then rose gradually through the 1970s and 1980s, returning to a just slightly higher level than at the beginning of the period (see Tables 1 and 2).[9]

8. For reasons that are unclear to me, Rigney and Barnes found a substantially lower rate of *American Sociological Review* citations to psychology journals, and a somewhat higher rate of citation to political science journals, than I did. They regard sociology as having "by far the greatest aggregate tendency to cite other social sciences" (1980:116), though it is not clear that their data show this. They find sociologists citing articles in the other four disciplines studied (psychology, anthropology, economics, and political science) 4.7 percent of the time, while anthropologists cite the others 3.2 percent, political scientists 3.1 percent, economists .9 percent, and psychologists .7 percent of the time. Their analysis, however, completely disregards citations to other social sciences (e.g., geography) and to interdisciplinary behavioral and social science journals (e.g., *Administrative Science Quarterly, Social Science Quarterly, Journal of Family Issues, Demography,* etc.). As a result, their figures for mean percentage of citations to other disciplines seem somewhat misleading. As Tables 1 and 2 show, citations to interdisciplinary journals constitute a large part of the citations outside of sociology proper, especially from the 1960s on. It appears to me that taking these "others" into account would challenge the claim that sociology has by far the greatest tendency to cite the other social sciences. Such "others" account for 23.2 percent of sociologists' citations in the Rigney and Barnes sample, compared to 46.5 percent of political scientists' and 36.6 percent of anthropologists'.

9. The citation count reported here is based on a sample of all articles in one randomly chosen issue per volume of the *American Journal of Sociology* and *American Sociological Review* between 1948 and 1988. These two journals are overwhelmingly the most important in the field, if frequency of citation is an indicator; the next closest, *Social Problems* and *Social Forces* rarely receive more than a fifth as many citations as the lesser of the *ASR* or *AJS*. In order to control for disparities in actual numbers of citations (especially because of variation in the page length of the journals), the analysis is focused on relative proportions of citations. Averaging the results into five-year clusters smoothes out the impact of individual articles (e.g., a single article in 1967 that included 67 citations to biomedical journals—27 percent of the total citations for the issue, and more than 60 more biomedical citations than in any issue sampled five years before or after it). The pattern of decline in citations outside the discipline from the late 1940s through to the middle 1950s is more pronounced in the *ASR;* an unusually high level of citations to psychology and psychiatry journals in one sampled issue of the *AJS* raises the out-citation rate for the 1953–57 period.

Table 1. American Sociological Review Reference Pattern, 1948–87 (in percentages)

	'48–52 (286)	'53–57 (279)	'58–62 (306)	'63–67 (658)	'68–72 (497)	'73–77 (678)	'78–82 (859)	'83–87 (983)	Average
Sociology	46	62	60	55	58	52	45	44	49
Psychology[a]	23	13	12	10	5	10	8	6	10
Interdisc. social science	4	3	3	6	5	5	5	5	5
Behavioral science[b]	2	1	3	5	4	3	5	4	4
Biomed. & phys. science	3	3	2	6	1	5	3	1	4
Org., admin., mgmt., labor	1	0	1	2	3	1	3	6	3
Economics	1	2	2	2	1	2	5	6	3
Population	0	2	1	2	1	0	4	6	3
Political science	0	2	0	0	4	1	3	2	2
Crime, deviance	1	1	1	1	0	2	4	2	2
Public opinion, policy	1	3	2	1	2	2	2	1	2
Education	2	1	1	3	1	3	2	1	2
Stat. and measurement[c]	1	2	2	1	4	1	3	3	2
Pol. econ., development	1	1	0	1	1	1	2	6	2
Anthropology	6	1	5	0	1	3	1	0	1
Law	0	1	2	1	1	1	1	1	1
History	0	0	0	1	1	2	1	2	1
General science	1	0	0	0	2	2	2	1	1
Gender, women's studies	0	0	0	0	0	0	0	1	0
Philosophy	1	0	0	0	1	0	0	0	0
Other	5	2	5	1	3	4	2	4	3

Note: Parenthetical figures in column heads are actual numbers (N).
[a] Includes psychiatry.
[b] Includes epidemiology, marriage and family, youth, adolescence, age.
[c] Unless codable under a discipline.

At the same time, there were substantial changes in the fields from which sociologists drew (and by implication, to which they related). The prominence of psychology, though still great, underwent a secular decline. Anthropology, similarly, became a much less frequent source of citations. On the other hand, economics and the interdisciplinary fields of organizational, administrative, management, and labor studies enjoyed substantial increases in prominence, particularly toward the end of the time period. Similarly, interdisciplinary social and behavioral science publications became more frequent sources and the field of political economy rose from a minor relation (consisting pri-

Table 2. American Journal of Sociology Reference Pattern, 1948–87 (in percentages)

	'48–52 (154)	'53–57 (161)	'58–62 (240)	'63–67 (195)	'68–72 (291)	'73–77 (753)	'78–82 (333)	'83–87 (372)	Average
Sociology	42	38	46	51	57	49	45	49	48
Psychology[a]	11	28	12	9	8	5	18	6	10
Interdisc. social science	9	5	3	3	5	10	6	6	6
Behavioral science[b]	1	1	0	3	5	4	3	8	4
Economics	3	2	0	3	2	2	9	5	4
Org., admin., mgmt., labor	1	3	2	5	1	4	5	0	3
Stat. and measurement[c]	2	1	6	3	6	2	1	2	3
Political science	1	0	1	1	3	2	3	1	2
Public opinion, policy	2	3	4	4	1	1	0	1	2
Education	1	2	4	4	2	1	0	3	2
Anthropology	2	3	4	5	0	2	1	0	2
History	0	0	3	1	1	3	1	4	2
General science	1	1	1	3	3	2	1	0	1
Population	2	1	0	1	2	2	0	1	1
Biomed. & phys. science	1	1	1	1	0	1	2	0	1
Pol. econ, development	0	0	0	0	0	1	1	3	1
Philosophy	0	0	0	0	1	2	0	0	1
Crime, deviance	1	1	0	0	0	0	1	2	1
Gender, women's studies	0	0	0	0	0	0	0	1	0
Law	1	0	0	0	0	0	2	0	0
Other	21	11	12	2	4	7	2	7	7

Note: Parenthetical figures in column heads are actual numbers (N).
[a] Includes psychiatry.
[b] Includes epidemiology, marriage and family, youth, adolescence, age.
[c] Unless codable under a discipline.

marily of articles in the *Journal of Political Economy*) into a significant source of citations (particularly with the rise of interdisciplinary Marxist journals and development studies). Population also grew substantially in the frequency of extradisciplinary citations. Education was a fairly stable source of citations, significant but not major. Political science was a very infrequent source of citations early on but became prominent in the later 1960s and has remained significant, though not always high. The importance of nondisciplinary statistics and measurement journals seems to have grown gradually through the period. Public opinion and public affairs journals were fairly frequently cited in the middle years of the period, the heyday of academic public opinion research, but much less so at either end. Crime, deviance, delinquency, and corrections drew considerably fewer citations early on than I expected. Some fields were never prominent sources of citations—at least during this period. Philosophy drew only a handful of citations, for example. Gender studies predictably received no citations in the early years, but also very few after the founding of *Sex Roles* and *Signs*. Finally, though it drew nearly four times as many citations overall as gender or philosophy, law still received only half those of the next closest discipline.[10]

The most interesting overall trend in the citation patterns is the dramatic secular rise in number and rate of citations (see Figures 1 and 2). Apparently disciplinary norms changed in the direction of requiring substantially more citations in each article. It is remarkable (from the point of view of the 1980s) how many articles in the *ASR* and *AJS* up to the early 1960s contained no references whatsoever. It seems unlikely that all the increase in citations is due to increase in relevant literature. Some must be due to attempts to "armor-plate" arguments with authorities, perhaps stimulated by rising levels of competition. Some, perhaps, is due to a continuing turn towards more papers attempting to put forward, modify, or test general sociological propositions and fewer describing research results without at least the pretense to such general "theory-building" cumulation. Whatever its causes, the shift in style is remarkable.[11]

10. Obviously, a variety of extraneous factors influence citation count statistics, making citation analysis a fairly blunt instrument for investigating disciplinary patterns. Some fields (e.g., history) are more apt to be cited from books, and thus to be undercounted in this analysis. Other fields (e.g., psychology and biomedical sciences) promote citation to more articles in each published piece, perhaps because of a shorter mean length of articles. Some journals are hard to classify—e.g., *Sociometry* and its successor *Social Psychology Quarterly,* which I have treated as sociology rather than psychology publications because of their affiliation with the American Sociological Association. I have classified journals under "statistics and measurement" only if they were not readily classifiable by discipline (as were, for example, *Psychometrika* or *Econometrica*).

11. This shift is more marked in the case of the *ASR*. There are a number of other, mostly minor, differences between the two journals. These can be noted in Tables 1 and 2, where fields are listed in descending rank order of total citations. A curious difference is the much greater number of citations to periodicals classified as other—a wide range of popular magazines, general intellectual periodicals, and journals from the humanities—in the *AJS* during the late 1940s and 1950s. It may be worth remarking that biomedical science journals, population studies and crime, deviance, and delinquency journals are all cited less often in the *AJS*. Anthropology, history and economics are all cited slightly more often in the *AJS*. The differences are fairly minor; much more striking is the basic consistency between the two patterns. Despite the differences of style and taste represented in each journal, they showed the same preponderance of in-discipline citation and a broadly similar distribution of citations to other disciplines and interdisciplinary fields.

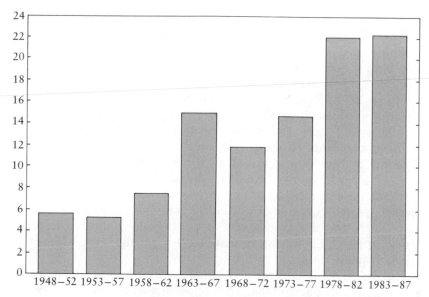

Fig. 1. *American Sociological Review*, Mean Citations per Article, 1948 to 1987.

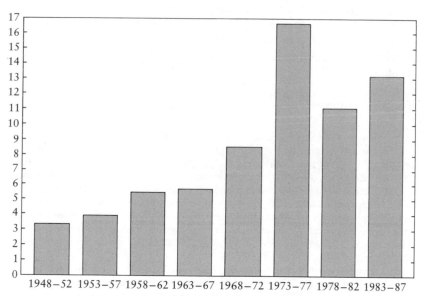

Fig. 2. *American Journal of Sociology*, Mean Citations per Article, 1948 to 1987.

Anthropology

Institutionally, anthropology has shared perhaps the closest relationship with sociology. Anthropology and sociology were taught in a single department in many American colleges and universities until the 1960s or 1970s.[12] Anthropology was the discipline most closely implicated in Talcott Parsons's and colleagues' efforts to develop a general theory of society (and, along with social psychology, figured centrally in the effort to create an integrated Department of Social Relations at Harvard). It shared a broadly functionalist orientation with sociology for many years, and a broadly evolutionary one before that (and in some quarters of each discipline, afterwards). Given this closeness, the overall rate of citation to anthropology journals seems surprisingly low (though this may be partly because anthropology is a field in which books, rather than articles, are the central form of scholarly publication).

The typical account of the division of labor between anthropology and sociology emphasizes that anthropologists deal with "primitive," "preindustrial," or "non-Western" societies. This is sometimes supplemented by the accounts that anthropologists use participant observation methods, and deal with culture, while sociologists use statistics and focus on social structure. The first two accounts are widely offered by both anthropologists and sociologists, while the third (culture versus social structure) is more often, but not exclusively, given by sociologists.[13] All three claims have an element of truth, in terms of statistical frequencies, but little or no standing as intellectual principles of division.[14]

12. Though some departments split earlier, a number—especially in smaller schools—are still joint today. The American pattern is the inverse of the British, where anthropology was the more established and larger discipline several decades ago, and sociology the subordinate sibling. Such prominent British sociologists as Peter Worsley, J. C. Mitchell, and John Barnes were trained in anthropology. Oxford University still has no professorship in sociology, although it has long had one in social anthropology (and although such distinguished sociologists as Mitchell, A. H. Halsey, Steven Lukes, Frank Parkin, and Bryan Wilson have taught there in other positions at advanced stages of their careers). The first professor of sociology at Cambridge was an anthropologist, John Barnes.

13. Anthropology itself has sometimes been split by debates over the priority of culture vs. social structure. The division is associated with that between American cultural anthropologists and British social anthropologists, with Leslie White and A. R. Radcliffe-Brown serving as standard bearers for at least one major confrontation.

14. Discussion in this text focuses entirely on the relationship of sociology to sociocultural anthropology. This minimizes one further impediment to intellectual integration between sociology and anthropology—the inclusion of physical anthropology, ar-

The first proposed principle of division would be better interpreted as making anthropology and sociology two branches of a highly interdependent undertaking. If the object is an understanding of human social arrangements, for example, then presumably both Western and non-Western, industrial and preindustrial, modern and primitive societies must be studied, and those studies related to each other. Of course, one might also call into question the intellectual merits of those distinctions. The primitive-modern typology has been especially widely questioned, largely because of its implied unilineal evolutionism (in fact, nearly every binary opposition is also used to distinguish elements within single societies as more advanced or archaic, as well as to divide up the world's societies). Such distinctions, along with most binary distinctions of overall social patterns (*gemeinschaft-gesellschaft*, status-contract, holistic-individualistic, etc.), also have been criticized as embodying a tendency to divide the world into "us" and "them." This is characteristic, for example, of the classical "orientalism" (Said 1976) that appropriated information about "Eastern" societies primarily in order to make contrasts with the West (whether negative, as in Montesquieu's idea of Persian tyranny; or positive, as in various Romantics' use of Third World societies to pose criticisms of modern Europe). It must be asked whether "preindustrial," "non-Western" and "premodern" do not group together a far greater range of heterogeneous social arrangements than do the countertypes against which they are defined. It is hard to imagine them being adequately rendered as positive rather than negative descriptions. In any case, a sociology that willingly accepts the exclusion of most of the world's societies from its purview must be considered both ethnocen-

---

chaeology, and linguistics in the later discipline. Giving a coherent account of this "four fields" approach in contemporary anthropology is becoming increasingly difficult, which helps account for problems anthropology departments sometimes have in wresting positions from deans and developing plans for future development. Though a variety of individual lines of work in anthropology are thriving at present, the discipline as a whole is in something of a protracted identity crisis. A hint of this can be seen in the move a few years ago to create a "Section on General Anthropology" as a subfield within the American Anthropological Association—a remarkable testimony to the fragmentation of the latter. One possible scenario is for increasing division of physical anthropology (which maintains close ties to ecology, evolutionary biology, and anatomy) and possibly archaeology from the rest of the field (Duke University has recently reassigned physical anthropologists from Arts and Sciences to its Medical Campus, distributed archaeologists to various departments and reconstituted anthropology as a Department of Cultural Anthropology). Such actions both achieve a greater internal integration within anthropology departments and remove the portion of anthropology that sociologists find most foreign (though in some cases, they also would leave numerically weak and thereby often politically disadvantaged anthropology departments).

tric and intellectually suspect. Yet that is precisely what American sociology has done, at least implicitly, aided and abetted by the separation of anthropology into a distinct discipline.

The meaning of this separation has been further challenged in recent years from the anthropological side by an increasing attention to "modern, Western, industrial" societies. This has been motivated partly by the disappearance or transformation of many of the traditional small-scale societies with low-productivity technologies that once formed the mainstay of anthropological research. Many anthropologists have accordingly turned their attention to relatively small-scale groupings within large-scale industrial societies—youth gangs, classrooms, intentional communities. A similar shift of attention has also occurred among anthropologists still working in the Third World. It has been motivated significantly by theoretical recognition of the arbitrariness and misleading nature of traditional notions of the self-contained primitive society or "tribe." Where canonical anthropological studies of forty years ago ignored the impact of Western colonialism, long-distance slave trade, and nascent state formation on the putatively small-scale and self-contained social groups they described, more recent anthropological research has been concerned with precisely those impacts. The very notion of tribe has been all but completely rejected, especially with regard to Africa. The interrelations of neighboring peoples within regions and their common subjection to colonial or state power have become central objects of study. Anthropologists working in the Third World today are more likely to participate in the interdisciplinary discourse of political economy as they address state level phenomena, the impact of international trade or capitalist businesses, and questions of the relative capacity of different groups to determine the conditions of their own lives.[15] Anthropologists have challenged the connotations of terms like "primitive," both in general insofar as they carry illegitimate or misleading value judgments, and in particular where the societies gaining anthropological attention are complex civilizations with long written histories, such as China or India.

From the sociological side, the notion of a neat separation of anthropology on the basis of its primitive, non-Western, or preindustrial subject matter has been challenged by a renewed involvement of sociologists in area studies programs, the resurgence of comparative his-

15. Of course, such anthropologists, and especially anthropologists looking at political economic issues in nonexotic societies, are prone to a certain amount of suspicion from more traditional anthropologists who view such work as "too sociological."

torical sociology, and the work of sociologists in development studies. It is still true, of course, that American sociology is remarkably biased towards American society, and prone to draw putatively universal conclusions from work in this single setting. Nonetheless, the comparative dimension is significant. In fact, a substantial comparative dimension was earlier at work under a rubric closely related to the proposed basis for separating sociology from anthropology. During the 1950s and especially the 1960s, "modernization" research and theory was an important part of the discipline. While it did lead sociologists to pay attention to non-Western societies, too often the paradigmatic approach led them to collapse variation into a model of unilinear development. The recent wave of comparative-historical sociology has been more skeptical of such overarching schemes, and more devoted to concrete patterns of variation among specific histories. Comparative sociology is split, however, between those whose work fits this model of contrasting a small number of specific historical cases, and those who pursue large-scale quantitative analyses of many cases. In the later model especially, the cases nearly always represent static snapshots of nation-state indicators.

The methodological argument for a division between sociology and anthropology seems even more suspect, though that does not stop it from being frequently voiced. Indeed, participant observation fieldwork is central to anthropological practice. Some anthropologists do, of course, work with historical documents and collect statistical information. Nonetheless, extended fieldwork remains central and largely definitive of the anthropological enterprise in the minds of both insiders and outsiders. It is understood by anthropologists not only as producing a rich variety of data, but as leading to a deep confrontation with "otherness" that is itself intellectually salutary. An important intellectual tradition is represented by the minority of sociologists who engage in participant observation fieldwork, though relatively few take on projects of the duration or intensity characteristic of anthropologists, at least on the classical model, and fieldwork or participant-observation oriented sociologists seem no more likely to work outside the U.S. (or more generally, their own society) than do others. Some other sociologists, to be sure, come close to reading these fieldworkers and practitioners of qualitative methods out of sociology, and qualitative methods have a second class status compared to quantitative ones in most major graduate programs in sociology. Nonetheless, defining sociology in terms of statistical methods would create so many anomalies as to be impossible. And while ethnography is central to anthropology, it is hardly exclusive to it.

Two other factors, both somewhat associated with the participant observation tradition, may account for a good deal of the impact it has on maintaining disciplinary difference.[16] The first has to do with a distinctive approach to learning the disciplinary craft. Anthropology, (like literature, law, and psychoanalysis) relies very heavily on case studies or classic works as exemplars; sociology relies much more on methodological recipes or strictures. A canonical series of ethnographies plays a central role in learning anthropology. These works—for example, Evans-Pritchard's *The Nuer,* or Malinowski's *Argonauts of the Western Pacific*—are subjected to continuing reanalysis. New theoretical approaches prove themselves, in part, by their ability to shed new light on or make better sense of such classic works, or contrasts among them. Though sociology has its classics, neither a case study method nor the use of such works as exemplars figures anywhere near as prominently as in anthropology.

The second distinguishing factor stems from the idea of confrontation with otherness, the deep recognition of difference.[17] Sociological work tends both to assume a high level of universal applicability for its generalizations, and to focus little attention on sharp lines of difference. This has been evident not only in the neglect of cross-cultural comparison, but in the failure to come to grips better and sooner with gender. Even when, under the influence of the feminist movement, sociologists do take gender seriously, it is often simply by adding a single variable to their analyses, not by considering the theoretical significance of gender as a basic category of consciousness (Harding 1987). The problem of making meaningful statements across lines of cultural difference is a central one for anthropology that has, however, at-

16. That is, while not providing an adequate intellectual rationale for a disciplinary division of labor, these two factors help to account for the persistence of disciplinary differences even as the topical contrast between anthropologists working in preindustrial societies and sociologists studying industrial ones is reduced. Halliman Winsborough (in discussion at the conference from which this volume stems) suggested that a factor that unifies the four fields of anthropology and separates them from sociology is the characteristic "round of life" of each field. Where sociologists worry about the availability of computers and large data sets, anthropologists worry about travel to remote locations and shipment of artifacts. I think there is something to this, though a range of changes from the spread of microcomputers to the increasing ease with which anthropologists can travel to and from field sites are probably reducing its impact.

17. It is true that this is not always the preponderant anthropological message. There is also an implicit argument as to the unity of mankind running through most anthropological work, and sometimes taking the upper hand. Kurt Vonnegut once commented that he studied anthropology at the University of Chicago twice, before and after his military service. The first time they taught him that everyone was the same, and the second time that everyone was different. The two themes meet, of course, in the notion of "finding oneself in the other."

tracted little sociological interest, especially in the United States.[18] This takes us into the realm of the third proposed rationale for the division of labor between anthropology and sociology.

It is not entirely clear why, but the study of culture has been strikingly marginalized in American sociology and, at least until very recently, regarded as more appropriate to anthropologists. Residues of this attitude can be found in most American introductory sociology textbooks. Culture is compartmentalized as the topic of a single chapter, seldom mentioned elsewhere in the book. Religion, for example, is apt to be discussed with little or no reference to the concepts introduced in the culture chapter. In such culture chapters, discussion is based largely on the work of Kroeber, Linton, Mead, and other anthropologists whose canonical works are two or three generations past.[19] In most books there is no mention of Lévi-Strauss, let alone of Sahlins, Geertz, and other leading contemporary cultural anthropologists. Likewise, there is no mention of recent work in literary criticism, philosophy, and history that ought to be seen as central to social studies of culture—for example, the writings of Foucault, Derrida, Lacan, Said, Jameson, or others sometimes lumped together (a little misleadingly) under the label "postmodernists." Of course, texts are biased indicators because their authors are generally forced to avoid theoretical complexity. This tends to minimize not only the attention

18. This actually suggests another significant difference between anthropology and sociology. In the last decade, anthropologists have been far more receptive to the various currents of "poststructuralist" and "postmodernist" thought—partly, in fact, because of their earlier greater involvement in cultural structuralism, but partly also for other reasons, including a general disciplinary receptivity to moral relativism, to the claims that knowledge is essentially power and that all particular intellectual orientations are equally arbitrary, and to a sense of the difficulty or inappropriateness of trying to assimilate the specificity of existence to any general theory.

19. Perhaps one should not blame the authors alone. Aiming for the mass market, publishers have created and the profession has accepted a lowest common denominator approach to introductory texts. This enforces a high degree of similarity and conventionality in offerings. Though all successful books are revised frequently to support the claim that they are up to date, publishers are highly resistant to major changes (and it has to be said that the sociologists whom publishers hire as reviewers tend also to be extremely conservative in their definition of appropriate contents). A publisher's staffer often checks other texts to ensure that precisely the same topics are covered. For example, in my own text, the publisher required that the culture chapter include a discussion of sociobiology—despite my insistence that this had little to do with contemporary sociology of culture. The grounds were that most of the other texts have something on sociobiology in the culture chapter. And, to be sure, at least one reviewer pointed out the absence of such a feature in my draft. At the same time, the publisher ruled out substantial expansion and updating of the section on language, minimized the treatment of new theoretical, anthropological and comparative historical work on culture and asked that I be sure that Margaret Mead and her recent critics stayed in.

paid to the sort of thinkers noted above, but the seriousness with which contemporary sociology of culture is addressed. Few books on the market, for example, feature the work of Pierre Bourdieu in any serious way; fewer still mention Raymond Williams. Nonetheless, the textbooks do tell us something about the discipline.

Especially in the U.S., sociologists have worked with a division of labor in mind that relegated the study of culture with a capital "C" (or "K") to specialists in literature, art, music, etc., and with a small "c" to anthropology. The first part of this division of labor involved a tacit assumption that the specificities of high culture were beyond sociological explanation, were simply matters of opinion or interpretation. In other words, sociologists bought (perhaps unconsciously and even in contradiction to what would have been their explicit, considered judgment) into one of the general, individualistic, self-understandings of modern Western culture, the ideology of artistic genius.

The second part of this implicit notion of a division of labor was enshrined in Talcott Parsons's (1951; Parsons, Bales, and Shils, 1953) division of the realm of human action into the three domains of personality, culture, and society. In a way, this was ironic for Parsons since he came much closer to developing a genuine cultural sociology than did any other major American sociologist of his generation. In Parsons's later work, especially, culture figures as central to the explanation of the continuity, coherence, and change of the social system. In any case, Parsons meant for studies of personality, culture, and society to be constantly interpenetrating (as they were in his own work). While he accepted a disciplinary division of labor, he sought to avoid the kind of separation and purported autonomy of psychology, anthropology, and sociology that has become the norm. Under Parsons's leadership, the Harvard Social Relations Department was oriented to producing students who could engage in what I am told (by Robert Wilson) Charles Dollard once described as the best kind of interdisciplinary collaboration—that which occurs when you have two disciplines inside one skull. On the other hand, Parsons tended, especially in his later work, to make culture into something of an overarching compendium of values, ideas, and orientations to action, a kind of general explanation for everything. This approach to culture did not encourage making it the focus of research so much as the most fundamental of independent variables.[20] In any case, the sociology of cul-

20. Nonetheless, some functionalists produced cultural studies that were much more concrete and historically specific than Parsons's own work (e.g., those of Eisenstadt 1973; Bellah 1957; Geertz 1973). And sociology offered other alternatives: phenome-

ture did not lack foundations on which to build, but it remained a remarkably isolated subfield. It is hard to imagine a sociologist declaring studies of social structure to be simply one topical subfield among many, yet this attitude dogged studies of culture and limited their impact on the discipline as a whole. "Mainstream" sociologists might follow Parsons in describing culture as a sort of general independent variable that exerted a determining force over social life "in the last instance," but they did not make it the object of their studies. The issue was less a shortage of theories raising issues of cultural analysis than the lack of a strong empirical research tradition closely linked both to those theories and to other problem areas in sociology. Some sociologists went out of their way to distinguish themselves from their "softer" brethren who took culture and interpretative research more seriously. Perhaps the foremost example of this is the attempt by the University of Wisconsin department to expunge the theoretical and cultural orientation of Gerth and establish a positivist, primarily quantitative sociology.

For whatever reasons, the sociology of culture became a small and not very active subfield, and until recently thought about culture figured only very slightly or in very general ways in the most influential lines of sociological work. The substantial attention accorded cultural issues by many of the theoretical founders of modern sociology, from

---

nology had a long minority following and included distinguished students of culture (e.g., Berger and Luckmann 1966; Berger 1969). American sociologists under the influence of Weber (including especially a number of Gerth's students from Wisconsin) conducted a wide range of culturally-focused research, including a good part of the community studies tradition (e.g., Vidich and Bensman 1968). Sociologists from Bell (1973, 1976) and Stanley (1978) to Riesman (1950), Slater (1970), and Bellah, et al. (1985) have offered cultural criticism of some note. Elias (1978, 1982) produced monumental historical analyses of cultural patterns and their change, though it took the revival of comparative historical sociology as well as of cultural sociology for them to become well-known in the U.S. Marxist sociologists and those influenced by them maintained a vital tradition of cultural analysis. Lukacs, though not formally a sociologist, wrote important social analyses of literature; Goldmann (1964) and Lowenthal (1961) kept his legacy alive. Hauser's monumental *Sociology of Art* (1982) was an effort to bridge Marxist historical and sociological analysis, though it has had little impact in American sociology. The Frankfurt school produced a host of major studies of culture, including both institutional analyses and formal and content-oriented critiques. The works of Adorno and Benjamin figure perhaps most prominently in this regard, but Horkheimer, Lowenthal, and Marcuse all published significant studies. Indeed, it would not be too much to say that more important work on the sociology of culture was done within the Marxist discourse than within that of the sociological discipline proper. The readership of Raymond Williams (e.g., 1958, 1981), for example, has been much wider in literary and Marxist fields than in sociology—especially in the U.S.

Comte through Parsons, was largely forgotten. Selective reading was powerful, especially when aided by a well-defined canon and a reliance on edited snippets and predigested summaries rather than serious primary source study. Two quick examples will suffice, since the aim here is only to be suggestive. First, Durkheim, arguably the most influential of all the founding figures, was for decades read almost without dissent among American sociologists as advocating a "pure sociology" that would be entirely objectivist and positivist, as foreign to problems of cultural interpretation as to individualistic psychology. This was plausible for the Durkheim of *The Rules of Sociological Method, Suicide,* and *The Division of Labor,* which figured centrally in the canon, but quite at odds with the Durkheim of *Primitive Classifications* and *The Elementary Forms of Religious Life.* An understanding of Durkheim's thought either in terms of its internal tensions or in terms of its development over his career had to be sacrificed in this treatment, as Jeffrey Alexander (1982) has recently shown (see also Alexander ed. 1988). Similarly, it remains possible for as sophisticated and important a theorist as Peter Blau (1986) to invoke Simmel as his unambiguous ally in opposing a purely structural sociology to cultural studies. This is because Simmel has been read (in sociology) almost entirely through certain small portions of his work, those focused on forms of social relationships, and especially on those forms that might be universal. Simmel's substantial inquiries into modern culture, like the more philosophical side of his intellectual work, have been largely ignored (see Frisby 1985). Considering its prestige at one time, it is remarkable how little a mark has been left on contemporary sociology by Sorokin's monumental attempt (1937–41) to explain overarching historical patterns of culture. It seems relegated, along with the efforts of Toynbee, Spengler, and Mumford, to some dark corner where we keep, without respect, the relics of grand historical syntheses. That Sorokin's were sophisticated sociological analyses, not just syntheses, seems to be forgotten.[21]

There may even have been deeper reasons for this sociological avoidance of the study of culture. To take culture very seriously might have meant an implicit challenge to the positivist self-understanding and the dominance of objectivist research techniques in sociology. Something of this was suggested in the debates over rationality and cross-cultural studies that followed the publication of Winch's *The Idea of a Social Science* (1958; see Wilson, ed. 1970; Hollis and

21. For more discussion of the sociology of culture, including more on its relationship to anthropology, see Calhoun (1989) and sources cited therein.

Lukes, eds. 1982). An extreme emphasis on cultural particularity and the internal, self-referential nature of linguistic meaning seemed to rule out most of the very project of cross-cultural analysis.[22] The majority of participants rejected such extreme conclusions, but never completely refuted the arguments on which they were based. Of course, the kind of analysis that Winch developed, following the later Wittgenstein, is not the only way of taking culture seriously. Anthropology offered both the *Kulturwissenschaft* tradition and the newer school of structuralism, for example, neither of which posed such intractable problems. Serious social studies of culture were undertaken by literary critics (e.g., Jameson 1981; Eagleton 1984), art critics (e.g., Gablik 1984) and historians (e.g., Thompson 1955, 1968; Maravall 1986, among many). There were exemplars from the established fields of cultural studies, particularly in the humanities. And indeed, various sociologists had been taking culture seriously all along (though often not under that name.)[23]

If it is hard to find good reasons for sociologists to ignore culture, it is correspondingly problematic that some anthropologists minimize their attention to the sociological and historical. But it should be said that by no means all anthropology—even excluding linguistics, archaeology, and physical anthropology—focuses predominantly on the cultural. There is a great deal of sociological work done under the disciplinary rubric of anthropology. Historically, this was particularly true of the British tradition of social anthropology, led by exemplars such as Radcliffe-Brown, Evans-Pritchard, Fortes, and Gluckman. It is true also of substantial segments of American anthropology, despite its more specifically cultural orientation, and, for that matter, of other national traditions.

In sum, differences between anthropology and sociology are quite real at the level of statistical patterns of styles of work and geographical distributions of work sites. Intellectually, however, sociology and anthropology seem only impoverished by any attempt to exclude domains as belonging to the other. If anything, current trends in the

22. Though it seems not to trouble most adherents, something of the same problem seems to beset much of the postmodernist and deconstructionist literature (see Calhoun, forthcoming). At its best, however, the poststructuralist emphasis is on identity *and* difference, and thereby would seem to require attention to cross-cultural relations.

23. A good deal of what attitude surveys attempt to describe and measure must be considered culture. See Wuthnow (1987, chap. 1) for a discussion of the affinity of this methodology with a subjectivist, individualist understanding of culture that he finds in the classical tradition of sociology (though perhaps he should see this as more an aspect than the whole of the work of Marx, Weber, and Durkheim).

disciplines seem to call the legitimacy of the strict division of labor argument still further into doubt.[24]

History

A generation ago, sociologists were apt to contrast their work to that of historians as scientific analysis opposed to mere description. In language descended from the *methodenstreit*, sociology was a nomothetic undertaking while history was idiographic. These accounts, and the philosophy of social science on which they were based, went out of fashion even before the recent resurgence of historical sociology and the rise of systematic and often quantitative "social science history." Nonetheless, they left an enduring mark on the implicit understandings of many sociologists.[25] Quite likely, they also contribute to the remarkably small number of citations we find to historical works.[26]

The minimal involvement of sociologists with history is all the more remarkable given the historical training and concerns of many of the founding theorists of sociology—notably Marx and Weber. Of course, there have been some historical sociologists at all stages of the discipline's history.[27] The fact remains that well under 1 percent of citations

24. I have in mind the rise of comparative historical sociology, on the one hand, and of anthropological work at state level and international phenomena on the other (e.g., the work of Eric Wolf 1983) as well as, simply, the growing number of anthropological studies of Western societies. It is not clear to me that there has been any great increase in studies of specific social settings within the Third World (as distinct from general discussions of the Third World) by American sociologists, though internationally there has been, and there has also been the rise of indigenous Third World sociology in many settings.

25. Echoes of the old opposition between idiographic and nomothetic sciences can still be heard in efforts to distinguish sociology from history. Many sociologists dismiss historians as engaged in mere description and storytelling (the nomothetic discourse always tending to reject the notion that narrative can be both a systematic and an analytic mode). The reliance on narrative was in fact attacked by "social science historians" in the 1960s. It has enjoyed a resurgence recently, however, particularly as it has been linked to notions of empowerment. Narrative not only gives voice to subaltern groups from the past, it encourages contemporary people to see themselves in these narratives of the poor and oppressed, to see not only poverty and oppression but humanity and the prospect for successful organizing and struggle.

26. Though once again, as in the case of anthropology, we are considering a discipline in which books, rather than articles, are the major form of scholarly communication.

27. This tends to be forgotten by historical sociologists convinced of the novelty of their endeavor. What is new, however, is not historical sociology but its institutionalization and a disciplinary view that treats it as something other than an idiosyncrasy. Before Skocpol, Wallerstein, and Tilly there were Moore, Bendix, and Smelser. Merton

in our sample were to history journals, and the vast majority of them were in the last fifteen years. It was during this period that historical sociology came into prominence. The rise of historical sociology depended in part on the prior flourishing of the "new social history," and the somewhat separate movement towards a "social science history." These were interdisciplinary undertakings from the start, though historians played the central roles. Senior statesmen in each discipline urged on the interdisciplinary communication.[28] E. H. Carr issued one of the more prominent and forceful calls for collaboration: "the more sociological history becomes and the more historical sociology becomes, the better for both. Let the frontier between them be kept open for two-way traffic" (1961:84).

This and similar calls were taken up by both historians and sociologists. Neil Smelser's *Social Change in the Industrial Revolution* (1958) was noteworthy for its attempt to link abstract sociological theory not only to historical narrative but to concrete analysis of primary source historical data.[29] Shortly thereafter the historian George Rudé (1964) used Smelser's theory of collective behavior to provide the theoretical context and conceptual framework for his pioneering investigation into eighteenth- and early nineteenth-century political crowds and rioters.[30] Without always drawing very explicitly on sociology, a number of other historians began to produce work that cer-

---

did major historical work on science; in approximately the same generation Elias stands as the most centrally historical sociologist; before them there was Sorokin and so forth back to the discipline's very historical founders.

28. History, Lloyd Kramer has recently suggested, has always been an appropriating discipline, ideology notwithstanding, so this was only one phase in a longstanding pattern: "The dominant institutional pattern has been the tendency of historians to define themselves along the increasingly precise lines of academic departments, limited specializations, and disciplinary boundaries. At the same time, however, much of the intellectual innovation among modern historians has resulted from their willingness to draw on other academic disciplines for theoretical and methodological insights, which has led to an expansion and redefinition of the political orientation of traditional historiography" (1989:97).

29. In this, it is interesting to note, Smelser's work was different from that of his Harvard predecessor George Homans. Homans's historical work was of great distinction, but it represented more of a parallel track to his sociology, a sort of second career with few direct linkages though some obvious shared tastes and styles. Homans never portrayed (nor I think conceived) his historical work to be an occasion for "applying" or "testing" his sociological theories.

30. Smelser's and Rudé's books shared a somewhat unfortunate common feature. In both, the theory tended to appear rather as abstract bread in opening and closing discussions, while the more satisfying meat of the sandwich was the concrete historical account in between.

tainly counts intellectually (if not disciplinarily) as historical sociology: Eric Hobsbawm, E. P. Thompson, and Keith Thomas in Britain; Herbert Guttman and Eugene Genovese in the United States. For the most part, these scholars remained essentially historians, as Smelser, Moore, Bendix, Eisenstadt, and others remained essentially sociologists, although they took up historical problems. Charles Tilly, in a slightly younger generation than most of those mentioned, was one of the first modern figures to achieve a distinguished position in both disciplines simultaneously and for the same work (that is, not like his teacher George Homans for two parallel lines of work).

This burgeoning of a new sort of work burst disciplinary boundaries, but it was not always a matter of cross-disciplinary borrowings or inspirations. It was the product largely of extra-academic forces and of changes in each discipline's internal preoccupations. Something of the variety of sources for the new lines of work can be seen in the various names under which they have traveled. The new social history had a great deal to do with the politics of the 1960s and the academic rehabilitation of Marxism. Social science history was a somewhat more staid affair, predicated on the borrowing of analytic techniques (and to a much lesser extent theories) from conventional nonhistorical social science for application to historical research problems. Historical (and comparative) sociology grew in the United States largely as a part of an internal struggle against a research tradition driven by technical advances as much as substantive concerns, against the extraordinary ethnocentrism of 1950s-style American functionalism, and against the neglect of struggle itself as a factor and radical change as a possibility in social life.[31]

The prominence of strife and polemic in the relations between the emerging comparative historical sociologists of the 1970s and the "establishment" of the profession should not obscure how much of a role—both positive and negative—more senior sociologists played in the development of comparative historical sociology. The field began

31. Only in a few cases, unfortunately, did this struggle take the form of systematic comparative and historical research which began as a minority even within the oppositional minority. Initially more prominent were abstractly theoretical, often epistemological, polemics. One of the attractions of comparative historical work was the opportunity to undertake empirical research tackling questions of the large scale common to theoretical discourse in the traditions of Marx and Weber. Most American sociological research at that time (as now) takes up much narrower questions. Historical and comparative sociologists sought to step into the breach between "abstracted empiricism" and "grand theory" described by C. Wright Mills (1959). Among other things, they sought to show the limits within which generalizations (commonly put forward at that time as universal laws) might hold.

to develop in its modern form in the 1950s. Early entries were largely concerned with assimilating foreign cultures and past times to a universal model of social functioning or change or both. Smelser's (1958) attempt to study a single course of historical social change in some detail was relatively unusual. More common were efforts to arrange contemporary societies in a hierarchical model of putative stages of modernization.[32]

Modernization theory gave double impetus to the development of modern historical sociology. First, beginning in the 1950s, it sparked a number of research projects that themselves produced works of some significance. From Robert Bellah's (1957) reexamination of the "Protestant ethic" thesis in Tokugawa Japan to more general, comparative studies like Shmuel Eisenstadt's (1963) work on empires, modernization theory produced major research. Modernization studies also tied historical sociology to the older tradition of economic history. It was in large part out of economic history, particularly studies of the early modern era and of the industrial revolution, that social history was emerging as a distinct subfield and, indeed, an increasingly central one in history departments (see Burke 1980:22–27). But modernization theory had an equally substantial *indirect* impact on historical sociology. By the late 1960s and early 1970s, it had sparked an intense reaction among researchers concerned to show the possibility of other paths of change, the autonomy of other cultures, and the different external and internal circumstances facing postcolonial and other currently less-developed countries as compared to the archetypical cases of Western development. Modernization theory made a major contribution to historical sociology by providing a very stimulating foil for critique and new research during the period of its collapse.

At about the same time, there was a reaction among younger historians against approaches that saw history as a narrative of the deeds of great men, the dates of battles, and the impact of abstract ideas. During the 1960s, the new wave of historians sought the recovery of a lost past in as much detail as possible. One faction of this thrust (what I have called "social science history") turned towards American sociology and demography, econometrics, and statistics, using computers to analyze records from parish registers and censuses to property-holding and voting patterns. Slaves became objects of cliometrics (Fogel and Engermann 1974) and rioters became objects of

32. See the critique in Skocpol and Somers (1980), and Skocpol (1984). Modernization accounts varied in the extent to which they treated the arrangement of contemporary societies into stages as a sort of pseudohistory of human evolution.

"the statistical analysis of contentious gatherings" (Tilly, Tilly and Tilly 1974). This quantitative group was largely American, though the Cambridge historical demography group was a major exception. At the same time, another faction, in which British and European historians loomed larger, turned to anthropology rather than statistics for inspiration.[33] Its efforts aimed at the recovery of past cultures, of people's ways of life seen from their own perspectives and as much as possible reported in their own words. Respect for those studied and a refusal to turn them into mere "objects of research" were central tenets from the work of E. P. Thompson through to the *History Workshop* group. Both statistical studies—perhaps the truest approach to Marxism's masses—and historical ethnography could claim to be "history from bottom up" (in the slogan of the *Journal of Social History*).

The achievements of what Bernard Cohn (1980) has called "proctological history" have been undeniably great. A wide range of source materials has been used to produce an enormous body of information. Nonetheless, the new social and social science histories often have yielded to an illusion of the pure resurrection of the past, forgetting the essential constitutive role of theory (see Selbourne 1980). The best studies, of course, went beyond mere discovery to analysis, explanation, and interpretation. But E. P. Thompson, for example, could deny and submerge the theoretical dimension of *The Making of the English Working Class,* claiming only to represent various lost voices, to eschew sociological categories, and to show us "real people and in a real context" (1968:9).[34] In general, theory seemed to many of the

33. One of the younger members of the Cambridge historical demography group, Alan Macfarlane (1981), is notable for combining fruitfully an anthropological approach with statistical research, a mixture that runs against the grain of interdisciplinary work in social history.

34. As Thompson phrased his aspiration: "I am seeking to rescue the poor stockinger, the Luddite cropper, the 'obsolete' hand-loom weaver, the 'utopian' artisan, and even the deluded follower of Joanna Southcott, from the enormous condescension of posterity. Their crafts and traditions may have been dying. Their hostility to the new industrialism may have been backward-looking. Their communitarian ideals may have been fantasies. Their insurrectionary conspiracies may have been foolhardy. But they lived through these times of acute social disturbance, and we did not. Their aspirations were valid in terms of their own experience; and if, they were casualties of history, they remain, condemned in their own lives, as casualties." (1963: 13). Thompson succeeds admirably in this goal, but he also relies on and develops implicit theory. The theory is sometimes subtle and helpful, sometimes problematic, but his effort to deny it and write as though it did not exist makes discerning the overall significance of his work more difficult, both in terms of broad patterns of historical change and in terms of comparative relevance to other instances of popular radicalism (see discussion in Calhoun 1982; Scott 1988).

new social historians to be at best a move of great abstraction away from the concrete lives they studied (echoes of the idiographic/nomothetic divide), and at worst a form of symbolic violence done to this concrete human world. This view was encouraged by the extremely abstract and antihumanist Althusserian structuralism much in vogue at the time. Indeed, Althusserian structuralism did almost as much to make general theory seem irrelevant to researchers in the Marxist tradition as Parsonsian functionalism did to those in mainstream sociology. The response of historians is represented, perhaps in extreme form, by E. P. Thompson's brilliantly witty if unfair polemic, *The Poverty of Theory* (1975). More generally, even where structuralism was not involved, the British and to a lesser extent American social historians (many of whom found inspiration in anthropology) often had an antipathetic relationship to sociology (see, e.g., Jones 1976; Samuel and Jones 1976; Thompson 1972).

The notion of theory as a form of symbolic violence, as virtually a continuation of the domination of elites over ordinary people by refusing to let the latter speak in their own voices, paralleled a theme of "poststructuralist" thought. Foucault in particular argued that theorizing as such was always an exercise of power (1977). At the same time, the notion of recovering lost voices prefigured a prominent feminist theme. Recovery of the vantage point of women, and of the voices of their own experience, has been a major and important project itself stretching across several disciplines.[35] Unlike the new social history, however, much of this feminist work has embraced theory as a central part of its intellectual work. Recently, literary theory has contributed substantially to this discourse on the interrelation of multiple voices, particularly through the work of Mikhail Bakhtin (1981) and others inspired by his writings on dialogicality. Those historians who have become involved with theory have been particularly likely to look to Bakhtin, the poststructuralists, and others outside the sociological mainstream.

The relationship between sociology and history has receded in the last few years; social history has been consolidated within the discipline, but cultural history has replaced it as the exciting new trend

---

35. The citation analysis gives an indication that feminist work has been a bit slow to penetrate the mainstream journals of sociology. The influential and highly visible journal *Signs*, edited in part by sociologists, is cited only a handful of times. Interdisciplinary periodicals on gender and women's studies account for a nearly negligible part of the overall citation pattern. Feminist work in sociology has often been the study of social circumstances and problems of women in sociologically fairly conventional ways, rather than an occasion for more basic reconsideration and reconstruction of disciplinary orientations.

(Hunt, ed. 1989). Anthropology and literary theory have moved into the ascendancy among interdisciplinary influences on history. In the case of anthropology, this is partly a continuation of longer-standing influences—for example, through the work of Keith Thomas and E. P. Thompson. In their work, the anthropological influence was very diffuse, more an orientation of attention to certain aspects of social life than direct use of any anthropological theory or analytic methods. During the 1970s, Natalie Zemon Davis began to publish a series of important works heavily influenced by the analyses of ritual and symbolism of Victor Turner, Max Gluckman, and Mary Douglas (see Desan 1989 on Davis and Thompson). It is perhaps no accident that her work lay in French history, for among French historians (both in France and abroad) a turn to the study of *mentalités* had shifted the focus of *Annales* school historians and a growing anthropological influence could be seen in a wide range of work—that of Darnton and Ladurie, for example (see Hunt 1986). At the same time, American historians (including Darnton 1984) began to be influenced by Clifford Geertz's anthropological writings, particularly his argument that cultural performances or systems constitute texts to be read. By the 1980s, the Geertzian influence began to be pervasive.[36]

The turn to a cultural history involved not just cultural anthropology but the rapidly diffusing influence of French poststructuralists, particularly Foucault (who is perhaps somewhat ambiguously classified thus) and Derrida (who is perhaps the paradigm for the label "poststructuralist"). Where Geertz had been criticized for the functionalism of his notions of cultural as a system (e.g., Chartier 1985), the poststructuralists emphasized internal contradictions and difference. Chartier, for example, argued for "a definition of history primarily sensitive to inequalities in the appropriation of common materials or practices"—for example, texts and rituals (1985:688). In both Geertzian and poststructuralist modes, however, the new cultural history was one that disputed the primacy—and perhaps even the stable existence—of society as an object of study. Its rejection of accounts of culture as mere reflection of social structure was extreme enough to distance it from the general project of a sociological theory

36. Indeed, Geertz's influence may have been greater outside of anthropology than within it. This is a not uncommon pattern of interdisciplinary influence. Allan Megill (1987:120) observes that the most cited historians (in the *Social Science Citation Index* and the *Arts and Humanities Citation Index*) are Michel Foucault, Erwin Panofsky, Ernst Gombrich, Frances Yates, Thomas Kuhn, and Mircea Eliade—all figures from the margins of professional history; none, indeed, was employed in an academic department or institute of history.

of culture and often resulted in a presentation of culture as a more or less autonomous, free-floating object of study. At the same time, for many in this discourse, culture was essentially an arena of contest for political struggle over meaning.

Some of the most influential work in the new vein came from intellectual history, which had been recast in part as cultural history, and which was particularly open to theoretical discussion. Hayden White and Dominick LaCapra played central roles. They argued that critical theorists and the sort of critical historians they saw themselves speaking for, "should recover those lost or repressed strands of Western culture that might challenge the reigning epistemological and ontological orthodoxies of our time" (Kramer 1989:100). Thus, their work was self-reflexive, taking up tensions within history, as well as oriented to tensions, repressions, and ambiguities in records from past times. They placed special emphasis on thinking about historical records as texts (especially LaCapra, 1983, chap. 1, where the emphasis is on the complexity of textual interpretation in a deconstructionist mode), and on pondering the nature of modern historical writing, especially narrative form (especially White 1987). Both White and LaCapra have challenged what they regard as problematic disciplinary habits. For White, the fundamental problem with historians' self understanding was their presentation of history as "a discipline that purports to serve as custodian of realism in political and social thinking" (1987:61). White has been influenced considerably by Foucault, who himself jousted with the disciplinary identity of history. An interrogator described him as " 'a barbarous knight,' galloping across the historical terrain, recklessly abandoning in his histories of prisons, of medicine, of hospitals, careful and meticulous research" (O'Brien 1989:29, quoting Jacques Léonard). Foucault replied in kind, describing the stereotypical historian as: "the virtuous knight of accuracy ('I don't have many ideas but at least what I say is true'), the doctor of inexhaustible information ('You haven't said anything about this thing or that, or even that which I know about and you are certainly ignorant of'); the great witness of Reality ('No grand systems but life, real life, with all its contradictory riches'); the heartbroken scholar who weeps over his little piece of earth just pillaged by barbarians: just as if after Attila the grass would not grow again" (quoted by O'Brien 1989:30, from Perrot ed., *L'Impossible prison*).

Sociologists have often felt that historians responded to their work with the same sorts of defenses of disciplinary identity. White summed up a Foucauldian as well as Nietzschean view a decade earlier, when he wrote: "Every discipline . . . is, as Nietzsche saw most clearly, constituted by what it *forbids* its practitioners to do. Every discipline is made up of a set of restrictions on thought and imagination, and none is more hedged about with taboos than professional historiography (1978:126).

One of the longstanding taboos for historians has been against self-conscious theorizing; even reflection on the categories used in historical writing has been substantially repressed. In recent years, this taboo has been broken not only by social history borrowing from social science, but by intellectual history borrowing from literary theory and philosophy. As Philip Abrams says, "the really significant development of the past twenty years has been the publication of a solid body of theoretically self-conscious historical work which has progressively made nonsense of earlier conceptions of history as somehow, in principle, not engaged in the theoretical world of the social sciences (1982:300).[37]

Prominent sociological theorists have offered encouragement to the joining of historical and sociological work:

> What history is, or should be, cannot be analyzed in separation from what the social sciences are, or should be [and] there simply are no logical or even methodological distinctions between the social sciences and history—appropriately conceived. (Giddens 1979:230)
>
>   Suffice it to say that the separation of sociology and history is a disastrous division and one totally devoid of epistemological justification: all sociology should be historical and all history sociological. (Pierre Bourdieu in Wacquant 1989)[38]

Such prominent historians as Eric Hobsbawm (1971) also argued that accepting that there is no principled reason for division between history and social science is only a first step toward the development of a truly adequate history of society (or sociological history). Fernand

---

37. Elsewhere Abrams suggests "that a long collective tussle with immediate matters of historical explanation has also been a way of discovering the problematic of structuring [his gloss on Giddens' structuration] and realising its capacity to integrate history and sociology as a single unified programme of analysis" (1982:xviii). There have certainly been some strongly dissenting voices among historians, notably G. R. Elton (1984) who finds little use for sociological history, even when done from primary sources by members of his own disciplines, and who would extend his attack to sociology and the other social sciences generally. At the same time, of course, there are a good many sociologists who neither understand the turn to historical work of many of their colleagues nor approve of it—especially if it means a turn away from the most sophisticated quantitative methods.

38. Charles Tilly, who frequently has cast himself in the role of explainer of sociology to historians and history to sociologists, ultimately suggests that the differences are more stylistic than substantive (see Tilly 1982).

Braudel (1980:69) wrote similarly that history and sociology are "one single intellectual adventure," and he has done an enormous amount to exemplify that unity in his empirical work. As Gareth Stedman Jones has commented, however, "there is no distinction in principle between history and any of the other 'social sciences.' The distinction is not that between theory and non-theory, but between the adequacy or inadequacy of the theory brought to bear" (1976:295).

Theory may be inescapable (as well as indispensable) to those who would interpret or explain history, though it may be left implicit, and thus harder to identify, challenge, and improve.[39] Sociologists should not assume, however, that it is automatically their own theories on which historians will draw. The relative weakness of sociology's involvement in the interdisciplinary discourse of cultural theory (especially in the United States) has weakened its disciplinary influence as well as its receptivity to significant new work.

At the same time, most theory that does not take care to be historically specific, and substantial about its relationship to time and place, limits itself to addressing formal conditions or possibilities for social life with no purchase on its actualities.[40] Yet if history and social theory need each other, they also challenge each other. To join them is harder than simply "applying" one to the other, or bringing different methods to bear on a given object of research. Objects of research are never "given" in any strong sense. When disciplines are brought together seriously, the taken-for-granted conceptual frameworks of each are challenged. Debate over interdisciplinary work in this as in other cases has turned on the dangers some groups of people felt and the sense of others that basic disciplinary problems would be solved simply by the mere existence of interdisciplinary work, rather than requiring serious rethinking of received disciplinary categories.

Partly for each of these reasons, there is a strong tendency for dif-

---

39. I use "theory" in a fairly broad sense here, including within its reference explicitly anti-theoretical positions such as those of Foucault and Derrida. The former made a number of declarations against the totalizing tendencies of theory, while the latter has gone to great lengths to avoid giving a clear-cut theory (or method) for deconstruction, and to avoid using any of his terms frequently enough in the same analytic sense so as to give them the status of "master" concept or key that opens all locks (see LaCapra 1983:152).

40. Both Weber and Simmel suggested something of this distinction between historically concrete actualities (full of content, multidimensional, and complexly determined) and the simplified and more abstract ideal types and forms that could be the objects of a universalizing sociology. Such forms describe a range of possibilities for social life, they specify conditions under which social life may take place, but they do not as such describe its concrete events or relationships.

ferent disciplines to "recapture" the subfields that make the most fruitful contact with neighboring disciplines. Thus, the Social Science History Association was founded in large part by historians seeking social science methods and social scientists seeking involvement in historical explanation. Over time, ironically, the quantitative historians and the (largely qualitative) sociologists moved past each other. While the former group was seeking something of an escape from conventional history, the latter group was seeking an escape from conventional sociology. Only for a while did they find both together. At the same time, each group grew large enough that it did not have the same need for extradisciplinary (and therefore somewhat unsettling) outsiders in order to establish a discourse. The same thing happened to the new social history. It ceased to be a radical alternative to mainstream history, and became one part of the mainstream. It also grew dramatically in numbers to the point where it was well able to sustain its own discourse without much involvement of nonhistorians.[41] In fact, social history itself became part of the "old guard," the object of attacks from poststructuralist cultural historians (see, e.g., Hunt, ed. 1989, and especially O'Brien 1989, on the Foucauldian dimension to this).

Historical sociology (or comparative historical sociology) has grown substantially, but it increasingly seems destined to be (a) contained within sociology, and (b) compartmentalized within the discipline.[42] Rather than challenging the limits of conventional sociology, suggesting the myopia implicit in ahistorical understandings of nearly every sociological topic, historical sociologists seem to have settled for acceptance as simply another special area within the discipline. The actual (rather than potential) relationship of sociology to history is thus not a general one, but rather, for the most part, a relationship

41. This is not to say, of course, that there are not such dialogues continuing and bearing considerable intellectual fruit. Rather, the point is that the definition and self-conceptualization of social history no longer involves any particular reaching outside of history as a discipline.

42. Its growth should not be overestimated, as the rate of citations to history journals suggests. The ASA's section on comparative-historical sociology is very eclectic; its membership far exceeds, for example, the number of sociologists actually doing primarily historical research, and especially doing it in ways which are in close relationship to the work of social historians. Despite the prominence of some of its practitioners, illustrated, for example, in the disproportionate number of works of comparative or historical sociology that have won the ASA's award for a distinguished contribution to scholarship in the last fifteen years, comparative historical sociology remains very much a minority orientation within the discipline. It is also probably undercounted by citation analysis techniques, because its practitioners are likely to write a smaller number of longer pieces than in many other specialties of sociology.

only on the part of a subset of sociologists specializing on historical topics. All too often, moreover, these sociologists simply draw data (or authoritative descriptions) from published historical works in order to construct what are often relatively conventional sociological analyses.[43] Many of these are not historical in any sense except being about phenomena that occurred in the past—that is, they are not about patterns of continuity and change over time. The real test of whether sociology has overcome its impoverishing self-distancing from history lies in whether sociologists in general *think historically,* as well as recognize the historical context of their work and use historical data. Does a sense of historical structuration and change become a basic part of the way we conceptualize the social world? Such a sense must affect the way we conceive of the relationships between structure and action, and between function and power.

The notion that history is idiographic while sociology is nomothetic shares a good deal with the notion that anthropology can be distinguished from sociology by its reliance on participant observation studies. These distinctions are meaningful as characterizations of styles of research. Historians and anthropologists are both more likely than sociologists to confront themselves with rich, dense data on many aspects of people's lives in concrete settings. This may make them sometimes resistant to theories and methods that demand great abstraction from such concrete specificity. It also makes them sensitive to issues of difference among peoples and ways of life. None of this, however, makes the disciplinary distinction a matter of principle. Indeed, the very notion of a purely idiographic discipline involves a misleading assumption that pure descriptive facticity is possible, that there can be descriptions untainted by theory.[44] A good social history without some

43. Though many historians profess a radically empiricist ideology, few things inflame the self-consciousness of historians at large more than being told that they are a class of empirical underlaborers piling up facts that sociologists will use to construct theoretically significant analyses. Such a description of the relationship between the two disciplines both neglects the very substantial work of systematic analysis undertaken by historians and, even more importantly, reifies facticity, losing sight of the work of interpretation and informed scholarship that goes into establishing sound historical judgement as to the facts. Such a view is hermeneutically naive in quite fundamental ways, whether presented by historians or sociologists.

44. In the same sense, Glaser and Strauss's (1966) reinvention of ethnography in the notion of grounded theory makes sense primarily as a rejection of excessively formalistic deductive theorizing. As a positive account of an approach it is quite problematic. Not least of all is an element of naive empiricism and an assumption that microsociological phenomena were somehow more immediately real than macrosociological ones. The general point, however, is well taken: nearly all the best sociological theory has been empirical work at the same time. This was true, for example, of Marx, Weber, Durk-

form of explicit or implicit sociology is no more imaginable than a good sociology with no sensitivity to specificities of time, place, or patterns of continuity and change (though goodness knows a fair amount of such sociology has been published).

Psychology

It is, of course, widely considered that psychology is not a social science at all, but either a behavioral science or a biomedical science, depending on the informant. Nonetheless, it is both grouped into the social sciences by many university administrations and creators of library cataloguing systems and is the most frequently cited of cognate disciplines to sociology. Part of this close relationship depends on the long-shared occupation of the field of social psychology. The proportionate role of psychology in this joint endeavor has increased over the last twenty years, particularly with the declining prominence of attitude survey methods. Nonetheless, a considerable number of sociologists both consider themselves social psychologists and (perhaps in smaller numbers) relate their work closely to that of colleagues in psychology departments. This linkage is all the more accentuated for social psychologists working in such topical interdisciplinary fields as human development and life-course studies, family studies, etc.[45]

---

heim, and Simmel, as of many theorists today, perhaps most notably Pierre Bourdieu. A case could be made also that Habermas's *The Structural Transformation of the Public Sphere* (1989) is among his most important statements precisely because it does include a substantial amount of concrete empirical analysis. Even where Habermas's theory is abstract, it is not simply deductive. Likewise, there is some empirical substance to much of Giddens' theorizing (though also a great deal of abstract prolegomenal discourse on definitions and relations among concepts); and his partially empirical *The Nation State and Violence* (1985) is among his more attractive works.

45. Though, conversely, in some such fields which were once clearly joint provinces of psychologists and sociologists, the sociologists have all but disappeared. Small group research is a good example. In the 1960s, not only were sociologists such as Bales and his colleagues prominent, they were in some cases pioneers in developing approaches most of us would now consider exclusively psychological—e.g., Phillip Slater (1967) in his use of Wilfred Bion's psychoanalytic approach to changing patterns of group relations. By the late 1970s, social psychology was thriving in psychology departments, but was on the decline in sociology. It has enjoyed an apparent partial resurgence particularly where its label has been used as a covering term for all microsociological studies, including those of symbolic interactionists (symbolic interactionism itself often being less a theoretical orientation than a euphemism for a mix of fieldwork, interpretive methods, and microsociology). And new attention to life-course studies and the emotions have helped to revive sociological social psychology.

Within sociology, social psychology has become something of a catchall category. In many curricula, it lumps together symbolic interactionism (perhaps the core of sociological social psychology but also an alternative label for qualitative microsociology), studies of groups and interpersonal relations, much of cultural sociology, studies of the life course, and the work of both Goffman and the ethnomethodologists—though it is arguable that neither is substantially "psychological." Much of contemporary sociological research into socialization pays little or no attention to psychological issues and may, indeed, counterpose its arguments to those of psychology (e.g., Kleinman 1985).

Perhaps the most important change in the relationship of sociology to psychology lies outside the joint subfield of social psychology. This is the declining concern of general (or macro-) sociological theorists for establishing a psychological grounding for or complement to their theories. For Talcott Parsons, it was essential that a connection be established between the social and cultural systems and that of personality. The connection was socialization processes.[46] Moreover, Parsons believed (along with a number of other theorists; see, e.g., Parsons, Bales, and Shils 1953) that a strong psychology must necessarily underpin any sociological theory by contributing to its understanding of what it means to be a human being.[47] This need not have anything to do with an attempt to reduce social phenomena to derivatives of individual phenomena or to generalize from elementary principles of behaviorism (as in Homans's work, e.g., 1964).[48] In Parsons's case, in fact, the most relevant psychology came from psychoanalysis, and he joined the "interpersonal relations" school of Harry Stack Sullivan, Clara Thompson, and others in modifying the Freudian inheritance in a sociological direction (see Parsons 1967).[49]

46. Indeed, courses in "socialization and personality" were long common in sociology departments. I also taught such a course in the late 1970s until my department renamed it simply "socialization," explaining that "personality" was not a topic of sociological concern.

47. This is a question not only of psychology, of course, but of philosophical anthropology. It is symptomatic of sociology's scientism that relatively few recent sociologists (in the U.S.) have turned to philosophy for help in developing an adequate conceptualization of what it means to be human. My impression, however, is that more have done so during the last few years than at any time since the 1920s.

48. As Camic (1989:44) has pointed out, behaviorism was one of Parsons's consistent polemical foils, especially in his early work. This is not appreciated as often or as clearly as his related opposition to atomistic individualism.

49. One little noted consequence of (or accompaniment to) the decline of functionalism in sociology has been a near disappearance of psychoanalysis from sociological

The main principle proposed to distinguish sociology from psychology is a seemingly straightforward appeal to levels of analysis: psychologists study individuals, sociologists study society (which many sociologists feel compelled to argue is an emergent phenomenon). Though its status may be problematic, this is perhaps the clearest of the principles adduced to distinguish sociology from another one of the social sciences. It is correspondingly ironic, then, that psychology is the other discipline by far most often cited by sociologists at all stages of the discipline's postwar history. The reason may lie, quite simply, in a shared ideology of science that unites psychology and sociology not in substantive work, but in the notion of reciprocal claims to distinct phenomena. However much sociologists may continue the Durkheimian tradition of inveighing against psychological reductionism and calling for a sharp division of labor, psychology shares much of the same understanding of science as mainstream American sociology. Both are highly empiricist. Moreover, both follow Auguste Comte's (1830–42) claim that each science must have its own distinctive subject matter, though not necessarily his more radical argument that psychology did not have such a subject matter and accordingly did not figure in his hierarchy of the sciences. Modern sociologists are inclined to be more generous and grant psychology scientific status as the study of "individuals" (or perhaps more sharply, of "mental life," or what goes on "inside" individuals).

Where Durkheim found it necessary to struggle against psychology to demonstrate the legitimacy of sociology, modern sociologists have worked in universities where the notion of disciplinary division of labor is much more firmly enshrined.[50] This does not mean that main-

---

discourse (though see the work of Chodorow 1978; and Smelser 1989). It is unclear how much this reflects the simultaneous decline of psychoanalysis in the face of behaviorism within psychology (and to a lesser extent in the face of psychopharmacology and psychobiology in both psychology and psychiatry), and how much it is a specifically sociological matter. It does seem that today's "neofunctionalists" are less inclined to resuscitate psychoanalysis than some other aspects of the Parsonian inheritance. In passing, it may also be worth noting that psychoanalysis was (and in some cases still is) closely related to functionalism's great macrosociological antagonist of the last twenty years, Marxism, particularly in Frankfurt school critical theory. Like neofunctionalists, many neo-Marxists—including a number claiming specific descent from the Frankfurt school—have been wary of too great an involvement with psychoanalysis. In both cases, this has sometimes contributed to a theoretical weakness by leading to avoidance of issues of socialization, personality, and emotional life.

50. Indeed, Durkheim's struggle against psychology on behalf of the nascent discipline of sociology was sufficiently important to him that he allowed it in many ways to distort his own work, leading him to stress the apparently objective side of society in

taining distinction from psychology and implied individualistic reductionism is not still important to many sociologists. Homans struggled against this basis for rejection throughout his career. More recently, one of the conditions of the renewal of interest in rational choice theory has been arguments (such as Becker's, see below under Economics) that rational action models do not depend on psychological accounts of rationality (or indeed any accounts of action as such), but rather on such external, supra individual factors as supply and demand. Durkheim (1895) premised his rejection of psychological foundations for sociology on the argument that social life was a phenomenon *sui generis,* an emergent phenomenon not explicable by reference to its constituent elements any more than life itself could be explained by simple reference to inert matter.[51] Blau (1986), Lenski (1987), and other contemporary macrosociologists often make similar claims.

Though not all sociologists find it necessary to be so radical, the idea of social life as an emergent phenomenon is widely repeated; it constitutes one of the main general claims sociology makes for its existence and shapes debates about the relationship of macrosociology to microsociology. Part of the underlying reason for this is simply that sociologists buy into the basic Western dualism separating individual from society and treating each as an autonomous substance. Even declarations of the mutuality of individuality and sociality tend to reproduce the substantivist dichotomy, for example, "self and society are twin-born" (Cooley 1909); though Cooley is still quoted, contemporary usage is often less subtle, substituting "individual" for "self," and seeing both society and individual as simply given. Macro/micro debates are often more or less simplistic reproductions of this dualism (see, e.g., several of the essays in Alexander et al 1987). One might think that levels of analysis should be conceived of as innumerable,

---

The Rules . . . (1984), for example, to the exclusion of the more subjective features. He did this even though he showed awareness of the problem of "internationalization" of social facts, and in other work evidenced a more basic (if philosophical more than psychological) concern for cognitive categories and what we would now call social psychology.

51. The claim of "emergence" is a very strong one, much stronger—and therefore more demanding if it is to be defended—than most of those who offer it seem to realize. That there are distinctive properties associated with large scale that are not present in constituent units does not demonstrate emergence. On the contrary, these are better understood as *collective* properties, not emergent ones. And whether relationship or connectedness should be considered emergent is debatable. Indeed, as Simmel (1908) suggested, there is good reason to argue that social relations are not external to individuals in the way Kant suggested that connection is external to things.

and distinguishable only on a more or less ad hoc basis, as part of specific research designs. Could we not, for example, imagine network analysis operating at the scale of interacting dyads and triads, and at every intervening "level" up to social structure on a global scale?[52] Why then does the debate always get posed in terms of a dualistic opposition? However many times it is asserted that individuals are social constructs, and that society is inconceivable without concrete human beings (though these may not always be individuals in the Western cultural sense), we seem unable to give up the opposition. The macro/micro debate characteristically dissolves into two main positions: (1) All good explanations must include reference (though not necessarily reduction) to the individual action that constitutes the social phenomenon; accordingly, macrosociology needs to rest on microsociology (Collins 1986; Coleman 1986, echoing Weber 1922);[53] and (2) macrosociology is entirely autonomous of the individual (or psychological) level of analysis (Blau 1986; Lenski 1987). I find more wisdom in the suggestion that the division is poorly posed and distorting of the issues involved (Giddens 1985a; Bourdieu 1980).

The level of analysis principle is problematic whenever it is taken to suggest some difference in substance rather than perspective. Simply observing modern disciplinary practices reveals that sociologists do not ignore individuals. Moreover, it is not clear that psychology is the study of individuals. Psychologists define a variety of objects of study: groups, interpersonal relations, intrapsychic phenomena, language understood in profoundly intersubjective ways, psychopharmacology, etc. Behavioral psychology generally takes individuals as units in the study of how operant conditioning cumulates, but usually in a purely external fashion, without much analysis of the cultural construction of individual as either autonomous or irreducible. As Richard Sennett (1979) has argued, it is quite meaningful to talk not only of social psychology, but of a "psychology of society."

In sum, the claim to a principled distinction of sociology from psychology based on the distinction of individual from society is challenged by the substantial attention that at least some sociologists pay to individuals, by difficulties in describing psychology as the study of

52. As Burt (1982) has summarized, the network perspective is premised largely on the assumption that the basic unit of analysis is the relationship; levels of analysis change with how many relationships are aggregated into the pattern under examination and must therefore be understood as involving collective rather than emergent properties (see also Nadel 1957).

53. Coleman and Collins are, of course, proponents of very different sociological theories, but both wish to place macrosociology on microfoundations.

individuals, and by difficulties in the very conceptual distinction of individual from society. As some sociologists turn their attention increasingly to problems of "agency" or "action," the implausibility of the disciplinary distinction grows (though talk of agency often produces a new dualism between it and "structure"). Sociologists have long studied the constructed quality of individuality and subjective dimensions of society. With regard to the latter, important strains of thought have maintained the importance of seeing subjectivity not simply in individual but in intersubjective terms (cf. Habermas 1988). A growing interpretive sociology of culture further erodes the claimed principle for distinguishing disciplines, because of its attention to subjectivity, even though it involves little reference to psychology.

Political Science

In some ways it is surprising that political science journals are not more often cited in our sample. They are cited more frequently towards the end of the period studied, which suggests perhaps the growing prominence of political sociology as a subfield of sociology. In addition, it probably reflects first the so-called behavioral revolution in which political scientists turned to largely quantitative empirical methods and, second, the growing attention in both political science and sociology to state formation and related problems. Nonetheless, political sociology has never been entirely absent as a subfield in sociology (though it was only very recently formed into a section within the ASA). For a number of years, however—roughly between World War Two and the middle 1960s—sociologists worked rather hard at maintaining the fiction of distinction between the objects of social and political analysis. Though it was not much explored at the time, some rationale for this might have been found in the classic oppositions of state and society, government and people. Of course, those oppositions were interesting precisely because of the questions they raised about relations *among* government, public discourse, and social integration. And such questions could not very readily be taken up when the division was used as the basis for a dichotomization of disciplines.

Internally, political science has been much more sharply divided into subfields than sociology. In particular, the four major subfields of U.S. political science—American politics (which includes also the judiciary and constitutional and public law as quasi-autonomous sub-sub-fields), comparative politics, international relations, and political theory—have almost nothing to do with each other. One of the oddities of this is that political theory as a speciality has almost entirely to do with the history of political thought, and especially normative theory, while the empirical theory that guides research (to whatever extent it does) is often quite separate (and at points quite likely to be heavily influenced by sociology). Relatively little attempt is made to relate normative and empirical theory—though more than in sociology, where normative theory is hardly discussed. One of the obstacles to bringing political theorists and sociological theorists into fruitful discussion is the fact that sociologists are not generally knowledgeable about classical social and political theory (e.g., Hobbes, Locke, Rousseau, Bentham, Mill), let alone about the ancients. This means that key reference points in normative theoretical discussion are lost to sociologists. This problem is often reinforced by the formal philosophical style of argumentation common in political theory but alien to sociologists. If there is to be better communication between the disciplines, it will depend significantly on sociologists learning more about social theory written before the invention of sociology as a discipline and before the work of our canonical founding fathers (whose work is greatly illuminated by such knowledge).

The differences between political scientists and sociologists cannot be said to inhere in contrasting styles of work as much as can those between sociologists and both historians and anthropologists. Especially in recent years, many political scientists have used analytic techniques similar to those used by sociologists. This has been true especially in American politics, where the "behavioral revolution" took deepest root. Indeed, the field of American politics is in practice defined rather oddly. It tends to exclude political economy of the U.S. and, to a large extent, the study of nonelectoral political movements. American politics is taken by many powerful senior political scientists to mean essentially (a) the study of voting behavior, and (b) the study of political institutions—e.g., congressional committees, patterns of bureaucratic appointments, etc. To a lesser extent, comparative politics at one time involved taking up the same sorts of questions crossnationally. Perhaps simply because a look abroad inhibits myopia of all sorts, comparative politics became much more open to contrasting intellectual approaches and a diversity of problems of study. There have been substantial relations between comparative politics and comparative sociology, especially with regard to such issues as the role of trade unions, social movements, and nationalism.

From the 1940s to the 1960s, many sociologists worked hard to maintain a double distinction of their work from politics. First, it was not political because they were "value-neutral" social *scientists*.[54] Sec-

54. Though this phrase of Weber's was commonly cited in explaining the distancing from politics held to be appropriate to sociologists, the substantive conceptualization

ond, their work was not political because that was a dimension of society that they delegated to political scientists. The former was a misleading ideology, of course (which is not to say that recognizing political biases and engagement means discarding entirely the ideal of distinguishing them from empirical findings). Enough has been said on that subject, I think, to let it rest.

The second aspect of the distinction is equally significant and less immediately recognized. Quite simply, it means that the very conception of society with which sociologists worked was apt to be distorted by the attempt to define politics as a removable institutional area within it. Much the same sort of thing was done with economic activity. Both were treated as separable institutional areas, segmentable along with religion, education, health care, and the family. In fact, because they were largely to be delegated to cognate disciplines, they often received even less attention.[55] What was obscured from consideration under such a plan was the role of political institutions (the state) and economic institutions (capitalism) in constituting what we mean by society in the modern world. The very fact that nation-states were the units in most comparative analyses went virtually unremarked and its implications nearly unexamined. The central role of capitalism was obscured by conceptions like "industrial society" and generally ignored.[56] It may be argued that family and religion were or are in some cases equally salient to defining and constituting in practice some social units, but the sense in which society came to be used as a singular noun in ordinary sociological parlance depended specifically and crucially on the state. Only the state could explain what was meant by a single society having multiple "peoples" within it, and admitting of dramatically different concrete forms of social organization at the community, ethnic, religious, or familial level (though reliance on the notion of society during the heyday of functionalism tended to reduce attention to such internal diversity by focusing on the presumed generally normative status of the mores of the dominant group).

Whatever the claims about division of labor, sociology and political

---

was more Durkheimian. As Aron (1968) has noted, it was really Durkheim and Comte who pioneered the apolitical conception of society.

55. In introductory sociology textbooks, for example, politics and economy were at most likely to receive attention in a single combined chapter, while other social institutions received full chapters. Even religion and education—clearly dealt with by other disciplines—were canonically held to need a full chapter each, though politics and economics did not.

56. Since the publication of a substantial literature of praising capitalism, and a shift in political rhetoric during the last ten years, it may be hard to recall that a generation

science are probably the most similar of social sciences in style of work. Some individual scholars—Seymour Martin Lipset, Philip Converse, Duncan Macrae, Theda Skocpol, and Ira Katznelson—have moved freely between the two fields; the boundary crossing remains very active among younger scholars.[57] Statistical methods, empirical theories, and theoretical orientations have been shared. Perhaps the most striking difference is the absence of a strong tradition of normative theory in sociology (and along with it the much shorter temporal depth of most sociologists' historical studies in social theory). As policy analysis has grown as a field it has frequently linked political science and sociology (see Macrae 1985), though economics remains political science's more common partner in that venture. Political science and sociology shared both the growth and the crises of the 1960s and early 1970s. They have shared in the revival of both academic Marxism and rational choice theory.

Interrelationships may grow still further in new areas. The revitalization of the theory of the state and its link to new avenues of empirical research is one of the most important (see Evans, Rueschemeyer, and Skocpol 1987) and has already been alluded to (see also Kurtz, this volume, chap. 2). The long overdue growth of sociological study of peace and war suggests increasing relationship to the field of international relations. Attempts to bolster democratic theory with a developed conception of critical discourse and the public sphere have come from both disciplines (Habermas 1989; Keane 1987; Calhoun ed. forthcoming). Development studies (or more generally, studies of the Third World) draw on both political science and sociology as well as economics. Though political science is more prominently represented in area studies programs, this is another meeting ground. Finally, "poststructuralist" work offering claims about the ubiquity of power in all social relationships and even in knowledge—Foucault is the most important—is shaping a range of interdisciplinary discourses in which both sociologists and political scientists (among others) are playing active roles. The most important instance of this is probably feminist scholarship (though the relative absence—or nonprominence—of feminist theory and theorists in sociology is striking; feminist theory is much more visible in political science, perhaps because of the greater emphasis on normative theory).

---

ago "capitalist" and "capitalism" were words which smacked of Marxism and at least implied criticism. Euphemisms like "the free enterprise system" were more common.

57. It seems more common for sociology Ph.D.'s to be employed in political science departments than the reverse (though I cannot say with any certainty that this is so).

Important as all these growing interdisciplinary discourses are, it remains remarkable how much the separation of political science from sociology has been maintained. There are journals such as *Politics and Society* and various broadly Marxist journals that try explicitly to join the fields. Graduate students cross departmental boundaries to take courses. But, if our citation analysis is to be believed, disciplinary literatures remain substantially separate (see also Crane and Small's findings, this volume, chap. 5).

Economics

One of the striking findings from our citation analysis is the substantial increase in references to economic literature since the late 1940s and 1950s. The earlier low figures are also surprising in themselves. Economic concerns had of course figured centrally for Marx, Weber, and Simmel, and only somewhat less centrally for Spencer and Durkheim. They had loomed large in the early work of Parsons (Camic 1989) but as Parsons's theory developed, and especially as it became more cultural and evolutionary, it turned away from economics.[58] Early American sociology had not been as heavily economic in orientation as that of Germany. Nonetheless, economic life figured centrally in Sumner's social Darwinism, in Giddings's accounts of community life, and in the work of other key figures in early American sociology. In his lifetime, Veblen was probably as influential in sociology as in any other discipline. By the postwar period, however, sociologists seemed to accept a disciplinary division of labor. The increasingly technical nature of economics may have had something to do with this. There was also, however, the sociologists' willingness to define their concern as having to do with the consequences of economic phenomena (e.g., the experience and social organization of poverty) rather than with the study of economic activity as such.

There are three dimensions to change in this pattern. First, a substantial and growing number of sociologists have turned to rational action or rational choice models as a primary theoretical orientation (e.g., Hechter 1987; Coleman 1986, 1990; see discussion in Wacquant and Calhoun 1989). These models have been most central to economics, and indeed in their characteristic form involve economistic assumptions about the nature of human action, though that is not strictly essential. Figures like Gary Becker have in fact made a partial

---

58. Parsons and Smelser's (1956) *Economy and Society* is perhaps the most neglected and underappreciated of Parsons's books, as Parsons himself once commented.

crossing from economics to sociology with their extension of economic rational choice models to sociological problems from marriage to fertility behavior, residential location to social movements.[59] In this sense, the current extensions of rational choice theory are making economic reasoning into a much more general approach to social life (as distinct from an approach to a restricted segment of social life); economic rationality is staking a claim to be a theory of comparable capacity for general understanding to the other classic social theories of sociology's heritage.

Second, many sociologists have become involved in the analysis of economic activity as a social process. For some, this has meant the long overdue development of the study of business as an institutional arena (and thus distinct from the search for general laws of organization; see Hirsch 1986; Jackall 1988; Calhoun ed. 1990). For others this has meant studies of markets (White 1983; White and Leifer 1987). For still others it has meant involvement in questions raised by the "new institutional economics"—for example, questions about the relationships between markets and organizational hierarchies (Williamson 1982; Powell and DiMaggio eds. forthcoming). This last is perhaps especially important, and has already involved the creation of a substantial arena of interdisciplinary discourse and a number of powerful analyses. It has direct, if older, sociological roots in the work of Selznick (1960), for example, and it recovers a pre-World War II closeness of relations between economists and sociologists. Though a fairly idiosyncratic work, Stinchcombe's *Economic Sociology* (1984) is something of a bridge between these first two dimensions to the growth of relations between sociology and economics. It combines rational choice theory with attention to ecological and other material conditions of social life, and to the institutional organization of economic activity.

Third, there has been the rise of political economy and development studies—two closely related fields in which sociologists have been central participants in recent years, not just borrowers from or supplementers to economics. Development studies obviously has a direct lineage back to modernization research, though it developed as part of the reaction to that school. It is an area in which sociologists are

59. Becker (1976) also contributed a key argument which helped convince many sociologists that rational choice theory did not involve a capitulation to *psychological* reductionism. He argued that the basic condition of scarcity, which made laws of supply and demand operative, allowed one to derive all the essential features of rational economic behavior without recourse to psychological accounts of individual procedural rationality.

linked to anthropologists and to some extent political scientists, as well as to economists. The rise of political economy and, in part, of development studies also owes a good deal to the politics of the 1960s (including the internationalism that manifested itself in such contradictory ways as the Peace Corps and the Vietnam War).

The reformulation of modernization theory started out as a challenge from Latin American economists, notably Raul Prebisch and his UNCTAD colleagues. From an early point, however, sociologists joined actively in the project of accounting for dependency and underdevelopment. One central figure, Andre Gunder Frank (e.g. 1967), was quite difficult to classify as either sociologist or economist (trained in part at Chicago in the interdisciplinary circle of Hoselitz and the journal *Economic Development and Cultural Change*). Sociological factors were at the core of *dependista* arguments. Perhaps most notable was the suggestion that Latin American countries, for example (almost all the early dependency theorists focused on Latin America), were not developing strong capitalist classes of modern industrial sectors precisely because of their links to the already rich countries. Instead of autonomous capitalists, countries like Brazil and Argentina had their best businessmen working as agents of American and European companies. Their political leaders were primarily intermediaries between their own countries and the governments of rich foreign countries on whose aid they depended. Governments in the poorer countries of the world had to be at least as attentive to the foreigners who gave them aid as to the wishes and needs of their own people. This made democracy—one of the supposed elements of modernization—hard to develop.

Dependency theory was not a final solution to problems of development nor a long-reigning dominant force in development studies. Nonetheless, its challenge to modernization theory was deep and effective. The way in which the contest was played out, however, with culturalist modernization theory as the main antagonist of a very sociological, class-oriented dependency theory, itself obscured some important issues. Certain material factors are crucial to development, even if they were not as sufficient as once was thought. Roads and other developments in physical infrastructure, for example, still matter, dependency or no dependency (Rostow 1980).

Development studies continues to involve sociologists in a broad interdisciplinary discourse with economists and others. Studies of peasant societies and of Third World states have been particularly active terrains for sociological work (see Alavi and Shanin eds. 1983). The most important sociological line of work in this field, however, has been the world systems theory of Immanuel Wallerstein (1974, 1980, 1989) and his colleagues. Initially an Africanist, Wallerstein turned his attention to a reexamination of the Europe-centered process of capital accumulation during the early modern period. His account of the modern world system drew most heavily on historical research, and it has remained significant in historical discourse as well as political economy. A more or less Marxist account ("more or less" because of its heavy stress on trade relations rather than relations of production), world systems theory was part of a dramatic revival in Marxist discourse during the late 1960s and 1970s.

The academic rehabilitation of Marxism was most influential in sociology of all the social science disciplines. Economics remained one of the most conservative. Yet, of course, Marxism involved economic analysis. Once sociologists began to take seriously the notion of capitalism as either a kind of social arrangement or a crucial force shaping social arrangements, even those who were not strict Marxists or who had left the Marxist fold found previously ignored economic elements to be central. Of course, classical sociological theory also offered important non-Marxist theoretical foundations for economic sociology, notably the work of Weber and Simmel.

Attempts by sociologists to adduce intellectual principles to explain their disciplinary division from economics are fairly rare. As in the case of political science, sociology is simply confronted with a larger, arguably older, and better organized field that will not go away simply because of sociological claims to include its subject matter. Economists are the least likely of all social scientists (unless psychology is counted as a social science; Rigney and Barnes 1980) to cite work outside their discipline, partly, it would seem, because of their large numbers and high prestige, and partly because of the relatively strong governance of economics by a paradigm that renders much of the rest of social science (and of the social context and organization of economic activity) irrelevant or at least distant.[60]

One area of interdisciplinary work that would seem to touch closely on economics, but often has not, is worth mentioning in this respect. This is the cluster of activity and publications that I have loosely grouped as "organizations, administration, management and labor."[61]

60. There are exceptions, of course. A notable one is Hicks's (1942) attempt to reformulate economics as a science of social welfare and to some extent social organization (a well-known, if not necessarily altogether successful venture, and one in which Hicks found little need to enlist the aid of sociology).

61. It could easily be argued that I have grouped together too heterogenous a set of publications and fields. How close, after all, are the linkages among the *Administrative Science Quarterly* and the *Monthly Labor Review*? One thing they do have in common

Journals and teaching in this area (or areas) are often linked to business schools or schools of industrial and labor relations, administration, and similar interdisciplinary hybrids. The prominence of such fields in general, and particularly in sociology, has grown substantially. Where work on the old problematic of bureaucracy was largely contained within sociology (and to some extent political science), the new field of organizational studies is increasingly dominated by work conducted in business schools (although often by sociology Ph.D.'s employed by them).[62] Interdisciplinary journals serving this cluster of activity now account for one of the largest sources of citations outside sociology proper. The very absence of strong attempts to distinguish in principle among sociology, economics, and political science may be one of the reasons why this area could flourish so readily across disciplinary borders. Of course, compared to the more uneasy tolerance of cultural studies or social history, it also has the advantage of a high-level of use of advanced statistical techniques and a general association with high-prestige academics whose status as social *scientists* is not in doubt. The relative prestige of journals like the *ASQ*, and their acceptance as genuine sociological publications, contrasts sharply with the way anthropological and historical journals are treated (e.g. by tenure review committees).

This does not have to do simply with the fact that organizational concerns were central to classical sociological theory and research, for so were historical and anthropological topics. It does not have to do with a long history of sociological linkage to economics and political science, it would appear, for those fields were cited less than anthropology in the early years of our sample, though by the later years they far exceeded it. In a sentence, then, my conclusion is that similar styles, compatible ideologies of scientism, and the rationalization of these by proclaimed principles of exclusion played the central role in minimizing the respectability of some areas of interdisciplinary work while elevating the status of this particular one.

---

is links not only to economics but to the concerns of business management, particularly as incorporated in the various programs of the university business schools which have risen to new prominence in recent years, especially, but not exclusively, in the U.S.

62. Ironically, though, sociologists teaching organizational studies in business schools have seldom been pioneers in developing an institutional sociology of business (see Calhoun ed. 1990). They have often been committed to a "scientific" paradigm for organizational studies, which narrowed its subject matter greatly, and sometimes, as in the case of population ecology, made it rather distant from managerial concerns and especially ideas of managerial action. The old problematic of bureaucracy has actually shifted in large part away from organizational sociology (except in textbooks) and toward political sociology (to the extent that it remains active in the research literature).

The Project of a General Understanding of Social Life
(by Way of a Conclusion)

In reviewing sociology's relations with several other disciplines in the social sciences, I have argued that there are no coherent, principled bases for justifying the disciplinary division of labor. That does not mean that the disciplines do not differ substantially; they do. Nor does it mean that having some disciplinary division of labor is simply a bad thing and that we should have only social science in general. Rather, given the scale of the social science enterprise today, some internal differentiation seems unavoidable. Moreover, there is something gained from the very defense of pluralism that disciplinary divisions produces. I should not want, for example, to see anthropology swallowed by sociology, especially if that meant a denial of resources to the kind of work done by anthropologists because it was such a minority tradition. Nor, in the same vein, would I want the larger and, in many quarters, more powerful disciplines of history, economics, and political science to have the opportunity to overwhelm or expunge the particular internal pluralism which is one of the attractive features of sociology. What I would argue is that elevating the divisions among disciplines to matters of principle discourages the recurrent reshuffling of boundaries and formation of interdisciplinary lines of work that are part and parcel of flourishing intellectual life. Moreover, each of the disciplines is itself impoverished by making a principled exclusion of that which is the turf of another. Our conception of society is damaged if we allow politics, or the economy, or culture, to be cut from it. Not only is it rent by gaps, but it is distorted in its fundamental nature. And conversely, work on politics, or the economy, or culture, is distorted and impoverished if those topics are reified and abstracted from the context of a general account of social life.

While the disciplinary division of labor does protect a certain pluralism, it ironically encourages an intradisciplinary monism—that is, an attempt to give a singular and unitary definition to sociology or any other discipline. For the most part, I think sociologists intuitively recognize this, and have come to tolerate a high level of internal pluralism. The tension between this and the idea that in principle there must be some principled unity to the field, however, often leads us to keep a certain amount of bad faith with ourselves. We make insupportable declarations to undergraduates; we devalue some subfields as "not really sociology"; we structure requirements in graduate programs as though there were some consensus about the minimum essential knowledge required to be a sociologist; we discourage crossdisciplinary work by both graduate students and young faculty still subject to tenure evaluations.

In fact, we act on a peculiar notion of the division of labor. With Durkheim, one might expect modern sociologists to see the division of labor as a source of interdependence and unity. But such interdependence would depend on a constant exchange—in this case of ideas—among the various units. Instead, we are like industrialists who, having established a division of labor among the producers of various components—wheels, axles, seats, engines—see no need for an assembly process in which the various components are brought into relationship with each other. On this analogy, the "car" we would attempt to create from the products of diverse labors within and without our discipline would be a general understanding of social life.

Strangely, given the very name of our discipline and the rationales we offer to defend its integrity, we do not seem really to care very much about a general understanding of social life. General sociology has been relegated primarily to introductory textbooks, and to a lesser extent to a sort of social theory that most practicing sociologists use but little in their work (and which draws too little on empirical research). Even the way generality is pursued in introductory textbooks indicates a telling problem. We divide up the discipline into a number of more or less discrete topics, each the subject of a chapter. These chapters are minimally integrated.[63] So the sense in which sociology claims to offer students a general understanding of social life is that it

---

63. That is, especially, they are not very much substantively integrated. Publishers introduce a variety of stylistic integrations—boxes with a running heading and other devices of format, for example. Authors provide a scheme (almost always the patently unrealistic notion that there are three basic theoretical orientations in sociology—functionalism, conflict theory, and symbolic interactionism) by which to make recurrent reference to schools of thought. But there is little attempt to link up what is said about the economy in its chapter to the way economic factors affect the family, or to the role of capitalism in producing social change, or to patterns of criminal activity and varying responses to them. Moreover, during the last fifteen years the number of chapters in a typical book has grown from about fifteen (dictated not by intellectual considerations but by the number of weeks in a semester) to more than twenty. This reflects a further fragmentation of the discipline, on the one hand, as more and more subfields require attention. On the other hand, it reflects our inability to recombine subfields. We cannot drop a chapter from the canonical table of contents. At one level, this is simply a matter of marketing; the publishers are afraid of losing customers among the highly conservative teachers of introductory courses. But it is also a matter of disciplinary consciousness. We are, quite simply, *habituated* to the idea that there will be separate chapters on socialization, family, and education; if we are now to add "life course" to them, there will just have to be an additional chapter. How much current work is being done in each subfield, or its relationship to any overall way of integrating the wealth of work in the discipline, is irrelevant.

offers them superficial information on a very wide range of topics concerning social life.

The difference from a typical history or anthropology course is instructive. The history course will usually focus on a particular period and place—in one sense a highly restricted approach to social life. It will not be called "Introduction to History" but "Colonial American History" or "Twentieth Century U.S. History" or, more broadly, "Western Civilization, Part II (since 1500)." [64] Within the definition of scope thus offered, the course will attempt to tie together aspects of political, social, economic, and intellectual/cultural history. Obviously, particular instructors, departments, or the whole field at certain times may have biases (e.g., traditionally minimizing economic and especially social history). Some courses may be topically defined as "labor history" or "women's history." [65] Nonetheless, the student is apt to learn about some instances of the phenomenon of "social life" or "human life" in a fairly rich way. He or she will be led to try to make connections among different aspects of such life, and to note contrasts and similarities between the historical instance studied and his or her own life. Similarly, in a typical anthropology class, the student will be presented with several ethnographic cases—the Swazi, say, the Tikopia, and the Tiwi—and perhaps studies that go beyond local groups to consider regions or states in China, Ghana, or Peru. The student will be asked to try to relate kinship to ecology, economy, religion, and power relations. Once again, much may be left out. Even so, what both these stereotypical history and anthropology courses offer is a confrontation with relatively rich concrete subject matter in a way that encourages the student to think about it in at least something of its fullness. This, I would suggest, is a central reason why history and anthropology succeed in winning more devoted undergraduate students, from among the most talented students, even in periods when the job prospects for new Ph.D.'s in those fields are much worse than for sociologists. [66]

64. The last might, at one time, have defined the broadest history course. More and more often, however, history departments (and the setters of liberal arts B.A. requirements) are offering courses in "World History" (still usually demarcated by dates suggesting the beginning of modernity or the end of the previous epoch). It is not clear whether such an approach does justice to the diversity of the world's peoples, but colleges seem unwilling to require non-Western history alongside Western.

65. In fact, increasing specialization within history is expanding the latter sort of offering—making history more like sociology—at the expense of the earlier idea of integration of different aspects of life in a period. This is partly, but by no means entirely, an effort to ensure attention to people or themes left out of more traditional courses.

66. At the conference on which this volume is based, William D'Antonio (see chap. 3, Tables 7 and 8) presented statistics showing the relative weakness of the GRE scores

Obviously the relative prestige of fields is also an issue, as is their perceived usability as pre-professional school majors. Sociologists should ask themselves why sociology is not seen as a more attractive prebusiness and prelaw major, and should consider whether the relative prestige of fields is not greatly influenced by the way that they are taught at the beginner's level.[67] I would suggest that history and anthropology, for example, present themselves in a particularly favorable way.[68] With regard to the dimension under consideration here, both do more to present a sense of the fullness of social life than is evident in the work of most historians (who are apt to write about highly specific features of a time and place—not nineteenth-century France, but "marriage patterns among industrialists in Lyon during the Second Empire") or most anthropologists (who still do write gen-

---

of sociology graduate students. There are several possible reasons for this: both sociology majors and sociology graduate students may be located disproportionately at non elite schools, sociology students may include a disproportionate number of those for whom GREs are poor indicators of ability, or a larger percentage of sociology majors may take the test. Be this as it may, it would appear clear that sociology is not attracting as many of the best students as it should or as other social sciences do. Not only are sociology students' GREs low, they have declined further from the discipline's peak than is the case for other disciplines (especially in the natural and physical sciences); we are thus losing ground relatively, not simply suffering a common decline. Even in the period 1977–87 when job prospects were much worse in anthropology and history than in sociology, anthropology students scored an average verbal and quantitative total of 1077; history students scored 1079; sociology students scored only 972. Students in anthropology and history even scored substantially higher on the *quantitative* half of the aptitude test. We delude ourselves, in short, to think that good undergraduates are not going into sociology only because they are careerists headed for professional schools or "harder sciences." Good students, oriented toward academic careers, interested in social issues, are simply choosing other fields in disproportionate numbers.

67. Even economics and political science, which do not generally confront social life in the rich fullness characteristic of anthropology or history, do teach introductory courses in a way decisively different from sociology. Political scientists teach about politics and public issues (even though they may do research, especially in American politics, which is remarkably depoliticized); economists teach about the economy (even though the work of most research economists is highly technical and abstractly removed from the day to day functioning of the economy). In economics particularly, the writing of an introductory textbook is far more of an effort of synthesis than in sociology, and correspondingly textbooks also serve as reference books within the discipline and are more often written by major figures than is the case in sociology. Of course economics has the benefit that students are prepared to face harder courses because they have a prior belief in the seriousness and practicality of the discipline. To some extent, sociology's attractive pluralism and internal diversity are the enemies of synthesis.

68. By "favorable" I do not mean that courses are simply more popular, but that they give a view of the discipline as more intellectually serious and satisfying. Sociologists—as indeed stereotypes suggest—often achieve superficial popularity—high enrollment levels—at the expense of intellectual substance and accordingly portray their field in a very unflattering light.

eral ethnographies, though much less often than in the past, being now more likely to write works focused on an aspect of or problem in the ethnography of a particular people, say, "linguistic indexicality and sense of self among the Bororo").[69] The very superficiality we impose upon ourselves in the attempt to convey generality through taking up so many different issues, rather than by relating aspects of a given instance of social life to each other, may contribute substantially to the way we are seen by powerful decision makers in government and the university community. Most people only know sociology through an introductory course, after all, not through research and theoretical works. And we often present ourselves at our worst in such courses.

Much the same can be said for the ways in which sociology is presented to the general public and informs public discourse. Sociology does a poor job in producing general, synthetic works that present research and theory to the educated public in an attractive form. Of course, this does happen occasionally and very successfully, as in the long tradition of sociological critiques of individualism, including those of Riesman (1950), Slater (1970), and Bellah et al. (1985). But these works only point to the difference between the sociological writing that attracts public attention and that which earns prestige and publication in the major journals. There are other exceptions, more closely related to disciplinary research agendas—for example, Coleman's *Adolescent Society* (1964), or Wilson's *The Declining Significance of Race* (1978), but not the number and range for which we should hope.

Our poor disciplinary self-presentation is not just willful and not entirely accidental. It is linked back to the general issue I have been discussing throughout this paper. Our urge to claim a specific place for sociology within the social sciences, and thus to proceed by distinguishing ourselves in a principled fashion from our competitors, is largely at fault. Why do we continue this effort that so impoverishes our self-understanding and work? I think, in closing, that a central reason lies in scientism. This begins with the notion to which we have

69. A related difference between anthropology and history, on the one hand, and sociology on the other is that sociologists are for the most part much less likely to see scholarship as a central criterion of evaluation distinct from research. That is, there is less emphasis in sociology on knowing the literature of a certain field which extends well beyond one's own specific research interest in it. Ironically, perhaps, the two specialties in sociology for which this is least true are theory and methods (and it is significant that both are conceived as specialist undertakings, not generalist knowledge). Unfortunately, perhaps, standards of "objective" research productivity are gaining ground in history and anthropology at the expense of direct respect for scholarship.

adhered since Comte that every science must have a distinct subject matter. This (as well as academic politics) is what informed Durkheim's overstated effort to distinguish sociology from psychology. It is, in the contemporary discipline, a key reason why we break our own field up in terms of topics and try to break up the social sciences in the same way. Scientism urges on us a belief in the objective certainty of empirical knowledge and makes us fearful of the suggestion that all knowledge is rooted in the perspective of the knower. Recognizing this does not obligate us to abandon the idea of truth or the project of empirical research. But we do need to see that truth—knowledge—depends on understanding, not just data. And surely, I hope, we want to understand social life in its richness and complexity. If so, we should focus less on disciplinary boundaries and recognize that both within and across disciplines there are different perspectives that shed light on an inherently common subject matter—human life—which is always social, yet always admits of certain tensions between individuality and sociality, which is always historical, and which is always culturally rooted and specific.

References

Abrams, Philip. 1982. *Historical Sociology.* Ithaca: Cornell University Press.

Alavi, Hamsa, and Teodor Shanin, eds. 1983. *Introduction to the Sociology of Developing Societies.* New York: Monthly Review Press.

Alexander, Jeffrey. 1982. *Theoretical Logic in Sociology, II: The Antinomies of Classical Social Thought: Marx and Durkheim.* Berkeley: University of California Press.

Alexander, Jeffrey, ed. 1988. *Durkheimian Sociology.* New York: Columbia University Press.

Alexander, Jeffrey, Bernhard Giesen, Richard Munch, and Neil J. Smelser, eds. 1987. *The Micro-Macro Link.* Berkeley: University of California Press.

Aron, Raymond. 1968. *Main Currents of Sociological Thought, I.* New York: Doubleday.

Bakhtin, Mikhail. 1981. *The Dialogic Imagination.* Austin: University of Texas Press.

Becker, Gary. 1976. *The Economic Approach to Human Behavior.* Chicago: University of Chicago Press.

Bell, Daniel. 1973. *The Coming of Post-Industrial Society.* New York: Basic Books.

———. 1976. *The Cultural Contradictions of Capitalism.* New York: Basic Books.

Bellah, Robert. 1957. *Tokugawa Religion: The Values of Pre-Industrial Japan.* Berkeley: University of California Press.

Bellah, Robert, Richard Madsen, William M. Sullivan, Ann Swidler, and Steven M. Tipton, 1985. _Habits of the Heart: Individualism and Commitment in American Life._ Berkeley: University of California Press.

Berger, Peter L. 1969. _The Sacred Canopy: Elements of a Sociological Theory of Religion._ Garden City, N.Y.: Doubleday.

Berger, Peter L., and Thomas Luckmann, 1966. _The Social Construction of Reality._ Garden City, N.Y.: Doubleday.

Blau, Peter M. 1964. _Exchange and Power in Social Life._ New York: Wiley.

———. 1969. "Objectives of Sociology." In _A Design for Sociology,_ ed. R. Bierstedt, 43–71. Philadelphia: The American Academy of Political and Social Science, Monograph 9.

———. 1977. _Inequality and Heterogeneity._ New York: Free Press.

———. 1986. "Introduction to the Transaction Edition." In _Exchange and Power in Social Life,_ vii-xvii. New Brunswick, N.J.: Transaction Books.

Bourdieu, Pierre. 1967. "Sociology and Philosophy in France Since 1945: Death and Resurrection of a Philosophy Without Subject." _Social Research_ 34:162–212.

———. 1980. _Le sens pratique._ Paris: Editions de Minuit.

Braudel, Ferdnand. 1980. _On History._ Chicago: University of Chicago Press.

Burke, Peter. 1980. _Sociology and History._ London: George Allen and Unwin.

Burt, Ronald. 1982. _Toward a Structural Theory of Action: Network Models of Social Structure, Perception and Action._ New York: Academic Press.

Calhoun, Craig. 1982. _The Question of Class Struggle: Social Foundations of Popular Radicalism During the Industrial Revolution._ Chicago: University of Chicago Press.

———. 1989. "Social Issues in the Study of Culture," _Comparative Social Research_ 11:1–29.

———, ed. 1990. _Comparative Social Research_ 12: _Business._ Greenwich, Conn.: JAI Press.

———, ed. forthcoming. _Habermas and the Public Sphere._ Cambridge, Mass.: MIT Press.

———. 1991. "Culture, History and the Problem of Specificity in Social Theory." In _Postmodernism and General Social Theory,_ ed. S. Seidman and D. Wagner, 244–88. New York and Oxford: Basil Blackwell.

Calhoun, Craig, and W. Richard Scott. 1990. "Peter Blau's Sociological Structuralism." In _Structures of Power and Constraint,_ ed. C. Calhoun, M. Meyer, and W. R. Scott. Cambridge: Cambridge University Press.

Camic, Charles. 1989. "_Structure_ After 50 Years: The Anatomy of a Charter." _American Journal of Sociology_ 95:35–107.

Carr, E. H. 1961. _What Is History?_ New York: Vintage.

Chartier, Roger. 1985. "Texts, Symbols and Frenchness." _Journal of Modern History,_ 57:682–95.

Chodorow, Nancy. 1978. _The Reproduction of Mothering: Psychoanalysis and the Sociology of Gender._ Berkeley: University of California Press.

Cohn, Bernard. 1980. "History and Anthropology: The State of Play." _Comparative Studies in Society and History_ 22:198–221.

Coleman, James. 1964. *The Adolescent Society*. New York: Free Press.

———. 1986. "Social Theory, Social Research, and a Theory of Action." *American Journal of Sociology* 91:1309–35.

———. 1990. *Foundations of Social Theory*. Cambridge, Mass.: Harvard University Press.

Collins, Randall. (1979) 1981. "Blau's Macrotheory." In *Sociology Since Midcentury*, 323–32. New York: Academic Press.

———. 1986. "On the Microfoundations of Macrosociology." *American Journal of Sociology* 86:984–1014.

Comte, Auguste. 1830–42. *Cours de philosophie positive*. In *Auguste Comte and Positivism: The Essential Writings,* ed. G. Lenzer. New York: Harper, 1975.

Cooley, Charles Horton. 1909. *Social Organization*. 1962 ed. New York: Shocken.

D'Antonio, William V. 1988. "Recruiting Sociologists in a Time of Expanding Opportunities." Paper presented at the Arizona conference, "Sociology and Institution Building," November 16–18.

Darnton, Robert. 1984. *The Great Cat Massacre and Other Episodes in French Cultural History*. New York: Knopf.

Desan, Suzanne. 1989. "Crowds, Community, and Ritual in the Work of E. P. Thompson and Natalie Davis." In *The New Cultural History,* ed. L. Hunt, 47–71. Berkeley: University of California Press.

Durkheim, Emile. [1895] 1984. *The Rules of Sociological Method*. New York: Free Press.

Eagleton, Terry. 1984. *The Function of Criticism: From the Spectator to Post-Structuralism*. London: Verso/New Left Books.

Eisenstadt, Shmuel. 1963. *The Political Systems of Empires*. Glencoe, Ill.: Free Press.

———. 1973. *Tradition, Change and Modernity*. New York: Wiley.

Elias, Norbert. [1939] 1978. *The Civilizing Process, I: The History of Manners*. New York: Pantheon.

———. [1939] 1982. *The Civilizing Process, II: Power and Civility*. New York: Pantheon.

Elton, G. R. 1984. *The History of England*. Cambridge: Cambridge University Press.

Evans, Peter, Dietrich Rueschemeyer, and Theda Skocpol. 1987. *Bringing the State Back In*. Cambridge: Cambridge University Press.

Fogel, R. W. and S. L. Engermann. 1974. *Time on the Cross: The Economics of American Negro Slavery*. New York: Little Brown.

Foucault, Michel. 1977. *Power/Knowledge*. ed. C. Gordon. New York: Pantheon.

Frank, Andre Gunder. 1967. *Capitalism and Underdevelopment in Latin America,* rev. ed. New York: Monthly Review Press.

Frisby, David. 1985. *Fragments of Modernity: Georg Simmel, Siegfried Kracauer, Walter Benjamin*. London: Heinemann.

Gablik, Susy. 1984. *Has Modernism Failed?* New York: Thames and Hudson.

Geertz, Clifford. 1973. *The Interpretation of Culture*. New York: Basic Books.

Giddens, Anthony. 1979. *Central Problems in Social Theory*. London: Macmillan.

———. 1985a. *The Constitution of Society*. Berkeley: University of California Press.

———. 1985b. *The Nation State and Violence*. Berkeley: University of California Press.

Glaser, A., and M. Strauss. 1966. *On the Discovery of Grounded Theory*. Chicago: Aldine.

Goldmann, Lucien. 1964. *Problèmes d'une sociologie du roman*. Paris, NRF.

Habermas, Jurgen. 1988. *The Philosophical Discourse of Modernity*. Cambridge, Mass.: MIT Press.

———. 1989. *The Structural Transformation of the Public Sphere*. Cambridge, Mass.: MIT Press.

Harding, Sandra. 1987. *The Science Question in Feminism*. Ithaca: Cornell University Press.

Hauser, Arnold. 1982. *The Sociology of Art*. London: Routledge.

Hechter, Michael. 1987. *Principles of Group Solidarity*. Berkeley: University of California Press.

Hicks, John. 1942. *The Social Framework*. Oxford: Oxford University Press.

Hirsch, Paul. 1986. "From Ambushes to Golden Parachutes: Corporate Takeovers as an Instance of Cultural Framing and Institutional Integration." *American Journal of Sociology* 91:800–37.

Hobsbawm, Eric. 1971. "From Social History to the History of Society." In *Essays in Social History,* ed. M. W. Flinn and T. C. Smout, 1–22. Oxford: Oxford University Press, 1974.

Hollis, Martin, and Steven Lukes, eds. 1982. *Rationality and Relativism*. Cambridge, Mass.: MIT Press.

Homans, George C. 1964. "Bringing Men Back In." *American Sociological Review* 29:809–18.

Hunt, Lynn. 1986. "French History in the Last Twenty Years: The Rise and Fall of the *Annales* Paradigm." *Journal of Comparative History* 21:209–24.

———, ed. 1989. *The New Cultural History*. Berkeley: University of California Press.

———. 1989. "Introduction: History, Culture, and Text." In *The New Cultural History,* ed. L. Hunt, 1–24. Berkeley: University of California Press.

Jackall, Robert. 1988. *Moral Mazes: The Social World of Corporate Managers*. Oxford: Oxford University Press.

Jameson, Fredric. 1981. *The Political Unconscious*. Ithaca: Cornell University Press.

Jones, Gareth Stedman. 1976. "From Historical Sociology to Theoretical History." *British Journal of Sociology* 27:295–305.

Keane, John. 1987. *Democracy and Civil Society*. London: Verso.

Kleinman, Sherryl. 1985. *Equals before God*. Chicago: University of Chicago Press.

Kramer, Lloyd S. 1989. "Literature, Criticism, and Historical Imagination: The Literary Challenge of Hayden White and Dominick LaCapra." In *The New Cultural History*, ed. L. Hunt, 97–130. Berkeley: University of California Press.

LaCapra, Dominick. 1983. *Rethinking Intellectual History: Texts, Contexts, Language*. Ithaca: Cornell University Press.

Lenski, Gerhard. 1987. *Human Societies*, 5th ed. New York: McGraw-Hill.

Lowenthal, Leo. 1961. *Literature, Popular Culture and Society*. Englewood Cliffs, N.J.: Prentice-Hall.

Lukács, Georg. 1962. *The Historical Novel*. London: Merlin.

Macfarlane, Alan. 1981. *The Justice and the Mare's Ale: Law and Disorder in Seventeenth-Century England*. Oxford: Oxford University Press.

Macrae, Duncan. 1985. *Policy Indicators: Links between Social Science and Public Debate*. Chapel Hill: University of North Carolina Press.

Maravall, Jose. 1986. *The Baroque Era*. Minneapolis: University of Minnesota Press.

Megill, Alan. 1987. "The Reception of Foucault by Historians." *Journal of the History of Ideas* 48:117.

Mills, C. W. 1959. *The Sociological Imagination*. Harmondsworth: Penguin.

Mullins, Nicholas. 1973. *Theories and Theory Groups in Contemporary American Sociology*. New York: Harper and Row.

Nadel, Siegfried. 1957. *The Theory of Social Structure*. London: Cohen and West.

O'Brien, Patricia. 1989. "Michel Foucault's History of Culture." In *The New Cultural History*, ed. L. Hunt, 25–46. Berkeley: University of California Press.

Parsons, Talcott. 1951. *The Social System*. New York: Free Press.

———. 1967. *Social Structure and Personality*. New York: Free Press.

Parsons, Talcott, Friedrich Bales, and Edward Shils. 1953. *Working Papers in the Theory of Action*. New York: Free Press.

Parsons, Talcott, and Neil J. Smelser. 1956. *Economy and Society*. New York: Free Press.

Powell, Walter, and Paul DiMaggio, eds. *The New Institutionalism*, forthcoming. Chicago: University of Chicago Press.

Riesman, David, with Nathan Glazer, and Reuel Denney. 1950. *The Lonely Crowd: A Study of the Changing American Character*. New Haven: Yale University Press.

Rigney, Daniel, and Donna Barnes. 1980. "Patterns of Interdisciplinary Citation in the Social Sciences." *Social Science Quarterly* 61:114–127.

Rostow, W. W. 1980. *The World Economy: History and Prospect*. Austin: University of Texas Press.

Rudé, George. 1964. *The Crowd in History: A Study of Popular Disturbances in France and England, 1730–1848*. New York: Wiley.

Said, Edward. 1976. *Orientalism*. New York: Pantheon.

Samuel, Raphael, and Gareth Stedman Jones. 1976. "Sociology and History." *History Workshop 5*.

Scott, Joan Wallach. 1988. *Gender and the Politics of History.* New York: Columbia University Press.

Selbourne, D. 1980. "On the Methods of the History Workshop." *History Workshop 9.*

Selznick, Philip. 1960. *Leadership in Administration.* New York: Harper and Row.

Sennett, Richard. 1979. *The Psychology of Society.* New York: Vintage.

Sica, Alan. 1989. "Social Theory's 'Constituency.'" *The American Sociologist* 20(3):227–41.

Simmel, Georg. 1908. "How Is Society Possible." In *George Simmel on Individuality and Social Forms,* ed. D. N. Levine, 9–14. Chicago: University of Chicago Press.

Skocpol, Theda. 1984. "Emergent Agendas and Recurrent Strategies in Historical Sociology." In *Vision and Method in Historical Sociology,* ed. Theda Skocpol. New York: Cambridge University Press.

Skocpol, Theda, and Margaret Somers. 1980. "The Uses of Comparative History in Macrosocial Inquiry." *Comparative Studies in Society and History* 22:174–97.

Slater, Philip. 1967. *Microcosm.* New York: Wiley.

———. 1970. *The Pursuit of Loneliness.* New York: Vintage.

Smelser, Neil. 1958. *Social Change in the Industrial Revolution.* London: Routledge and Kegan Paul.

———. 1989. "Self-Esteem and Social Relations: An Introduction." In *The Social Importance of Self-Esteem,* ed. Andrew Mecca, Neil J. Smelser, and John Vasconcellos, 1–22. Berkeley: University of California Press.

Sorokin, Pitirim. 1937–41. *Social and Cultural Dynamics.* Boston: Porter Sargent.

Stanley, Manfred. 1978. *The Technological Conscience.* Chicago: University of Chicago Press.

Stinchcombe, Arthur. 1984. *Economic Sociology.* New York: Academic Press.

Thompson, Edward P. 1955. *William Morris.* London: Merlin Press.

———. 1968. *The Making of the English Working Class.* Harmondsworth: Penguin.

———. 1972. "Rough Music: Le Charivari Anglais." *Annales ESC* 27:285–313.

———. 1975. *The Poverty of Theory and Other Essays.* New York: Monthly Review Press.

Tilly, Charles. 1982. *As Sociology Meets History.* New York: Academic Press.

Tilly, Charles, Richard Tilly, and Louise Tilly. 1974. *The Rebellious Century.* Cambridge, Mass.: Harvard University Press.

Vidich, Arthur, and Joseph Bensman. 1968. *Small Town in Mass Society.* Princeton: Princeton University Press.

Wacquant, Loïc. 1989. "Towards a Reflexive Sociology: A Workshop with Pierre Bourdieu." *Sociological Theory* 7:26–63.

Wacquant, Loïc, and Craig Calhoun. 1989. "Intérêt, rationalité, et histoire: à propos d'un débat americain sur la théorie d'action." *Actes de la Recherche en Sciences Sociales* 78(June):41–60.

Wallerstein, Immanuel. 1974. *The Modern World System.* New York: Academic Press.

———. 1980. *The Modern World System, II.* New York: Academic Press.

———. 1989. *The Modern World System, III.* New York: Academic Press.

Weber, Max. [1922] 1968. *Economy and Society.* Berkeley: University of California Press.

White, Harrison. 1983. "Where Do Markets Come From?" *American Journal of Sociology* 87:517–47.

White, Harrison, and Eric Leifer. 1987. "A Structural Approach to Markets." In *Structural Analysis of Business,* ed. M. Schwartz and M. Mizruchi. Cambridge: Cambridge University Press.

White, Hayden. 1978. *Tropics of Discourse: Essays in Cultural Criticism.* Baltimore: Johns Hopkins University Press.

———. 1987. *The Content of the Form: Narrative Discourse and Historical Representation.* Baltimore: Johns Hopkins University Press.

Williams, Raymond. 1958. *Culture and Society.* London: Chatto and Windus.

———. 1981. *The Sociology of Culture.* New York: Shocken.

Williamson, Oliver. 1982. *Politics and Markets.* New York: Free Press.

Wilson, Bryan, ed. 1970. *Rationality.* Oxford: Blackwell.

Wilson, W. J. 1978. *The Declining Significance of Race.* Chicago: University of Chicago Press.

Winch, Peter. 1958. *The Idea of a Social Science.* London: Routledge and Kegan Paul.

Wolf, Eric. 1983. *Europe and the Peoples Without History.* Berkeley: University of California Press.

Wuthnow, Robert. 1987. *Meaning and Moral Order: Explorations in Cultural Analysis.* Berkeley: University of California Press.

5

American Sociology since the Seventies: The Emerging Identity Crisis in the Discipline

DIANA CRANE AND HENRY SMALL

The current state of any discipline is a perennial subject for speculation among its members, who are generally anxious about its present welfare and prospects for the future. Typically, these concerns are centered around the following issues: Is the discipline producing theories that speak to major issues in the field, which in turn can serve to counteract the effect of pressures within particular specialties that tend to diversify and fragment the interests of members of the field? Is the discipline generating theories and findings that are of sufficient importance to attract the attention of neighboring fields as well as providing knowledge that can be applied to the solution of practical problems?

Most social scientists are actually conducting research in no more than two or three fields at a particular time. Consequently, their perspective on their discipline as a whole is inevitably incomplete and biased in terms of their own interests and experiences. In this paper, we will use the technique of co-citation analysis as a means of obtaining a "map" of the configuration of specialties in sociology since the early seventies in order to observe the nature and location of the changes that are taking place. A variety of sophisticated techniques have been developed for compiling and analyzing citations contained in research publications. Using these techniques, information scientists have shown that much of science and social science is interconnected within and across disciplines (Small and Griffith 1974). In 1987, there were 8,530 fields. In this vast terrain, sociology is a tiny speck consisting of 58 fields.

We will compare research fields in American sociology in the early seventies with those in the mid-eighties[1] in order to examine the

---

1. Citation data are not available for the social science literature prior to the 1970s.

changes that have taken place in the total configuration of fields as well as in the relationships among these fields and their links to basic and applied fields outside sociology. We will also look at a number of characteristics of fields in sociology, such as their size and the recency of the literature that cites and is cited in them, as indicators of the extent and nature of the growth of sociological knowledge. On the basis of this information, we will assess the reasons for these changes and the directions in which the discipline is likely to move in the nineties.

How does this type of analysis compare with the information that can be obtained by examining textbooks in sociology or by consulting a disciplinary handbook, such as Smelser (1988)? Co-citation analysis locates the specific areas of the field that are currently attracting attention from those who are conducting research. By contrast, as Calhoun shows (see this volume, chap. 4), the selection and organization of subjects in sociology textbooks is dictated by considerations of marketing and the conservative prejudices of teachers of introductory sociology rather than by how actively a particular subfield is being researched at a particular time. Similarly, the contents of disciplinary handbooks are likely to be determined more by editors' preconceptions of the discipline than by the scope and nature of current research. Articles reviewing a particular field tend to be comprehensive, describing all the different lines of research in a field, rather than restricting their attention to the most active areas.

The Sociology of Scientific Disciplines

The concept of a scientific discipline is an ambiguous one. The existence of research areas centered around a small number of fairly specific questions is not problematic. It also seems reasonable to assume that clusters of related research areas constitute specialties whose members are linked by a common interest in a particular type of phenomenon or method (such as crime, the family, population, etc.). Disciplines, in turn, are composed of clusters of specialties; members of disciplines, however, are affiliated as much by political and social interests as by intellectual concerns. Moreover, members of recognized disciplines are bound to one another by a professional association that organizes scientific meetings and acts as the representative of its members to organizations and institutions outside the discipline. Nonetheless, from an intellectual point of view, there are few issues on which members of a discipline are unanimous. While subgroups that crosscut various specialties will agree about the use of certain types of methods or theories, other subgroups are likely to favor alternative approaches (Coleman 1986).

The issue of what constitutes a discipline becomes even more ambiguous if one examines its historical evolution. For example, American sociology emerged in the early years of this century and was institutionalized "before it had a distinctive intellectual content, a distinctive method, or even a point of view" (Oberschall 1972:189). By the late thirties, the American Sociological Society had attracted about 1,000 members (Oberschall 1972:241). In the postwar period, intellectual debates, regardless of substantive foci, were centered around the viability of a functionalist orientation and the emerging methodology of survey research. For about two decades, the intellectual center of the discipline was focused around the work of a half-dozen leading theorists. Their students, trained in a few departments in major universities, moved to less prestigious institutions where they disseminated the ideas of their mentors.

By the early seventies, as the numbers of sociologists expanded rapidly (Waller 1989), this highly coherent intellectual environment had disappeared. It had been replaced by a variety of conflicting theoretical perspectives (Mullins 1973) and by specialties that were increasingly independent from one another in terms of distinctive theoretical approaches and methods (Collins 1986; Ben-David 1973). Members of some specialties interacted more frequently with researchers outside sociology who were studying similar phenomena from other disciplinary perspectives.[2] Collins (1986) argues that, as a result of the greater size of the discipline and its proliferation of specialties, members of the discipline are now less able to perceive accurately the contours of the discipline as a whole. Consequently, he suggests that a paradoxical situation has emerged in which sociologists tend to be pessimistic about the future of their discipline as a whole but optimistic about the future of their own specialties. According to Collins, their pessimism about the future of the discipline is exacerbated by philosophical and methodological controversies about the feasibility and quality of social scientific research.

Given that the concept of a discipline as an intellectual entity is difficult to define precisely, what are the characteristics of a discipline that can and should be examined? Recent literature on the sociology of science provides some indications. Historians and philosophers of science have attempted to differentiate between different types of disciplines. For example, Kuhn (1970) has argued that most social sci-

2. For example, the work of sociologists of science was often of greater interest to historians and philosophers of science than to sociologists in other specialties.

ence disciplines lack fields with clearly defined paradigms that can direct research toward the solution of specific problems, as occurs in the natural sciences. Price (1970) argued that social scientists differ from natural scientists in their use of the scientific literature. According to Price, natural scientists base their research on a small body of recent literature on a narrow topic, while social scientists, and particularly humanists, draw from sources that are less likely to be recent and more likely to come from a wide range of fields.

Pantin (1968), a philosopher of science, has hypothesized that scientific fields differ in terms of the numbers of variables that must be examined in order to understand empirical phenomena. Restricted sciences, such as physics and chemistry, are those in which scientists concentrate their attention upon small numbers of variables and are able to develop mathematical models that can be tested very precisely. In unrestricted sciences, such as biological and social sciences, the large number of variables limits the extent to which mathematical models can be developed. Understanding of the phenomena requires information from a wide variety of specialties.

All of these conceptualizations of disciplines are similar as they indicate that sciences and social sciences differ in terms of the nature of the questions to be investigated; this in turn has implications for the relationships between specialties within the discipline and between specialties within and outside the discipline. Restricted disciplines, such as most physical sciences, would be expected to exhibit a high degree of linkage between different research areas within the discipline but less linkage to other disciplines. Unrestricted sciences, such as most social sciences, would be likely to exhibit relatively diffuse links among research areas both within and outside the discipline.[3] However, a social science discipline, such as economics, that deals with a small number of quantitatively defined variables would be expected to behave more like a restricted than an unrestricted area.

To summarize, there are two central issues concerning the nature of academic disciplines: (1) How do disciplines grow and change? Specifically, how do new research areas emerge and how do specialties expand? (2) What holds disciplines together? What provides linkage between the different specialties of which the discipline is composed?

In order to examine these issues, we will compare sociology with another discipline, economics. First, we will explore the hypothesis that sociology fits the Price-Kuhn characterization of social science disciplines by comparing it with a social science discipline, namely,

3. Whitley's (1976) concepts of umbrella and polytheistic disciplines are analogous.

economics, that is less likely to fit that stereotype. Specifically, we hypothesize that sociology is less likely to generate the precisely defined questions that spawn research areas and consequently is less likely to produce research publications based on a small body of recent literature. This means that there should be fewer research clusters in sociology than in economics and that they should be based on less recent publications. It also suggests that books, which are a less rapid means of knowledge dissemination than journal articles, should be more important in sociology than in economics. In other words, the lack of "exemplars" in sociology is expected to be reflected in the numbers and characteristics of research clusters and in the preference for books rather than articles as an outlet for publications.

Second, we will attempt to test the implications of Pantin's argument concerning restricted and unrestricted sciences. Specifically, we will hypothesize that in an unrestricted science, such as sociology, links between clusters within the discipline will be relatively weak while in economics, a restricted science, such links will be stronger. By contrast, the same theory leads us to expect that sociology will be weakly linked to a larger number of areas outside the discipline, while economics will be strongly linked to a few areas outside the discipline, presumably those that are applying ideas from that field.

Finally, we will examine the changes in the major concerns of the disciplines since the early seventies and in the relations between fields within these disciplines.

Methodology

Mapping the structure of scientific specialties and disciplines requires an enormous data base, much larger than it is feasible to generate by means of interviews and questionnaires. Such a data base is provided by the *Science Citation Index* (SCI) and the *Social Sciences Citation Index* (SSCI). These indexes show the numbers of citations that publications in the sciences and the social sciences have received in any given year in the journals that are included in the data base.[4] Since the social science journals are primarily American,[5] it is appropriate to

4. Books can be *cited* references but cannot be *citing* references since they are not scanned for citations.

5. In both economics and sociology, less than 25 percent of the citing journals were foreign or international. According to Garfield (1977), the selection of journals for the SSCI is deliberately biased in favor of English-language journals since these have been shown to have the most impact in terms of citations. Baughmann (1974) showed that 95 percent of the cited sociological literature is in English. Fletcher (1972) showed that

conclude that we are obtaining the structures of these disciplines as viewed by American researchers.

Co-citation analysis is a technique for clustering the data contained in these indexes. From extensive clustering studies of several consecutive years of the SCI, the primary structural unit that emerges in the natural sciences is the narrow subject matter specialty (Small 1976; 1977). Specifically, the co-citation technique measures the frequency with which two documents are cited simultaneously in references from journal articles. It then applies a single-link clustering algorithm to form clusters using this information. The technique identifies research areas in terms of two lists of references: (a) a list of references that are co-cited by a group of articles—the *cited* references; and (b) the list of references that contain the co-citations—the *citing* references.

In other words, clusters formed by the algorithm used here consist of a relatively small group of co-cited documents and a larger group of citing documents, each of which cites one or more of the co-cited documents. These two sets of documents are believed to represent a research area, a group of researchers engaged in the joint exploration of related problems.[6]

Relations between research areas can be examined using citations between research areas, that is, the citing papers that cite documents in two or more clusters. These links between areas can be used to prepare graphs showing the connections between fields within a dis-

---

79 percent of the nonjournal citations in the economics literature were to Anglo-American literature. Comparing the number of journals used for the two disciplines in the study with the number of journals located in comprehensive listings of journals for these fields (Sichel and Sichel 1986; Turner and Turner 1990, quoted in Waller 1989), we found that the economics journals used in the 1972–74 study represented 52 percent of the economics journals reported in Sichel and Sichel (1986) for the period, 1900–1970; the economics journals used in the 1987 study represented 64 percent of the economics journals listed in Sichel and Sichel from 1900 to 1986. Comparing our lists of journals for sociology with the numbers of sociology journals reported by Turner and Turner showed that our list for 1972–74 contained 29 percent more journals than Turner and Turner and, for 1987, 81 percent as many journals as Turner and Turner for 1900–86. Comparing the 1987 list of economics journals with a 1986 list of core journals in economics (Diamond 1989), revealed that 96 percent of the core journals were included in the 1987 list.

6. A questionnaire study by Small (1977) of a cluster in the natural sciences (collagen research) revealed the existence of a small group of researchers who were regarded as leading researchers in the area and had extensive informal contacts with one another. A study by Mullins et al. (1977) also found considerable evidence that two other clusters in the natural sciences represented groups of researchers who were aware of one another, collaborated with one another, and communicated with one another.

cipline or between disciplines. Links of this sort can be used to identify specialties (clusters of research areas) and disciplines (clusters of specialties).

Multidimensional scaling, a technique for determining the relative distances between clusters by comparing their relative positions on two dimensions, has been found to be useful in determining the relative distances between clusters in maps of this kind. On the basis of co-citation frequency, the relative distance between a particular cluster and others with which it is linked can be estimated. In other words, the fewer the number of co-citations between two clusters, the further apart they are considered to be. A high number of co-citations between two clusters indicates proximity.

Our analysis of sociology and economics in the early seventies is based on a computer file, which was created by merging three years of the annual SSCI (1972, 1973, and 1974). All articles cited ten or more times in this three-year file were selected for clustering. Since most scientific papers are cited fewer than five times in their entire history, this means that only very frequently cited papers are being examined. The idiosyncratic citation behavior of some scientific authors is likely to have little effect upon the patterns being observed here.

While most of the clusters that emerge in the 1972–74 SSCI file represent substantive areas, a few represent methodological topics such as path analysis and multidimensional scaling. In such cases, researchers are presumably involved in applying or perfecting these techniques. Most of the clusters were relatively small. Of the 1,208 clusters in the 1972–74 SSCI file, 517 were cited by fewer than 30 documents, 548 by 30 to 99 documents, and 143 by 100 or more documents.[7] Clusters cited by fewer than 30 documents were excluded from the 1972–74 data base.[8] Our analysis deals specifically with 80 of the 691 clusters that were cited by 30 or more documents: 44 clusters identified with economics and 37 clusters identified with sociology (see Table 1)[9].

In order to be able to classify clusters by discipline, we classified journals in the SSCI file using the disciplinary classifications that ap-

7. By comparison, 1,610 clusters were formed using all documents cited 15 times or more in the 1973 *Science Citation Index* file, capturing 50 percent of the cited items. The mean size of these clusters was 5.0 cited documents and 67.8 citing documents; the largest cluster contained 51 cited documents and 519 citing documents.

8. For a study of social science clusters cited 100 times or more, see Griffith and Small (1976).

9. For more information about these procedures, see Small and Crane (1979).

Table 1. Types of Clusters by Discipline and Year

	1972–74	1987
Economics		
Economics[a]	16	21
Low disciplinary economics[b]	28	53
Interdisciplinary economics[c]	—[d]	27
Total	44	101
Sociology		
Sociology[a]	1	0
Low disciplinary sociology[b]	36	23
Interdisciplinary sociology[c]	—[d]	35
Total	37	58

[a]Over two-thirds of the citing articles in the cluster were published in journals identified with the relevant discipline. There were a minimum total of thirty citing references in each cluster.
[b]Between one-third and two-thirds of the citing articles in the cluster were published in journals identified with the relevant discipline. There were a minimum total of thirty citing references in each cluster.
[c]Between one-quarter and one-third of the citing articles in the cluster were published in journals identified with the relevant discipline. There were a minimum total of twenty-two citing references in each cluster.
[d]Excluded from 1972–74 analysis.

pear in *Ulrich's International Periodicals Directory* (1973, 1987). For the early seventies, we identified seventy-one economics journals and eighty-five sociology journals in the SSCI data file. We classified clusters as belonging to sociology if over two-thirds of the citing articles in the cluster were published in journals in that discipline (hereafter the disciplinary journal concentration, DJC). Using these criteria, only one sociology cluster emerged in the 1972–74 data base and none in the 1987 data base. A cluster was classified as "low disciplinary sociology" if from one-third to two-thirds of the citing articles were published in journals in that discipline. A substantial number of low disciplinary sociology clusters were identified in the 1972–74 data base (see Table 1).

In the early eighties, the Institute for Scientific Information changed its procedures for clustering documents. In the new system, references from the *Science Citation Index* are combined with references from the *Social Sciences Citation Index* for clustering purposes. The new clustering procedures produce five levels of clusters. The first level corresponds to the research area, a specific set of problems that has attracted the attention of a group of researchers; the second level corresponds to a specialty, a cluster of research areas. The third and fourth levels represent individual disciplines and clusters of disciplines (e.g., the social sciences) respectively. Again, a single-link clustering algorithm is used at each level. The initial clusters at level 1 are formed on the basis of lists of citing articles that co-cite articles on the list of cited articles. The clusters identified on the first level are used to form clusters on level 2; those identified on the second level are input for the third level and so on. For example, Figure 1 (3d level) shows the connections between social science specialties in several disciplines, including two of the specialties that we will be discussing, specifically, a specialty identified with economics (shown in Fig. 4) and a specialty identified with both sociology and economics (shown in Fig. 6).

In order to locate clusters containing citing references from sociology and economics journals, we obtained all clusters from the file that contained citing references from articles appearing in 242 journals that were identified as belonging to sociology and economics using *Ulrich's International Periodicals Directory* and that were cited by thirty or more documents. Because of the strikingly small number of low disciplinary sociology clusters that emerged in the 1987 data base, a new category was added for that period, "interdisciplinary sociology." In this category, the criteria for defining a cluster as belonging to either sociology or economics were lowered to a minimum of 25 percent of citing references in the respective discipline and a minimum total of twenty-two citing references.[10] In both the earlier and the later data bases, labels for the clusters were obtained from lists of key words drawn from article titles by ISI staff.

While co-citation data have the enormous advantage of providing an overall view of the content of a discipline at a particular time, the technique has certain limitations. One problem that has been discussed is whether or not the technique locates a reasonably exhaustive set of research areas and how it compares in this respect with other information retrieval methods (Sullivan et al. 1977). Using citation indexes for a single year, it appears that co-citation techniques are unlikely to retrieve all the relevant research activity, because not all papers cite the core references of a given research area. In addition, it may take time for new developments to be cited and to form research areas.

10. In Figures 4, 5, and 6, we show a few clusters identified as high interdisciplinary economics and sociology in which the proportion of citing references in the respective discipline is as low as 15 percent.

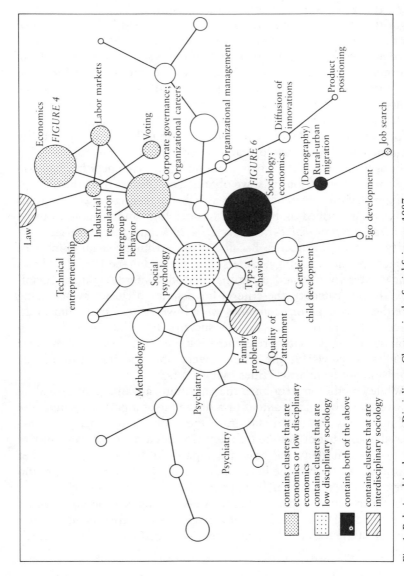

Fig. 1. Relationships between Disciplinary Clusters in the Social Sciences, 1987. In this figure and in figs. 4, 5, and 6, the size of a circle is an indication of the relative size of the cluster. Unlabeled clusters have no citation links with either economics or sociology.

A more subtle issue is that of the threshold or the number of papers that are included in the data base for clustering. The threshold was determined in two steps. First, a minimum citation threshold of seven was applied, selecting all papers cited seven or more times. Then a fractional citation threshold was applied, where each citing item was weighted by the reciprocal of the length of its list of references. This procedure corrects for differences in citation practices between fields. In the 1972–74 data base, the final threshold was ten. The 1987 threshold was higher than that of the earlier data base. This means that a substantial increase in the numbers of clusters observed, as occurred in economics, is probably a conservative estimate of actual growth. A decrease in the numbers of clusters, as occurred in sociology, would be anticipated if the size of the field had remained stable.

Characteristics of Sociology and Economics as Disciplines

Assuming that sociology behaves like a social science and economics like a natural science, we hypothesized that sociology would be less likely than economics to generate precisely defined questions or exemplars that spawn research areas. This in turn implies that: (1) sociology would be less likely than economics to produce new research clusters; (2) research clusters in sociology would be based on older publications than those in economics; and (3) sociology clusters would include more references to books (a less rapid means of knowledge dissemination) than those in economics.

In the early seventies, based on the citing references, sociology produced fewer clusters (thirty-seven) than economics (forty-four) in spite of the fact that the numbers of journals in the two disciplines were not substantially different. Although there were fewer economics journals (seventy-one) than sociology journals (eighty-five),[11] the economics literature produced more clusters (see Table 1). The 1972–74 social science citation file produced sixteen economics clusters and twenty-eight low disciplinary economics clusters as compared to one sociology cluster and thirty-seven low disciplinary sociology clusters.

In 1987, there were more economics journals (134) than sociology journals (108) in the SCI-SSCI file. While the number of economics journals was one and one-quarter times the number of sociology journals, there were more than three times as many economics and low disciplinary economics clusters than low disciplinary sociology clusters. When we included additional clusters defined using less stringent

11. Includes criminology and demography journals.

Table 2. Disciplinary Affiliations of 1987 Clusters Identified by Citing and Cited
         References

	Citing references N (%)	Cited references N (%)
Economics		
Economics	21 (21)	84 (83)
Low disciplinary economics	53 (53)	15 (15)
Interdisciplinary economics	27 (26)	—
Not economics	—	2 (2)
Total	101 (100)	101 (100)
Sociology		
Sociology	—	22 (38)
Low disciplinary sociology	23 (40)	18 (31)
Interdisciplinary sociology	35 (60)	2 (3)
High interdisciplinary sociology	0	1 (2)
Not sociology	0	15 (26)
Total	58 (100)	58 (100)

criteria, the number of economics clusters was almost twice the number of sociology clusters (see Table 1). In other words, if the DJC can be regarded as a measure of the discipline-like character of a cluster, then it appears that economics behaves more like a discipline than sociology. In terms of its appearance in a well-defined set of specialized journals, economics has a higher degree of internal connectivity than sociology and in this sense is more "coherent" as a discipline. Put another way, the literature in economics is much less scattered than the literature in sociology.

Another indication of the relative diffuseness of the sociology literature is that when the clusters in the two disciplines are categorized in terms of *cited* references (Table 2), almost all the low disciplinary economics clusters are categorized as economics. By comparison, low disciplinary and interdisciplinary sociology clusters based on citing references are as likely to be categorized as not belonging to sociology as they are likely to be categorized as sociology on the basis of *cited* references.

In addition, the relative sizes of the clusters in the two fields has changed in favor of economics. In 1972–74, the mean size of the economics clusters (i.e., the number of citing items) was slightly smaller than sociology (65.9 compared to 69.1). In 1987, the mean size of economics clusters (not including the clusters defined at the lower threshold) was 83, compared to 59 for sociology. Thus, the mean size of the sociology clusters had decreased by 14 percent while the mean size of the economics clusters had increased by 26 percent.

Table 3 presents some statistics on the sizes of the clusters in the two disciplines (here we have combined all types of clusters), the age of the items cited, and the fraction of cited documents that are books. These characteristics reflect the extent to which members of the discipline are concentrating their attention on problems defined by a small number of recent research papers.

Cluster age was measured in two ways: year of publication of cited documents in a cluster, and use of Price's Index, the percentage of cited

Table 3. Characteristics of Clusters in Economics and Sociology, 1972–74 and 1987

	1972–74		1987	
	Economics	Sociology	Economics	Sociology
No. of clusters	44	37	101	58
Mean size (cited items)	5.3	5.5	7.4	5.1
Mean size (citing items)	65.9	69.1	72.6	54.8
Mean year (cited items)	1965.4	1963.6	1974.5	1973.0
Mean 'age' (cited items)[a]	7.6	9.4	12.5	14.0
Mean year (books)	1965.6	1962.9	1973.9	1972.8
Mean year (articles)	1965.3	1964.0	1974.0	1972.7
Percentage of cited items that are books	24.5	39.0	24.7	67.5
Percentage of cited items publ. in last five years				
All items:	52.8	46.5	19.3	18.8
Books:	43.9	43.6	20.2	19.5
Articles:	55.7	48.4	19.0	17.2

[a]These figures were calculated by subtracting the mean year of all cited items published in each discipline from 1973 and 1987 respectively.

documents published during the last five years. The more recent the mean date of publication (or the larger Price's Index), the more rapidly new knowledge is being created and old papers are being rendered obsolete.

In the 1972–74 data base, the mean year of cited items for both disciplines (1965.4: economics; 1963.6: sociology) was substantially older than the mean year of publication for the twenty largest clusters in the 1973 *Science Citation Index,* which was 1969.9. However, the literature cited by the economics clusters was more recent than the literature cited by the sociology clusters (see Table 3).

Again, in the 1987 data base, the mean year of all cited publications was more recent in economics than in sociology. However, both disciplines were clearly building on literature that is relatively older than was the case in the earlier period. The mean age of the cited literature has increased by 49 percent in sociology and by 64 percent in economics. This implies that in both fields work being published in the late eighties was based on ideas that were originally developed in the early seventies. In the earlier period, work that was published in the early seventies was based on work from the mid-sixties. For the entire 1987 data base, the mean year of all cited items was 1977.4.

Another way of examining the recency of the literature being cited in a discipline is to examine the percentage of the literature being cited that was published in the five-year period prior to its citation. In both sociology and economics, these figures have declined by 28 percent and 34 percent respectively. The average figure for the 1987 data base is 33.4 percent. Again, this suggests that both disciplines are building on older rather than newer literature. The reasons for this phenomenon may be due to an increase in the average age of members of these disciplines, as a result of a decline in recruitment in recent years (Waller 1989), and to the sharp decrease in funding that both disciplines experienced in the early eighties (Zuiches 1984).

Finally, reliance on journal articles rather than books is characteristic of the natural sciences and is believed to be a factor in the speed with which knowledge grows and changes in those disciplines. The percentage of cited items in clusters that are books is markedly higher for sociology than for economics in both the earlier and the later periods. What is most striking is that the difference between the two disciplines in this respect has almost tripled since the early seventies. However, the high percentage of books cited in sociology does not explain the increase in age of cited documents in that field since articles and books cited in the discipline do not differ substantially with respect to date of publication. On the other hand, since books can be cited but are not scanned for citations, the fact that the sociological literature is so heavily oriented toward book publishing may have affected the numbers of clusters identified with sociology that we have been able to observe in this study.

Sociology and Economics as Restricted or Unrestricted Disciplines

According to Pantin (1968), disciplines vary in the number of variables that are considered in relation to a specific research problem: restricted disciplines concentrate upon a few quantitatively defined variables; unrestricted disciplines incorporate ideas from a wide range of fields. As we hypothesized sociology to be an unrestricted discipline, we expected that its research fields would be characterized by diffuse ties to a large number of other fields both within and outside the discipline. That is, sociology is a perspective or a world view that has permeated a number of adjacent disciplines; in turn, its disciplinary core is relatively small.

By contrast, as we hypothesized that economics approximates a restricted discipline, we expected that research fields in economics would be characterized by dense ties to closely related fields and relatively few ties to fields in other areas within and outside the discipline. In other words, the disciplinary maps of sociology and economics should look quite different.

Economics and Sociology: 1972–74

In the early seventies, at a minimum of three co-citations between clusters, the economics and low disciplinary economics clusters formed one large network that included all but three clusters in the field (see Fig. 2). At a minimum of seven co-citations between clusters, this network consisted of two large groups of clusters and three small groups of clusters. One of the large groups of clusters included areas dealing wth investment policies and consumer economics. The other large group of clusters included areas dealing with public goods, income distribution, and pollution control. The smaller groups of clusters dealt with consumer demand, monetary theory, and market structure.

When linkage between clusters in low disciplinary sociology in the seventies was examined using a minimum of three co-citations between clusters, sociology formed one large network from which only one cluster was excluded (not shown). At a minimum of seven co-

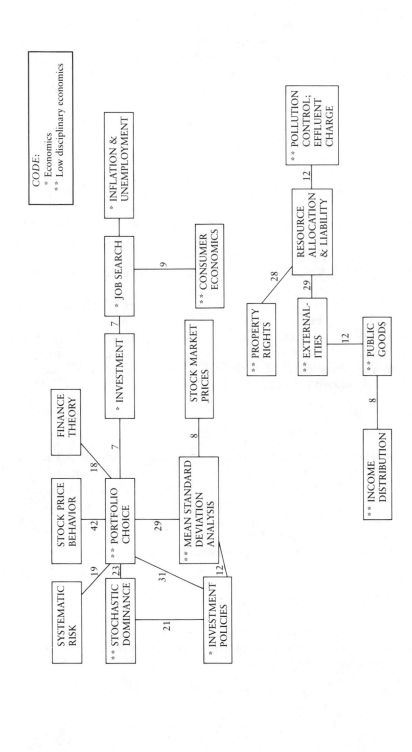

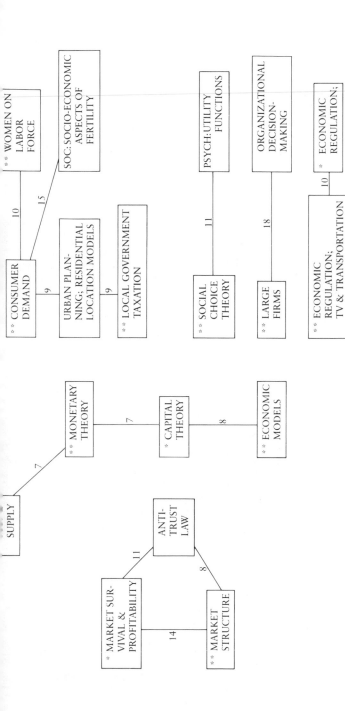

Fig. 2. The Disciplinary Structure of Economics, 1972 to 1974. This figure shows connections at seven or more co-citations between clusters. Clusters that are not labeled * or ** are not cited with sufficient frequency in economics journals to be classified as either economics or low-disciplinary economics. The numbers on the lines connecting the clusters represent the number of times references in each of the connected clusters were co-cited. A high figure represents a large number of co-citations and hence indicates that the two clusters are building on ideas that are closely related. The following clusters, identified as economics, were isolates: processes of price mechanism, competitive equilibrium, manufactured exports, effective protection, profit functions, trade model, optimal laws and pricing, linear expenditure system, and international trade pricing. The following clusters, identified as low-disciplinary economics, were isolates: X-efficiency, savings flows, economic growth, education investment, econometric analysis, developing countries, advertising, spectral analysis of time-series data, and ocean resource exploitation.

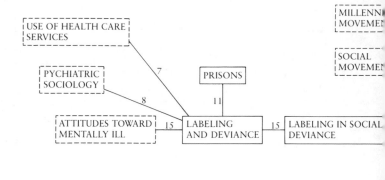

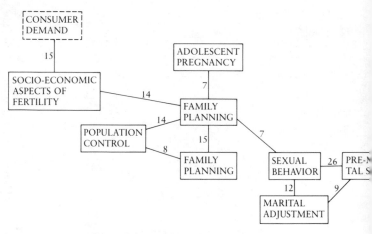

Fig. 3. The Disciplinary Structure of Sociology, 1972 to 1974.
This figure shows connections at seven or more co-citations between clusters. The numbers on the lines connecting the clusters represent the number of times references in each of the connected clusters were co-cited (for further explanation, see Fig. 2). The following clusters, identified as low-disciplinary sociology, were isolates: analysis of social problems, evaluation of sociological theory, occupational grading, phenomenological sociology, population dynamics, social stratification, societal transition, sociological theory construction, sociology of religion.

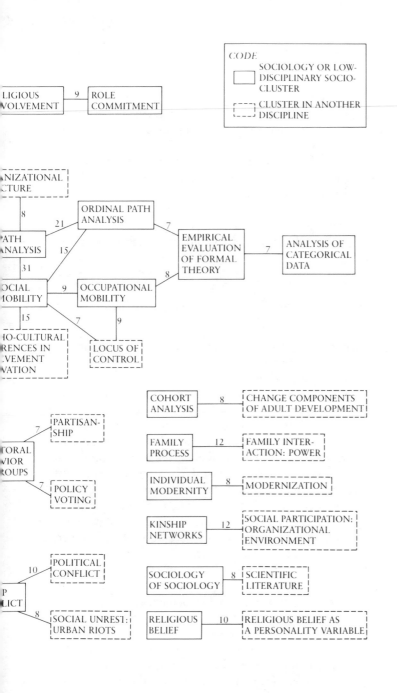

CODE

☐ SOCIOLOGY OR LOW-DISCIPLINARY SOCIO-CLUSTER

┌┄┐ CLUSTER IN ANOTHER
└┄┘ DISCIPLINE

LIGIOUS
VOLVEMENT — 9 — ROLE COMMITMENT

NIZATIONAL
CTURE

— 8

PATH
ANALYSIS — 21 — ORDINAL PATH ANALYSIS — 7 — EMPIRICAL EVALUATION OF FORMAL THEORY — 7 — ANALYSIS OF CATEGORICAL DATA

15

31

OCIAL
MOBILITY — 9 — OCCUPATIONAL MOBILITY — 8

15 — 7 — 9

HO-CULTURAL
RENCES IN
VEMENT
VATION — LOCUS OF CONTROL

COHORT ANALYSIS — 8 — CHANGE COMPONENTS OF ADULT DEVELOPMENT

7 — PARTISAN-SHIP

TORAL
VIOR
ROUPS

7 — POLICY VOTING

FAMILY PROCESS — 12 — FAMILY INTER-ACTION: POWER

INDIVIDUAL MODERNITY — 8 — MODERNIZATION

KINSHIP NETWORKS — 12 — SOCIAL PARTICIPATION: ORGANIZATIONAL ENVIRONMENT

10 — POLITICAL CONFLICT

P
LICT

SOCIOLOGY OF SOCIOLOGY — 8 — SCIENTIFIC LITERATURE

8 — SOCIAL UNREST: URBAN RIOTS

RELIGIOUS BELIEF — 10 — RELIGIOUS BELIEF AS A PERSONALITY VARIABLE citations between clusters, the network consisted of three groups of clusters, each containing a few tightly linked clusters and several peripheral ones. The largest groups of clusters were concerned with: (1) population control and the family; (2) social and occupational mobility and path analysis; and (3) labeling and deviance. A small group of clusters dealt with religious involvement and belief. Eight fields were linked only to fields in other disciplines (see Fig. 3).

According to this configuration, the most quantitative areas dominated the discipline in the early seventies. The study of social mobility was strongly linked to methodological areas and to formal theorizing. Demography and the study of marriage and the family formed a second large cluster. The less quantitative fields, such as religion and group conflict, were considerably smaller and presumably less influential.

Interdisciplinary Relationships of Economics and Sociology:
1972–74

Another way to assess the nature of a discipline is to examine its relationships with other disciplines. As we have seen, unrestricted disciplines such as many biological and social sciences draw upon information from a wide variety of fields in order to understand and explain their subject matter (Pantin 1968). If sociology is an unrestricted discipline and economics a restricted discipline, sociology clusters should have more links with clusters in other fields than economics clusters. When each cluster was taken as a starting point, and all clusters directly linked to it by a cluster co-citation strength of seven or more were recorded (i.e., its "nearest neighbors"), the mean number of nearest neighbors per cluster was larger for sociology than for economics, indicating that, overall, sociology clusters were involved in more links than economics clusters (see Table 4). However, 42 percent of sociology's links were to clusters outside the sociology set, whereas this was the case for only 30 percent of economics' ties. Thus, economics had a substantially higher number of links within the discipline (70 percent) than sociology (58 percent).

If the criterion for relatedness is reduced from a minimum of seven to a minimum of three co-citations between clusters, the contrast is even more striking: economics and low disciplinary economics had ties to thirty-three clusters outside the field while low disciplinary sociology was linked to eighty-four clusters outside these fields (see Table 5). Again, this suggests that economics is more cohesive as a

Table 4. "Nearest Neighbor" Analysis: Economics and Sociology, 1972–74[a]

Number of nearest neighbors	Economics	Sociology
Total number of nearest neighbors	57	62
Mean number of nearest neighbors per cluster	1.3	1.7
Number of nearest neighbors not in discipline	17	26
(percent of total)	(30%)	(42%)
Number of nearest neighbors in same discipline	40	36
(percent of total)	(70%)	(58%)

Source: From Small and Crane (1979).
[a] At >7 co-citations in each link.

Table 5. Number of Links between Economics, Sociology, and Other Disciplines, 1972–74[a]

	Economics	Sociology	Psychology	Inter-disciplinary psychology	Other disciplines	Total
Economics	—	2	0	4	27	33
Sociology	2	—	1	17	64	84

Source: From Small and Crane (1979).
[a] At >3 co-citations in each link.

discipline than sociology, which has many more links to other disciplines.

In addition, there were relatively few links between economics and sociology or between psychology and sociology (see Table 5). The relative absence of links between clusters identified with journals in sociology, economics, and psychology suggests that information and ideas did not diffuse readily between these three disciplines during this period. Economics was more closely allied with fields such as management, law, and political science than with sociology and psychology. Sociology had weak affinities with low disciplinary psychology but virtually none with psychology itself. Many of the links to fields outside sociology appeared to be to clusters in anthropology, political science, and psychiatry.

Economics and Sociology: 1987

Because of differences in the ways in which the two data bases were constructed, analysis of the content of the clusters and of the relations between clusters uses a different format for the 1987 data base. Clusters at the lowest level (research areas) were linked at the second level (the specialty level). In turn, links between specialties at the second level created disciplines and subdisciplines at level 3. What is missing in this procedure is information on the links between all of the clusters at level 1, regardless of whether they merge into specialties at level 2. Consequently, some of the kinds of analyses that were done for the 1972–74 data base could not be repeated for the later period, and hence some types of comparisons cannot be made.

In 1987, economics consisted of one large specialty (Fig. 4), seven medium-size and small specialties, five dyads, and twenty-seven isolates (three of them linked to clusters in other disciplines).[12] The large specialty (Fig. 4) appeared to represent the present core of the discipline since it included over one-third of the economics clusters and one-third of the low disciplinary economics clusters. It incorporated most of the fields that had been present in the three large clusters in the earlier period, including research on the stock market, monetary theory, and income distribution. New elements in this specialty were concerns with budget deficits and exchange rates.

One of the largest of the remaining specialties, consisting of seven fields (not shown), dealt with corporate governance (an expansion of a field labeled "large firms" in 1972–74) and was linked to a specialty outside economics dealing with organizational decision making. The latter appeared to represent studies in business management.

Another medium-size specialty (industrial regulation) was in part an outgrowth of a specialty that had also existed in the earlier period, economic regulation. Three small specialties were new: technological entrepreneurship, technological change, and labor markets combined with intraindustry trade. Two others dealing with the labor theory of value and labor unions were linked to sociology (see Figs. 5 and 6).

12. The seven medium and small specialties were (in order of size) corporate governance (not shown); industrial regulation (see Fig. 1); technological entrepreneurship (see Fig. 1); technological change (not shown); labor markets (see Fig. 1); labor unions (see Fig. 6); and labor theory of value (see Fig. 5). The five dyads were: capital income taxation and U.S. agriculture; income growth in OECD countries; job search (see Fig. 1); voting (see Fig. 1); and local government expenditures (the last two were linked to clusters in other disciplines). The twenty-seven isolates were: household capital; public choice; labor contracts; market socialism; British industrial revolution; runaway pricing; money demand; demand behavior; classical economics; piecewise monotonic maps; monopoly power; aggregate import demand model; demand for money; crude-oil market; market price (socialist economies); state audit budgets; free banking system; macroeconomic policy; firm size; employment decisions; dynamic equilibrium in markets; trade union labor contracts; modeling interprovincial migration; state economic development; and three clusters linked to other disciplines—property crime (criminology), anticipated utility approach (management), and rural-urban migration (demography).

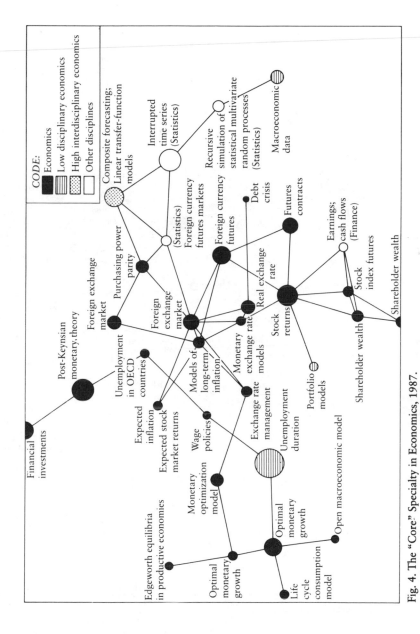

Fig. 4. The "Core" Specialty in Economics, 1987.
Disciplinary affiliation of clusters is based on disciplinary affiliation of journals in which the references *cited* in the clusters appeared. Distances between the clusters were determined by multidimensional scaling.

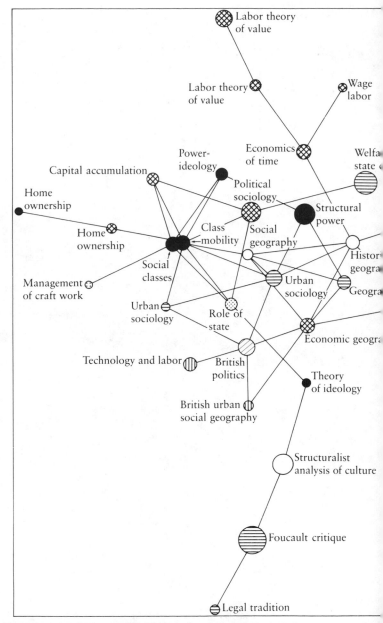

Fig. 5. Major Specialties in Sociology, 1987, Part I.
Disciplinary affiliation of clusters is based on disciplinary affiliation of journals in which
the references *cited* in the clusters appeared. Distances between the clusters were determined by multidimensional scaling, using citing references. For items labeled * the cited
references were evenly divided between economics and sociology.

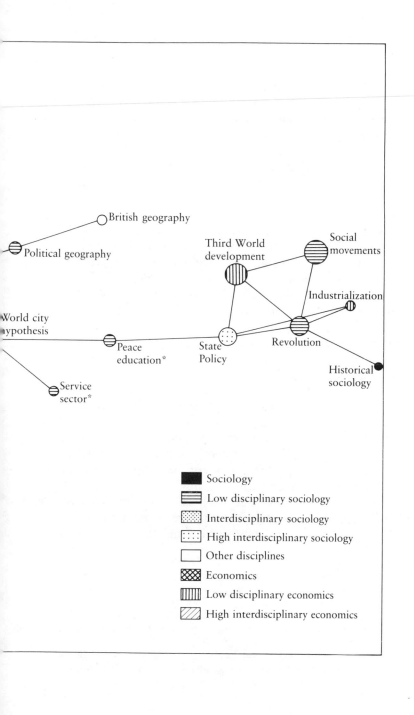

British geography

Political geography

Third World
development

Social
movements

Industrialization

World city
hypothesis

Peace
education*

State
Policy

Revolution

Historical
sociology

Service
sector*

◼ Sociology
▤ Low disciplinary sociology
▦ Interdisciplinary sociology
⬚ High interdisciplinary sociology
☐ Other disciplines
▨ Economics
▥ Low disciplinary economics
▧ High interdisciplinary economics

It is also interesting to examine the sources of knowledge within the clusters, as an indication of whether or not economics is itself generating the knowledge its practitioners cite. In the specialty shown in Figure 4 and in corporate governance (not shown), clusters were more closely identified with economics on the basis of the references co-cited in the cluster than on the basis of the references that co-cited them (cf. Table 6). Using the *cited* references, over three-quarters of the clusters were identified with economics whereas, using the *citing* references, the clusters were more likely to be identified as low disciplinary or interdisciplinary economics. As we will discuss below, this suggests that economics exports knowledge to other fields but imports relatively little.

In comparison with economics, the disciplinary structure of sociology was much more diffuse. It lacked a sizable core that incorporated a number of major subfields. Instead, sociology shared its subject matter with several other disciplines, as indicated by the numbers of clusters entirely identified with the other disciplines and applied fields, such as economics, geography, peace science, and gerontology.

The discipline consisted of three large specialties, each containing seven to ten clusters (see Figs. 5 and 6), three dyads, and one four-group cluster. There were also twenty-seven isolates, some of which were linked to clusters affiliated with other disciplines.[13]

Regardless of whether one looks at the disciplinary affiliations of the clusters from the point of view of the "producers of knowledge" (those who are cited in the clusters) or the users of knowledge (those who cite the references in the clusters), the majority of the clusters were classified as low disciplinary or interdisciplinary sociology (see Table 6). In terms of citing references, none of the clusters in the two largest specialties were identified with sociology (i.e., over two-thirds of citing references from sociology journals). The majority were classified as interdisciplinary sociology, meaning that sociology comprised less than a third of the citing references. In terms of references that

13. The third specialty, criminology, is not shown. The three dyads were: religious commitment; family taxation–marital dissolution; and premarital sex (demography). The quadruple was British sociology of science. The following isolates were linked to clusters in other disciplines: sexual aggression; Mexican immigration; corporate interlocks; occupational prestige; social psychology; gender; adolescent pregnancy; and economic sociology. The remaining isolates were: sociology of action; sociology of computers; hazards model (demography); mortality differences (demography); racial prejudice; rural deprivation; migration; sexual differences in addict careers; community dynamics; political values and generational change; social class inequalities in education; criminal punishment; fertility transition (demography); and underground economies.

Table 6. Disciplinary Classification of Clusters in Major Specialties of Economics
and Sociology, 1987[a]

A. Percentage of Clusters Identified as Economics in Two Major Economics Specialties

| | Identified as economics on the basis of | | |
	Citing references %	Cited references %	Total N
Figure 4	28	76	33
Corporate governance[b]	30	70	10

B. Percentage of Clusters Identified as Sociology and Economics in Two Major
Sociology Specialties

| | Identified as sociology on the basis of | | Identified as economics on the basis of | | |
	Citing references %	Cited references %	Citing references %	Cited references %	Total N
Figure 5	0	18	0	18	39
Figure 6	0	25	0	46	28

[a]Using the disciplinary affiliation of the journal in which the reference appeared.
[b]Not shown.

were cited in these clusters, about one-fifth of the clusters were identified with sociology but as many or more were identified with economics (18 percent and 46 percent respectively; see Table 6). By contrast, over three-quarters of the clusters in the largest economics
specialty (Fig. 4) were classified as economics on the basis of the references cited in those clusters (see Table 6). These statistics suggest
that it would be erroneous to consider the two largest specialties in
sociology as core fields in that discipline.

In the third specialty (not shown), which represented criminology,
this pattern was reversed, with four out of the seven fields being categorized as low disciplinary sociology (one-third to two-thirds of the
citing references were to sociology) on the basis of the citing references. However, criminology, being an applied field, does not qualify
as a core field in the discipline. There were, however, no alternative
candidates.

The largest sociology specialty (see Fig. 5) contained two separate
groups of clusters, one dealing with class issues from a Marxist perspective and the other dealing with social movements, industrialization, and revolution from the same perspective. These two fields were

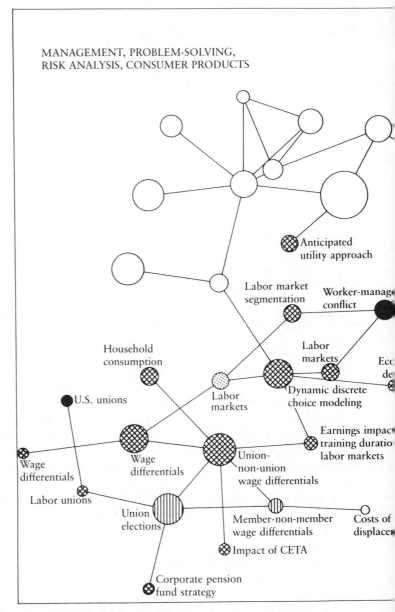

Fig. 6. Major Specialties in Sociology, 1987, Part II.
Disciplinary affiliation of clusters is based on disciplinary affiliation of journals in which the references *cited* in the clusters appeared. Distances between the clusters were determined by multidimensional scaling, using citing references.

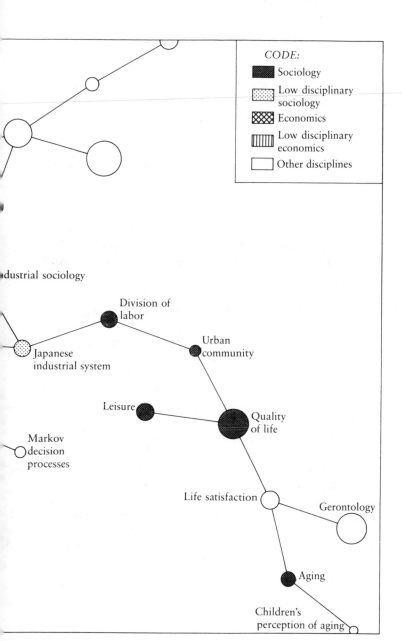

industrial sociology

Division of labor

Urban community

Japanese industrial system

Leisure

Quality of life

Markov decision processes

Life satisfaction

Gerontology

Aging

Children's perception of aging

linked by clusters belonging to other disciplines, including geography and peace science.

The second largest sociological specialty dealt with labor markets, industrial sociology, and the division of labor (see Fig. 6). On one side, it was linked to a set of economics clusters dealing with labor unions and wage differentials among different categories of workers. On the other side, it merged with a set of clusters on leisure, the quality of life, and aging. In two of the latter, the cited materials were from the sociological literature but the majority of the citing materials were not.

The remaining clusters were of two types. One type consisted of isolates, dyads, or triads that represented entire fields, such as the sociology of computers, racial prejudice, community dynamics, the sociology of Jewry, the sociology of religion, and the sociology of language. Some of these clusters were so small as to be below the cutoff point of 25 percent representation of sociological references among the cited items (e.g., sociology of the professions, sociology of education, and American sociology of science). Even methodological subjects such as log-linear models were represented only in clusters in which the sociological component was less than 25 percent. Other clusters were linked to clusters outside sociology. In other words, these sociology clusters were embedded in specialties that included clusters from other disciplines. Much of what appeared to be sociology of health care, sociology of marriage, sociology of sexual behavior, social psychology, gender, and methodology was nested in other fields.

As suggested by these data, the situation of sociology today represents a distinct contrast to sociology in the early seventies. In the earlier period, sociology had a well-defined core consisting of quantitatively oriented fields, such as social mobility, methodology, demography, and the family. In 1987, the study of social classes and class mobility was no longer linked to methodology and formal theory. Instead, it was linked to Marxian economics, studies of political ideology, and the role of the state, and, more distantly, to European theorizing, in one direction, and the study of revolution, historical sociology, and economics in the other direction. Fields like demography and the study of the family were quite separate fields (see Fig. 1). It is significant that Figure 5 does not appear in Figure 1, but at that interdisciplinary level it is linked to another set of specialty clusters, representing the study of social problems and criminology (figure not shown). In Figure 6, the sociology clusters are concerned with issues related to work and leisure and form a bridge between the economics of labor unions, on the one hand, and gerontology, on the other.

Another curious finding from this study is that topics such as organizational theory and management and social psychology, both of which have traditionally been studied by sociologists, were also being pursued by sizable groups of researchers who were not sociologists and who apparently interacted very little with sociologists.

By contrast, economics retained its coherence, as indicated by the existence of a large core specialty and by the fact that a large proportion of the cited references in its clusters were identified with economics.

Interdisciplinary Relationships of Economics and Sociology: 1987

In contrast to the situation in 1972–74, when there were minimal links between the two disciplines, the extent to which economics and sociology were linked at the specialty level in the 1987 data was striking. As we have seen, economics specialties were linked to sociology specialties, including four clusters dealing with Marxist issues (see Fig. 5) and several clusters dealing with wage differentials among union and non-union workers (see Fig. 6). In Figure 6, a chain of sociology clusters linked economics and gerontology. Economics clusters were also associated with sociology specialties such as criminology and demographic aspects of migration. In Figure 5, several disciplines, including economics and sociology, were linked in such a way that no specific area of the diagram was associated with a single discipline.

However, it was clear that sociology was making more use of economics than vice versa. Thirty-eight percent of the sociology clusters cited references from economics while only 6 percent of the economics clusters cited sociology references.

Finally, it appears that while economics frequently exports knowledge, as indicated by the disciplinary affiliations of the citing references, it is less likely to import it. This is shown by the fact that clusters identified with economics, low disciplinary economics, and interdisciplinary economics on the basis of *citing* references are much more likely to be identified with economics on the basis of *cited* references (see Table 7). For example, among clusters that are classified as interdisciplinary economics on the basis of the references that cite the cluster (the users of knowledge), 74 percent are classified as economics on the basis of the references that are cited in the cluster (the producers of knowledge). In other words, economics mainly exports knowledge and does so as part of a package that is almost entirely

Table 7.   Cluster Classification of Sociology and Economics, 1987: Comparison of
Disciplinary Affiliations of Clusters Based on Citing and Cited References

Clusters identified by citing references:	*Percentage of clusters identified as sociology on the basis of cited references*
	(%)
Sociology	0
Low disciplinary sociology	52
Interdisciplinary sociology	30
Total (N)	22

Clusters identified by citing references:	*Percentage of clusters identified as economics on the basis of cited references*
	(%)
Economics	100
Low disciplinary economics	87
Interdisciplinary economics	74
Total (N)	84

comprised of economics. By contrast, sociology both imports and exports knowledge. When it exports knowledge, it is more likely to be associated with material from other disciplines. Among the clusters defined as low disciplinary sociology on the basis of the citing references, only 52 percent are defined as sociology on the basis of the cited references. Among clusters defined as interdisciplinary sociology on the basis of the citing references, only 30 percent were defined as sociology on the basis of the cited references.

It is useful to compare this view of sociology with the portrait of sociology that emerges from the most recent volume of reviews of the field, the new *Handbook of Sociology* (Smelser 1988).[14] As is generally the case with books of this kind, the *Handbook* suggests more coherence than appears to exist in research fields that are constituted on the basis of recent citations. Many *Handbook* chapters were represented in the citation analysis by only one or two clusters (e.g., re-

14. The Smelser volume reviews the following fields: the new theoretical movement; social structure; data collection; causal inference; inequality and labor processes; race and ethnicity; sociology of age; gender and sex roles; jobs and work; environments and organizations; political sociology; trends in family sociology; sociology of education; sociology of religion; sociology of science; medical sociology; mass media institutions; spatial processes; deviance and social control; social movements; and development and the world economy.

ligion, social movements, race, and ethnicity), and, in some cases, were too small to meet our cutoff criterion for inclusion in the field (e.g., American sociology of science). Others, as we have seen, were enmeshed in the literatures of other fields (e.g., health care, marriage, sexual behavior, methodology, and gender). Still other specialties did not appear on the basis of the citation data to be closely related to the sociology literature (e.g., medical sociology, mass media, organizations, and theory, other than Marxist). There is little in the Smelser volume to suggest that sociology and economics are currently sharing a number of research sites (see above). There is also little that suggests the degree of prominence that Marxist perspectives assume in the citation data, where Marxism permeates the study of a number of key areas. The lack of consensus in the discipline as a whole is indicated by the torrent of critical commentary devoted to the volume in a special symposium in *Contemporary Sociology* (Calhoun and Land 1989).

Conclusion

Three major sets of findings emerge from this analysis. First, compared to economics, the number of research areas identified with sociology between 1972 and 1987 shows a conspicuous lack of growth. This may partly be explained by the funding crisis that affected all social sciences, and particularly sociology, under the Reagan administration in the early eighties (Zuiches 1984). This crisis was more serious for sociology than for economics, since sociologists generally collect their data, usually at considerable cost, while economists are able to rely on statistics gathered by national and local governments (Morgan 1988). It is likely that sociologists have not been able to explore fully the implications of existing knowledge because of lack of funds.

Second, in the aging of the respective sources in the literatures of the two fields, sociology actually resembles economics. In the early seventies, the sociology and economics literatures were building on references that were, on the average, between seven and nine years old. Both fields are now building on cited references that date on the average from the early or middle seventies and that were thus between twelve and fourteen years old in 1987 (the date of the second set of data). One explanation may be that the average sociologist and economist is older than was the case in the early seventies. Older researchers may be more likely to cite older materials and less likely to keep up with new literature or, if they do, less likely to cite it. Alternatively, lacking resources to do new studies that constitute a substantial advance over earlier studies, researchers in both disciplines continue to cite older works.

A third set of findings concerns the virtual disappearance of core areas in sociology and its increasing embeddedness in the literatures of other disciplines, including economics, a discipline with which sociology had virtually no ties in the early seventies. These results might conceivably be an artifact of the use of a different approach for producing the relationships between the co-citation clusters, but the fact that economics retains its core while sociology does not argues against this interpretation.

Hargens (1991) argues that the lack of concentration of the literature in sociology is due in part to the relatively small number of articles published by high visibility journals like the *American Sociological Review* and the *American Journal of Sociology*. Unlike the *American Economic Review*, which publishes more than twice as many articles per year as the *ASR*, the latter is not representative of the wide range of research published in the discipline and, consequently, does not function as a focal point for the field.

While ideas from sociology are increasingly being incorporated in a wide range of fields (including journalism), at the same time it seems to be losing a clearcut identity based on the study of a number of well-defined subject areas. The enormous advances in sociological methods that have been made in recent years have not been matched in theory. New theoretical approaches are influential in specific fields but do not provide a unified perspective for the discipline as a whole.

An important task for general theory is that of creating ways of conceptualizing society as a whole that can provide a reference point for researchers in a wide variety of sociological specialties. In the past, the major sociological theorists performed this task of locating metaphors that could be used to exemplify the major issues of their time. Marx, for example, characterized the industrializing societies in the nineteenth century in terms of the conflicts between exploited workers and management who controlled the means of production. At the beginning of the twentieth century, Durkheim used a metaphor that he obtained from studying primitive societies, namely, the idea that all societies are integrated in terms of varying levels of commitment to dominant norms and values. Parsons also conceptualized society in terms of social integration but used the analogy to a biological organism as his metaphor. Society, like a biological organism, was a system whose elements responded to crisis by restoring their equilibrium. These conceptualizations of society were shared by large numbers of

sociologists for several generations. Today, these ideas are not adequate to the task of symbolizing the complexities of postindustrial
societies with their increasingly global cultures that are saturated with
information and images.

A major problem with finding new metaphors is the fact that sociological theory and research, both on the level of general theory and in
the various research specialties, have tended to put more emphasis
upon social structure than culture. In contemporary societies, since
the implementation of television and computers on a wide scale, cultural variables have exerted an increasing influence on economic and
political structures. However, fields within sociology that are concerned with cultural institutions, such as science, religion, and the
mass media, have not come up with new models of the interface between culture and social structure that are relevant to the discipline as
a whole.

Clearly, economics has followed a different trajectory from sociology, which has its own advantages and disadvantages. It has continued
to refine a theoretical outlook that was developed in the nineteenth
century and has not incorporated perspectives from other disciplines
(Hirsch et al. 1987). Unlike sociology, economics is a deductive science; this tends to discourage the collection of empirical data that
might challenge assumptions based on theory. Consequently, while
economics is highly coherent, observers argue that it has remained
static and unresponsive to social change, in spite of a very substantial
increase in new research areas (see Table 1). In the seventies and
eighties, economics researchers concentrated so heavily on the construction of elegant mathematical models in the absence of empirical
data (Morgan 1988)[15] that some authors claimed it was losing touch
with the realities of contemporary economies. According to Hirsch et
al. (1987:320), "economists pay a heavy price for the very simplicity
and elegance of their models: empirical ignorance, misunderstanding,
and, relatedly, unrealistic and bizarre policy recommendations."
Rather, Hirsch et al. (1987:332–33) argue that "sociology's very lack
of definition . . . its theoretical cacophony . . . its perennial identity
crisis can be viewed as selected *advantages*."

However, without a substantial core to generate new knowledge,
the likelihood that the discipline will continue to influence other fields
in the social sciences seems slight. It is significant that economic theory

15. Morgan (1988) compared economics with four other disciplines: sociology, political science, chemistry, and physics. He found that economists were much more likely
to publish articles based on mathematical models without any data in major disciplinary
journals than were members of the other disciplines.

is currently influencing sociological research but not vice versa. Sociology's lack of identity may also affect recruitment: students come to sociology for personal reasons rather than because of the powerful attraction of sociological theories. They are also likely to leave without degrees because the realities of the discipline do not match their personal agendas. There has been a steady decline in all types of degrees conferred in sociology (B.A., M.A., and Ph.D.) since the mid-seventies (Berger 1989; Waller 1989), while degrees in economics have continued to increase (Waller 1989).

Alternatively, the fact that sociologists exchange knowledge as much with their peers in other fields as with fellow sociologists may be an indication that sociologists are at the vanguard of a new style of organization of social science knowledge. The increasing interdisciplinarity of some aspects of the social sciences would seem to call into question the present organization of academia by discipline, a mode of organization that was created in the nineteenth century when the conditions within these fields were entirely different. University departments at present are organized around substantive issues and methods, in spite of the fact that there is considerable overlap among disciplines. The highly segmented nature of university departments, which is reflected in the requirements they impose on students pursuing doctoral degrees, is not at all isomorphic with the configuration of links between academic disciplines (see Fig. 1). Research specialties in each discipline are not confined to specific regions of this map. Instead, the high level of intermingling of specialties from different disciplines suggests that, unlike the situation that prevails when these disciplines are taught, researchers from these fields do not respect each other's territories. If this scenario were to predominate in the future, the social science *discipline* would be replaced by the *social sciences*, which would resemble the biological sciences in their lack of respect for disciplinary boundaries and their propensity to generate new interdisciplinary fields. In the past fifty years, spurred on by enormous amounts of federal research funds, the biomedical sciences have proliferated into a multitude of new fields.

Finally, it is possible that sociology itself is actually not one discipline but many. This is suggested by the fact that the most exciting and testable new theories are associated with particular specialties rather than with the discipline as a whole. Unfortunately, sociology is not now large enough to sustain so much diversity. If it were to subdivide along the lines of the biomedical sciences, each new field would be too small to be viable as a separate discipline. However, in the future, should it manage to attract a higher level of funding for research, this may be the direction in which the discipline will move. If the discipline was able to expand substantially in terms of numbers of researchers and publications and then to subdivide into several distinct subdisciplines, each one would have a more coherent image in terms of theory, substance, and method than now exists in sociology as a whole.

References

Baughmann, J. C. 1974. "A Structural Analysis of the Literature of Sociology." *Library Quarterly* 44:293–309.

Ben-David, J. 1973. "The State of Sociological Theory and the Sociological Community: A Review Article." *Comparative Studies in Society and History* 15:448–72.

Berger, J. 1989. "Sociology's Long Decade in the Wilderness." *New York Times* May 22: E6.

Calhoun, C. J., and K. C. Land. 1989. "Symposium: Smelser's Handbook: An Assessment." *Contemporary Sociology* 18:475–513.

Coleman, J. 1986. "Social Theory, Social Research, and a Theory of Action." *American Journal of Sociology* 91:1309–35.

Collins, R. 1986. "Is 1980's Sociology in the Doldrums?" *American Journal of Sociology* 91:1336–55.

Diamond, A. M., Jr. 1989. "The Core Journals of Economics." *Current Contents (Social and Behavioral Sciences)* 1 (January 2):4–11.

Garfield, E. 1977. "On the Literature of the Social Sciences and the Usage and Effectiveness of the *Social Sciences Citation Index.*" In *Essays of an Information Scientist*, Vol. 2. 550–55. Philadelphia, Pa.: Institute for Scientific Information.

Griffith, B. D., et al. 1974. "The Structure of Scientific Literatures. II. Toward a Macro- and Microstructure for Science." *Science Studies*, 4:339–65.

Griffith, B. D., and H. Small. 1976. "The Structure of the Social and Behavioral Sciences' Literature." *Proceedings of the First International Conference on Social Studies of Science*, Nov. 4–6.

Hargens, L. L. 1991. "Impressions and Misimpressions about Sociology Journals." *Contemporary Sociology* 20:343–49.

Hirsch, P., et al. 1987. "'Dirty Hands' versus 'Clean Models.'" *Theory and Society* 16:317–36.

Kuhn, T. 1970. *The Structure of Scientific Revolutions.* 2d ed. Chicago: University of Chicago Press.

Morgan, T. 1988. "Theory versus Empiricism in Academic Economics: Update and Comparisons." *Journal of Economic Perspectives* 2:159–64.

Mullins, N. C. 1973. *Theory and Theory Groups in Contemporary American Sociology.* New York: Harper and Row.

Mullins, N. C., et al. 1977. "The Group Structure of Co-citation Clusters: A Comparative Study." *American Sociological Review* 42:552–62.

Oberschall, T. 1972. "The Institutionalization of American Sociology." In *The Establishment of Empirical Sociology: Studies in Continuity, Discontinuity, and Institutionalization,* ed. T. Oberschall, 187–251. New York: Harper and Row.

Pantin, C. F. A. 1968. *The Relations Between the Sciences.* Cambridge: Cambridge University Press.

Price, D. J. de Solla. 1970. "Citation Measures of Hard Science, Soft Science, Technology and Nonscience." In *Communication Among Scientists and Engineers,* ed. C. E. Nelson and D. Pollock, 3–22. Lexington, Mass.: D. C. Heath.

Sichel, B., and W. Sichel. 1986. *Economic Journals and Serials: An Analytic Guide.* New York: Greenwood.

Small, H. G. 1976. "Structural Dynamics of Scientific Literature." *International Classification* 3:67–74.

———. 1977. "A Co-citation Model of a Scientific Specialty: A Longitudinal Study of Collagen Research." *Social Studies of Science,* 7:139–66.

———. 1978. "Cited Documents as Concept Symbols." *Social Studies of Science* 8:327–40.

Small, H. G., and D. Crane. 1979. "Specialties and Disciplines in Science and Social Science: An Examination of Their Structure Using Citation Indexes." *Scientometrics* 1: 445–61.

Small, H., and E. Garfield. 1985. "The Geography of Science: Disciplines and National Mappings." *Journal of Information Science* 11:147–59.

Small, H. G., and B. C. Griffith. 1974. "The Structure of Scientific Literatures. I. Identifying and Graphing Specialties." *Science Studies* 4:17–40.

Smelser, N., ed. 1988. *Handbook of Sociology.* Newbury Park, Calif.: Sage.

Sullivan, D., et al. 1977. "Co-citation Analyses of Science: An Evaluation." *Social Studies of Science* 7:223–40.

Turner, J. H., and S. Turner. 1990. *The Impossible Science: An Institutional Analysis of American Sociology.* Newbury Park, Calif.: Sage.

Waller, D. 1989. "Size, Resource Concentration, and Mutual Dependence in U.S. Economics and Sociology: An Examination of an Aspect of the Organizational-Technological Model of Knowledge Production." Unpub. University of California at Riverside.

Wepsiec, J. 1983. *Sociology: An International Bibliography of Serial Publications: 1880–1980.* London: Mansell Publishing.

Whitley, R. 1976. "Umbrella and Polytheistic Scientific Disciplines and Their Elites." *Social Studies of Science* 6:471–98.

Zuiches, J. J. 1984. "The Organization and Funding of Social Sciences at the National Science Foundation." *Sociological Inquiry* 54:188–210.

6

Universities without Contract Research

SAMUEL Z. KLAUSNER

Universities Should Not Contract for Research: A Position Statement

Universities should neither seek nor accept research contracts; not for engineering research, nor for research in medicine, the social sciences, nor any other area. "Contract" (a purchase of services on a problem set by a sponsor) is the key term. "Grants" (a gift to a researcher to investigate a, usually, disciplinary problem) are another matter. Universities should assist in establishing research corporations. These corporations could contract for research with foundations, the government, and industry. University representatives might control the corporate board. University faculty and students might be prominent among its researchers.

This paper argues for a managerial separation between a university's academic activity and research contracting. The university should accept fiscal responsibility for "boutique" research, such as relatively small grants for individual or group efforts. However, the stewardship of large-scale research diverts academic programs. Academic management is not always efficient for managing research. Furthermore, sponsorship, the exercise of patronage, is the exercise of power, whether in the arts, in the sciences, or in politics. University recipients of external funds, in turn, become patrons within the academy who then delegate and appropriate power at level after level in the university hierarchy. We have not only academic kings but also princes, dukes, and just plain influential squires. Externally sponsored loci of empowerment have an influence, for good or bad, on university life.

The intent of this organizational recommendation is to encourage, not discourage, faculty research, to improve the climate for research, and to free the university for its academic mission.

Institutional separation of knowledge production for immediate social needs—the contract research function—and responsibility for the
training of new cadres and the search for fundamental knowledge—
the academic function—is overdue. This argument rests less on the
cultural tension between these functions than on the distinction between the institutional arrangements required for the production of
practical knowledge and the arrangements for the socializing of citizens, the university's teaching mission. Such divided labor is a normal
accompaniment of increasingly intense societal activity. As Durkheim
argued nearly a century ago, the "organic solidarity" among specialized institutions perfects the achievements of each.

The internal blurring of the distinctions between the research and
teaching functions of the university reflects the external blurring of
the distinctions between the university and governmental, industrial,
and foundational research sponsors; that is, between the university,
on the one hand, and the polity and economy, on the other. Nowhere
is this more significant than in the social sciences, whose task it is to
study the polity and the economy, not to merge with them.

Each social institution contributes in its own unique way to the
national welfare. Each has its own problems and needs. The subjection of the university to the needs of the polity distorts the university.
Research sponsors wield a big stick, a stick given to them by the research community in its hunger for support. As Ruscio (1984:353)
says, "The fate of academic science is in the hands of institutions outside the university, especially government ... [S]cientists ... find
themselves caught between independence and dependence, between
the desire to maintain a critical distance from their benefactors and
the need to draw on their benefactors' largesse." What does the sponsor want from the university that is so frightful? Do we not have an
interinstitutional contract, freely entered into by two mature and
knowledgeable parties?

Philosophical agreement on the significance of separating teaching
and research activities will, in part, be conditioned by one's understanding of the university's role in society. I, for example, would dig a
moat between the academy, on the one side, and the economy and
polity, on the other. The university might well develop more "useful"
as well as better "theoretical" knowledge for society were it more
insulated from the immediate interests of government. Those who prefer that a university be a community of free scholars, pursuing knowledge for its inherent cultural value and, like a religious institution,
standing outside the material structures of society, tasked (to use a

current neologism) to critique the norms and values of the society, should be pleased with a renewed separation. Such independence would permit the critique of knowledge implicit in economic and political action, a less immediate but more profound national service. By contrast, those who assign to the university a mission contributing directly to the political and economic welfare of the nation will resist the institutional insulation as isolation. They probably do not resent the strong shaping (it is always shaped to some extent) of their university by the economy and polity, and, perhaps, by religion.

In practice, the separation of teaching and contract research is an American problem. The Soviet Union has excluded the insulation of the academy from the polity on ideological grounds. Religious societies, similarly, reject separation. Smaller nations, especially developing nations, need the immediate contributions of all of their intellectuals for their development. Only an affluent people may encourage a search for knowledge that is not immediately utilitarian. Such a people has a global responsibility to do so.

The American government expects, with a clear conscience, to call the tune for universities. The university is a citizen, and it is responsible for performing the role government officials may allocate to it. Prager (1984:1056), a physiologist, speaking as a member of the White House Office of Science and Technology declares, "University research and training are integral to constructing an enterprise that is responsive to the needs of the country in terms of human well-being, national security, economic stability and industrial and commercial competitiveness." This rhetoric of laudable goals echoes on the campus as arrogance or as call to duty, depending on faculty members' ideology.

Donchin (1985), describing the Forum on Research Management, a group assembled to coordinate and facilitate government sponsorship of university research, explains the "conflict between government and universities" as a matter of scientists working with a "support model" in which the funding agencies select researchers according to scientific criteria, while government operates with a "procurement model" implying no obligation toward basic research. The latter means the federal government is in the business of acquiring research results.

The National Science Foundation was established in Congress during the late 1940s precisely as a vehicle for government funding of basic research, to meet long range social needs. Over the years the Foundation has been drawn increasingly toward applied research on national problems. Social research in the NSF has been directed into those styles of research that appear "scientific" as well as "useful" to its natural science leadership (Klausner 1986).

The Economic and Social Research Council in Great Britain, described by Posner (1986), treats other than research activities of the universities as ancillary. The Centre National de la Recherche Scientifique, the Deutsche Forschungsgemeinschaft, and the Max Planck Gesellschaft take a similar approach to the university.

Rosenzweig (1982), writing on the research universities and their patrons, holds that many scientists and university officers exempt government-university relationships from the ordinary rules of democratic politics. Government cannot be a true partner when the government is at one and the same time a patron, adversary, buyer, and regulator.

Of the roughly twenty-five hundred institutions of higher learning in the United States, perhaps not more than a hundred are engaged significantly in research contracting. These are among the "research universities." Examples in this paper are drawn from a variety of fields, including sociology. Since most of the issues are not discipline-specific, special problems of the social sciences will be mentioned, *pari passu.*

The Evolution of the Research University

Roger L. Geiger's (1986) history of the development of the research university prior to the Second World War is an excellent guide. Research universities emerged from the academic flock in the late nineteenth century. In the lead were old private schools such as Columbia, Harvard, and the University of Pennsylvania and large public institutions such as the University of Illinois, Michigan, and California. The newer universities, such as the Massachusetts Institute of Technology (MIT), Johns Hopkins, and Stanford, were, perhaps, even bolder in their pursuit of sponsored research. Research sponsored by private patrons and foundations was nurtured by all of these schools long before the days of contracting when research would promise a product for a payment.

The Morrill Act of 1862, with its land-grant funds, encouraged colleges to add utilitarian studies, such as engineering, to their classical programs. The elective system assured a place for such utilitarian activities in the curriculum. Eventually, students were to be accepted without preparation in classical languages. Johns Hopkins, founded on a German university model, established graduate education in research as a dominant form of vocational preparation.

Research university leadership took a leaf from the books of corporate businessmen. They became academic empire builders. Trustees, as potential contributors, were recruited from the corporate world and took an active part in the governance of the research universities. Presidents and trustees talked of running these schools in a businesslike fashion. The numbers of administrative officers grew. Deans and their administrative staffs appeared to mediate between faculty and the president or the provost or the rector, whichever the case might be. Faculty resented the loss of their authority to these administrative specialists.

Research opportunities were used to compete for the small pool of research professors. By the last decade of the nineteenth century, Columbia instituted sabbaticals to facilitate professorial research and improve its competitive recruiting position. The research faculty's fame attracted middle-class students who sought professional education or training in applied science.

The faculty, in becoming more professionalized, acted less and less as English dons, engaging students at dinner and into the night, and became more and more absorbed in their research. Student social systems, each with its mini culture and exclusiveness, emerged around residential arrangements: Harvard "houses," Yale "colleges," and eating clubs at Princeton. Intercollegiate athletics became more central to university life and a meeting point for student and alumni interests.

Campus class stratification was also apparent in the segregation of women students. Further, restrictions on Jewish admissions in schools such as Harvard, Yale, and Columbia were supported by the undergraduate students, alumni, and top administrators, while generally rejected by the new, and not numerous, research faculty.

At the turn of the century, tuition still made up the bulk of university income (63 percent at the University of Pennsylvania and 90 percent at MIT). The now administratively distinct undergraduate colleges provided most of the tuition income. They were also a future source of alumni contributions and political support. Yale, Harvard, and Princeton were among the first to launch appeals for alumni support. Summer sessions increased the efficiency of facilities use and added to tuition income. Philanthropic contributions from individual patrons and from newly emerging foundations, such as John D. Rockefeller's General Education Board, paid for research facilities. State universities were subsidized by appropriations from the state legislatures.

Research in Dedicated Institutes: The Competition

Government and industry, early on, did not see the research universities as a resource. The federal government conducted its research through agencies such as the Geodetic Survey, the Division of Entomology, the Army Medical Services, the Bureau of the Census, the Bureau of Mines, and so forth. The National Academy of Science, and its associated National Research Council, coordinated the intelligence of researchers in and out of government. Early in this century, some larger foundations established independent research facilities, such as the Rockefeller Institute for Medical Research and the Carnegie Institute of Washington's Mount Wilson Observatory. The Brookings Institution, formed in 1927 from the National Bureau of Economic Research and the Institute for Government Research, and similar independent research institutes, competed with universities for the allegiance of economists. It offered them a research setting away from the training of neophyte students. Industries, such as General Electric (1900), DuPont (1902), and Eastman Kodak (1912), had already built their own laboratories.

Research universities competed with each other and with non-research campuses, as well as with government, industry, and foundation-sponsored laboratories. To attract and keep faculty, research universities reduced teaching loads to six or eight hours a week compared to the twelve to sixteen hours in the nonresearch schools. A reduction in the student-teacher ratio attracted students. Graduate students, aiming for a research career, provided labor for research projects.

The freestanding nonprofit research institute, yet another competitor for the research dollar, gained ground outside of the universities after the Second World War (Orlans 1972). Government was among the sponsors of such research and development centers. RAND was initiated, under an Air Force contract to McDonnell Douglas, and soon became, oxymoron that it is, an independent "captive" institute, obliged to work for a single agency, the Air Force. Eventually, RAND management persuaded its sponsor to allow it to accept contract work from others up to roughly 20 percent of its total volume of business. Some, such as Battelle, established as nonprofits, became public for-profit corporations.

The government also sponsored extramural institutes in cooperation with university consortia. The Associated Universities, Inc., founded in 1946, conducted Brookhaven National Laboratories. Participating were Columbia, Cornell, Harvard, Johns Hopkins, MIT,

Princeton, Pennsylvania, Rochester, and Yale. For practical purposes, Brookhaven served the needs of the Atomic Energy Commission. The Universities Research Association formed in 1965 in conjunction with both the Atomic Energy Commission and the National Aeronautics and Space Administration (NASA) was probably one of the largest of the university consortia. Its programs were interdisciplinary and problem centered. Through these consortia, the universities became "captive" to government sponsorship. This meant that they were subject to agency definitions of research needs. A few faculty were both beneficiaries and agency research advisors.

Early University Research Sponsors: The Paradigm of a Joint Endeavor

The Government as Sponsor

Rosenzweig (1982) estimated that in 1940 the total available from the government for university research was $31 million, an amount that grew to over $3 billion by 1979. From the outset, government interest was utilitarian.

The Social Science Research Council, established in 1924, helped university-affiliated social scientists stake out a university position in this competition with the independent and government institutes. With the support of Herbert Hoover, the American Association of University Professors (AAUP) encouraged universities to place their research institutes at the service of government agencies. Foundation efforts sometimes paved the way for government support of university-based research. The Laura Spelman Rockefeller Memorial Foundation, for example, promoted university social science institutes (see Bulmer, this volume, chap. 9).

Meeting the competition of dedicated research facilities required cultural adjustments. Natural science laboratories in research universities increasingly turned to utilitarian work. Social science laboratories worked towards a "social technology" for a planned society that could assure the material welfare of Americans.

The Rockefeller Foundation's support of urban social studies at the University of Chicago established the trademark of the Chicago school of sociology. Chicago's social scientists were a prominent presence in Washington. Charles E. Merriam and William F. Ogburn, among others, led the Hoover-sponsored research published as *Recent Social Trends*, and they continued as savants for the Roosevelt New Deal. As cultural descendants of social workers and clergy, these Chicago professors had a strong commitment to social welfare. Throughout the Second World War and afterward, they advocated that each government agency have its own inhouse social scientists who would be, perhaps (to stretch an idea a bit), its spiritual guides. The social sciences would lead in social reconstruction (see Buxton and Turner, this volume, chap. 11).

By contrast, the Rockefeller attempt to bring Yale into the world of applied social research by establishing its Institute of Human Relations failed. Tension between the Foundation's interest in improving the welfare of mankind and the university's pursuit of knowledge for its own sake was not resolved. Yale was in but not of New Haven. It was simply not interested in community service. Nonetheless, the pull of patriotism in the Second World War committed Yale to the Human Relations Area Files project.

The Roosevelt administration was more utilitarian in its approach to research than was the Hoover administration. Projects were justified in terms of job creation, rarely in terms of the needs of science. Social scientists in Washington gave way to natural scientists. The latter dominated the National Academy of Science and the National Resources Committee, groups that advised government on the support of university science.

The models of government contracting for research at the university, set in the prewar years, gelled as the level of support achieved a critical mass during the war. The 1943–44 contracts of the Office of Scientific Research and Development would triple the level of all prewar scientific research. Social scientists were honing new methods, if not new institutional arrangements, within the Office of Strategic Services. The four volume report *The American Soldier* demonstrated the power of large-scale surveys. Psychological testing for any personnel classification, introduced by Yerkes during the First World War, was continued in WWII, especially in the Army Air Corps flight crew selection. "Large scale" and "large budget" were the words as the wartime scholars returned to their universities.

European academics were also conducting research for government. Soviet faculty served in various specialized institutes outside of the universities. In the Netherlands and in France, the bulk of contract research has been accomplished in government laboratories and independent institutes. In Britain, defense and other government research has tended to be conducted in government laboratories. The British Advisory Council in its 1956–57 annual report advised the universities to avoid government contracts. The pressure to be utilitarian, the council warned, could hamper the free pursuit of knowledge.

The National Science Foundation was chartered specifically to promote basic research in universities. Yet, within the first decade of its existence, the 1950s, Congress insisted on policy-oriented efforts. An associate director of NSF charged that government interference in universities produces a "warping and distortion" of the educational pattern (Paul Klopsteg, foreword to Kidd 1959). He advised universities to seek uncommitted funds for their day-to-day operations and capital expenditures. His was a voice in the wilderness.

Foundations as Sponsors

Although foundations tended to prefer program support (i.e., funds not earmarked for specific projects) in the early days, the Rockefeller Foundation moved to project grants in the interwar period. This allowed the Foundation to focus its efforts on particularly promising areas and to select the specific faculty whose work they would support. Those professors who could negotiate with the Foundation were at an advantage. With professor-Foundation ties, the university became less of an academic actor in building its programs and more a management structure through which funds were funneled and, hopefully, stewarded. Harold J. Laski, who had been teaching in American universities during the midtwenties and was somewhat aghast at the role of foundations in university life, wrote in *Harper's* (1928) that he thought foundations would obtain domination over university life. Laski anticipated that the system would turn research into simple fact gathering and influence the advancement of the professor "who is active in 'putting goods into the shop window.'"

Following the Second World War, foundation grants were dwarfed by government funding. Good foundation policy meant seeking out areas neglected by government and industry. They found their niche in supporting specific academic programs, curricular innovation, conferences, and dissertation programs. The major foundations, Ford, Rockefeller, Russell Sage, Commonwealth, and others, maintained targeted social science efforts.

Industrial Sponsors

Industry was not far behind the foundations in its support of university research, especially of research in engineering and business schools. Industrial sponsorship of social science tended to be funneled through the business schools. Before 1935, an industrial research dollar was a dollar deducted from profits or reinvestment capital. Immediate commercial justification was needed. Even after 1935, when corporate gifts became tax deductible, stockholders wanted to serve their commercial interests. Universities evolved centers around a concern shared by several corporations, usually in a common problem area. The Wharton School Industrial Research Unit began offering analyses of labor-management relations in 1919. The Harvard Economic Service was established to forecast business conditions for private subscribers. MIT was probably more active than other universities in pursuing industrial research.

In the case of industrial research, even more than in the case of foundation- or government-sponsored research, the university was marketing a service. The basic research component of that service was fleeting. The universities were contributing to product development and, perhaps, some market testing. As in manufacturing, the Harvard forecast could be produced over and again using the same template. Such a repetitive service could and would eventually be provided by business on a for-profit basis.

Interestingly, it was industrial leaders, George Swope of General Electric and Frank Jewett of Bell Telephone, who slowed the trend at MIT toward industrial service and insisted on a basic research program. They brought in Karl T. Compton, a theoretical physicist, to boost basic research. Contract research at MIT was placed under an institute, the Division of Industrial Cooperation. That institute would deal with proprietary rights and with the commercialization of patents based on faculty research products. The new California Institute of Technology, resisting this constraint by its industrial customers, sought a range of patrons, and a number of them from the California business community gave small yearly gifts. The university, in this way, could control the researcher and lessen pressure toward immediate commercial exploitation.

In the four decades since the end of WWII, the university research paradigm has changed but little. Commercial sponsorship of university-based social research institutes flowered in these years. Several of the leaders had developed a taste for large-scale research through war service in the Office of Strategic Services. In 1948, the Institute for Social Research (ISR) at Michigan, with its component Institute for Survey Research and the Center for Group Dynamics, was formed. Now, in the mideighties, with four research institutes, 450 people, and a $15 million annual budget, ISR has maintained some degree of budgetary independence of the university. The university also keeps ISR at a distance. The Regents' bylaws provide that the institute will pose no financial burden on the general funds of the university. The institute will be wholly supported by grants and contracts. If the funds cease, no person not previously employed by the university will continue. Salary and service will terminate regardless of rank (Cannell and Kahn 1984:1257).

Columbia's Bureau of Applied Social Research operated under the university's contracting system but, never quite academically acceptable, it was denied its own tenured appointments. Paul F. Lazarsfeld, the leader of the effort at Columbia, was able to advance social research methodology through business patronage. The National Opinion Research Center at Chicago still competes with the for-profit groups in the social survey field. The Human Resources Research Organization (HumRRO) was established at George Washington University in 1951 and became an independent nonprofit organization in 1968 following student unrest over its army contract (Cannell and Kahn 1984:1269).

These research groups fit neatly into the business development point of view of research university administrators. They pursue contracts with government, commerce, and industry, and grants from foundations. They sustain the volume of business needed to justify electronic data tabulation equipment and to hold a technical support staff. Their projects meet the test of economic relevance.

Fundable Professors: The Faculty Adapts to Sponsorship

A university's drive to develop puts a premium on "fundable" faculty. In recruitment the funding track record becomes particularly relevant. Routinely, candidates for tenure present the personnel committees with a list of the grants and contracts they have been awarded. Candidates may even list the dollar amounts of the awards, testimony to their entrepreneurial and administrative acumen. The professional schools—engineering, medicine, and business—lead the way here, but arts and sciences faculties are not far behind. Honorific grants, such as a Guggenheim, attest to outside judgment of the academic quality of the candidates' work. The record of contract awards, however, does not leave the personnel committees the same evidence for assessing the academic worth of the projects.

Contract research is offered to the universities because that is where the researchers are concentrated and because, in earlier decades, universities had the capital to assure the viability of a large-scale project. Were the universities not to contract for research, some research professors would associate themselves with the independent nonprofit and for-profit institutes. If they did, university administrations might question their loyalty. Ruscio (1984) states a variant on Gresham's Law in which private interest drives out public interest in academe. The universities anticipate that professors may be drawn off into consulting. The limitation on outside work—the rule by which not more than one day a week of consulting is permitted—is both a benefit and a barrier to academic recruiting. It is a benefit because it permits professors in high demand to supplement their income and so reduce any incentive to leave the university. It is a barrier because it tells professors that outside work is a privilege that may be given, or taken away, by the administration. In practice, professors are not in violation by working for an outside sponsor during the winter break or over the summer. Under most plans, therefore, a third of the year may be legitimately invested outside of the university. This could increase professors' salaries by more than a third if their external rate is higher. Universities protect themselves against "disloyalty," or conflict of interest, by establishing a right of "first refusal." By this rule, a faculty member is required to offer a contract to the university before offering it to an outside corporation.

The existence of nonprofits large and solvent enough to accept responsibility for large projects, and which attract academic research talent, is a post–World War II phenomenon. Major for-profit organizations, such as Arthur D. Little and Booz Allen and Hamilton that were founded earlier but expanded significantly in the postwar years, have now entered the field. The largest of these have been engineering service firms. Some of them include a social science research division. The most productive academic talent has been slow to throw in their lot with these firms, partly because of the task-assignment authority to which they would have to submit. Those who make a career of full-time association with such institutes are often lost to academic research. This is one indirect impact of the competitive climate in universities.

The university struggle in this competition for talent is more often focused on the issue of authority rather than the diversion of academic talent. The terms of a 1982 contract between Washington University in St. Louis and Monsanto Company for $23.5 million for medical school research leading to "marketable biomedical discoveries" illustrates this. The terms included unlimited consultation to Monsanto by medical researchers, apparently waiving the limitation on "outside" consulting by defining it as "inside." Further, the researchers promise not to divulge commercially relevant information from Monsanto-sponsored studies. As Rule (1988:434) has stated, "higher education is treated as an 'infrastructure' for industrial development." Michael Shapiro (1983), professor of law at the University of Southern California, argues that the university has an incentive to hire people who can get patents that may be assigned to the university. He illustrates this with the $5 million contract between DuPont and Harvard to set up a laboratory for geneticist Philip Leder. DuPont was granted first rights to anything Leder produces.

Research contracting, though, has a direct political impact on university faculties. It bolsters the bargaining power of those who receive large contracts. Where research sponsorship was viewed in the early days as a means of faculty recruitment, the faculty member as an institute director now negotiates with the sponsor, who now chooses the kind of research to be accomplished, and with the administration to assure the manpower, the positions, and the physical facilities for conducting the research. This becomes a battle of the titans and one consequence is the proletarianization of the faculty. The contract research staff assumes an industrial employer/employee relationship with the university through the principal investigator. The administration, in asserting its control over the enterprise, strengthens the authority of the university bureaucracy. The faculty members, lacking the power of the institute director, nevertheless find themselves subject to the more enveloping administrative authority. The administration increasingly sets work and pay conditions without meaningful consultation. A faculty senate may emerge and the AAUP may enter the act, but the process moves ineluctably toward classic labor relations. At some point, most activist bargaining agents enter on behalf of the faculty and the status of employer/employee crystallizes in the negotiated labor contract.

Government and industrial contracts are sought, actively sought, by faculty who believe large-scale research to be fundamental to advance basic knowledge. The professor electing this career line enjoys team research and the responsibilities of administration. The line between such principal investigators and business entrepreneurs or corporate executives is quite thin. These individuals may, indeed, "commute" between academic and government or industrial positions.

In the physical sciences, the linear accelerators of nuclear physics and the wartime Manhattan project are examples of such "big science." In the social sciences, large-scale collections of social information have been considered necessary for testing basic propositions about society. Talcott Parsons, theoretician that he was, hoped for such data. He prepared a paper for the Social Science Research Council in support of the inclusion of the social sciences in the planned National Science Foundation. Parsons argued there for large-scale social data collection, a precursor of the effort to discover strategic social indicators for societal monitoring (Klausner and Lidz 1986). The Coleman report on American education exemplifies the large scale cross-sectional survey. The Income Maintenance Experiment, ultimately not carried out by a university group but by Mathematica, Inc., illustrates the type of social experiment government has in mind. Both of these were tests of social policy, though Coleman, good methodologist that he is, did rescue some of the data to advance methods of contextual analysis.

Social research bureaus in universities gather data from large population samples. Survey methodology has been at the core of the Michigan and Columbia efforts. The Wisconsin Institute for Poverty Research carved out a special niche defined by a social problem and the methods of microeconomics. These activities prepared students in quantitative analysis, probably drawing some talent from classical historical sociology, social theory, and work dependent on ethnographic methods. More to the point, the availability of funding for surveys has reduced the role of these other types of sociology in the education of sociologists, including the education of those who will specialize in quantitative analysis. By and large, the university social research center is dwarfed today by the independent nonprofits and for-profit companies in the survey field.

The large-scale survey field has become increasingly service oriented. As Lyons (1969) points out, government looks to social researchers for data in support of operations. Government sponsors know what questions to ask. Questions, or at least question areas, are polished by inhouse social scientists. The requested work is shaped by issues defined in legislation. Politically defined social problems, not problems of theory, guide the contract "performances." The contractor is directed to collect information that the operating personnel and Congress may use to evaluate programs, and evaluation is framed by the administrations of the operating agencies. The Request for Proposals (RFP) has become less and less a request for new ways of thinking and more and more a request for efficient ways of obtaining the expected data with assured statistical reliability. This is the prerogative of a purchaser of services but, in all likelihood, it deprives the Congress of perspectives that might be substantively, if not politically, helpful. Such research favors the technician who can select a sample, secure a good questionnaire return rate, and supervise efficient coding of the responses and data entry. The conceptually creative becomes a luxury.

Fundable Programs: The Curriculum Adapts to Sponsorship

"Fundable" professors work in "fundable" areas. The fundability of areas, particularly government fundability, is determined more by the political process than by disciplinary logic. The economic tie is a political tie.

The federal government provided 72 percent of the research funds of universities in 1979. Though this was but 9.8 percent of all federal R&D funds, the research universities are now becoming economically dependent on the federal government and bound to its programmatic definitions. Sponsored research accounts for a third of the budgets of the major research universities. The federal government is the major sponsor.

The impact on sociology is telling. That the programs of both the National Science Foundation and the National Foundation for the Humanities support sociology reflects the tensions between its humanistic and scientific character. Governmental and industrial support is, almost entirely, for the scientific version of sociology, particularly the positivistic, objectivistic measurement version, over the more historical, philosophical, and moral aspects of the field. The agencies that let contracts, as mentioned above, seek quantitative data as a basis for policy. The bureaucracy believes the philosophical, conceptual definitions of social problems to have been settled in the political process that generated the authorizing legislation. As Smelser (this volume, chap. 1) writes, the "empirical science model of social study . . . will call the tune." The inner tension of the field should be resolved in the light of disciplinary, not political, dynamics.

University curricula come to reflect Washington priorities. The new specialties to be developed tend to be politically promoted. Such specialization has an ephemeral quality, producing an infertile series of short-term commitments, rising and falling with the life-cycle of social issues. One example is the Social Security Administration's responsibility for a research program in "disability," which received significant budgetary support, largely for the social sciences and for social work, from the midfifties until the midseventies. Public opinion was justifiably concerned with discrimination against the disabled. Programs were sponsored for training and hiring the disabled and for architectural design of access to facilities such as schools. Ramps for wheelchairs appeared along public thoroughfares and bus-lifts became accepted by public transit operators. Funds flowed to universities for the training of disability counselors and for evaluations of the counseling. Special journals carried the reports and associations of disability workers arranged conferences.

By the time the programs were in place, the funds began to dry up. Graduates specializing in disability counseling could not compete with clinical psychologists or psychiatric social workers for positions. Faculty engaged during this budgetary thrust became relics of a period of government problem-oriented largesse. They survived professionally by adapting their skills to other work.

Foreign area studies, another example, have tended to remain interdepartmental programs. They have rarely achieved budgetary independence within the university along with tenured faculty positions. Staff brought in to meet area study needs could remain on "soft" money, marginal to the standing faculty (Winsborough, this volume, chap. 7; Calhoun, this volume, chap. 4). It is not unusual for a university to decide to offer or not to offer work in a foreign culture if, and only if, a patron is found.

Sponsorship alone is not sufficient to direct a field. Sociology has not developed in all of the directions for which clients offered funds. The field of military sociology is an example. The fields at the intersect of sociology and business or finance also have remained underdeveloped. Consequently, the disciplinary area of the sociology of the economy is undeveloped. Lester Kurtz (this volume, chap. 2) mentions a budget of $59.9 million in 1988 for the Army Research Institute for the Behavioral and Social Sciences, more than the combined social science budgets of the NSF and NIMH and DOE. The matter here is not the disciplinary possibilities, as such, but the social ideologies of those attracted to the field. One could imagine sociologists being quite enthusiastic about access to large-scale data sets, to cross-national comparative material, and the study of a social institution significant enough to dominate a number of societies, historical and contemporary. Yet, the prudent novice assesses the career advantage of a field with few courses to teach, few prestigious journals to carry the research reports, and a weak section within the professional society.

The concrete-problem perspective drives government sponsors toward multidisciplinary designs. A response to an RFP by an interdepartmental team tends to be considered a stronger contender in the applied field. A program of research on manpower may require a psychologist, a sociologist, an economist, and someone from the business school familiar with program administration.

Denis Prager (1984), a government official, calls for the university to develop new and innovative organizational approaches to interdisciplinary research. Disciplinary departments, he says, may even disappear or form relationships with research institutions outside the standard disciplinary establishment. No longer will a university's faculty only be full-time and tenured. Faculties will come in different shapes and sizes with members coming from government, other universities, and from industry on short-term loan or part-time arrangements (cf. Crane and Small, this volume, chap. 5).

Because of the nature of university authority, the principal investigator can rarely guarantee the performances of these associates. The interdisciplinary issue is not simply intellectual, but is a management challenge. The difficulty in coordinating staff, with what Winsborough (this volume, chap. 7) calls a differing "round of life," is patent. Coordination is easier when the several actors are members of a center and subject to the authority of the director.

The intellectual interdisciplinary issue deserves attention in its own right. Is knowledge ever really integrated in these efforts? Collegial disciplines tend to offer diverse types of technical-operational support to a project. Conceptual integration is rarely attempted. Typically, the RFP is prepared by a member of one discipline in the light of the "inputs" of colleagues in other disciplines. The intellectual coordination generally resolves into a subdivision of tasks and their allocation among associates. A clinical psychologist may assist a survey researcher in framing a question. An engineer may assist a medical researcher using "high-tech" equipment. University disciplinary organization limits such cooperation and, for epistemological reasons, should do so.

The division of disciplines in the pursuit of knowledge is wellfounded (Calhoun—this volume, chap. 4—offers another view). Late in the last century, a Kuhnian "scientific revolution" in psychology established the rule of empirical, rather than simply logical, methods that subsequently severed the common department of philosophers and psychologists. Disciplinary boundaries reflect methodological differences and, essentially, frame of reference differences. Certainly, demography and sociology are both concerned with society. Demography, for its part, along with its mate, human ecology, is conceptualized in a space-time frame of reference. Sociology evolves its concepts in a symbolist frame of reference. Demography and sociology, for this among many other reasons, emerge as distinct social sciences.

Outside of philosophy, little thought is given to how one bridges space-time and symbolist knowledge. This is not the place to argue that case but, in brief, let it be said that merely juxtaposing specialists within a research project does not resolve the epistemological problem. The sum of disciplinary abstractions does not reconstitute concrete reality. Thus, university resistance to interdisciplinary work does not prove the obtuseness of the modern university or the politics of turf. It attests to professorial insights into the underlying epistemological problem.

In a decidedly polemic work criticizing the research university, Von Blum (1986) discusses the decline in teaching associated with the increase in research in the university, the courses not taught, the unavailability of teachers to students. Despite the administrative separation of undergraduate colleges from graduate research operations and announced awards for teaching, research publication remains the major criterion for tenure decisions. Bad teaching, as reported by student evaluations, can hurt, but good teaching alone does not merit tenure.

The humanities and, secondarily, the social sciences, other than economics, are particularly vulnerable to budget "crunches." Cummings (1984), writing on university budget cuts, says that those programs most closely aligned with the private sector, that is, business, economics, finance, science, and engineering, seldom suffer the losses typically sustained by the social sciences and the humanities. The fact is that those social scientists who ally themselves with sponsors, private or public, are less vulnerable.

Incompatibilities between Academic and Research Administration

University Authority Is Not Research Authority

Research centers contribute more than funds to universities. As Winsborough (this volume, chap. 7) argues, they may divert intradepartmental strain, slowing the process of departmental "mitosis," and may be repositories of capital equipment and skills needed by members of several departments. Clearly, they are important for student training and as facilities for research faculty.

However, I have suggested some dilemmas when contract research subjects faculties and curricula to the policies of political and economic institutions. Managing research under an academic administrative regime can ill serve both teaching and research. There are managerial incompatibilities, such as exercising authority over colleagues, mentioned above, when they happen to be a hierarchically organized research team. In his description of the HumRRO decision to leave

George Washington University, Meredith Crawford writes, "We were finding that the administrative procedure of the university rendered it very difficult for us to make a prompt response to new contract possibilities. Also, university accounting procedures do not lend themselves to our work on a number of different contracts" (Cannell and Kahn 1984:1269).

Generally, a for-profit company that promises to deliver a product need not reveal its budgetary arrangements to the customer. A nonprofit corporation is responsible for seeing that the budgeted funds are expended as agreed as well as for providing "deliverables" according to a time schedule. The university, as a contracting agency, guarantees what it is not in a position to guarantee. University trustees, who carry the ultimate responsibility, do not attend to research operations. Their attention is on fund raising, authorizing programs, rubber-stamping personnel decisions, and so forth. In fact, neither the president, nor the provost, nor the dean leaps in when a project falters. The responsibility for research performance is delegated to the research unit and its director.

Quality control in an industrial corporation follows the path of authority from management to staff and line. Sanctions include the threat of dismissal. The university institute director has the authority to control the nontenured faculty, and certainly the members of the staff without faculty status, reporting to him or her. Tenured faculty, though, are protected. How often has a dean withheld funds from tenured researchers or from the research institute for nonperformance? The university rarely returns the sponsor's money or appoints a second investigator if the report is poor or not delivered at all.

This peculiar control, or "uncontrol," system of universities does not affect administration of grants. Granting agencies do not expect more than fiscal monitoring on the part of the university. A research grantor is assisting a faculty member in achieving his or her own intellectual aims. The grant is a gift. (Sometimes a sponsor will use a contract arrangement for such a "gift" and sometimes a grant arrangement is used when some return is expected. Such departures tend to occur when a research monitor wants to circumvent rules authorizing expenditure by the sponsoring agency, but these exceptions need not detain us here.)

In his work on nonprofit institutes, Orlans (1972) points to universities' lack of review procedures. The university's responsibility ends, in practice, with a signature on a research proposal. That signature follows a review of the proposal to assure that the commitments are consistent with university policy, especially the academic objectives of the institution. The only reasons for refusal of university approval that I have encountered have been insufficient indirect cost recovery, or other financial difficulty, or an attempt by the sponsor to control personnel appointments. Issues of "human subjects" or faculty time commitments usually seem to be negotiable.

University Personnel Policy Is Too Ponderous

University personnel policy is too ponderous for research appointments. The faculty, responsible for the cultural crafting of the disciplines and uniquely competent to judge the candidate's credentials, must agree on the area of an appointment and on the candidate. After five or six years in the probationary role of Assistant Professor, the young academic is evaluated for tenure, again by the faculty, hallowing a system designed to insulate the academy against outside pressures as well as against the pressures generated by the politics of the university itself. An appointment or a tenuring procedure can consume the better part of an academic year.

A research project, by contrast, may have a specialized requirement not fitting any perceived personnel needs of departments. The ability of a university research institute to offer departmental appointments affects its recruitment success. In addition, team research requires a large number of technical support personnel for whom there may be no alternative positions on the permanent staff. Further, the researcher's service may be needed only for a few months and does not justify the tedious process of establishing a position before recruiting even while the budgetary clock is running.

The university, for its part, adapts by establishing nontenure accruing positions, such as research professorships (soft money appointments), or adjunct professorships (for those holding a position elsewhere). Engineering schools have a goodly number of research associates filling such roles without the protection of tenure. In the social sciences such roles are filled disproportionately by women. Medical schools appoint clinical professors who offer patient services with nominal teaching responsibilities. The patients of a teaching hospital are a research population, cases for training, and income opportunities for the medical staff and for the school.

With all these adaptations, universities assemble a variety of "second-class citizens," individuals who neither enjoy the prestige nor the rights in governance of the faculty. The campus may sustain a cadre of workers who are socially alienated from the faculty. Paradoxically, they may also have higher earnings than some of the faculty.

Moreover, administrative officers are engaged without faculty procedures. A research center may skirt the procedures for academic appointments by administrative hiring. Even technical personnel may be engaged on an administrative line. In some research universities, the budget for administration exceeds that for instruction and the number of administrators exceeds that of academic personnel.

Administrators, though, are not the second-class citizens referred to above. They are outside the "class" stratification system of the standing faculty. Like another "caste," they have specialized professional duties. Mobility across the faculty/administrator line is exceedingly rare except for the chief administrators, deans and the provost, who are usually promoted from the faculty, though not necessarily from the faculty of the same university.

The authority of administrative officers to shape university life is mounting. Admissions officers select the undergraduate student body. Financial officers recommend faculty salaries and student tuitions. Development officers and university information personnel interpret the university to the wider public, and facilities officers allocate space among the "budgetary units." Officers who monitor contracts and grants have a striking role in setting research policy. They may define the status of the research staff, negotiate overhead, and write the patent policy governing the commercialization of the products of research. While, technically, these functions are reviewed by a faculty consultative committee, in practice the administrators' advice becomes policy. The politics of faculty/research administrative relations are adversarial—as they should be.

The abdication of administrative responsibility by faculty and the entrance into these power vacuums by administrators have a long history. The growth of administrative needs of the entrepreneurial university has required the delegation of authority to specialized experts. The administration of university instruction has, for a long time, included business and control functions, the organization of curriculum and teaching, the management of the library, its acquisitions and staffing, and of laboratories and their equipment. Business functions even in small colleges include accounting, budget preparation and control, expenditure of university funds for salaries and material procurement, the collection of revenues, management of invested funds, employment of nonacademic personnel, and so on.

The introduction of research contracting during the Second World War complicated the business functions, particularly in requirements for managing changing project payrolls, tax deduction control, and more complex benefit packages. John Russell (1954), writing on the finance of higher education shortly after the war, warned that business administration was outstripping academic administration. The campus culture could not but change and the faculty would become not only a numerical minority, but increasingly unable to exercise the authority to set policy.

Management Must Be Tailored to Function

The lack of coherence between academic and research administration is not limited to the nature of authority and personnel policy. On the one hand, academic administration is geared to activities that are quite stable. These include yearly iterations of arranging course programs, assigning space, keeping student records, and, by and large, dealing with the same personnel. Each research project, on the other hand, is unique, with its own staffing, its own peculiar relation to data sources, its own space and equipment needs, and its own project budget.

Administrators have attempted to adapt academic administration to research administration incrementally. Contemporary MBAs are often led to believe that they command a general science of administration, applicable regardless of what is being administered. Hospital, church, academic, industrial production, and research administration, among others, all basically present the same types of problems. The fact is, though, that administrative structures, as well as policies, should vary with respect to the functions being administered. Science administration is not church administration and academic administration is not research administration.

Universities Are Not Competitive

It is one thing to bid on contracts and another to win them. To bid and not to win is to invest time and treasure in proposal preparation and to settle for less and less desirable contracts, unless the bidding institution can convince agencies to see it as a sole-source offeror or has learned how to collude in "wiring" an RFP.

University institutes working in the applied fields are not competitive with nonprofit and commercial research corporations. Work is more expensive in universities. Partly because of the grafting of academic on research management, work is less efficient. I have argued that academic staffing and curricular planning are distorted by the adjustment of academic management to research. The obverse also holds. Academic management reduces the efficiency of applied research.

Basic research is appropriately inefficient. Endless thinking, trial and error, and immersion in the library are at its heart. Applied research is also basic when it seeks an understanding of the laws governing concrete systems. Most applied research, however, is a production-line activity.

Applied social science is more and more called upon for data to document a situation, not for a theoretical analysis of that situation. Social researchers may float a questionnaire and produce the marginals, the tabulated frequencies of responses to each item. The costs to this point can be readily estimated. For university researchers this is but propaedeutic for data analysis, for analytic cross-tabs, or for a regression analysis testing the interdependence among variables. Analysis is open ended, difficult to budget, and, in all events, raises the budget estimates out of the competitive range. Analysis also requires the most professional participation and increases the ratio of "chief" to "Indian" time. One of the ironies of this situation is that universities "spin-off" nonprofit and for-profit corporations and then find themselves competing with them for contracts. This is Stanford's experience with the Stanford Research Institute. Bad pushes out good research in the economics of competitive bidding. Marginals or fact gathering replaces analysis or the discovery of new knowledge.

A clear line of hierarchical authority is needed for efficient conduct of a team project, but university faculties are not in a command formation. Personnel cannot be shifted between projects without their assent. In a commercial corporation such assent is considered a given of the labor contract. Interdisciplinary projects bring together people not accustomed to working together. Colleagues are asked to snatch time from busy schedules to contribute to a proposal that sometimes is given more as a courtesy than as a personal priority. The principal investigator is often unable to write an integrated proposal from the diverse contributions. Professors are reluctant to sustain the volume of service work needed to amortize research equipment and provide steady employment for a technical work force.

Few university social survey groups can sustain the computer-assisted telephone interviewing systems that are stock-in-trade for commercial groups engaged in "quick-and-dirty" market research. They either subcontract telephone interviewing or appeal to student training to justify doing it "the old fashioned way."

Lower-level technical employees tend to be inexperienced students to whom the university has an educational responsibility. University institutes cannot be justified as profit centers for universities. As student training laboratories they merit an instructional budget. Cheapness of graduate student labor is illusory. These apprentices, as poorly paid as they are, produce much more slowly than practiced and better paid technical personnel. Some of the graduates go on to academic positions and establish similar institutes in other universities. Perhaps more of them find their way to the competing independent nonprofit and for-profit institutes.

The behavior of institute directors provides the major evidence for the incompatibility of academic and research administration. The successful director knows how to use the informal, rather than the formal, organization. The principal investigator knows who to call to cut "red tape." The lively existence of the informal system reduces pressure to amend the university's formal administrative apparatus.

Marketing the University

Bidding for Research

As Karabel (1988) points out, scholars have at least four audiences: colleagues, decision-making elites, subordinate social groups, and educated publics. The researcher's publics are primarily colleagues and decision makers, the latter mostly in government and industry.

The race to get government and industry to pay for research is triggered as much by developmental interests as by the need of the researcher or any of the other audiences for knowledge. To stay in the race, research universities resort more and more to market strategies. Organizational success is measured by growth. In a free enterprise system of consumer sovereignty, growth entails marketing. Marketing involves both shaping a product and awakening demand. Research is recast as a service. Universities may create institutes as devices for attracting funds as they develop instructional programs to attract potential donors. The research marketer reads the *Commerce Business Daily* and bids for contracts.

The grants and contracts and the development offices encourage faculty to pursue research opportunities. Administrators and faculty with experience in government agencies bring to the proposal writing their insights into the project review criteria. University offices located in Washington lobby for the interests of their school. In 1983, Catholic University and Columbia University lobbied Congress directly for $5 million for physics research facilities, effectively an end-run around peer review.

Faculty may be under pressure to corral some volume of work to justify their low teaching load. One engineering school, located in a university where the other schools have a two course teaching load, maintains an expectation of four courses, two of which are expected to be "bought off" with research contract funds.

Meister (1981), writing on contracting for behavioral research from the perspective of a government official, expects universities to solicit his business. He does not expect researchers to follow their personal interest. The sponsoring agency specifies the topic it wants investigated. In the bidding process, university researchers are under what he calls a "self-generated pressure" to bid on whatever topic a government agency may wish to study.

The issue is not quite as stark as Meister suggests. Contract terms are negotiated between an agency and a researcher. A researcher in demand can insist on "space" and allow a bit of "fat" in the interstices of the contract performances, to pursue his or her scientific interest. Additional academic leeway is achieved through time contributed by the researcher and through subsidies given by the university in the form of space and equipment and, perhaps, communication and computing support. One measure of the extent to which academic payoff is achieved within a contract would be the number and quality of peer-reviewed publications emerging from various contracts.

Bidding for Students

Marketing is not limited to research services. Student recruitment officers market the university as they try to attract a freshman class with defined characteristics. Promotional policies of admissions offices in the large research universities are informed by market analyses, which derive from the same educational entrepreneurial orientation that press universities toward bidding for research contracts. The "competitiveness" of the school becomes a marketable attribute. Indeed, in private universities, competitiveness correlates with level of tuition, paralleling the price/demand relation in the commercial market.

The "rankings" of schools and departments become part of the sales "pitch" to prospective students, faculty, and contractors. Von Blum (1986) describes an "obsession for national rankings." Nearly all of these rankings tend to be based on "soft" data. Faculty and department rankings may be reputational, where department heads are asked to rank departments in their discipline, or rankings may be based on a publication rate without correction for field, or quality, or even the age distribution of the faculty. School rankings are, in part, based on indicators such as the student/faculty ratio, the amount spent per student, or the geographic diversity of the student body.

The student/faculty ratio is obtained by dividing the number of students by the total academic staff. A large research university may have a number of faculty who teach very little, with undergraduate classes being assigned to junior faculty or even to graduate students. The student/faculty ratio in such a school would mislead the potential undergraduate. Expenditure per student is often computed by dividing the total university budget by the number of students, when only a fraction of the budget is devoted to instruction.

Marketing for "input" continues at the "output" end. Placement of the graduates is a PR "plus." Academic offerings may then be shaped by anticipated manpower needs, the availability of jobs, in a particular time period. In this marketing climate, education becomes vocational training just as research becomes a service.

Selling the Product of Research

Patenting the product of research brings the university into merchandising. The university provides the context in which the discovery is made and claims a share in the profits, just as an industry would were the discovery to have been made in corporate laboratories. No one doubts institutional entitlement. The claim might even be extended to other commercially exploitable "intellectual property" of the faculty, such as textbooks. That is, to what extent is a text produced on university time and to what extent on the professor's own time?

Linnell (1982), writing on faculty income, reminds us that ownership rights in intellectual property are guaranteed by the Constitution (Article I, Section 8). Federal patent legislation of 1980 (Pub. L. 96–517) gives universities the right to retain title to inventions made with federal support. The issue of the control of the product of research where many parties contribute to the outcome has been argued in court (e.g., *Maher v. Roe*, US 464 (1977)).

Research universities have appointed patent administrators. A hundred or so of these specialists belong to the Society of University Patent Administrators. That society reviewed 498 patents and found that only 5 percent earned over $100,000 in the six years between 1969 and 1975. Another 30 percent earned between $10,000 and $100,000 and that the remaining 65 percent earned under $10,000. Thus, a university patent policy is really aimed at the first 5 percent.

The university, in agreement with the researcher, may exercise its patent right by contracting with a for-profit firm to commercialize the patented products (Dimancescu and Botkin 1986). Only last year Harvard decided to assume that function, a direct entry of the university into product development. Presumably, Harvard will not enter production but will conclude agreements with industry for this purpose—though New York University's spaghetti factory does come to mind.

The issue or proprietary knowledge, or secret research, may precede the patent question. Universities have generally eschewed any limitation on the professor's right to publish. Yet if they test a product in the commercial market, the knowledge has an economic impact. The right to sell knowledge is the right not to sell. The secret research issue has been raised mainly with regard to defense contracting in a period in which faculty and students did not agree with national goals. Secret research for industrial and political clients has rarely been challenged. The implications, however, for the free flow of ideas are not different in the latter case. In the social sciences much economic research for private industry is, by its nature, proprietary and, thus, its place in the academy dubious.

Recent federal administrations have expected the universities to produce useful, patentable products for transfer to industry for commercialization. The Stevens and Wydler Technology Innovation Act of 1980 mandated technology transfer from government laboratories to private industry. The process is monitored by a Center for Utilization of Federal Technology in the Department of Commerce. In 1988, the National Science Foundation sponsored a National Cooperative R&D Laboratory Project and found that in 1987–88, 38 percent of university laboratories and 52 percent of government laboratories were involved in technology transfer to industry.

This commitment draws universities away from basic scientific research. The gamma correlation coefficient between technology transfer and basic research, in the NSF study, was $-.21$. The correlation between technology transfer and industrial funding of R&D was .71, and the correlation between technology transfer and time devoted to patents was .39 (Rahm et al. 1988). Marketing and intellectual creativity do not play well together.

The University May Lose Money on Research

Cost Sharing Is a Promise Not to Profit

Grants are budgeted in order to prevent universities from profiting. Cost-sharing arrangements and indirect cost-recovery negotiations limit the university charges. Cost sharing is expected by a granting agency that feels that it is supporting and sharing in the pursuit of knowledge and so should not be expected to carry the whole burden. The applying institution may have to show that it is providing 5 or 10 percent of the cost. The sharing may be expressed in limits on indirect cost recovery. A sponsor may be willing to pay only 15 percent overhead rate when the actual indirect costs may reach 40 or 50 percent or more of the total direct costs or of wages and salaries.

Cost sharing does not appear explicitly in contract budgeting. It is likely, though, that the university and the government will agree to use the same indirect cost-recovery rate for contracts as is negotiated for grants. Further, in its effort to be competitive, implicit underwriting of indirect costs is accepted by the university. Rare is the contract budget that presents a true space cost or library-resource cost.

To compensate for the insufficient recovery, the university transfers money from other accounts into research support. It is difficult to specify the path of cross-subsidization, given university accounting practices. Not inconceivably, tuition could be lower were research subsidy not needed. During the Second World War, government contracted with universities for instructional services and the universities realized a significant operating surplus. Research subsidization also repays the university in other ways, such as retaining its excellent faculty and attracting graduate students.

If grant and contract research are deficit activities, why do university administrators continue to seek this work? One reason has just been stated, namely, the retention of good faculty and students. In the competition between universities for graduate students, the ability to offer stipends, sometimes based on work on sponsored research, is crucial. Perhaps more fundamental is the character of nonprofit budgeting. Any income received is to be spent. Paradoxically, therefore, the more income a university enjoys, the higher its cost, or expenditure per student, when that is computed by dividing income by the number of students. The amount of the cash flow is sometimes more important than the "bottom line." Research income accounts for 30 or 40 percent of the university cash flow. The occupants of these positions constitute a vested interest. In addition, the university has fixed facility costs, such as for a library, and research helps carry that burden.

Research funds may contribute to construction programs, and these buildings may offer classroom space. Research funds help build up an inventory of research equipment, facilitating the work of scholars even after the project is completed, assuming that the government sponsor does not reclaim the equipment. The diverse funding sources are a hedge against recession in any particular area. Universities receiving income from tuition, research, alumni contributions, foundation grants, endowments, and state subsidies are cushioned against particular economic shocks. The true budgeting picture, taking account of these contributions to the university, has yet to be computed.

The Negotiated Overhead Rate

Reimbursement for indirect costs is not simply a fiscal arrangement but has political consequences for the university. The rate of reimbursement is negotiated between the government and the university under government rules about what is reimbursable. Facilities charged to overhead earnings are pervasive. Overhead earnings contribute to the library, to the president's office, to campus communication systems, and to the support of nonfunded scholars and students. The Office of Management and Budget Circular A-21 rests on the theory of the pervasive use of government funds. In this policy circular, the OMB asserts that its regulatory interest extends throughout the university. Thus, for example, the entire faculty, even those with no direct federal support, complete time allocation forms indicating the proportion of their time in teaching, research and administration.

Indirect cost recovery produces some tension among rival university claimants to the funds. A researcher whose project earns these monies may try to acquire them to support his or her other research needs. This has been a major issue for social researchers whose efforts are labor intensive. When overhead is calculated as a proportion of salaries and wages, labor intensive research is particularly taxed. The university allocates these funds to general university services, even subsidizing nonfunded faculty research. Schools—particularly medical schools—are in a better position than is a department or a project to control these funds. However, the central administration may adjust its contribution to the schools in the light of overhead retained, undercutting the advantage of the research centers.

The Dinosaur

We have two images of diversity with respect to universities and their sponsors. In one of these, the university institute seeks a variety of sponsors and so tries to minimize its dependence on any single sponsor. In the other, the university becomes one of a number of institutions banded together for a mammoth effort. The power of any given member of such a consortium tends to be limited.

The first type produces internal organizational diversity. The variety of sources of funding means a variety of organizational representatives, a student body, a cadre of researchers, managers of a securities portfolio, and so forth. Is there a critical size for a university? Might the critical size be different for the promotion of research than it is for student instruction?

Research budgets vary from the small grant in aid to the individual professor to the contract for establishing and maintaining institutes. Large grants or contracts are given by government agencies that prefer transfer payments over an increase in staffing. Government knowledge development functions are, in this way, delegated to the universities.

Earlier, when foundations were the major sponsoring agencies, the issue of value of "project" as against "block" grants was debated (Bulmer, this volume, chap. 9). A "block" grant would transfer authority to the university, especially the department, to select grantees, that is, projects, and so maximize academic considerations. Actually, it does not work out in this way. The large contract funds a distinct research unit or program. The larger it is, the more independent of the department its director will be. The projects to be funded are quite carefully designated in the sponsor's terms.

In the competitive bidding for contracts, the "buyer's" needs become paramount. If the interest of an original major sponsor flags, the institute turns to diversification for self-preservation. When this occurs, programmatic influence shifts toward the institute. Such institutes may strive for independence of the university.

The dinosaur of the system is the second image, the consortium, described appreciatively by Dimancescu and Botkin (1986) as the new alliance that effects collaborative research agreements among government, industry, and universities. Early consortia were designed to bring together a critical mass of talent, such as the Associated Universities that supported Brookhaven Laboratory, for the development of nuclear energy and its applications in medicine, warfare, and in shaping the earth. Recent consortia are designed to harness national wealth and intelligence in support of the economy. The support of industrial activity in the competition between nations is a major output. Their organization has been facilitated by the withdrawal of government enforcement of antitrust laws, a step taken during the Carter administration and formalized later in the National Cooperative Research Act.

Dimancescu and Botkin (1986) advocate a university mission to fuel the economy. Those removed from this "economic mainstream" should, they say, reevaluate their research agendas. The role model is

Rensselaer Polytechnic Institute. Now under the presidency of a former director of NASA, it hosts the Center for Manufacturing Productivity. Current policy looks toward the reduction of its undergraduate program in favor of graduate studies and engineering research. The new look at Rensselaer is to be symbolized architecturally by a modernistic multistoried research facility to stand at the entrance to the campus, in contrast to the old red brick structures.

Separate Research from Teaching

The time has come for a recommendation. Contract research in university institutes, I have argued, blurs the boundary between the academy and the economy and polity. One response would be to place contracting outside of the university, in a university-like research institute. The impact of government and industry on university faculty and curriculum could, in this way, be limited. Further, a more tailored administrative design for academic and research activities, respectively, would benefit both. Reasons for supporting such an outside corporation range from internal management considerations to matters of the university's role in society, its relations to other parts of the society, and concerns about its main mission.

The issue is the classic sociological one of the structural differentiation of social organizations. Talcott Parsons theorized about the evolutionary differentiation of the household as a productive unit into economic organizations, specialized in production, on the one hand, and the family, on the other, specialized in the reproduction of social members and their emotional socialization and support. He asked whether these specialized institutions, especially the family, were weakened in the process and concluded that each is stronger and more functional in its specialized form. This restates in evolutionary terms the position of Durkheim cited at the beginning of this paper.

In the case of research universities, the emergent units would be specialized, on the research side, in the production of knowledge—the manipulation of cognitive symbol systems. The academic side would specialize in socialization—educating the citizen. The great system benefit would be in what Durkheim termed the "organic solidarity" of the differentiated units. This requires an integration between the distinct structures. The now distinct university and the university-linked research institutes would negotiate a relationship. The character of that relationship is, however, a question for another paper.

There exist precedents for placing research contracting outside of the university. The Electronics Research Laboratories of Columbia became the nonprofit Riverside Research Institute in 1967, and the Draper Laboratory at MIT became independent at about the same time. The Human Resources Research Office of George Washington University became the Human Resources Research Organization in 1969. These moves were made in response to immediate political pressures, such as student protest against defense research in the Vietnam period. Student protests may have played a part in triggering the move. Yet, one may believe that for more basic social evolutionary reasons, these were changes waiting to happen. The real reason may not be far from those suggested in this paper.

Universities and their faculty should participate in such endeavors but the effort should also be contained. The university must not be subordinated to the political economy.

A Research Corporation for the University: The Form It Might Take

While it is not possible to design the research corporation here, a preliminary sketch of its structure might take the following form. The corporation would be external to the university's administrative structure, though not necessarily physically removed from the campus. It would have its own corporate charter, its own president and officers. University representatives might sit on its board. The corporation would negotiate with the university for purchase of a variety of services. These might include space, library, computer and data processing, and accounting services. The charges for these should be realistic so that the university does not subsidize the corporation.

The research corporation would employ faculty and students on terms consistent with the university policy on outside consulting. Their performance requirements would be set by and monitored by the corporation and their salaries should be competitive with those offered by industry for comparable work. The corporation could have nonprofit and for-profit divisions, each accepting its own type of contracts. The for-profit division might even contribute to the university, perhaps offering scholarships and grants to university faculty for basic research. The social sciences should have their own, separately managed unit so as to avoid dominance by the engineering and medical sciences component.

The research corporation could conceive of itself as servicing the economy and polity. It could patent its products and might even participate in production and marketing enterprises.

The university, for its part, could still be home to grant research.

The income from the research corporation could help with cost sharing. Those currently employed by the university in the administration of contract research need not fear for their jobs. They could be absorbed into the research corporation. The disentanglement of research and academic administration would simplify both. The university would be better able to continue as a community of free scholars offering intellectual critique to the society and educating its citizens. The research corporation would be the institution in which academy, polity, and economy meet to serve the general welfare.

References

Cannell, Charles F., and Robert Lewis Kahn. 1984. "Some Factors in the Origin and Development of the Institute for Social Research, the University of Michigan." *American Psychologist* 39:1256–66.

Connery, Robert H., ed. 1970. *The Corporation and the Campus: Corporate Support of Higher Education in the 1970s*. Proceedings of the Academy of Political Science, vol. 30, no. 1. New York: The Academy of Political Science, Columbia University.

Cummings, Scott. 1984. "The Political Economy of Social Science Funding." *Sociological Inquiry* 54:154–70.

Dimancescu, Dan, and James Botkin. 1986. *The New Alliance: America's R&D Consortia*. Cambridge, Mass.: Ballinger.

Donchin, Emanuel. 1985. "The Forum on Research Management: An Experiment in University-Government Dialog." *American Psychologist* 40: 826–30.

Geiger, Roger L. 1986. *To Advance Knowledge: The Growth of American Research Universities, 1900–1940*. New York: Oxford University Press.

Kidd, Charles V. 1959. *American Universities and Federal Research*. Cambridge, Mass.: Belknap Press of Harvard University Press.

Karabel, Jerome. 1988. Commentary on Bulmer and Sica, presented at conference on "Sociology and Institution-Building." Arizona, Nov. 16–17.

Klausner, Samuel Z. 1986. "The Bid to Nationalize American Social Science." In Klausner and Lidz, *The Nationalization of the Social Sciences*, 3–40.

Klausner, Samuel Z., and Victor M. Lidz. 1986. *The Nationalization of the Social Sciences*. Philadelphia: University of Pennsylvania Press.

Laski, Harold J. 1928. "Foundations, Universities and Research." *Harper's* 157:295–303.

Linnell, Robert H., ed. 1982. *Dollars and Scholars: An Inquiry into the Impact of Faculty Income upon the Function and Future of the Academy*. Los Angeles: University of Southern California Press.

Lyons, Gene M. 1969. *The Uneasy Partnership: Social Science and the Federal Government in the Twentieth Century*. New York: Russell Sage Foundation.

Meister, David. 1981. *Behavioral Research and Government Policy: Civilian and Military R&D*. New York: Pergamon Press.

Orlans, Harold. 1972. *The Nonprofit Research Institute: Its Origins, Operations, Problems and Prospects*. New York: McGraw-Hill Book Company.

————.1973. *Contracting for Knowledge*. San Francisco: Jossey-Bass Publishers.

Posner, Michael. 1986. "Do We Need Research Councils?" *The Political Quarterly* 57:156–71.

Prager, Denis. 1984. "Trends in Governmental and Academic Institutions Affecting Science." *American Psychologist* 39:1056–59.

Rahm, Diane, Barry Bozeman, and Michael Crow. 1988. "Domestic Technology Transfer and Competitiveness: An Empirical Assessment of Roles of University and Governmental Laboratories." *Public Administration Review* 48:969–78.

Rosenzweig, Roger M. 1982. *The Research Universities and Their Patrons*. Berkeley: University of California Press.

Rule, James B. 1988. "Biotechnology: Big Money Comes to the University." *Dissent* 35:430–36.

Ruscio, Kenneth. 1984. "Prometheus Entangled: Academic Science in the Administrative State." *Public Administration Review* 44:353–59.

Russell, John Dale. [1944] 1954. *The Finance of Higher Education*. Rev. ed. Chicago: University of Chicago Press.

Shapiro, Michael. 1983. "New Genetics Industry Tests University Values." *The Center Magazine* (May/June) 16:43–50.

Von Blum, Paul. 1986. *Stillborn Education: A Critique of the American Research University*. Lanham, Md.: University Press of America.

7

Sociology Departments and Their Research Centers: An Essential Tension?

HALLIMAN H. WINSBOROUGH

Disciplines, Departments, and Research Centers

The subject of our inquiry is sociology. Chapters in this volume deal with that subject in various of its incarnations, but two notions of the elements of sociology predominate: sociology as a collection of people (or of groups of people) and sociology as a collection of intellectual things.

Many chapters, including this one, deal primarily with sociology as collections of individuals and their attendant social paraphernalia, that is, with sociology as a profession, a labor process, a training and socialization regime, a public, a faculty, a department (see especially Buxton and Turner, chap. 11; D'Antonio, chap. 3; Reiss, chap. 8; Klausner, chap. 6). In these views the boundaries of any one collection are fairly distinct. Ambiguity, and perhaps marginality, arises from the overlap. From this perspective, sociology is, perhaps, the union of all these collections.

In many of the other chapters, sociology is mostly discussed as a body of knowledge (see especially Smelser chap. 1; Crane and Small, chap. 5) that can, perhaps, be used or influenced for various aspects of public policy or institution building (see especially Halliday, Introduction; Sica, chap. 10, Kurtz, chap. 2; Bulmer, chap. 9). In these works the elements of sociology are intellectual things—writings, ideas, propositions, findings, definitions, meanings, symbols—that are partitioned to form topics, areas, subdisciplines, and disciplines.

Although a partition of such intellectual elements and a hierarchial

This work was done at the Center for Demography and Ecology, which receives core support from the Center for Population Research of the National Institute for Child Health and Human Development (HD 5876).

arrangement of the partitions is a traditional approach to organizing knowledge, it is interesting to note how modern "network" images have penetrated into our discussion. Crane and Small, for example, use the articles published by sociologists as an operationalization of that body of knowledge. They use co-citations as a way of defining the structure and boundaries, or their lack, of our subject. One is reminded of Mary Hesse's "network" image of a scientific theory (Hesse 1974). Calhoun's notion of the body of sociological knowledge seems to be a web of meanings and symbols that are connected by a complex of dependency and reference. Thus Calhoun's position is less similar to current philosophy of science, and more to ideas in the theory of knowledge, as in Quine and Ullian (1970).

These network images suggest that the partitioning of knowledge is a complex and uncertain activity. The division into disciplines, subdisciplines, courses, and topics is likely to do violence to some real connections between elements, just as it is hard to find a "pure" clique in a sociogram. It is interesting that Calhoun's image, as well as Crane and Small's, suggests that sociology isn't a clique at all but an "unstructured" discipline with boundaries necessarily open to—indeed merging with—neighboring fields.[1] I suspect that the partitioning approach to knowledge is most appropriate to teaching and exposition, while the network approach is most natural to research and analysis.

Despite a predominance of focus on one or another of these notions of sociology—as groups of people or groups of intellectual things—I suspect most authors in this volume would agree that the relationship between these elements is central to the idea of a discipline, for the notion of disciplinarity implies a set of specific, active, relationships between a collection of organizations and a set of partitions of the body of knowledge. All of the collections of individuals we would want to say are part of sociology have as their avowed purpose some actions with respect to sociology as an intellectual product. They variously learn, discover, invent, revise, conserve, transmit, defend, attack, enjoy, or utilize sociological knowledge.

Each kind of action probably leads the actors to partition and organize the intellectual material of sociology in a somewhat different way. A graduate student reading an assigned article may not worry much about whether it is "really" sociology or economics. The editor of a journal in sociology would be likely to worry about that distinction when considering the same article for publication. The "best" organization or partition of the intellectual material is dependent on

1. Perhaps there is a pattern to this openness, with neighboring fields being anthropology in the 1940s, psychology/psychiatry in the 1950s, political science in the 1960s, economics in the 1970s, history in the 1980s, maybe anthropology again in the 1990s.

the action to be taken toward it. That organization is also constrained by the social context. A sociologist teaching in a department of psychiatry partitions the field rather differently than one working in a business school.

I believe that some of the conflict in our field comes about because of the different views, or partitions, of the intellectual material that are encouraged by the organizations we live in. I will argue that membership in an academic department leads one to see the organization and extent of sociological knowledge differently than does membership in a research center.

In what follows I will investigate these differences and their origins by looking at the demography of each kind of organization separately. Focusing on the births and deaths of departments and centers lends—I hope not spuriously—a "natural selection" justification to what might otherwise be a hopelessly functionalist argument. In so doing I will stress the importance of the mundane in creating these differences of opinion about the lofty domain of the architecture of knowledge. Specifically, I will stress the influence of differences in the "round-of-life" among people in various groups on their notions of what the intellectual organization of sociology is or should be.

Other than being a demographer by trade, my qualifications for writing a paper on this issue are modest: a bit of experience is all I have. I have lived in four departments divided evenly between public and private, large and small, good and less good. I have been involved in a dozen research institutes or centers: three in demography, three in survey research, four interdisciplinary ones, and two in other areas of sociology. I was there at the birth, or close to it, of one department and four centers. I was a mourner at the death of two or three centers but only a distant observer at the demise of departments. My last twenty years have been at University of Wisconsin–Madison, so the sample of experience is quite biased to the large midwestern state university. I write this following a three-year stint as chair, so some "halo" of that ambiguous role remains.

This experience permits little generalization beyond departments of sociology and research centers allied to them. When I mean to make more general statements, I shall be explicit.

Definitions

What Are Departments?

Regular departments. No doubt the idea of an academic department, whether of sociology or some other field, is self-evident to readers of this volume. Let me highlight those aspects that are most important to the task at hand. Departments are the elemental administrative unit in a university. Departments initiate the hiring of faculty and recommend faculty members for tenure. Faculty members are connected to one or more departments. The organized faculty of a department is a recognized actor in university affairs with a clear membership and with duties and responsibilities that are often spelled out in state statute or university rules.

The faculty of a department always has the responsibility to design and conduct a teaching program in the academic discipline that the department represents. Usually the department faculty controls some of the requirements for degrees in their discipline. Although research is important in many places, it is the teaching activities that are the essence of the department. There are many departments without research but none that I know of without teaching responsibilities. Thus, a department's primary activity with respect to the intellectual material of its field is exposition and instruction.

Of course most departments encourage, indeed require, their faculty to engage in research. The research itself, however, is seen by the department as the responsibility of the individual faculty member, not the department as a corporate group. Departments do not, as research centers may, choose which research topics will be undertaken and assign research tasks on those topics to specific faculty. To do so would be seen as an egregious violation of the scholar's independence.

Within the social sciences, departments undertake to provide some modest support for faculty research through assignment of space, provision of some secretarial assistance, and routine office supplies. Sometimes a department can make some research equipment available. Sometimes the department controls space designed for research use such as small groups labs or video rooms. Departments are most successful in providing research facilities for their faculty when most of the faculty need the same kinds of things.

By and large, however, the faculty member must look outside the department for research assistance. The university may provide some access to research money or facilities—computer time is a prime example. Often, however, the faculty member must go outside the university to the foundations or the federal government for research support.[2]

---

2. The primary exception to my assertion that research support must be sought outside the university is probably found in departments with rural sociology. There, funds for research assistance may be "wholesaled" to the department by the experiment station and the department given authority to divide the pot as it sees fit.

Because departments have a corporate responsibility for teaching and not for research, it is the teaching activity of departments that provides the official partition of the body of knowledge in most universities. Knowledge is partitioned into disciplines by the course rosters of the various departments. That roster is defined by history, modified by negotiation, changed by student demand, and manipulated by course requirements. Courses belong to departments. It is the department's responsibility to teach them, especially the popular ones and those that are required by another department. New courses are usually reviewed to be sure they don't trespass on another department's domain.

There is a reciprocal influence between the kinds of people on the faculty of a department and its roster of courses. The course roster of a department constrains who the department can hire. Chairs of sociology departments argue most effectively with deans for new positions or for replacements most persuasively in terms of courses. For example, a chair argues with the dean that if the department is to continue teaching the delinquency course, there must be a replacement for the retiring criminologist. Or a chair may argue that the next hire must be someone in gender studies because the potential enrollment in the women's roles course exceeds the capacity of the faculty to provide offerings.[3]

The other side of the coin is that who is on the faculty determines parts of the course roster. Most faculty want to teach something in their area as well as courses they were hired for. That is appropriate so long as the course will garner sufficient enrollment and so long as no other department has a similar course, that is, so long as the area "belongs" to sociology.

Things go in a circle because topics go together. If a sociology department hires someone to teach statistics, it is more likely to get an additional course on status attainment than a seminar on Merleau-Ponty. Once in the roster, the course on status attainment gains a life of its own and subsequently may become justification for a new hire.

Of course the "naturally occurring" development of knowledge has an influence on the local definition of the domain of the field. A chair can argue that there must be a position for someone to teach and do research in historical sociology because that is the way the field is

3. How much weight this argument carries may depend on where the alternative enrollment opportunities are. In many places deans' budgets are influenced by the enrollments in their colleges. If the alternative enrollments are in the dean's college, the argument won't carry much weight. If they are in another college, the chair will at least get a hearing.

developing. Most deans will listen closely to such arguments, weigh the evidence carefully, and provide a position, if the dean is convinced and solvent, because the reputation of the department among its peers is important to the university.[4] Nonetheless, I have never met a dean in this situation who didn't ask, "What will this person teach?" and give the answer a heavy weight in deciding whether or not to find the money. If the candidate wants to teach courses already taught in the history department, the outcome is problematic. Joint appointments may be required; favors must be traded among departments.

What is the image of knowledge that results from this focus on teaching? First, knowledge is partitioned into the parts owned by the various departments. Second, within departments, knowledge is ordered from elementary to advanced. Beginning courses are broad, focused on principles if there are any, and not too deep. Advanced courses are presumed to depend on prior courses and deal in more depth with a narrower subject. Finally, the organization of knowledge responds to demand from students. Courses that don't enroll enough students don't get taught. Currently popular subjects yield well-attended courses.

In a department, then, faculty are the human elements of a discipline while courses partition and organize the intellectual elements. In most universities, departments "own" courses and are responsible for seeing that they are taught. Thus, ownership, responsibility, and exposition define the relationship between human and intellectual elements of the field in the context of most academic departments.

Quasi-departments. As universities tried to maintain a limited roster of departments in the face of the burgeoning enrollments in the post-World War II period, there developed a plethora of not-quite-departmental organizations, or quasi-departments. Many of them developed as a device for breaking through the department-oriented partition of knowledge in order to meet demand for a program of courses that would usually be taught in separate departments. Some of them are career-oriented programs, perhaps on their way to becoming professional schools. Some are a response to a partition of knowledge arising outside of the university and are, perhaps, departments in the making. Women's studies, various ethnic studies programs, area studies programs, and environmental studies are examples. A few are in response to alternative partitions of knowledge arising within the

4. This observation was made by Joseph Galaskiewicz at the conference on "Sociology and Institution Building" Arizona, Nov. 16–17, 1988, and independently by Gerald Marwell.

university. Perhaps regional science is an example. A few such programs are moribund departments.

Some of these units are departments in all but name, having independent teaching programs, awarding their own undergraduate and graduate degrees, and independently hiring faculty whose "tenure home" is in the unit. The Committee on Human Development at Chicago was an example. Some units take over only a few departmental functions. At Wisconsin we have an international relations undergraduate program that gives a degree but has no faculty, just a set of required courses drawn from the offerings of regular departments. A nonfaculty adviser counsels students through the requirements. It is a wonder of cost-effectiveness.

The typical quasi-department teaches courses and gives degrees but lacks an independent faculty. The faculty are drawn from regular departments that control hiring and awarding of tenure. Sometimes the faculty who participate in these units is not well defined. Membership comes and goes over time. Duties, responsibilities, and organization of the faculty group are less clear than in the case of a regular department.

Quasi-departments are interesting, often problematic, units that can tell one a lot about what's going on in a university. Nonetheless, they are not the topic of this paper except as they may be departments-in-the-making or departments in their death throes.

What are "Centers"?

Centers are primarily places for doing research. One of their most important assets may be offices where faculty hide from undergraduate students and concentrate on their research tasks.

Although a department's primary asset is its faculty, research centers usually have other assets as well, assets designed to promote a specific kind of research work. Centers collect resources used directly for research such as computers, survey research facilities, small groups laboratories, libraries of specialized materials, and sometimes specialized data. They collect a staff skilled in direct research activities such as programming, interviewing, running libraries, or drawing samples.

Centers develop research support services such as people to do specialized typing and document preparation, people who can keep the books on large research grants, and people who understand and are up to date on the ever-changing university and government rules about grant submission and management. In many centers I know of, these services are the ones that strike the newcomer as most unexpectedly valuable.

The majority of the scholars involved in research centers are also faculty, but often some center members are not. Many research centers are host to postdoctoral fellows. Many also have relatively permanent research scholars who are not members of the teaching faculty. Over time, these nonteaching scholars may develop an image of the intellectual material of the field that is increasingly conditioned by the environment of the center they work in. As they act in terms of this image, they may look less and less like sociologists to the faculty not so unremittingly influenced by the image of the field engendered by that center. Some centers also have research support staff who are not sociologists but whose training, accomplishments, and publications in their own field make them scholars of considerable distinction. Scholars in all these ambiguous situations are sometimes treated badly and can be the source of considerable conflict between departments and centers.

The scholars associated with a center usually do not constitute a recognized governmental body as they do for a department. Often the faculty participate in center decisionmaking, but often considerable authority is exercised by the director. In some instances, it is not completely clear who is and who is not a "member" of the center. Indeed, a reasonable number of quite important research centers have no place in the organization chart of their university. This ambiguous organizational arrangement can mean that those scholars in centers who are not also faculty have only the least professional of links to the university—that of employee.

Since centers do little formal teaching, they are outside of the official university partition of knowledge. Sometimes they are explicitly "interdisciplinary," gathering together people from various departments with an interest in the same topic. Such topics are often about things that are perceived, both outside and inside the university, as having troubles that might be ameliorated by the fruit of social science research. Often the organization of knowledge that generates the center's topic comes from outside the university, that is from a governmental body, a foundation, or a private donor (see Bulmer, this volume, chap. 9).

Another major type of center develops to provide facilities for the specialized research methods of a part of a department. Although such centers are often within a single department, the partition of knowledge they represent is often different from that of the department's teaching program. Thus, a survey research center specializes in those topics that can be studied using surveys. The topics may predominate in a few courses in several departments but be completely unrepresented in the other offerings of those departments.

For both of these kinds of centers, and for others as well, the center member's relation to the partition of knowledge that the center represents is likely to be a bit ambivalent. The scholar is likely to feel ownership of, and responsibility for, the specific work he or she does in the center. Such a scholar may feel a certain possessiveness of the method in methods-based centers or ownership and responsibility for his or her own disciplinary perspective in the interdisciplinary center. But the center member is less likely to feel responsible for, or possessive of, the work of the center in general. The major relationship of the center member to the general partition of knowledge represented by the center is exploitative: "This rubric provides funds to support my work." The primary relationship to the topic, when narrowed to the scholar's specific research interest, is inquiry, investigation, and examination.

The specific image of knowledge fostered in the center may vary with the kind of center it is. Those centers that cross departmental boundaries encourage the view that the official partition of knowledge may be too rigid. Those centers that cover subareas within a department suggest that a monolithic view of the field may be too unitary. Whatever their kind, centers challenge the official partition of knowledge based on courses.

Centers are thus collections of capital, human and otherwise, that scholars may employ to multiply their research efforts. Centers do a lot of other things as well. Important among them is their role in the training of graduate students. Their essence, however, is research.

The Demography of Departments and Centers

The Birth of Departments

The birth rate for departments is low, though it was not always so. Currently, aside from smaller universities filling out their roster of traditional departments, most new departments come about in one of two ways. The first is by a mitosis in which, for example, sociology and anthropology divide, statistics splits off from mathematics, or the geneticists decamp from zoology to set up shop on their own. In these circumstances, a traditional subdiscipline achieves independent status.

The second source for births is the development of an entirely new department or, perhaps more frequently, an applied "school" that lies in the interdisciplinary interstice between several established disciplines. The development of a quasi department is often the first phase of life for these interdisciplinary creations. Industrial relations, policy studies, and human development are examples. In these circumstances it is less that a subarea achieves independence and more that something new is created.

In both instances, the driving force behind the birth seems usually mundane. Let me illustrate this belief with two stories; one about each kind of birth. I will begin with a mitosis.

A mitosis. Twenty years ago I was in the sociology and anthropology department at Duke University that was in the process of dividing. The department had claimed to cover the two fields for many years but had only one anthropologist for most of that time, in contrast to about fifteen sociologists. While I was there, the complement of anthropologists increased substantially, and there developed a running discussion about separation. Separation occurred a few years after I had left the department, so my information on the last stages is word-of-mouth.

During the time I was a participating observer, the pressure for separation was not from the quarters I expected. The pressure had almost nothing to do with intellectual differences. Neither did it have to do with power in departmental decision making, even though the department had a headship as opposed to a chairship and thus a lot of clout was in the hands of the boss sociologist.

So far as I could tell, the source of separatism came from the departmental administrative staff, both faculty and nonfaculty. The development of anthropology increased their work load well beyond that suggested by the increased numbers of faculty, students, and courses.

The administrative staff was used to, and quite good at, dealing with the routines and the emergencies that make up a sociologist's round-of-life. The routines and emergencies of an anthropologist's life are quite different.

The department head was used to dealing with sociologists' NIH grants coming through or being cut a few days before the semester began, thus requiring a juggling of teaching schedules. He had no idea what to do when an anthropologist, stopping through London on the way to India to spend a year drawing on a grant of counterpart funds, discovered that the entry visa had been withdrawn. How was the head to get the scholar and his or her family home? How was the head to pay the scholar's wages for the rest of the semester?

The departmental secretary was used to getting counter-sorters and computer terminals repaired quickly. She could "cool the mark" with the best of them when an irate interviewee called to complain about questions in a graduate student's schedule. But she was quite uncertain about how to free ten trunks of Brazilian feather costumes from quarantine in Miami.

The director of undergraduate studies was used to finding substitutes for sociologists missing class for a few days to go to conferences, and so on. She hated trying to organize a timetable with coherent offerings when nearly half the faculty was gone most of the time.

In each instance, the new kind of problems required a repertoire of responses that was more extensive than the people could manage. They felt like "generalists" and desperately wanted to find some "specialists" in the problems of anthropologists so they could go back to being specialists in the problems of sociologists. They were eager for a separation. When the anthropologists began to express some desire for a separate department, "in order to hold our heads up at meetings," the response was very rapid.

Indeed, it seemed that there were no economies of scale in having the joint department. The university was going to have to add enough administrative salary to the joint department to support a separate department quite well. It was this fact that seemed to make a difference in whether or not that university got a separate anthropology department. The round-of-life of sociologists and anthropologists requires administrative services that are sufficiently different as to obviate economies of scale.

I think this perspective accounts for why anthropology hangs together despite often being an uncomfortable aggregation of four quite different areas; archaeology, linguistics, cultural and physical anthropology (see Calhoun, this volume, chap. 4). They are all away a lot. They all go to quite remote places. They all want to bring back lots of things and are going to need a good deal of space to put the collection when it gets home. The round-of-life of people in each of these disparate areas requires fairly similar administrative services.

From this perspective it is not hard to see why departmental mitosis is fairly rare. After a while, faculty are sorted into bunches that need similar administrative services. Unless there is a round-of-life revolution in a subdiscipline, there are only costs to division. Besides, research centers can provide an alternative way to cope with some of the special needs of subdisciplines.

A potential transition. My second story is about the transformation of an interdisciplinary, quasi department into a regular department. In this case, the story isn't over yet.

There is a move afoot in Madison to give our La Follette Institute for Public Affairs the authority to hire and recommend faculty for tenure. That would require the Institute to take the final step in becoming a department. Heretofore the Institute had no independent faculty. All Institute faculty were hired by, and had their tenure home in, other departments. They held joint appointments in the Institute.

The precipitating event occurred when the economics department declined to hire a distinguished economist for the Institute because he wasn't "theoretical" enough. The Institute director wanted and needed the hire quite badly, had been through a number of similar turn-downs by economics, and had finally decided he had to gain his freedom. So he began to call in some chips. He has some big ones.

Our legislature is quite interested in the fate of the Institute. It has given the Institute a separate line in the budget and funded it quite well. In no small measure that is because a number of the more able legislators see their current job as a stepping-stone to better state or federal administrative jobs. They want a place to take courses, participate in research, maybe teach a class, and otherwise build their vitae.

As a consequence of the legislative interest, the dean has gone out of his way to make the Institute grow. He appointed the new, strong director from the same economics department that is providing roadblocks. He assured regular departments that appointments shared by La Follette would not cost them positions or money. Add to this the fact that our new chancellor has her Ph.D. from a public policy school and it is clear that there is a lot of power as well as emotion on the side of a birth. But it is not a shoo-in.

Under University of Wisconsin (U. W.) rules, if the Institute is to recommend a tenured hire it must have a regular, organized, department-like faculty to vote for the recommendation. If the Institute has a regular faculty, its governance structure will change. The powerful directorship will become merely a chairmanship. Under U. W. rules, budget and personnel issues are under the control of the tenured part of the formally organized departmental faculty. All other departmental issues are controlled by the whole of the faculty.

Some of the current faculty affiliates do well teaching in the small master's degree program but aren't especially productive. They will have a much increased say in the development of the Institute if they are part of a formal faculty. That prospect is not to everyone's taste. People talk about the "quality control" in hiring provided by the necessity of joint appointments with older and, to date, stronger departments.

If the essence of a department is its teaching, the deciding vote in whether or not the Institute becomes a department may hang on enrollments. Can enrollments be brought to the level to justify a department? I expect they can. That will require developing new courses, doing some marketing for the master's program, and probably introducing some undergraduate courses. In a university in which differential support among departments is at least partially enrollment-driven, and in a time when undergraduate enrollments are not rising, other departments are not going to be delighted to share "their" students with La Follette. Becoming a department thus has some political costs as well as gains.

Once he has calmed down, the director may decide he would rather La Follette remain an institute. The price for tenure-granting authority is high. He loses control of the future as the directorship becomes a chairmanship and as regular faculty take over a lot of his current power. Further, he will have to turn his attentions away from building an increasingly impressive research program to developing the service teaching mission.

The major point of this story is to illustrate the ways that development of a new "interdisciplinary" department is unlikely. In this example there is a lot to be gained by the director and the university in establishing a new department. But there is a lot to be lost to the director who must carry through the transition.

In most places, the organization of the quasi-department is less rigidly specified than it is for a regular department. Of course, the flexible structure of the quasi-department is one of its attractive features from an administration's point of view. It permits more administrative intrusion than most departments would stand for, allows a strong entrepreneur his or her head in starting something new, and makes possible the participation of clients for the unit—for example, legislators or granting agencies—in a way prohibited for regular departments. Thus, the transition of a quasi-department into a regular department is fraught with opportunity for frustration.

No doubt many other factors come into play in the birth of a department, whether by mitosis or by transition. Chief among them is probably the experience of other universities about similar units. Nonetheless, these mundane factors—Are there administrative diseconomies of scale? Is the straitjacket of departmental essence and organization worth it?—are likely to play a critical role.

Although the causes of departmental births may be mundane, the consequences are of some importance. As a department, anthropology is a force to contend with at Duke University. Its voice is heard along with that of other departments in university affairs. Its quality gets averaged in with that of other departments in calculating the university's reputation. Its courses are part of the roster; anthropology has a nameable place and a declared unity in the official partition of knowledge. All this despite the fact that it comprises four quite separate-seeming subjects, and thus would have seemed a most unlikely candidate for departmental status.

The Birth of Centers

If departments are born rarely, centers appear with some frequency. There are four kinds of center births. First are those centers that develop instead of a new department. Second are those centers created to conduct interdisciplinary research on a specific topic. Third are those generated primarily as a way to capture money. Last are those centers that develop defensively. I shall discuss each of these kinds of births in order and this section will end with a discussion of the probabilities of a center birth in a number of the subareas of sociology.

Centers instead of departments. As research technology grows and changes, so the round of the lives of faculty in the subdisciplines diverge. (They may also converge. More on that later.) It is the research part of life that diverges. Teaching has thus far been remarkably resistant to technical change. Over time, the existential differences in research life have become considerable. They were outlined some years ago by John Lofland in a wonderful piece, "How to Make Out in Graduate Sociology: One Observer's View" (Lofland 1971). Lofland encouraged graduate students to consider these existential differences in choosing an area of specialization, arguing that it is possible to love the ideas of a subarea but hate its round-of-life.

As the round-of-life differences translate into differing needs for space, things, and administrative services, so might there develop pressures for departmental mitosis. If funds are found to establish a center, many of those needs may be satisfied without a radical separation. A modest amount of seed money may engender a reasonable amount of research money, perhaps enough to support a subarea. Some centers, survey centers for example, can provide services to developing technologies in a number of disciplines. Thus, several separations may be avoided at one stroke.

In this way the possibility of centers intervenes in the process of disciplinary mitosis. I'm not proposing a great deal of self-consciousness on anyone's part in this process. At most a dean decides to allocate some seed money on the vague feeling that, if it isn't done now, it is going to cost more in the future.

It takes the concatenation of several circumstances for centers to develop through this in-lieu-of-mitosis-fashion. Obviously, first and foremost is the divergent technology of research. Second is sufficient external research support so that the center can approach self-supporting status. Finally, the research technology influences the culture of the subdiscipline in ways that make center development more or less likely. Differences in these things, I would argue, account for most of the differing propensity of subareas to form centers in lieu of mitosis.

Interdisciplinary centers for topical research. Centers also form around the needs/desires/opportunities for interdisciplinary research. Here the departmental boxes are too restrictive rather than too broad. A center becomes a device to bring together people with similar substantive interests across organizational boundaries, not only those of the department but also sometimes of schools, colleges, and divisions. Often the subject or problem to be addressed is the name of such centers: Institute for Research on Poverty, Family Studies Center, Urban Studies Center, and so on.

The organizational tension of the academic department exists in spades in these interdisciplinary research centers. People from differing departments often have differing rounds-of-life and differing technical research needs. The costs for servicing the several rounds-of-life are usually underestimated. Thus, interdisciplinary research centers can be unstable. They can survive if they are very well endowed or if, over time, they select members who share a research round-of-life as well as an interest in the subject. An example, perhaps, is the Institute for Research on Poverty at Madison. It is quite interdepartmental, drawing faculty from economics, sociology, social work, home economics, and political science. Nearly all the faculty, however, do their work through the secondary analysis of large data files.

Some of these centers develop into, along with, or out of quasi-departments. Taking on the teaching mission usually signals a substantive, as opposed to round-of-life, coherence for participating faculty. A good teaching program will present courses covering the several research traditions and thus may form a basis for stability for an interdisciplinary unit. Often, however, the faculty involved will find the research facilities in their departments of origin more suited to their research style than the interdisciplinary center can provide. Thus it is that quasi-departments have difficulty building an independent research record. Thus it is that interdisciplinary units become either broad-scale teaching programs or narrow-style research units.

Centers for money. Of course money is central to forming a center. Although many centers are nearly self-supporting through the grants and contracts their faculty win, every center, I believe, requires a modest, independent budget. That way faculty can make contributions to the collective with the reasonable expectation that, over time, he or she will get more than they give. Finding this modest independent budget can be hard. Training grants, which in their older form provided a fair amount of "institutional" support, were probably a major factor in beginning a number of centers. (I have begun two from that base.)

Money can be a sufficient as well as a necessary condition for center birth. Sometimes a private donor who is interested in supporting some kind of research feels the need for the gift to result in a nameable thing. So a center gets formed and named after the donor or one of the donor's relatives or heroes.

Sometimes, a foundation or agency decides to support certain kinds of centers. Scholars apply for the money simply to increase their research facilities. Usually such grant programs follow rather than lead the growth of centers in the area. It is the productivity of the independently developing centers that attracts the granting authority (see Smelser, chap. 1). That is certainly what happened with the initial foundation interest in supporting demography centers and with the following federal programs.

One of the great puzzles in many universities is what happens to the overhead from grants. I have known one or two centers whose sole excuse for existing seemed to be as a vehicle to capture the overhead money generated by grants that would have existed anyway (see Klausner, chap. 6).

Sometimes centers are very nearly personal property. Sometimes they are simply naming of the research enterprises of a single faculty member and hence should probably be called Professor Grant Swinger's Center much as the analog in, say, biochemistry would be called Dr. Bench Scientist's lab.

Founding or adding to such centers can be a way for a university to deal with outside raids without having to raise wages to astronomical proportions. Negotiations about how much will be added to Dr. Scientist's lab in the face of an outside offer are routine in the physical and biological sciences. The sums involved can add up impressively. As a recent chair of a department that survived some outrageous raiding attempts, let me recommend this device to social scientists. The analogy to the physical and biological sciences and the implicit demand for equal treatment from the administration can make such a request difficult to turn down. Besides, there is a lot of legitimacy in asking for the tools to do your work.

Defensive centers. Finally, centers can develop defensively. When a department has developed several centers, some of the residual people may need to band together to keep the other centers from appearing to represent the totality of departmental research. Such centers can provide legitimate places for the university to allocate additional funds. They can be vehicles for the establishment of seminars, working paper series, and lecture series. They also provide collegiality and a sense of identity. The latter can be quite important for graduate students lost in the anonymity of a large department. All of these good things happen in centers that develop for other reasons. There, however, they are secondary gains. In the defensive center they may be the primary ones. The areas that develop defensive centers are likely to be ones more central to the field. They are likely to represent the "main" research technology of the department and the one for which the department itself has the most resources.

Centers for subareas. The various subareas of sociology are subject to the risk of center formation in different measure for the differing kinds of births. Here follow my assessments of the attributes of some of the areas that make them more or less likely to create centers in these various fashions. For areas likely to create centers, I will comment on the image of knowledge created in them.

Survey research. Survey research needs a lot of administrative services. It takes many part-time, often itinerant, helpers to do interviewing and coding. Their training and skill is central to the quality of the work and their able overseers are jewels to be treasured. One must deal with samplers as though they were gods or they will go away and double their salary in business or industry.

Because of the personnel commitments, it is best to have a steady amount of business to keep the staff working. There are risks of disruptive booms and busts unless the size of the enterprise is fairly large. It may be necessary to take on some routine projects to keep body and soul together. These aspects of funding require a pretty able planning and accounting section.

Research funds for survey research are fairly plentiful.

The work needs a fair amount of equipment. Keypunches, counter-sorters, and tabulators were the tools in my youth, and they were replaced by computers of diminishing size and cost but increasing complexity. These days one needs a lot of telephone lines and a lower travel budget.

The technology of survey research yields two important cultural traits that help center formation and persistence. First, survey research is a sequence of structured emergencies. A lot can go wrong, so it is hard to get away for very long. The faculty are usually around and, along with the staff, band together to fight the forces of entropy. That can produce solidarity. Second, survey research is a sociable activity. You have to talk to people to do it, so survey researchers are usually personable and concerned with communicating well. Those things help keep centers from flying apart.

All in all, survey research is a great in-lieu-of-mitosis center maker that often serves several departments.

I think the situation of the survey center emphasizes a fairly eclectic image of knowledge. Most centers do work on many topics, some undertaken simply to keep the wolf from the door. There isn't a shared theory or model of process that is common to the topics studied. In most survey centers there does develop a pride in craft that is shared. Knowledge about that craft is highly valued.

The temporal dimension looms large in survey research. A good deal of the work is done to find out what is going on now, as opposed to previously. Today's poll is likely to find something different from yesterday's. As with historians, survey people can show a certain impatience with the idea of eternal verities.

Historical sociology. Historical sociology is a striking contrast. In this field one does major parts of the work alone. Like an anthropologist, one needs to be away from home a lot. Historical sociologists go to civilized places, though, places with archives. Also unlike anthropologists, historical sociologists can get a good deal done in a summer. One needs the skill, persistence, and perhaps contacts to find out where the good material is, to get through the bureaucracy and past the tutelaries. Then the historical sociologist is on his or her own. One needs little technology in the field, although the laptop computer is an increasingly useful tool. One may use local finding guides and the local photocopiers. Once home, a well-lighted and private place for the word processor is the major requirement.

Research money for historical sociology seems hard to get. Most of the funds are for travel and, with great good luck, support for faculty time. There is not much margin to make a center on.

The field seems to be neutral with respect to cultural and personality traits that make centers. Although there are few historical sociology centers, historical sociologists sometimes join in other kinds of centers and seem to have a good time. Even so, unless the historical sociologist is one of the newer hybrids that does modern statistics on large quantities of ancient data, a center can't be much help.

Critical sociology. Marxists are a contradiction. They need to talk to each other quite a lot but don't seem to get along very well. I suppose it is the dialectical method. Criticism as a way of life doesn't make for stable friendships. Maybe that's why one doesn't find Marxists in very big bunches.

I think this contradiction is at the heart of the success of Eric Wright's Havens Center at Madison. The Havens Center brings in well-known, left-oriented scholars for one to three weeks. The visitors give lectures, go to seminars, and engage in dialogue. It is long enough for everyone to get well criticized but only occasionally long enough for people to get really angry. The center seems to increase productivity quite considerably. It also requires some specialized services to take care of the string of visitors, many of whom are from abroad. Life in that center can seem like an endless succession of potluck dinners.

Of course there is very little external research money for left-oriented sociology. Only under fairly special circumstances do Marxists make centers.

Social psychology. Experimental social psychologists are puzzling. They have shared needs for laboratories, for a subject pool, for computer programs specializing in the statistics of measurement, and analysis of experiments. They tend to occur in bunches but, since the long march from M. I. T. to Michigan and the formation of the Institute for Social Research, they haven't made many centers. Experimentalists in sociology and psychology seem to get along well enough, but even when the two departments share a building there seems to be little institution building for reasons that are unclear. One might conjecture that the federal building programs of the early 1960s built a lot of small groups labs. Classes provide a sufficient subject pool. Perhaps then there isn't much to be gained by organizing. It is all built in.

Other kinds of social psychologists join and make centers quite facilely. Indeed, social psychology at Michigan produced a quasi department of considerable stature, but it was primarily a teaching organization.

Most often the centers formed by social psychologists focus on specific problem areas; aging, mental health, disaster studies. There has been a good deal of research money in these areas but fairly little in the way of common technical needs. Some of these centers are money-generated and others are interdisciplinary centers that have narrowed their research style. Rarely do they seem in lieu of departments.

Overall, social psychology as a subdiscipline is in itself so diverse in its research technology and administrative needs as to make a single center an unsatisfactory arrangement. Most social psychologists seem best off joining a center that shares their research technology, whether it be that of survey research, demography, or whatever.

Organizational studies. Organizational studies has produced a few centers, but I have known only one closely. It was started several years ago at Wisconsin when we had a number of quite active people in the field who did projects together in an interlocking network. The principals formed a center that held a very successful brownbag seminar, but there didn't seem much more that it could do for its members. Perhaps this is because this area is so central to sociology that its administrative requirements are the departmental norm rather than a case of deviant needs. I'm inclined to put the organizations center I know of under the category of ones that developed defensively.

Demography centers. In another era demographers needed sets of census volumes, rotary calculators, and adding machines. Centers hired clerks to run the equipment and maintain libraries of the foreign or furtive government documents. Within sociology, this pattern of needs was fairly unique to demographers. Demography centers formed rather early. Sometimes they included participants from other departments as well. Of course, demography has always been fairly well supported by outside grant money, first from foundations and then from the federal government.

As data came on magnetic tape rather than in census volumes, it became more difficult to do certain kinds of demography outside of a center with its holdings of data files, computers, programmers, and so on. During roughly the same period—in the 1960s—demographers broadened their data base to include surveys as well as censuses. A number of demography centers broadened to become facilities for secondary analysis. At the same time, the analysis of secondary data spread to other subareas of sociology, and the needs of demographers became more similar to those of people in some other fields.

There have been demography centers for about fifty years. Many generations of graduate students have grown up working in them, using their research facilities, and observing their properties. As these students have taken jobs elsewhere, they have begun new centers or joined existing ones. They know what worked where they were trained and what didn't work so well. They make and modify the centers they are in. Centers have become the expected state of nature of demographers. They are institutions.

As with survey research, demography centers serve scholars in several fields. Thus, demographers are likely to have a somewhat eclectic view of knowledge. Unlike survey research, demography has a fundamental process model whose logic generates the technology of the center. The renewal process lurks somewhere behind nearly every piece of work in demography. Common concern with this process links scholars from the several disciplines in a demography center in a way found less frequently in survey centers.

In the preceding pages I have presented research centers as quite useful tools for faculty to use in getting their work done. If centers are such a flexible response to the research needs of scholars and departments, why don't they develop willy-nilly? I believe the answer is because centers are a real bother. They can consume a good deal of faculty time to manage and the value added to the research act may not be worth the opportunity cost of that time. Thus, there is a limit to the birth rate of centers.

The Death of Departments

Mortality among departments appears to be pretty low. It certainly creates a lot of surprise when it happens. Aside from some failed experiments (perhaps demography at Berkeley is an example), most of the mortality in the social sciences seems to be in geography.

There are a number of odd aspects to the mortality of geography departments. The first is that it is entirely an American phenomenon. Geography in the rest of the world seems in fine shape. Second, the mortality seems to have come in two waves, the first occurring in the early 1950s and the second more recently. The epidemic of the 1950s began when Harvard closed its department. My informants tell me the Harvard department was quite small, rather poorly managed, and had recently lost some distinguished scholars to leading European universities. Unlike many other geography departments of the time, the Harvard department had ignored the burgeoning area studies movement and so was not well connected with the rest of the university. When an ugly scandal arose, the president simply closed the department down. There followed a kind of contagion in the Ivy League; Yale, Princeton, and a number of smaller schools abandoned the field.

The more recent wave of closing seems rather unconnected. Michigan closed its department following the departure, in rapid succession, of three very distinguished people. Many of the remaining faculty had split appointments; the department may have suffered from too much connection to other parts of the university. The remaining people apparently made poor use of the replacement positions allocated by the dean; he got angry and closed the department.

The more recent demotion of the department at Chicago to a program has a similar story. Chicago, like Michigan, had had one of the leading departments. Three losses of distinguished scholars to a small department generated a crisis.

Between the Chicago and the Michigan closings came a closing at Pittsburgh. There, a dean tried to reinvigorate an aging department of modest distinction. The faculty searched for a new chair to lead the resurrection but, after several years, couldn't arrive at a consensus. The dean finally suggested an able administrator who was a geographer before he took the job of running a Pittsburgh Area Study research program. The faculty turned him down and the dean closed the department.

The most consistent thing about these stories is how unsatisfactory they are in explaining why geography departments were closed down. Anyone in the academy could tell a number of stories with a similar plot—a small department that lost important people, subsequently behaved badly, and angered an administrator—but the stories are about departments that didn't get shut down. Why geography? I wish I could tell you that it was because of low enrollments since I hold teaching to be the essence of a department, but that won't wash. Michigan had a hard time finding seats in other courses for the freshmen who would have previously taken the geography survey course.

Is the idea of geography a residue from an older partition of knowledge? Will geography, perhaps like rhetoric, disappear from the face of the university? Apparently not, since there has been no change in the total number of departments over these waves of mortality. Other schools have added geography; most recently University of Southern California, University of California–Davis, and Duke.

It has been proposed that the issue is the lack of a general understanding of what the field is all about. In other countries where geography is a regular and important part of the secondary curriculum, there have been no problems. In the U.S., closings have frequently been preceded by committees inquiring into whether geography is "really" a discipline.

Why is geography so weak that an angry administrator can close it down when, under similar circumstances, he or she wouldn't touch economics, Greek, or comparative literature? Maybe it is nothing more than the image of the National Geographic—that ubiquitous, solidly middlebrow purveyor of good maps and pictures, "Where the Gauguin maids / In the banyan shades / Wear palmleaf drapery" (T. S. Eliot, *Fragments of an Agon*). Probably not, but it may be that a discipline is well advised to watch its "positioning," as the marketing people say.

The Death of Centers

Unlike departments, centers die regularly. This would seem to be part of their virtue as a species.

Some kinds of centers are more fragile than others. Centers that are focused on a single individual are especially fragile because an individual's tenure in a given university is limited. Centers that depend on a specific grant program may have a higher than average mortality rate because sponsors are fickle.

Centers may also die of success. With success and increase in size and function, the tasks of organizing a center change. Rather than depending on shared norms, informal and face-to-face contact, and collegial meetings, the larger organization demands rules, structured relationships, and an increasing division of authority as well as labor. Academic collegial groups are notoriously flat in their organization charts. It is unusual for an academic to be especially skilled in managing an organization with lots of levels. But the pay rate for non-faculty employees is likely to be quite dependent on how many people he or she manages. The nonfaculty staff may press for more hierarchical levels. Thus, the drift to organizational complexity is driven by more than management necessity, and the academic leader is increasingly out of his or her element. Mismanagement, bad feelings, and the weight of bureaucracy are the main predators on successful centers.

I have known one fairly distinguished center that died for lack of money. The issue wasn't research money at all. The faculty participating in that center were individually quite well funded. Rather, the problem was that the very modest amount of "extra" money went away. The center had been built on a training grant in the days when such programs provided a certain amount of program funding as well as money for trainees. There were just enough funds so that the participating faculty could feel that they were not playing a zero-sum game when they cooperated with their colleagues and engaged in a little resource sharing. There was also just enough money so that a faculty member could accept the center directorship and provide a rational-choice explanation for an otherwise hopelessly public-spirited decision.

It is nonetheless the case that center mortality in fact can lead to mortality of the center's name by many years. Some centers are firmly fixed in the organization chart of the university and so hang around in name long after they have ceased to function in fact. If there is a little bit of endowment income for the center, modest funds ground into the budget, or a traditional allocation of space, that may be sufficient incentive for a department to preserve a fiction of existence. It would not matter very much except that such defunct centers can take up space in the organizational landscape of the university and prohibit the development of other centers in the same neighborhood. A last story will illustrate this point.

When I came to the University of Wisconsin in 1967 the Social Systems Research Institute was in the last throes of death. It had been a successful interdisciplinary center organized by Guy Orcutt, a physicist turned economist. Its intellectual focus was on the construction of large-scale systems models in the social sciences. It was an elaborate institute with perhaps eight "centers," each in a single department. They focused, for example, on research in special areas such as social organizations, demography, and the labor force. Many of the younger faculty associated with the institute went on to very distinguished careers after the institute died. One was Congressional Budget Officer. More than a handful are now National Academy of Science members. SSRI died of its success and of its dependence on one, apparently quite charismatic, person for energy and leadership.

By the time I arrived in 1967, Orcutt had been at the World Bank for a couple of years and SSRI was moribund. There was still a board of directors and, as someone hired in sociology to refund and energize the "center" in population, I was put on the committee. It was like a wake. All the other members had been caught up in the intellectual social movement. They had no idea how to resuscitate the organization. Indeed, it almost seemed as though a failed institute was a necessary homage to the departed leader. There was a very modest amount of university money left in the budget and most of the committee meetings were about how to spend it. As I tried to explore a possible interdisciplinary role for the demography center, I was told firmly that was SSRI's mission. Deans seemed to confirm that SSRI owned the interdisciplinary turf and that demography should confine itself to sociology; and so we did. A few years later SSRI was collapsed into economics and the modest funds merged with the department budget. The name is retained for a preprint series of work in econometrics and mathematical economics. By that time the die was cast for a demography center primarily within sociology.

The Tension between Centers and Departments

In many places there is a good deal of tension between departments and their centers.

From the point of view of the department, centers consume the time and energy of faculty. If centers are some physical distance removed from the department, as they often are, and if centers provide office "hideouts" for faculty, as they often do, participating in a center can seem like deserting the department. Since centers are usually formed by faculty having somewhat deviant research interests or rounds-of-life, this retreat can seem like a fracturing of the department along preexisting fault lines that threatens its viability. Since making a center usually takes money, especially grant money, this splintering can seem like the rich abandoning the poor. Particularly, it can seem like an abandonment of the teaching activities that are central to the department's existence.

On the other hand, center members are likely to feel that they are just trying to get the somewhat unique research facilities that the university won't provide through the department. Teaching may be the essence of a department, center members reason, but research is how it becomes famous. Center members argue—correctly, if things are working right—that center people use less than their fair share of the departmental resources. What, then, is the complaint?

Whatever may be the justice of these feelings by department members and center members, the result of the round-of-life differences is that center and noncenter department members meet each other less frequently over the coffee pot, while collecting their mail, or getting yellow pads than they would if there were no centers. Less interaction produces less amicability and also less chance to exchange information about what is going on—information that lessens the chance of subsequent misunderstanding.

Department–center conflict arises most acutely over faculty hiring.
If the demography center wants someone in population and development in Africa, the survey center wants someone in measurement, and
the courses on gender roles are over-subscribed, there is likely to be a
squabble in faculty meeting over hiring priorities. Unless there develops a tacit agreement to "take turns" in seeking a position from the
dean, the squabble may become a sustained war in which each side
vetoes the other's access to positions. This outcome can be especially
likely if the department-generated view of the domain of sociology
leads members to define measurement types, for example, as outside
of the fold and hence not warranting a "turn." Such a situation is less
likely in a large and complex department, but disagreements about
what is within the fold are likely between centers and departments of
any size because there are differences in the image of, and relation to,
sociological knowledge fostered by the two kinds of enterprises.

Departments teach what is "known." Courses conserve and collect
disparate research questions and findings, build them together historically and theoretically, and produce a course. The activity is synthetic, a property it shares with theory building. The teaching activity
is also centripetal, pointing toward the disciplinary core (see Calhoun
[this volume, chap. 4] and Kuhn [1977] on the importance of textbooks in this process). The parts of courses justify themselves in terms
of the central topic that the course is about. Courses justify themselves
by pointing toward that general topic which is the subject of the department as a whole. It is that central subject that the department
"owns" in the official division of knowledge of the university. Teaching that is too centrifugal, too outward pointing, leads to quasi-
departments.

Research centers investigate what is "unknown." Research searches
out the unexpected phenomena. It decomposes processes into their
parts to understand cause and effect. It tests and hopes to extend or
replace accepted knowledge. Research is also centrifugal, outward
pointing. Understanding is sought through connections to whatever
ideas help, without regard to whether they are part of the sociological
sphere. Hence, full-time researchers in centers may seem questionable
sociologists to department faculty. Hence, sociologists in centers have
useful and productive working relationships with economists, political scientists, and so on.

In the above I am assuming center member and department member
are roles that may be jointly held. Members of one center are thus
quite likely to take the role of department member when fussing about
another center.

Peroration

The title of my paper is a kind of stuffy pun that expresses my understanding of this situation. I think the conflict between departments and centers is essential in that it is a conflict between the essences of the enterprises. The essential teaching activities of the department are synthetic and centripetal; the essential research activities of the centers are analytic and centrifugal. These things are antagonistic: the one building, the other tearing down; the one looking inward, the other straining outward.

The conflict between the two enterprises is also essential in the sense of "necessary." They represent the inherent strains in what it is we are supposed to do. If we only look inward and build our theories, we create an empty ideology or schizophrenic delusion. If we only look outward and take things apart, we create an empty collection of facts or a compulsive ritual. Both inward and outward looking are necessary for a healthy discipline; both analysis and synthesis are necessary for scholarly progress. Thus, the tension between departments and their research centers is an institutionalization of that tension between "convergent" and "divergent" thinking—between being a traditionalist and an iconoclast—which Kuhn noted in his essay "The Essential Tension": "Since these modes of thought are inevitably in conflict, it will follow that the ability to support a tension that can occasionally become almost unbearable is one of the prime requisites for the very best sort of scientific research" (Kuhn 1977:226). As it is for scholars, so is it for scholarly institutions.

References

Hesse, Mary. 1974. *The Structure of Scientific Inference,* chap. 2. Berkeley and Los Angeles: University of California Press.

Kuhn, Thomas. 1977. *The Essential Tension: Selected Studies in Scientific Tradition and Change.* Chicago: University of Chicago Press.

Lofland, John. 1971. "How to Make Out in Graduate Sociology: One Observer's View." *Kansas Journal of Sociology,* 7:102–15.

Quine, W. V., and J. S. Ullian. 1970. *The Web of Belief.* New York: Random House.

8

Trained Incapacities of Sociologists

ALBERT J. REISS, JR.

Sociology's claim to scientific status is precarious despite Comte's pronouncement that it is the queen of the social sciences. We have long since abandoned Comte's theory of society for other frames of reference, models, and methods of inquiry. His legacy of positivism, however, retains a firm grip on our discipline, despite pointed criticisms by ethnomethodologists and grounded theorists. Empirical studies abound. One might even say that within our discipline there is less agreement on theory than on methods of inquiry.

These global characterizations aside, my sole purpose in what follows is to focus attention on how the core methods and techniques that sociologists employ for data collection shape sociological conceptions of individual, organization, and society. This shaping comes about because our data are the product of sample *respondent* surveys with designs centered on external rather than internal validity. The emphasis on external validity places a premium on national and large-scale sample surveys organized through bureaus and centers of survey research.[1]

Examination of methodological training in academic sociology discloses how we train incapacities into each generation of sociologists. The principal required courses teach sample respondent questionnaire

1. Because the focus of the symposium upon which this volume is based is on academic sociological training, the organization of surveying in large public and private organizations is not examined in this paper. Sociologists depend quite heavily upon data collected in periodic surveys like opinion polls, government surveys such as those on employment, health, and crime, or commissioned special surveys. Private survey firms are quite commonly used to collect data for sponsored academic sociological research. The collection of survey information in these organizations lies with technical specialists, who generally lack expertise in the substantive knowledge that is the occasion for the survey. The substantive expert often lacks knowledge of the consequences of technical decisions. Just how to pool substantive and technical skills effectively in research undertakings is an interesting and largely unexamined area of scientific inquiry. The matter has been given only limited attention, most recently in attempts to assign responsibility for fraud in scientific inquiry.

or interview surveys as the prototypical model for data collection and probability statistics as the primary analytical method. Courses in field and observational methods are required less frequently. This essay explores how the curriculum in methods results in trained incapacities by neglecting to train in methods for the direct observation of social life.

Observation is integral to all human activity. Each of us is both observer and observed. The meaning attached to those observations is problematic if one's aim is to describe *social reality.* As Goffman (1974:1–2) noted:

> Presumably a "definition of the situation" is always to be found, but those who are in the situation ordinarily do not *create* this definition, though their society often can be said to do so; ordinarily, all they do is to assess correctly that the situation ought to be for them and then act accordingly.

He goes on to observe (1974:8):

> Let me say at once that the question "What is it that's going on here?" is considerably suspect. Any event can be described in terms of a focus that includes a wide swath or a narrow one and—as a related but not identical matter—in terms of a focus that is close-up or distant. And no one has a theory as to what particular span and level will come to be the ones employed. . . . A similar issue is found in connection with perspective. When participant roles in an activity are differentiated—a common circumstance—the view that one person has of what is going on is likely to be quite different from that of another.

Methods for the direct observation of social life record information on behavior and events *as they occur* in their natural social settings. In direct systematic observation, the scientist, or persons the scientist selects and trains, collects and records information or employs technological means of direct surveillance to record events as they occur.[2] In systematic social observation, the categories for collecting observations arise from the descriptive and analytical categories guiding the investigation. Observers are trained in collecting and classifying observations under these rubrics. Methods of direct observation that are

2. Methods of direct observation are by no means the sole province of the scientist. It is practiced by different occupational specialists. Clinicians are schooled in direct observation, as are professional journalists. Other examples are intelligence agents and law enforcement officers. Nonetheless, no occupation relies exclusively on direct observation.

less systematic, such as those characterized as solo, participant, or field observation, rely more upon each observer's definition of what is observed, although the observer typically has a disciplinary perspective that guides the observation. Less commonly used technological modes of direct observation that observe and record behavior and events as they occur are the camera, the audiotape, and electronic modes of surveillance.

Major contrasting methods do not collect observations of behavior or events in social life as they occur. Therefore we shall speak of them as indirect methods of observation. Typically, the data are verbalizations recalled[3] by subjects of the investigation. Subjects act as observers of themselves and others but not of what they observe going on at the time. Instead, they supply information in response to investigator or interviewer cues; thus, they are spoken of as respondents. Metaphorically speaking, interviewers ask respondents to report traces of past behavior or to aggregate information about themselves. Although survey interviewers can be asked to record observations about the respondent's behavior during the interview, study directors rarely ask interviewers to do so.[4]

It must be noted that sociologists, like historians, do not always themselves collect the direct observations that they use as evidence. By contrast, others, such as journalists and photographers, may provide firsthand observer accounts. One must be careful, however, to distinguish whether the information in a medium is a record of direct or indirect observation. For example, journals and diaries are valuable sources of direct observations of events for a time and place but they also include indirect observations.[5]

3. Trial lawyers and detectives also are among those skilled in eliciting information from respondents. Unlike social scientists, however, they may be quite interested in having the person being interrogated behave in a desired way, e.g., make a confession or by response and demeanor influence a judge or jury. Trial lawyers are especially interested in having the subject's behavior observed by those responsible for reaching a decision.

4. To illustrate the point, psychiatrically trained clinicians might rely upon direct observations of demeanor, gestures, tone of voice, and other behaviors to determine how their patient feels when making a given verbalization. Correspondingly, interviewers will ask and record what respondents say they think, feel, etc., or perhaps, more typically, how they think they felt, etc.

5. The writings of Jefferson and Alexis de Tocqueville are instructive in this respect. Jefferson's *Memoir* (1829) and Tocqueville's *Democracy in America* (1840) contain almost no direct observer accounts. Their journals do. See especially Tocqueville's *Journeys to England and Ireland* (1958) for first-hand observer accounts of social life in England and Ireland mixed with opinion, self-observations, explanation, and evaluations.

Observation in Traditional Science

The preferred method of data collection for scientific investigation is *direct observation*. Ordinarily, the biological or physical scientist does not substitute indirect for direct observation when direct observation is feasible. The history of science is writ large with inventions that facilitate direct observation, such as the optical telescope and the microscope. The history of science also is writ large with recording the direct observations of the human senses. Darwin's (1890) journal attests to the power of direct observation and documents the role his observations played in developing his theory of evolution (1880). Direct observation and recording may be the method of exploration and discovery, par excellence. Scientists seem intent upon seeing or experiencing directly the nature of phenomena—what is there.

The importance of direct observation in science is so critical that much effort is placed on penetrating the unseen world, turning the unseen and inaccessible into the seen and accessible. Recent complex technology testifies to the central importance of direct observation. Through sensors, signal transmission, and computer reception, the structure of matter turns into images. Technologies have been invented to look directly at soft tissue as well as bone structure, abandoning the indirect measures that had to suffice until such methods of direct observation were invented. These examples are intended to make clear not only that direct observation is the preferred method of data collection in the traditional sciences but that indirect modes are ordinarily adopted only when there are constraints on direct observation. A main constraint in sociology is that we have not yet learned how to observe directly or of how to turn that which is observed indirectly into direct observation.

Care must be taken not to confuse reconstruction, inference, and explanation with observation. The data of the archaeologist or the paleontologist, for example, include direct observations of where an observable specimen was found, and so forth, as well as the specimen. What cannot be observed directly is what is reconstructed and explained using the specimen, its location, and other elements as data. Furthermore, what constitutes an experiment is often thought of mistakenly as indirect observation. The experiment may be regarded as an ordered set of direct observations that fit a model of causal inference. One can directly observe and record the experimental conditions and apparatus, the experimental intervention, and some outcome of that intervention. It is these data that are direct observations.[6]

---

6. Put another way, one should not confuse a method, such as an experiment, with an observational mode. Data collection is only one element in an experiment. Similarly,

To say, then, that the preferred method of scientific data collection is direct observation is not to undermine the importance of indirect modes of observation. It *is* to emphasize that scientists ordinarily make great efforts to penetrate that which cannot be seen or experienced directly by the scientific observer through methods that approximate direct observation.

Methods of Social Observation

The preferred method of data collection of traditional science contrasts sharply with the preferred method in sociology. It seems only somewhat of an overstatement to conclude that sociology builds its body of knowledge on indirect rather than direct methods of data collection, that is, sociologists do not use methods that observe the phenomena of social life as they take place. Survey research, the major form of sociological data collection, is an indirect mode of social observation. It is used in preference to direct modes of field observation, field experiments, technological modes of observing and recording, and systematic social observation. The argument advanced in this paper is that sociologists use indirect modes of data collection because that choice results less from constraints on direct observation methods than from their trained incapacity in the use of such methods.

As a part of explicating that thesis, we must first deal with the argument that the preference for survey methods is a matter of constraints on direct social observation methods rather than of a trained incapacity in their use. Several kinds of constraints are commonly mentioned.

Some advance the argument that the substitution occurs because sociologists are constrained from direct observation by institutions of privacy. Law and custom set limits to what human beings and their technology can observe directly. There are such constraints on the large and diverse surveillance technology that records behavior as it occurs (Marx 1988). Some additional limits are imposed on the invasion of personal privacy by survey investigators. The consent of human subject committees and of human subjects are required for inquiry into matters considered private. To be sure, when one cannot have access to a situation to observe directly, interviewers may learn something about matters that occur there, provided that persons consent to talk about them.[7] For example, one cannot enter the polling

---

what constitutes the observables should not be confused with how one collects information on them.

7. The more general problem is access to what is not generally observable. Institutions of privacy restrict access to private matters, both internal and external to human

booth to observe voting behavior, but one can ask people how they voted outside the polling place.

Clearly, there is a place for learning about behavior by questioning people about what they observe about their behavior and that of others,[8] especially when it appears to be the only means of access. Yet when surveys are used to collect data, all too commonly the conditions of limited access do not prevail. Even when privacy considerations enter, it is surprising how often one can find settings where such conditions are not a constraint because consent is obtained. It is surprising, for instance, how little sociologists directly observe students in schools, particularly in classrooms, in contrast with the number of questionnaire and interview surveys of teachers and students about their behavior. Even more striking, perhaps, is how students often are used to gather information on matters that could not be observed in that setting precisely because they are co-opted (and in ways that are more invasive of their privacy). Moreover, many matters that must be regarded as private in private places are not so in public places where they can be observed, such as conversations.

Were sociologists to take direct social observation seriously, they would soon discover that much observation can be done by placing observers in organizational roles where they can observe behavior or by using technological means of observation. For example, hundreds of observers have been trained to systematically observe citizen and police behavior in the company of police officers. In addition, persons who regularly occupy organizational roles can often be trained to provide information by direct observation and reporting.

Solo participant observer field studies and multiple observer systematic observation studies of behavior in police organizations are good examples of the power of direct observation. Solo participant observer studies of police detectives and patrol officers have facilitated the comparative study of policing. Data exist for the jurisdictions of Canada (Ericson 1982), England (Cain 1973; Chatterton, 1976; Grimshaw and Jefferson 1987; Holdaway 1983), the Federal Republic of Germany (Kürzinger 1979), the Netherlands (Punch 1979), and the

---

subjects and their organizations. Beyond gaining access to private matters are the problems of gaining access to that which we do not know how to observe directly, e.g., what goes on in the heads of people, and of how to gain access to matters that are held secret. The institution of spying and of spy satellites raise interesting questions about social observation without consent and, one might add, of social observation without social scientists.

8. The word "observe" is used advisedly since the responses are either self-observations or reports of observations about other matters.

United States (Banton 1964; Bittner 1967; Buckner 1970; Manning 1980; Muir 1977; Rubinstein 1973; Skolnick 1966; Westley 1970).

Systematic social observation was developed by this author (1967) in studies of police patrol behavior. The method samples encounters, events, or behaviors. Multiple trained observers collect information using standardized observational instruments (Reiss 1968, 1971a, 1971b, 1976, 1979). Subsequent innovations make it feasible for observers to encode and record elements of events as they occur (Sykes 1974). Among the systematic observation studies of the police are observations of women on patrol (Bartlett 1977; Bloch and Anderson 1974; Sichel et al. 1977), of police response time (Bieck and Kessler 1977), and of police field interrogation practices (Boydstrum 1975). Multiple observers also have been used to monitor the implementation of randomized field experiments in methods of police training to reduce their use of violence (Fyfe 1988) and police interventions in domestic violence crises (Boruch et al. 1990).

In addition, systematic social observations have been combined with sample surveys of the police and the public (Reiss 1967; Ostrom et al. 1973). These investigations provide opportunities to compare the two methods of data collection. They are instructive about the two methods, though they do not resolve the issue of whether they tap dual or multiple realities. Maureen Cain's report of her study of policing by a county force in England is instructive of the gains when participant observation is done in addition to survey interviews. She reports (1973:9–10):

> The main hypotheses of the research were tested by means of a structured interview.
>
> In addition, it was decided to spend a period of "participant" observation with the police. This part of the research was first intended simply to enliven the rather bald discussion of tabulated responses: very rapidly it became apparent that it also served the purpose of establishing *rapport*, so that in many cases it would be fair to say that it was the observation work which made the interview possible. I would guess, though there can be no evidence for this, that it also improved their validity. As time went by, and I became more of a participant and less of an observer, a third, very important value of the observation work became apparent.... The observational records made it possible to "go behind" the interview data so that the responses given are themselves explained in terms of the structure of the policeman's life space and the sense which he makes of it.
>
> By the end of the research a fourth position had been reached. As my knowledge of on-going police work became more complete the

inappropriateness of many of the questionnaire items became increasingly evident on two levels. First, some of the situations and
sentiments about which questions were asked were more meaningful
in the researcher's world than in the policeman's. Second, even when
the situation or feeling under discussion was one which was recognized by the policeman, it was not always presented or expressed in
his concepts or language so that he was constantly having to make
conceptual leaps, assumptions that what the researcher was *really*
on about was a situation or feeling about which he *did* have knowledge and experience. The extent to which men were prepared to
make this effort was no doubt a function of their varying relationships with the researcher, which affect such things as their assumption that she really knew what was relevant but expressed it differently—in which case they would answer what they thought she
meant—or the more negative assumption that an outsider, and this
outsider in particular, could never understand police work and these
ridiculous questions proved it, in which case the man might give a
meaningless answer to a (for him) meaningless question.

It is mistaken to contend that sociologists should be trained in either
methods of social observation or in survey research methods. Indeed,
the design of systematic social observation investigations is formally
similar to the design of sample surveys (Reiss 1968, 1971b, 1976).
Any methods curriculum will encounter considerable overlap in training
for both methods of data collection and analysis. The trained incapacity, then, lies as much in providing experiences in doing observational
studies, particularly systematic social observation investigations, as it
does in providing methods training in designing observational studies
and in observer techniques and skills.

As well as the issue of privacy, a second major argument advanced
against direct observation is that sociological phenomena cannot be
observed directly because of the nature of the phenomena. On the face
of it, this is a rather peculiar argument should one take literally the
emphasis on what is social in the sense of inter-individual rather than
intra-individual. Perhaps one reason why the argument is made is precisely because so many sociological studies use the individual as the
source of their data on the social and come to regard the primary data
of the social to be attitudes, opinions, and motives rather than the
behavior of individuals, groups, and collectivities. What appears to
have happened in sociology is that the methods of data collection
shape sociological knowledge rather than the knowledge we seek
shaping the methods of data collection.

Setting aside these considerations, a case can be made that sociologists have made more contributions to the development of direct

rather than indirect methods of data collection. Sociologists may be hard put to identify their contributions to the development of survey data collection because the basic elements, for example, sampling, questionnaire and interview schedules, and interviewing, developed largely outside our discipline.[9] Correspondingly, there is more evidence that sociologists contribute to the development of direct methods of data collection, despite their underutilization. Ethnomethodology and systematic social observation both have been developed largely by sociologists.

There is a third argument that seems on its face to lack substance. That argument holds that the censuses and probability surveys are the only ways one can collect *quantitative* data. Correlatively, it is argued that observational methods provide only *qualitative* data. There is ample demonstration by now, as we illustrated above, that observation of natural social phenomena can be organized as systematically as the sample respondent survey. Systematic social observation and sample survey methods differ principally in that survey data are collected by interviewers from respondent observers, whereas direct observations of natural social phenomena are made by independent observers. Data from systematic social observation surveys can be quantified and analyzed in the many ways that individual survey data can be analyzed. The units of observation are by no means confined to individuals as the source of the data.

A fourth argument often advanced against observation studies is that their external validity is low. This argument rests in turn on erroneous presumptions about sampling frames, sampling units, and sample size and confounds these with arguments about relative costs. The external validity of solo observation studies is certainly problematic, even when there is convergence from a number of independently conducted solo investigations. There is no reason, however, why one cannot sample and observe units for any territorial aggregate and generalize from those observations. Indeed, probability samples of organizational units are often sampled in the United States for sample surveys. There are national, state, and local sampling frames for many different kinds of organizations, such as schools, businesses, military units, arts organizations, law enforcement departments, and courts, to give but a few examples. Moreover, within these organizations one can sample a given type of organizational unit, such as classrooms in schools or organizational transactions, hearings in a court, or encoun-

9. A case can be made, however, that sociologists have made substantial contributions to the analysis of individual level data from surveys, especially from panel surveys.

ters between police officers and citizens.[10] Although the logistical
problems of sampling may be greater for direct observational surveys
than for sample respondent surveys, the formal problems of external
validity are no different.

Closely paralleling the argument about sample size is the argument
that observational surveys preclude a comparative or macrosociology.
The argument is elusive since it appears to rest on a naive presumption
that one can observe the macrocosm by a single investigation using a
single method.[11] An understanding of the social macrocosm, whatever
that may mean, will hardly rest on being able to observe it all at once,
so to speak, or by any single means of observation. It is at best a slow
and painstaking cumulative effort. The argument of this paper is that
direct observation, when possible and permissible, is a preferable
means to that end.

A fifth argument advanced is that observational surveys are more
costly while indirect methods are cheap. This seems like the kind of
argument that is as difficult to refute as it is to support. One can readily get into arguments about how one should calculate costs. Should
costs be calculated per unit of information, per investigation, per total
costs for a given result? Direct observational means, whether by an
observer or by technological means, may well have low unit cost per
unit of information. The unit cost of information on consumer pur-
chases by observing or monitoring transactions may be much lower
than that based on interviewing buyers. Yet one would be hard put to
argue for the exclusive use of one or the other on the basis of unit
costs for a piece of information.

What does seem clear is that although the cost of sample surveys
has risen considerably, by comparison with physical and natural science costs of data collection and analysis, it is still on the cheap. Big
science is costly, and sociologists, while hard put to justify big science
costs, may nonetheless preclude the development of their knowledge

10. A methodological issue arises whenever the observational units differ greatly in
the size of their component elements, e.g., when one samples schools that differ greatly
in number of classrooms. The problem can be dealt with by appropriate weighting
schemes (Kish 1965:564–72). Sample surveys of respondents are not without their
problems of sampling frames and respondent selection. National samples in the U.S.A.
depend upon selecting area units and then sampling some organization within that unit,
such as households or businesses, and then selecting respondents within those units.
The external validity of sample surveys of household respondents, for example, depends
upon randomizing respondent selection.

11. One is tempted to draw attention to how naive such a presumption would be for
the physical macrocosm. There are multiple means for its observation, none of which
observes the macrocosm.

by low-budget research. Fewer low-cost investigations and more high-priced ones might be a preferable strategy.

Evidence of Trained Incapacities

To provide evidence of trained incapacities for social observation is no simple matter. One runs the risk of using indirect modes of observation to advance one's argument. Hence, a disclaimer is necessary. The argument advanced in this paper does not contend that respondent sample surveys or organizational records are defective means of data collection. Rather, the intent is to show how heavy reliance on methods of indirect observation shape our discipline in ways that direct observational methods would not.

A caveat is also in order. The evidence on trained incapacities offered in this paper derives as much from my experiences as a sociologist and my participant observer roles as a department administrator, a screener of applicants for positions in departments, a reviewer of grant applications, and a reader of our journals as it does on systematic research. To give some indication of the imbalance that I sense, I made a few tabulations of the methods used in papers presented at annual meetings of societies that report empirical research and in papers published in sociology journals. All of these observations lead to the conclusion that methods of direct observation play a very small role in the training of sociologists and in their empirical work. Indeed, when observational methods are taught they almost always focus on what their instructors regard as field methods yielding qualitative reports. Direct observations are infrequently quantified and systematic social observational methods are infrequently taught.

For those who like descriptive statistics, I assembled a few to illustrate this imbalance in methods of data collection for empirical studies in our discipline. Only a very small proportion of papers presented by sociologists at annual meetings and an even smaller proportion of papers published in the major sociological journals are based on direct observational methods. A sample was drawn from several thousand abstracts of papers presented by sociologists at the annual meetings of the American Sociological Association, the Society for the Study of Social Problems, and the American Society of Criminology. All non-empirical papers were eliminated. Papers devoted exclusively to theory and critique were removed, as were papers on the same subject presented at more than one convention. Of the remaining papers, only 3 percent reported that the data were collected by direct observations under the control of the investigator. Less than 1 percent of the total quantified the observations.

Case histories of individual or historical events based on historical or individual accounts comprised an additional 13 percent. While some of these were based on direct observation, such as news media accounts of journalists who viewed the events, most such accounts were by interview, not by observation. Journalists, like sociologists, treat their respondents as their observers. A respondent sample survey or census was the main method of data collection for 48 percent, and organizational records were the principal source of data for 36 percent of all papers presented. The organizational records used were not generally based on organizational observer or member accounts of events as they took place but were derived from organizational accounting procedures. Of course, there is variability in these proportions among the scholarly meetings, but the imbalance is clearly evident in all.

The results from a review of articles published the last two years of issues of the *American Sociological Review, Social Forces,* and the *American Journal of Sociology* confirm a similar imbalance as far as direct observational methods are concerned. Because some issues were devoted to particular topics, there are noteworthy fluctuations from issue to issue and across journals in the proportion of articles using other methods of data collection. An issue devoted to research on complex organizations, for example, relies more on organizational records than on survey research, despite the growing use of survey methods of data collection for such studies.

It is more difficult to get a sense of the methodology curriculum for graduate training in sociology because there seems to be considerable variability in what the required courses may be. Quite clearly, the analysis curriculum is dominated by a statistics requirement. Statistics courses, in turn, are dominated by the statistics of probabilists rather than Bayesians. In recent years, the teaching of econometric techniques has become more common and path modeling may even have reached the lower reaches. My impression is that survey methods dominate the methods curriculum and serve as the bridge to the analysis curriculum. Social statistics textbooks do much to confirm this impression, judging from their illustrative examples. Although quite commonly a "methods of research" course is required, surprisingly little attention is given to observational methods of data collection. Among the latter, attention focuses primarily on participant observation as a prototype method of what is called field investigation. Nonetheless, the common designation of these as field methods may be re-

vealing as it shifts attention to what Everett Hughes used to speak of
as getting data "on the hoof." The experience of observing "in the
field," whether or not as a participant, shifts the emphasis to direct
observation and recording of social organization and human behavior
based on the experience of the observer qua observer.

What is surprising, perhaps, is how little attention we sociologists
pay to training our graduate students in the design and execution of
randomized laboratory and field experiments, the model method of
data collection and analysis for bench scientists. Setting aside laboratory experiments, we have witnessed the growth in recent years of
randomized field experiments, particularly in the evaluation of techniques of social intervention, some of which have been noteworthy.
Among those worthy of mention are randomized law enforcement interventions in domestic violence (Sherman and Berk 1984), assignment to supported work programs (Hollister et al. 1984), and inmate
release-to-work programs with monetary rewards (Rossi et al. 1980).
Although such experiments require methods of social observation to
determine whether the assigned treatment is delivered, this requirement of the design unfortunately is often omitted. What is more, it is
common to select outcome variables that are not directly observed by
the experimenter. Rather, reliance is placed upon survey-collected outcome variables or those produced by the organizational processes
being evaluated. In the spouse assault experiments, for example, the
deterrent effect of the randomized treatment of arrest when compared
with other police interventions is subsequent police arrests and the
spouses' self-reports of whether they were assaulted by the offending
cohabitant. This latter example is chosen deliberately because one
may readily argue that it is virtually impossible to observe subsequent
assault. Yet that is far from correct, at least so far as the subsequent
arrest of offenders is concerned. At the very least, the police can report
on their direct observation of indicators of assault and often observe
first hand the outcome of the assault, for example, whether the spouse
has visible injuries. The example is also chosen because it may illustrate that one will want to use a variety of methods of data collection
to approximate the variable one seeks to measure. Surely as part of
the validation, direct observation of subsequent assault, whether by
police-trained observers or employees of the observation data collection team, seems essential. A comparison of police observations of
assault and reports of victim testimony of assault at the time of the
incident seems a likely way to test the validity of victim self-reports to
a survey interviewer. To be sure, there will be those victim reports of
events that are not reported to the police, a matter that complicates

not only validation of self-reports but of the criterion variable. There are, however, analytical ways of handling partial validations of a criterion variable and capture-recapture models for analyzing outcome variables based on multiple sources of data (Reiss 1985).

These observations on training and empirical research are not necessarily persuasive to those who hold any one of a number of positions on methods of measurement. For example, some will argue that everyone is an observer of oneself and others, and the respondent sample survey collects those direct observations. One problem of course is to what extent are they direct observations? Typically, these observations are aggregate observations in which the presumption is that the respondent knows how to aggregate the specific observations that are the raw data for what is reported. This presumption is clung to despite considerable evidence that individuals make considerable errors in reporting statistics of aggregation. This is true even when that aggregation is for an individual in a close relation to the respondent. It is worth noting that generally one avoids aggregating as part of the direct observational process.

Others will contend that establishing the validity of measures and their error properties in respondent methods of data collection is tractable without reliance on direct observation methods of data collection. Without being drawn into the abstract world of triangulation and meta-analyses, it is hard to imagine that one would forgo validation by direct observation where that is feasible.

Consequences of Relying upon Indirect Rather Than Direct Methods of Social Observation

I approach the problem of determining the consequences of opting for indirect rather than direct methods of data collection and probabilist methods of analysis for the discipline of sociology perhaps with more resolve than conviction, since the data for a convincing case are not at hand by any means of data collection! Yet I shall offer a number of conclusions for consideration, leaving open the question of whether they are inherent in any of the methods of data collection rather than in their practice.

One of the consequences of probability sample surveys is that data are collected and findings produced, at least in practice, for population aggregates rather than natural social units. This follows in part from the way that survey populations are sampled in terms of the units and characteristics of a population of units. More importantly, it appears to follow from the limitations of population respondent surveys to discover, bound, and characterize natural social units.

A second consequence is that survey methods of data collection are a quite limited means for understanding social processes. For some social processes, in fact, one may need to have continuous observation to understand the process. This may be the case, for example, if one wanted to understand the course of conflicts or of how disputes are resolved.

A third consequence is that exploration and discovery are more consistent with direct observation than with indirect observation methods. Exploration and discovery by the survey or analysis of institutional records depends quite heavily upon how one conceptualizes and operationalizes variables and upon techniques of analysis such as latent attribute or cluster techniques.

Though it is difficult to stipulate just how and why direct observation is a means of discovery, it perhaps occurs more readily when the scientist is the observer. But it also seems to stem from the fact that direct observation and recording can produce a more detailed description of an individual unit. A colleague of mine contends that the concepts of a science generally emerge only out of painstaking and quite tedious, repetitive, and detailed observation and recording of phenomena. Such description leads eventually to detailed classification systems around which the science is initially constituted, whether those of a periodic table, a Linnaean classification of living things, or a planetary system. Description rather than analysis is the initial core of any science. The bottom line, so to speak, is that we have too little painstaking description in sociology. For example, it might take many, many more detailed descriptions of marital conflicts to understand how to classify them, or we may need many, many more detailed community studies to describe the structure of community.

To be sure, detailed description and continuous observation pose genuine problems of data reduction. Whether one is scanning the universe with an optical or radio telescope and maintaining a photographic record of it or making a detailed audiovisual recording of some ongoing event such as judicial proceedings, one quickly finds that the volume of observations is incredibly large—like a stellar galaxy. Yet this may only attest to the fact that we may need to return again and again to this one continuous observation to understand one instance of court proceeding and make some things problematic about court proceedings in general.

Perhaps a fourth consequence is that the respondent probability sample survey focuses unduly on external rather than internal validity—upon generalization rather than upon understanding the nature of variability. Whether this is inherent in the method of data collection is unclear, as one can readily argue that it is a consequence solely of current practice. Yet a core concern of internal validity is the development of measures and providing estimates of their error properties. It is hard to see how this can be done simply as a survey exercise and independent of measures obtained by direct observation. Direct observation seems integral to the development of measures.[12]

A fifth consequence is more difficult to characterize. It arises because observation is the core of all methods of data collection. Methods vary only in who makes the observations, how, and by what means. What I have characterized as direct means of observation depend upon direct sensing of phenomena as they occur in time and space. One major means of doing so is for scientifically trained observers to have human sensory contact with the phenomena under observation. The other relies upon technological sensing of those phenomena. Although there has been a premium on visual contact and description, direct human sensing includes all of the senses. The major technological means of sensing may sense and record more than one dimension related to the senses—for example, image, color, and sound. They are also capable of recording other elements, such as time.

Direct methods of data collection do not require prior classification of what is observed or recorded. This is rather different from what is required in the social construction of events by respondents to sample survey cues. Language is not essential to capture and record direct observational language that enters into the social construction of the observed. What constitutes an experience may not yet be fashioned into words, and social reality can be captured in some sense independent of observer constructions. More may be seen and recorded than exists in the mind's eye of the observer; videotapes, for example, while captured from some observational perspective, do not depend directly upon observer constructions. Though captured in time and capturing time, they can be open to ever new social constructions.[13] Videotapes may be analogous to stored tissue samples that can be reexamined over time. One suspects that we have yet to explore the advantages of

12. Sociologists, unlike psychologists, devote very little of their effort to developing standardized tests and measures. There is almost no attention paid to the error properties of measures. The typical survey reports only sampling error, perhaps the least important of the measurement errors in any sample survey. When error profiles are constructed, sampling error generally comprises only a small part of the total error accounted for by the profile.

13. Some dozen years ago a replication of some of the surveys of the *American Soldier* in World War II was planned with the soldiers of the contemporary military as the

direct recordings of behavior as it occurs and in ways that they can be preserved for successive generations of scientists to observe again and again. They may constitute our museum specimens rather than the data tapes we so laboriously document and store for secondary analyses. The social constructions of data tapes perhaps are far more dated than would be visual and audio recordings of events as they occur.

Epilogue

It is difficult to state conclusions for a discursive essay. We sociologists seem to blind ourselves to the frontier of observational methods where social events and behavior are recorded as they occur. These records can be maintained for repeated observation and analysis over long periods of time. Were we to develop an archive of direct social observations, we may come to understand better the nature of our changing social universe and our changing social actors.

In this essay, I have tried to find answers to two puzzling and related features of our methodological landscape. The first is almost paradoxical. How are we to understand the enigma of data collection in the sociological investigation? Why do we show a distinct preference for indirect as compared with direct methods of social observation when direct observation often is feasible and more consonant with a science of sociology?

The other puzzle is, why do those who opt for direct observational methods persist in regarding them as qualitative methods and eschew quantification? Underestimating quantification results in neglecting to use and further develop systematic social observation.

If there is substance to these remarks, they support the contention that we train methodological incapacities into sociologists. Our goal should be to develop a more balanced methods curriculum by training our students to develop and use methods of direct observation.

References

Banton, M. 1964. *The Policeman in the Community.* London: Tavistock.
Bartlett, H. W., and A. Rosenblum. 1977. *Policewoman Effectiveness.* Denver: Civil Service Commission.

---

respondents. What surprised those who began to plan the replication was that almost none of the survey items made sense to contemporary soldiers if asked verbatim. Many had lost their contextual meaning as well. Just what would constitute a comparable item was moot. The abandonment of the effort merits a footnote only to remind us of how ephemeral are many survey questions. It stands also as a cautionary tale for direct methods of social observation. How to capture social reality so that it can be understood in and over time is a central methodological issue.

Bieck, W., and D. Kessler. 1977. *Response Time Analysis: Methodology and Analysis.* 2 vols. Kansas City, Mo.: Board of Police Commissioners.

Bittner, E. 1967. "Police Discretion in Emergency Apprehension of Mentally Ill Persons." *Social Problems* 14:278–92.

Bloch, P., and D. Anderson 1974. *Policewoman on Patrol.* Washington, D. C.: The Police Foundation.

Boruch, R., K. Larntz, and A. J. Reiss, Jr. 1990. "Guidelines on Doing Good Randomized Field Experiments." *Research in Brief.* Washington, D.C.: National Institute of Justice.

Boydstrum, J. E. 1975. *San Diego Field Interrogation.* Washington, D. C.: The Police Foundation.

Buckner, H. 1970. "Transformations of Reality in the Legal Process." *Social Research* 37:88–101.

Cain, M. 1973. *Society and the Policeman's Role.* London: Routledge & Kegan Paul.

Chatterton, M. 1976. "Policing in a Midlands City." Ph. D. diss. Manchester University, England.

Darwin, C. 1880. *Origin and Species by Means of Natural Selection.* 6th ed. London: J. Murray.

———. 1890. *Journal of Researches into the Natural History and Geology of the Countries Visited During the Voyage Around the World of H. M. S. Beagle Under the Command of Captain Fitz Roy, r.n.* New York: Appleton.

Ericson, R. V. 1982. *Reproducing Order: A Study of Police Patrol Work.* Toronto: University of Toronto Press.

Fyfe, J. J. 1988. *The Metro-Dade Police/Citizen Violence Reduction Project: Final Report.* Washington, D. C.: The Police Foundation.

Goffman, E. 1974. *Frame Analysis.* New York: Harper & Row.

Grimshaw, R., and Jefferson, T. 1987. *Interpreting Policework: Policy and Practice in Forms of Beat Policing.* London: Allen & Unwin.

Holdaway, S. 1983. *Inside the British Police: A Force at Work.* Oxford: Blackwell.

Hollister, P., P. Kemper, and R. Maynard, eds. 1984. *The National Work Supported Demonstration.* Madison: University of Wisconsin Press.

Jefferson, T. 1829. *Memoir, Correspondence, and Miscellanies.* From Papers of Thomas Jefferson by F. Carr. Charlottesville, Va.

Kish, L. 1965. "Sampling Organizations and Groups of Unequal Sizes." *American Sociological Review* 30:564–72.

Kürzinger, J. 1979. "Private Complaints and Police Behavior." In *Police and the Social Order: Contemporary Research Perspectives,* ed. J. Knutsson, E. Kühlhorn, and Albert J. Reiss, Jr. Stockholm: National Swedish Council for Crime Prevention.

Manning, P. 1980. *The Narc's Game: Organizational and Informational Limits on Drug Law Enforcement.* Cambridge, Mass. M. I. T. Press.

Marx, G. 1988. *Undercover: Police Surveillance in America.* New York: Twentieth Century Fund.

Muir, W. K., Jr. 1977. *Police: Streetcorner Politicians.* Chicago: University of Chicago Press.

Ostrum, E., et al. 1973. *Community Organization and the Provision of Police Services.* Beverly Hills, Calif.: Sage.

Pate, T., A. Rerrara, A. Bowers, and J. Lorence. 1976. *Police Response Time: Its Determinants and Effects.* Washington, D. C.: The Police Foundation.

Punch, M. 1979. *Policing the Inner City: A Study of Amsterdam's Warmoesstraat.* London: Macmillan.

Reiss, A. J., Jr. 1967. *Studies in Crime and Law Enforcement in Major Metropolitan Areas,* vol. 2, *President's Commission on Law Enforcement and the Administration of Justice.* Washington, D. C.: G. P. O.

———. 1968. "Stuff and Nonsense About Social Surveys and Observation." In *Institution and the Person,* ed. Howard Becker et al. 351–67. Chicago: Aldine.

———. 1971a. *The Police and the Public.* New Haven: Yale University Press.

———. 1971b. "Systematic Social Observation of Natural Social Phenomena." In *Sociological Methodology 1971.* ed. Herbert Costner, 3–33. San Francisco: Josey Bass.

———. 1976. "Systematic Observation Surveys of Natural Social Phenomena" In *Perspectives on Attitude Assessment: Surveys and Their Alternatives,* ed. A. W. Sinaiko and L. A. Broedling, 123–24. Champaign: Pendelton.

———. 1979. *Police and the Social Order: Contemporary Research Perspectives.* 271–305. Stockholm: The National Swedish Council for Crime Prevention.

———. 1985. "Some Failures in Designing Data Collection That Distort Results." In *Collecting Evaluation Data,* ed. L. Burstein, H. Freeman, and P. Rossi, 161–77, Beverly Hills: Sage.

Rossi, P. H., R. A. Berk, and K. Lenihan. 1980. *Money, Work, and Crime.* New York: Academic.

Rubinstein, J. 1973. *City Police.* New York: Farrar, Strauss & Giroux.

Sherman, L. W., and R. Berk. 1984. "The Specific Deterrent Effects of Arrest for Domestic Assault." *American Sociological Review* 49:201–271.

Sichel, J. L., L. Friedman, J. Quint, and M. Smith. 1977. *Women on Patrol: A Pilot Study of Police Performance in New York City.* New York: Vera Institute of Justice.

Skolnick, J. 1966. *Justice without Trial: Law Enforcement in Democratic Society.* New York: John Wiley & Sons.

Sykes, R. E. 1974. "A Pilot Study in Observational Measurement: A Research Report on Turnover and Work Group Interaction." *Observation* 4. Minneapolis: University of Minnesota.

Tocqueville, Alexis de. 1958. *Journeys to England and Ireland,* ed. J. P. Mayer. New Haven, Conn.: Yale University Press.

Westley, W. 1970. *Violence and the Police: A Sociological Study of Law, Custom, and Morality.* Cambridge, Mass.: M. I. T. Press.

9

The Growth of Applied Sociology after 1945: The Prewar Establishment of the Postwar Infrastructure

MARTIN BULMER

The institutional establishment of sociology depends in part on its public reception. Sociology is not an activity pursued in isolation in the setting of an ivory tower, but one that contributes to the self-understanding of society and to the maintenance of that society. Indeed, many figures in the Pantheon of the discipline in the nineteenth century had lively practical interests and involvements that were reflected in the problems that they addressed and the topics that they selected for investigation. When, around the turn of the century, the gradual institutionalization of sociology in American and European universities gathered pace, these practical interests and involvements still influenced scholarly orientations and interests. Whether in the early interests among Chicago social scientists in their city (see Diner 1980) or in the setting up by German social scientists of the *Verein für Sozialpolitik* (Oberschall 1965), there was an enduring commitment to the production and application of socially useful knowledge. In the British context these links were particularly strong, with the close links between empirical researchers such as Charles Booth and See-bohm Rowntree through the tightly knit British political elite even hindering the development of sociology because of the attractions of the embrace of public affairs (see Abrams 1968).

In the second half of the twentieth century there has been a qualitative change in the relationship between sociology and practice. What was previously implicit and understated has become explicit and integral to the self-conception of the discipline. Applied sociology, in its various forms and not always called by that name, has arrived on the scene, attracting large external support from foundations, governments, and the private sector. Sociology, in varying degrees, is thought to be "useful" and deserving of encouragement. Sociologists in turn have not been slow to respond to the demands made upon them, serving as contract researchers, consultants, advisers, officials, and even, in a few rare cases like Gunnar Myrdal, Patrick Moynihan, and Ralf Dahrendorf, political actors in their own right. The aim of this chapter is to focus upon certain aspects of these trends in American sociology and to trace the origins of these developments in antecedent developments during the period between the two World Wars.

This focus is linked to broader questions in the sociology of the social sciences, concerning the connections between the conditions that produce certain types of sociology, the institutions by means of which and in which sociology is established, and the ways in which sociology connects with particular audiences. As Neil Smelser implies (see this volume, chap. 1), American sociology today may be distinctive, and certainly different in certain respects from sociology in western European countries such as France, West Germany, and Great Britain. This is not only due to significant differences in the histories of these societies, but to the means by which sociology became established and the audiences to which sociological work was addressed. One aim of this chapter is to illuminate some of these broader issues, still current in assessing the place of sociology today, by means of a case study of some aspects of the interwar period in the United States.

The Significance of the Interwar Years

Around 1920 there began to be apparent in American sociology a markedly more empirical orientation, and during the 1920s the organization of empirical research also began to change, at first slowly (see Hinkle & Hinkle 1954; Ross 1979; Bannister 1988; and, for an example, Johnson and Johnson 1980). These changes were associated with the growth of a more applied orientation. Although this book concentrates upon developments in the period after 1945, it is the argument of this chapter that a transformation of the applied orientation within American sociology began to take place around 1920, and that the tendencies that became explicit after the end of World War II had their origins in interwar developments of major significance. The beginning and ending dates are imprecise, but a focus upon the half-century starting in 1920 permits certain general trends to be identified that are not so clearly apparent if one's concern is exclusively with the postwar period.

What were the conditions out of which this growth in "applied" or "useful" sociology developed? This chapter cannot and does not purport to be a rounded historical account of such sociological developments between 1920 and 1945. Rather, focus is upon four institutional infrastructures that permitted different types of applied sociology to develop: the internal differentiation and scientific development of sociology, the growing role of philanthropic foundations, the expansion of a national consciousness, particularly through the media, and the tentative interest of government in social science.

"Applied sociology" has come to have several meanings. Most familiar is the distinction between basic and applied research, taken over from the natural to the social sciences. A variant of this, focused upon the intended audience for research, is the distinction between discipline research and policy research (Coleman 1972), the latter being "applied." An alternative approach eschews definition and approaches the matter in terms of different models of application: the engineering model and the enlightenment model, put forward by Morris Janowitz (1970). The former likens the role of the applied social scientist to the engineer or doctor, applying theoretical knowledge produced by others to the solution of discrete social problems. The latter involves no such sharp distinction, but the gradual percolation of sociological ideas and findings into the stock of social knowledge of a society, rather than the use of sociological studies to provide "technical fixes" for discrete problems.

To the classic formulation may be added models drawn from both critical and clinical sociology (see Street and Weinstein 1975; Rossi and Whyte 1983). A different distinction directs attention to the difference between analysis and prescription, holding that applied sociology is inescapably concerned with both (see Lynd 1939; Rule 1978), whereas discipline-oriented sociology may not be. Or applied sociology may be defined not so much in terms of its sponsorship, substance, or intellectual frame as in terms of the *use* that is made of it. Even if it is not possible to distinguish what is basic from what is applied research, it is possible to make statements about the utilization of social science in public affairs (see Lazarsfeld, Sewell, and Wilensky 1967; Lazarsfeld and Reitz 1975:35–36). In the interwar period, the predominant definition, to the extent that it was made explicit at all, was in terms of *use,* and this is the one adopted in this chapter.

The expansion of sociology, including applied sociology, took place from a small base. One measure of its scale, admittedly a crude one because it does not directly equate to membership of the profession, is the membership of the American Sociological Society (as the association was known until 1959). From 115 founder members in 1905, membership had risen to 1,530 by 1930, fell to 996 by 1937 due to the Depression and contraction of academic openings, and stood at 1,034 in 1940. One should not infer too much from this fall in the 1930s, since other avenues of employment opened up. In the federal government, a group of some fifty to sixty sociologists worked in the Department of Agriculture under Carl Taylor, while Philip Hauser, on his appointment to the Bureau of the Census in the mid-1930s, brought in a considerable number of sociologists to do demographic research. The post-1945 take-off into self-sustained growth altered the scale of the discipline. By 1949, there were two and one-half times the members there had been in 1940; from 1950 to 1959, membership increased to 6,500; and by 1970, it had reached 13,000 (Rhoades 1981:11, 19; ASA, 1989:2). William D'Antonio discusses in more detail aspects of this postwar expansion in chapter 3 of this volume, but undoubtedly one feature was the increased demand for sociology from outside academic sociology itself, and increasing resources made available, particularly after 1960, to meet this demand. Yet this was not a new phenomenon; it had already begun in the interwar period.

The Internal Differentiation of Sociology

The accomplishments of applied research were a significant part of American sociology in the interwar period. Between 1920 and 1945 ten studies may be cited by way of example to give some flavor of the range of such work: Robert Park, *The Immigrant Press and Its Control;* W. I. Thomas, *The Unadjusted Girl;* Clifford Shaw, *The Jack Roller;* John Landesco, *Organized Crime in Chicago;* Clifford Shaw and Henry McKay, *Juvenile Delinquency and Urban Areas;* Willard Waller, *The Sociology of Teaching;* Robert and Helen Lynd, *Middletown;* F. J. Roethlisberger and W. J. Dickson, *Management and the Worker;* Gunnar Myrdal, *An American Dilemma;* Samuel Stouffer et al., *The American Soldier.* There are other fields, such as rural sociology and demography, where one might have cited less well-known but significant examples. To be sure, the line between pure and applied work is blurred. Many of the studies cited could be classified as either or both. This, however, emphasizes the point that Janowitz was making about "enlightenment," that there is no hard and fast line between "pure" and "applied" sociology. Classics such as *An American Dilemma* or *The American Soldier* contributed both to theoretical understanding *and* to practical issues of race relations in the first case, military organization and the social psychology of groups in the second.

The ten works cited above range across the study of crime, social deviance, education, work, race relations, the military, and the press. This range, and the specialization that is involved, points to the first infrastructural condition for the development of applied sociology, which was internal to the discipline. The transition between the first and second generation of American sociology—between the generation of W. G. Sumner, E. A. Ross, Albion Small, and Franklin Giddings (1870–1910) and the generation of Robert Park, Ernest Burgess, William Ogburn, Howard Odum, Robert Lynd (1910–1940)—is often stated in terms of the contrast between a generation of armchair scholars and a generation of empirical researchers. Though this is an oversimplification, it contains an important truth about the character of American sociology. Around 1910 to 1915, American sociology became markedly more empirical in its orientation, and it is this characteristic above all that distinguishes American sociology today from some continental European sociologies.

The change may be linked to the growth of a belief in the potential of the social sciences as sciences.

> Around 1912 . . . a distinctly new voice appeared in the social science literature, and it swelled to a powerful chorus after World War I. Social scientists began to call for a more objective version of empiricism and social intervention. The new program was more quantitative and behavioristic and urged that social science eschew ethical judgments altogether in favor of more explicit methodology and examination of the facts. While the call for objectivity sometimes expressed itself in a renewed commitment to empiricism, it was also apparent in efforts to revise general theory. (Ross 1979:126)

These views had their greatest initial impact in psychology and economics, and individuals such as James B. Watson and Wesley Mitchell saw themselves as developing these subjects in a scientific direction. The influence of the natural science model was wider, however, and spread through the disciplines. Indeed, the professionalization of applied psychology before and during World War I marked the beginnings of the serious application of academic social science to issues of public policy, originally as part of the testing of army recruits for the War Department (Sokal 1987). There were differences in emphasis—psychologists sought individual data, economists aggregated time series—and sociologists at first did not put so much emphasis upon methodology. But there were definite links between a more empirical orientation, an applied orientation, and a somewhat more rigorous methodology.

William Ogburn may serve as an example. A student of Franklin Giddings at Columbia at the beginning of the century, he demonstrated his proficiency in quantitative aggregate data analysis while working at the War Industries Board during World War I. After the war he achieved recognition as a leading theorist as the author of *Social Change* and pursued studies of the family and electoral behavior. After his move from Columbia to Chicago in 1927, Ogburn was successively president of the American Sociological Association and of the American Statistical Association. His apotheosis as a proponent of applied quantitative research was reached as research director for President Hoover's Committee on Recent Social Trends (1933), still the most monumental study by social scientists of American society, which exemplified both President Hoover's faith in scientific expertise and Merriam and Ogburn's conviction that social science had an important practical contribution to make (see Karl 1969).

Just as sociologists at the time were divided over many of the issues involved in such a shift, so interpretations of the period differ. A recent illuminating study of the period concentrates on the work of Ogburn, Luther Bernard, and Stuart Chapin. The development of "objectivism" and "scientism," according to this recent account, coincided with a growing interest in efficiency, adjustment, and social control, which in Ogburn's case meant "putting sociology at the service of the highest bidder, thus setting the stage for a service-intellectual conception of the discipline" (Bannister 1988:237). My own study of empirical sociology at the University of Chicago in this period puts more emphasis upon the aim of establishing sociology as a science, at least in the German sense of the term *wissenschaft* (Bulmer 1984).

Undoubtedly, changes in the character of sociology derived from both symbolic shifts and real changes. The rhetorical element that Alan Sica (chap. 10) identifies was displayed, for example, by Charles Merriam's espousal of the "science of politics" and of the quantitative study of political behavior in the 1920s (Karl 1974) and in Ogburn's scientistic presidential address to the American Sociological Association in 1929. Nonetheless, these changes had a real basis as well.

The reality was the increasing effectiveness and power of explanations of the natural world by scientists, which in areas such as psychology bordered on the social sciences and influenced scholars as different as J. B. Watson and W. I. Thomas. Thomas, for example, studied physiology and experimental biology with Jacques Loeb and brain anatomy with the psychiatrist Adolf Meyer, and he was considerably influenced by them (Coser 1977:292, 300–301). Questions of audience cannot be ignored, though this influence was stronger on applied than on basic research. Ogburn's reliance on what he saw as objective social measurement in the compilation of *Recent Social Trends* combined a belief in science with a perception that policy makers, and above all the engineer-President, Herbert Hoover, would find most convincing results presented in this manner (Bulmer 1983).

The application of sociology from 1920 onwards was also fostered by a process that has received rather less attention, but that was a necessary condition for the emergence of applied sociology. Sociology today is differentiated into a considerable number of subdisciplines or special sociologies, such as the sociology of education, development studies, social psychology, rural sociology, the sociology of politics, of organizations, of health and illness, of social welfare, of crime, and so on, each with its own course at advanced undergraduate and graduate levels, in some cases its own higher degree programs. In almost all cases there are specialist journals for communication between those working in an area. Some implications of this differentiation are the subject of Diana Crane and Henry Small's work (see chap. 5).

Specialization is now the norm. Before 1920 such specialties were scarcely apparent, and even by 1945 their development was uneven. By that date some subfields, such as rural sociology and criminology, were well established, and others such as the sociology of education or the sociology of health and illness only existed in embryo. Yet their coming into being was closely linked to the successful applications of the sociology that they embraced.

The dates of the establishment of journals give some indication of the degree of crystallization of a field: *The Journal of Criminal Law and Criminology* in 1910; the *Milbank Memorial Fund Quarterly* (now *Health and Society*) in 1923; the *Journal of Educational Sociology* (now *Sociology of Education*) in 1927; *Rural Sociology* in 1936; *Sociometry* (now *Social Psychology Quarterly*) in 1937; and the *Journal of Marriage and the Family* in 1939. The earliest established journals were those to which various disciplines contributed and that were not purely sociological. For instance, few contributors to the *Journal of Educational Sociology* at the outset taught in mainstream sociology departments.

Developments in sociological specialties and their relation to applied work can be exemplified very briefly through two case studies, criminology and education between 1920 and 1945. The sources of American criminology were various, including urban reform movements, a concern with child welfare, psychiatric approaches to the treatment of offenders, and a more sociological approach. One example of the last was the work of Ernest Burgess and his students at the University of Chicago. In part, this was a response to social conditions of the day, as in John Landesco's study of gangs and Clifford Shaw's life histories of juvenile delinquents. The work, however, was set within a sociological frame and an urban social theory, made explicit in the studies of delinquency areas. A wide range of methods was employed, including the use of official statistics, documentary records, newspapers, observation, interviews, and life histories.

What is most interesting were the close links with bodies seeking to influence policy. The Institute of Juvenile Research, within which Shaw worked, had other branches that dealt with various aspects of penal policy and sought to influence local practice. Burgess's famous work on parole prediction was done for the Illinois Crime Commission, and this involved close ties with academic criminal lawyers also concerned with influencing criminal justice policy. Shaw and MacKay contributed a notable essay on the causation of delinquency to the federal Wickersham Crime Commission of 1931. Like the Illinois Commission, this had little immediate impact, but it was important in affecting the climate of opinion about penal policy. Thus, developments within a subfield of sociology that were important for the future direction of the discipline were also spilling over into policy debates involving academic and practicing lawyers and penologists. The *Journal of Criminal Law and Criminology* was a principal means by which this constituency communicated with each other. The words *"and Police Science"* were added to the masthead in the 1930s, reflecting the academic interest in this subject (Chicago had one of the first chairs in the subject in 1929, followed shortly by Berkeley), and another channel by which social science might feed into practice.

The case of educational sociology was different. Educational sociology, unlike the sociology of education, was primarily undertaken by people working within the educational world in teachers' colleges and education departments of universities. To that extent, it was embedded, if not in professional practice, in the education of professional educators. The first course in "Educational Sociology" appears to have been offered at Columbia by Henry Suzallo in 1907–8, and by the mid-1920s nearly half of American normal schools and one-third of university and college departments of education taught the subject (Szreter 1980). The National Society for the Study of Educational Sociology was established in 1923, and the *Journal of Educational Sociology*, from 1927, was its official journal, edited by George Payne of New York University.

Yet the subject connected only slightly to mainstream sociological teaching and research in departments of sociology. A monograph like

Willard Waller's *The Sociology of Teaching* (1932) was altogether exceptional in being the product of a mainstream sociologist. No comparable work was produced in departments of education, unless one includes the rare pioneering studies of schools and school government carried out by George S. Counts in Chicago in the late 1920s. The subject was conceived as a branch of applied sociology that would yield rational educational knowledge of help to educators and research workers. In contrast to criminology, the general standard of research was low and much writing on the subject confined to textbooks—a much-favored medium of publication between the wars—with emphasis on exegesis and moral prescription (Brim 1958:8–10). There was little attempt to formulate questions in the theoretical terms of sociology or to connect to the mainstream of social science, so that the answer to questions was of interest both to the educator and to the sociologist. An effective sociology of education, as distinct from educational sociology, did not develop until after 1950, despite the apparent proliferation in teaching of the subject.

One should not generalize too readily from these two case studies. Criminology, at least at Chicago, was well integrated with the mainstream of the subject and connected with academic peers in related disciplines like law and psychiatry. Educational sociology, by contrast, though strongly established, occupied an intellectual ghetto. Other specialties tended in one direction or the other: social psychology was often taught from within mainstream departments, but rural sociology had a ghetto position in separate institutions or separate departments, was strongly committed to a form of empiricism, and became quite well established in the interwar period, but it was insulated from the mainstream of the discipline. With the post-1945 growth of sociology, many of these barriers were broken down, normal schools and land-grant colleges were upgraded to universities, and special sociologies developed more fully, often supported by newly established specialist journals, and taught more extensively in departments of sociology.

The scientific aspirations of sociology also flowed together with those whose interests lay in the investigation of social conditions. Writing in 1897, George Vincent, then teaching sociology at Chicago but later President of the Rockefeller Foundation, distinguished between the philosophical and scientific sides of sociology on the one hand and the "social technological" side on the other. The latter had its origins in various sources, including the early British poverty surveys of Charles Booth (and later Seebohm Rowntree), which provided the inspiration for the early American social investigators such as Jane

Addams, Florence Kelly, and W. E. B. DuBois (Bulmer et al. 1991). The Social Survey Movement, as a movement for community reform, began in 1905 with the Pittsburgh Survey, directed by Paul Kellogg, a journalist and social worker. Backed by the Russell Sage Foundation, this was the first of a whole swathe of studies in which communities were studied and to a considerable extent studied themselves (Chambers 1971, chap. 3). Funded by the Department of Surveys and Exhibits at Russell Sage, and headed by Shelby M. Harrison, over two thousand local surveys were carried out over the next twenty years (Harrison 1931; Eaton and Harrison 1930). Though this is the main lineage, there were other developments, including the Country Life Movement, and the Institute of Social and Religious Research, which emerged in 1921 from the ruins of the Interchurch World Movement and funded 75 projects up to 1934, including the Race Relations Survey of the West Coast directed by Robert Park and the Lynds' first study of Middletown (Converse 1987:25–31). These developments all form part of the prehistory of applied sociology.

Applied sociology also grew out of attempts to make the social sciences more rigorous and more quantitative. Postwar developments in psychology and in business research were the first step. A market for the social sciences in the business world began to develop, which Paul Lazarsfeld was later to exploit to very good effect. The Psychological Corporation was set up after World War I by James McKeen Cattell to make the expertise of psychologists available on a professional basis to commercial users. A second tributary lay in psychological measurement of attitudes, particularly the pioneering work of L. L. Thurstone in the late 1920s, which influenced Samuel Stouffer (see Stouffer 1930) and figured in the arguments between proponents of quantification and the case study at the University of Chicago of that period (Bulmer 1984). The beginnings of market research about the same time were also important in fostering the demand for this type of applied social research in the business world.

By 1960, the most familiar tool of applied sociology, though by no means confined to that type of inquiry alone, was the modern sample survey. The foundations of its use in the worlds of government, business, the media, and in academic disciplines such as sociology and political science were laid in the interwar period. The start of market research, and the joint application of sampling in the selection of respondents and more systematic design and analysis of questions by practitioners such as Archibald Crossley, Elmo Roper, and George Gallup, laid the technical basis of sample surveys. Initially, however, their work outside the commercial sphere was confined to election studies, the most famous being Gallup's triumph over the *Literary Digest* poll in predicting the outcome of the 1936 presidential election. There then followed during World War II the extensive use of survey research in three groups within the armed forces, one of which (headed by Samuel Stouffer) produced *The American Soldier*. After hostilities ended, three leading university-based centers of survey research developed, the National Opinion Research Center on the campus of the University of Chicago, the Institute of Social Research at the University of Michigan, founded by Rensis Likert, and the Bureau of Applied Social Research at Columbia University, founded by Paul Lazarsfeld. The latter two produced not only much important research in sociology, social psychology, and political science, but provided the training ground for a new generation of survey researchers who went out to colonize the social sciences and create new or expanded centers in places as far apart as Berkeley, Urbana, and Chapel Hill. (The existence of such centers also gave rise to tensions in the academy that are dissected in the chapters in this volume by Hal Winsborough (chap. 7) and Samuel Klausner (chap. 6)). A full account of these developments is available in a fine study by Jean Converse (1987), as well as in earlier autobiographical accounts (especially Lazarsfeld 1969).

The Role of the Foundations

Among the most important institutions contributing to the growth of the social sciences before 1945 were the great philanthropic foundations, which funded basic and applied social science research throughout the period, starting in the early 1920s. The major foundations established in the early years of the twentieth century by John D. Rockefeller, Andrew Carnegie, and Mrs. Russell Sage had a disproportionate influence upon the early expansion of empirical social science. The importance of the Russell Sage Foundation in making possible the Social Survey Movement from 1908 onwards is well known. In a sense, however, this was less influential in the long term than the work supported by Rockefeller and Carnegie, for they channeled support into social science departments and divisions of universities, thus making a more enduring impact upon the direction of development of the developing social sciences.

A shift of attention to the foundations represents a shift from the internal dynamics of the social sciences to consider some of the external circumstances that shaped the social sciences. To what extent were developments in the social sciences a product of external forces over which the social sciences themselves had little control? The issue is whether, as Jerome Karabel (1988) has put it, "the powerful institutions, both private and public, that support social scientific research, push it in directions that diverge from those that would have been followed in response to its internal intellectual logic."

This question, like that of the "scientism" of sociology, is one of keen controversy on which there is much disagreement. The original literature on the subject often consisted of bland and sometimes self-serving accounts by retired foundation officials of their own foundation and its stewardship, which lacked a critical edge. In turn, radical scholars critical of the role of foundations attribute to the foundations hegemonic aspirations and a distorting influence (see Arnove 1980, and also the exchange between the author and D. Fisher (Bulmer and Fisher 1984, in response to an earlier article by Fisher (1983)). Others argue that by the 1920s foundation officials had achieved a degree of autonomy from their trustees, and could initiate programs and policies more in line with their own interests and those of their academic advisers, which reflected the preoccupations of the academic world as much as it shaped them. Counterfactuals are of limited usefulness in the history of the social sciences, but in this case it may be worth asking: what would the social sciences have looked like by 1940 if the major American foundations had not existed?

The most important single foundation was the Laura Spelman Rockefeller Memorial. Robert Hutchins said in 1929 that "in its brief but brilliant career [it] did more than any other agency to promote the social sciences in the United States" (Hutchins 1930:1). Established in 1918 for charitable works, Beardsley Ruml became its director in 1923 and phased out support for emergency relief and religious bodies, while reducing support for social welfare. He redefined its role as that of strengthening the basic social sciences, embracing sociology, anthropology, and psychology with parts of economics, political science, and history. Understanding major social issues required adequate theoretically grounded explanations of human behavior, which only these social sciences could provide.

Ruml, an applied psychologist who had moved into philanthropy, argued that the social sciences were in an unsatisfactory state, as they were largely deductive and speculative, using second-hand observations, documentary evidence, and anecdotal material. He used the resources of the Memorial to try to strengthen empirical research in the social sciences, mainly in the United States but also in Western Europe, by providing resources for research facilities and assistance, providing scholarships for young researchers, and establishing research institutes on university campuses. During his directorship of the Memorial between 1922 and 1929 (when it was wound up and effectively became the Social Science Division of the Rockefeller Foundation), $45 million was disbursed, some $20 million for social science research. Ruml's strategy envisaged the systematic expansion of the social sciences over at least a decade. His strategy ushered in and set the pattern for the beginnings of the modern system of large-scale, grant-aided research for sociology from foundations and government that was so greatly expanded after 1945.

Ruml's orientation was quite strongly toward applied social science research. After gaining a Ph.D. in psychology at the University of Chicago, he had worked as an applied psychologist with Walter Bingham and Walter Dill Scott at the Carnegie Institute of Technology in Pittsburgh before moving with his colleagues in 1917 to Washington D.C. to develop psychological tests for the Committee on Classification of Personnel in the Adjutant-General's office in the War Department. After the war he joined Scott and others in the Scott Company of Philadelphia, a brief experiment in running a firm that offered a psychological consulting service. In his proposal for a change of direction for the Memorial, Ruml emphasized the benefits that flowed from the application of social science research, citing as examples industrial companies in Philadelphia and the federal Civil Service Commission, and making use of tests that were in turn a practical outcome of wartime work (Bulmer and Bulmer 1981:366).

The strategy of the Memorial was to support research that would bring practical benefits through application. Additions to social scientific knowledge would lead to the furtherance of public welfare. Industries, municipal and state governments, and welfare organizations would all benefit from the expansion of "laboratories" investigating different aspects of society. An aim of considerable importance was the wider dissemination of work done by specialist scholars, so that they came to play a part in the thinking of the population at large.

Support for social science took three forms, depending on whether it was for institutions, research organizations, or individuals. In the case of the first two, support was in the form of block grants, not support for specific programs or projects as is the usual pattern of funding today. The ten largest recipients of Memorial support across all the social sciences (receiving half of total funding) were, in descending order, the University of Chicago, Brookings, Columbia, the London School of Economics, Harvard, Minnesota, Vanderbilt, Iowa State, Yale, and the University of North Carolina. In addition, major

funding was provided to establish and maintain the Social Science Research Council from 1923, and for fellowships and the endowment of
chairs at selected institutions. The fellowship scheme was intended to
train younger scholars as the social science generation of the future;
many of the key actors in the period after 1945 had been recipients of
such Memorial support at the start of their careers. In addition, the
scheme (and its successor, administered by the Rockefeller Foundation) provided opportunities for both American and European scholars to study abroad, taking Louis Wirth to Germany, Herbert Blumer
to France, and bringing Paul Lazarsfeld on his first extended visit to
the United States which led to his migration. Endowment of chairs
was more selective, but among those supported were Edward Sapir
and Edwin Sutherland for periods at Chicago, and Elton Mayo at
Pennsylvania and Harvard, which meant he didn't need to return to
Australia.

Institutional support for sociology was concentrated at a few
places, the University of Chicago, the University of North Carolina,
and the London School of Economics, in particular. During this period Chicago dominated American sociology, since the subject was
barely taught at Harvard, in decline at Columbia after flowering at
the beginning of the century, and only developing slowly as a research
endeavour at the major state universities. At Chicago, the Memorial
provided half a million dollars in 1927 for recruiting extra staff and
over a million dollars for the erection of the Social Science Research
Building. Similar support at LSE for general endowment, buildings,
and library facilities permitted the expansion of virtually the only center at which sociology was taught in Britain until the 1950s.

The Memorial was most innovative, however, in the creation of research organizations. Ruml's aim was to promote empirical research,
often with an applied orientation, and to train younger scholars in
empirical methods. The means by which this was to be done was empirical research organized through a research committee or institute,
of which notable examples came into being at Chicago and North
Carolina. The Local Community Research Committee at the University of Chicago (Bulmer 1980) and the Institute for Research in Social
Science at Chapel Hill (Johnson and Johnson 1980) provided the infrastructure that underpinned the empirical sociological research carried out under Park and Burgess at Chicago and Howard Odum at
Chapel Hill. This is not to say that it brought such research into being,
but it was a necessary condition for its success.

The funds for research organizations were used for a variety of purposes. Academic staff were freed for full-time research by provision of

replacement teaching. Graduate traineeships for research were used to give students research experience and pay their way through graduate school, which in this period was the preferred form of research assistance. Some statistical, clerical, and field staff were, however, employed on projects requiring more extensive data collection and analysis. The grants paid for supplies and equipment, for the preparation of manuscripts, and for some subsidy of publication by university presses. The sociological research done under these auspices included a good proportion of the classic Chicago urban studies of the 1920s as well as work by Clifford Shaw on delinquency and John Landesco on gangs, but Memorial support was little known because the Memorial discouraged public announcements or acknowledgments of its benefactions. At Chapel Hill, Odum built the Institute for Research in Social Science into a major secondary center nationally and the leading center of sociology in the South, although it was handicapped by the smallness of the starting base, the provincial ambience, and the exceptional local sensitivity of research topics such as religion, industrial relations, and race.

The Carnegie Corporation also supported some social science work, sharing in the funding of the National Bureau for Economic Research and initiating the studies of Americanization to which Robert Park and W. I. Thomas contributed, the latter without acknowledgment. During the 1930s it initiated the study of race relations by Gunnar Myrdal, which resulted in *An American Dilemma* (Lagemann 1987; 1989). Nonetheless, the scale of Rockefeller Memorial support was considerably greater and had a much more direct impact upon the developing social science disciplines. It also established the social sciences as a major topic of interest within the Rockefeller Foundation, insulating the Foundation from involvement in research on controversial topics but committing them to support in the longer term.

Interpretations of the influence of the Memorial upon the course of social science vary. Some radical commentators have charged that foundations such as the Memorial used support for social science as a means of producing knowledge that would tend to support the economic interests of the benefactors and the strata of society to which they belonged (see Fisher 1980). It has been argued that bodies like the Memorial exercised considerable intellectual influence upon developments in the social sciences. "The power of the foundation is not that of dictating what will be studied. Its power consists in defining professional and intellectual parameters, in determining who will receive support to study what subjects in what settings" (Arnove 1980:319). Such connections are easier to assert than to demonstrate, however. In certain fields prone to domination by a particular social group—the influence of white scholars in the study of race relations in the South is the prime example (Stanfield 1985)—foundations did exercise control and intellectual influence of a direct kind. But in relation to broader trends in the social sciences such as the move toward an empirical and applied orientation, it is difficult to argue that the foundations were the determining factor.

Ruml fashioned the Memorial into an instrument for support for social science, but the system of block grants was among other things a means of distancing the Memorial from the subjects of inquiry that it was sponsoring. In 1924 the trustees adopted a series of six negative and six positive principles to guide their giving. These firmly enunciated the principle that support would be provided to "responsible educational or scientific institutions" who would "sponsor the research and assume responsibility for the competence of the staff and the scientific spirit of the investigations" (quoted in Bulmer and Bulmer 1981:379). In other words, reliance was placed upon the standards of the leading educational and scientific institutions of the country to guarantee the quality of the resulting product. Critics of the influence of foundations are thus criticizing support for activities at leading elite universities, and by implication the role of those universities in society, as much as the content of the work that was supported.

This brings us back to the proposition that powerful institutions such as foundations may push sociology in directions that it would not otherwise have chosen to take. Recent work on foundations has begun to unravel the complexity of the activities of foundations and their officials at this period, which are certainly not reducible to some Gramscian formula of their being the bearers of the ideas of a dominant class. (For a useful brief review of this literature see Kohler 1987; for an insightful discussion of the Gramscian thesis in the American context see Karl and Katz 1987; two notable recent monographs are Wheatley 1988 and Lagemann 1989). A more convincing analysis might be to treat foundation officials as representatives of a new stratum of professional experts, a *cadre* in the French sense, who sought to use the social sciences to enhance the traditional foundation aims of social efficiency and social control. Ruml, for example, was a close associate of Charles Merriam, who became a leader of the behavioral revolution in political science and an architect of the Social Science Research Council (Karl 1974). Ruml was at least as much influenced by Merriam, and his colleagues in psychology, as being an intellectual innovator himself. He was an *institutional* innovator, an entrepreneur of organizational ideas whose monument is the pay-as-you-go tax system that he invented during World War II.

Changes that foundation support facilitated were not necessarily those that their architects intended. The conception of the application of knowledge was primitive and poorly articulated. Aside from applied psychology, one influence was clearly Ruml's admiration for the early work of Elton Mayo and his belief that this was a fruitful model for an applied social science. At the Memorial he talked as if the transition from theoretical to empirical research and from "speculation" to research would enhance the potential applicability of results, without having any very clearly worked out idea as to how this would occur. The Social Science Research Council was clearly intended to perform this function, but may not have lived up to expectations, for in the early 1930s, when Dean of Social Science at Chicago, Ruml inveighed against the artificiality of disciplinary boundaries and their baleful effects on productive interdisciplinary cooperation.

It was in the 1920s that the term "interdisciplinary" first appeared (Frank 1988). The promotion of interdisciplinary research was an important aim of the Rockefeller Foundation in particular, though it is unclear once again how far the foundation provided the impetus and how far it was responding to the prompting of social scientists as various as psychologist Robert Woodworth, anthropologist Margaret Mead, political scientist Harold Lasswell, and sociologist William Ogburn, who edited one of the first collections of papers on the subject (Ogburn and Goldenweiser, 1927).

To some extent there was a conflict between the growth of the social sciences and their separation into distinct disciplines, which was accentuated in the interwar period. There was a desire on the part of some scholars and some outside the academy to address social problems and issues seen to be common to the social sciences and not to confine theoretical problems within a particular discipline. (There was less effort in this period for the overall theoretical integration that Craig Calhoun advocates in chapter 4, but it followed shortly after World War II with the creation of the Harvard Department of Social Relations.) Paradoxically, at a university like Harvard, where sociology was weakly established before 1940, interdisciplinary work flourished, particularly at the business school, but also in the medical school, in anthropology, and public health. As Buxton and Turner point out (see chap. 11), the shift in Rockefeller policy in 1934 from broad funding of institutional programs to funding specific projects had a major impact, tending to reduce the scope for interdisciplinary activity.

Though much of the appeal to interdisciplinarity was rhetorical, it did have some real substance. Arid and theoretically barren though its product was, *Recent Social Trends* (1933) was an impressive documentation of the state of American society by authors from different social science disciplines. Elton Mayo's work on industrial organization was pathbreaking research that cut with a sharp theoretical edge across disciplines. The emergence of criminology as a distinct area of study brought together psychology and psychiatry, sociology and law in fruitful conjuncture, with sociology tending increasingly to dominance. There were several pioneering attempts to bring together the study of personality and social structure. W. I. Thomas, political scientist Harold Lasswell, the anthropologist Edward Sapir, and the psychiatrist Harry Stack Sullivan, for example, were involved in an SSRC-sponsored effort to bring social psychiatry closer to the social sciences (Perry 1982:232–50). John Dollard, who wrote his Chicago dissertation under William Ogburn, brought the two fields together in his mature work. Lawrence K. Frank, who assisted Ruml at the Memorial, was an important source of ideas in his own right on the development of child psychology. At the same time, much of the sociology of the day was not oriented to these interdisciplinary concerns.

The precise extent of the influence of foundations at this period is difficult to pin down. Just as the social sciences did not merely mirror what the foundations wanted, neither did the foundations simply mirror developments in the social sciences. A subtle process of influence and shaping was at work, of feedback between the foundations picking up certain tendencies present in the social sciences, giving them support, and thus reflecting them back more strongly to the constituent disciplines. Lewis Coser (1965) suggested that the foundations acted as gatekeepers, and that an elective affinity developed between foundation officials and large-scale research entrepreneurs. This was true of Merriam and Howard Odum, whose apotheosis came when they joined William Ogburn in producing *Recent Social Trends,* which was a presidentially sponsored inquiry actually funded by the Rockefeller Foundation. Yet, paradoxically, foundation support was not enough to secure the triumph of their influence. *Recent Social Trends* was overtaken by events and sank into oblivion politically. Despite his influence among political scientists and as a teacher of younger scholars, Merriam's own department was wasted by Robert Hutchins's animosity in the 1930s. And for Howard Odum, though he labored mightily and created a major center at Chapel Hill, lasting intellectual distinction seemed to elude him, so that although an important figure historically, his enduring impact outside the South is limited.

In a contrasting case, Carnegie support for Myrdal's work on *An American Dilemma,* shows that accepting foundation money did not commit an author to an uncritical social position. Indeed, Myrdal seems to have been recruited precisely because he was thought to be able to provide a more objective outside analysis grounded in social science (Lagemann 1987). In that case, intervention by a foundation broadened rather than narrowed the range of empirical and normative questions that sociologists addressed. By the same token, Myrdal's work would not have been possible without the range of already existing research that he drew upon and synthesized (Jackson 1985, 1990). In short, in both less and more successful projects, foundation support was a necessary but not a sufficient condition for the development of effective empirical social science.

The Expansion of a National Consciousness

A further, more diffuse, influence contributing to the expansion of applied social science in the 1920s and 1930s was the growth of a national consciousness and the mass media. One is inclined to forget that the United States in the interwar period, as well as having a more diversified system of higher education, was also a more localized and regionalized society than it later became. For the majority of the population, the main frame of reference immediately after World War I was not a national one.

The research programs at Chicago and Chapel Hill were focused upon the locality not just because of an interest in urban and rural social structure and process, but because the local societies in which those groups of sociologists were located provided the intellectual horizons within which research was conducted. Many of the early Chicago studies were conducted under the aegis of the *Local Community* Research Committee (my emphasis), with a focus upon urban ecological structure and on social life within natural areas of the city. Even studies that were not primarily urban in focus were usually conducted within a local urban setting.

Howard Odum's aims at Chapel Hill centered on the study of conditions in the state and the region (Johnson and Johnson 1980:161). Indeed, Odum's most lasting contribution to sociology was his work on regionalism and regional planning in the South. He developed an approach that emphasized distinct differences in both cultural and natural attributes between different but interdependent areas. (The interdependence was very apparent in sociology itself, for most of the ideas and tools of the discipline that he used were drawn from outside the South.)

The growth of applied sociology and applied social science for local and regional policy-making elites was a significant development, though these were not necessarily produced for those occupying elected office. Research in criminology in Illinois, for example, was very much oriented to the reform of the penal and judicial system, particularly in Cook County, an exemplification of Neil Smelser's point about the importance of the reform impulse in understanding the growth of American sociology.

As sociology began gradually to make some impact on policy makers at the national level, it tended to be cast in a more scientific than reform mold. The work of sociologists in the Department of Agriculture and the Bureau of the Census, for example, represented the provision of technical expertise to aid policy formulation, as did Shaw and McKay's analysis of the causes of juvenile delinquency for the Wickersham Crime Commission in 1931. This was not the only way, however, in which sociology reached out to a wider audience.

The spread of popular journalism and radio began to break down regionalism, with consequences for social science. It made people more aware of the changing nature of their society and posed questions about it to which sociologists appeared to have answers.

> Similar transitional eras had occurred at earlier stages of American history. What gives the twenties its particular cast is the rapid development of new communications media, which made people conscious that their society was in transition. . . . The beliefs of generations who considered themselves rural or urban, Victorian or modern, isolationist or internationalist, individualist or collectivist, competed for the attention of the uncommitted young, whether they were small-towners, first generation immigrants moving from ethnic enclaves to suburbs, or middle class city dwellers seeking to adopt the trappings of upward mobility that once were reserved to the wealthy elite. (Karl 1983:78)

This change in consciousness meant a readier market for sociology. At first this was reflected most directly in market research and opinion polling, but the enhanced importance of the media was significant in the 1930s by stimulating communications research, which was so important in Lazarsfeld's early American career and in the renaissance of sociology at Columbia (see Shils 1948:34–40).

As well as constituting a subject for research, the new media provided a means for disseminating the results of social science. Although the attention devoted to social science was meager compared to the post-1945 period, an audience among "the educated public" began to develop, initially, perhaps, more for works of psychiatry and anthropology, such as the writings of Margaret Mead, but also for a few sociological studies such as *Middletown*.

In a broad sense, the growth of sociology between the wars, and more strongly after 1945, as well as the development of tools of inquiry like the sample survey, was in part a response to the growing national (rather than local or regional) consciousness, a means of holding up a mirror to American society so that it could regard itself. One manifestation of this was the salience of social studies teaching in American schools, another the very large numbers of undergraduates who take courses in sociology. Another way of pinpointing this transformation would be to say that sociology shifted from addressing an audience of fellow academics and a few key elite opinion formers to a wider audience, in some contexts a mass audience, which found in sociology one means of trying to understand what it meant to be and to sustain a national society.

What did not develop to any significant extent was a sociology directly oriented to social movements and subordinate social groups, such as women or industrial workers, in the way that some branches of "critical sociology" have grown in more recent times. Race, however, is a partial exception. American sociology, with its central focus on race and ethnicity, was a means of illuminating the condition of black Americans and also an avenue of upward mobility for a small number of black scholars such as Charles Johnson, Franklin Frazier, and Ralph Bunche. This tradition of research had a major impact upon the American public through Myrdal's *An American Dilemma*.

Indeed, the best-known popular writer on the position of African-Americans between the wars, W. E. B. DuBois, editor of *The Crisis*, had begun his scholarly career as a sociologist and pursued it for thirteen years between 1897 and 1910 before abandoning academic work for journalism and political action (Bulmer 1991). At this period, however, sociology was not an instrument for radically challenging the status quo in American society, and sociologists had few links to bodies such as trades unions or the policy-making levels of the New Deal Democratic party where such an influence might have been felt.

The Federal Government

The contrast between the pre-1945 and post-1945 peacetime worlds is most striking in the role of the federal government. Despite the New Deal, "the uneasy state" (Karl 1983) was slow in extending its sway, the federal government was weak, and moves to extend the authority of the center were slow, cautious, and contested. The speed with which the wartime apparatus in Washington was dissolved in 1918 was one sign: both the psychologists in the Army (Ruml among them) and the economists in the War Industries Board (Ogburn among them) had their activities brought to an end as soon as hostilities ceased. The arguments over the scope for planning in the New Deal made evident the deep-seated suspicion of expansion of the role of government in Congress and the country. Karl and Katz (1987) have pointed to the ambivalence of Congress about expertise, and the reluctance, prior to 1945, to countenance financing it, preferring to rely on private foundations. Robert Wiebe has observed that until the middle of the twentieth century "the most useful image of (American) government was that of an empty vessel, a container into which power flowed and formed but which provided nothing of its own. Always an exaggeration . . . the image nevertheless expressed an approximate truth of high importance" (1975:132).

The New Deal years were generally "years of disappointment" for social science (Lyons 1969:125), notwithstanding the fact that two of the members of Roosevelt's "Brains Trust" (A. A. Berle, Jr. and Raymond Moley) were social scientists, and that sociology made some slight inroads, for example, through the Bureau of Agricultural Economics in the Department of Agriculture, which also later became the government location of Rensis Likert. Attempts at national planning that involved social scientists failed (Karl 1963).

All the same, there were signs of change. Partly but not entirely as a result of falling stock values, the philanthropic foundations had acknowledged during the 1930s that they could not continue to underwrite the generality of developments in medical science, natural science, and social science research. In 1934 the Social Science Division of the Rockefeller Foundation abandoned its practice of making block grants, which to a considerable extent had allowed university social scientists to determine how to allocate the resources provided, in favor of project grants of a more delimited kind specified in terms of areas of interest to the Foundation. It gave notice to the state and federal governments that the task of underwriting the cost of scientific research was too great for private bodies to bear.

There was little sign of response before World War II, but this change was important in the longer term for the model of support for science adopted by the National Science Foundation (NSF) after 1945. This owed a great deal to Rockefeller experience (Kohler 1978) and in turn influenced the arrangements for the support for social science when these were subsequently added. There were also tensions between the natural and social sciences. Social science was not represented in the embryonic machinery for science policy, the Science Advisory Board, that was established in 1933, and which subsequently failed. Indeed, antagonism of social scientists within the federal government to the SAB on grounds of their exclusion was one source of hostility between natural and social scientists in the 1940s that led to the exclusion of social science from the NSF (Miller 1982). Though the parallels are important, the differences between natural and social science were significant, the former characterized by a high degree of central organization, the latter by increasing proliferation and fragmentation, and a less straightforward path into the Washington world.

Conclusion

This partial examination of certain interwar trends suggests that the seeds of postwar institutional developments were present earlier, even if the scale of sociology remained comparatively small. This paper has not considered sociology departments in universities in any detail (cf. Shils 1980). The influence of war itself is clearly a major variable, which also is not discussed here except in passing. Our concern has been with the institutional form and means of support for sociology, concentrating on work that had practical usefulness and so encouraged further support for the discipline. If there is a single conclusion to be drawn, however, it is of the persuasiveness of the "enlightenment" model of knowledge utilization.

Morris Janowitz's formulation of the interaction between social science knowledge and utilization recognized the complexity both of social science knowledge itself and of the impact that it has upon society. In the early period of the discipline, an applied orientation might characterize work as diverse as empirical studies in rural sociology, the Lynds' first study of Middletown, early criminological research, and Robert Park's view that sociology could illuminate public opinion and thus contribute to social control (in its original sense; see Janowitz 1975). *An American Dilemma* illustrates the strength of the "enlightenment" model, for this was a work at once contributing to theoretical social science and making major statements about the philosophical significance of race in American society, combined with commentary on public policy on race issues.

A concern with practical outcome, rather than with the intentions of the sociologist, was most usual at this period. It was a period where Janowitz's "enlightenment" model is particularly illuminating, since there was the absence of a hard and fast distinction between pure and applied research. Indeed, the collection of essays in this book as a whole continues a theme related to "enlightenment" that Janowitz opened up two decades ago in an earlier collection, which focused on varieties of political expression in sociology (Janowitz 1970). Just as no sharp line can be drawn between useful and useless sociology, so the varying applications of sociology in the interwar period helped to shape the outlook of the actors in the postwar world and to determine the directions that it would take. The precise chronology is difficult to pin down, and occurred first among elites and opinion leaders, but the significance of the interwar period is clear.

Sociologists are addressing themselves to an audience or audiences. In the interwar period, those audiences began to expand. Though E. A. Ross had cut something of a public figure, few of the founding fathers sought to reach out to a wide audience. In the interwar period, sociology began to develop specialist audiences within fields such as education, social work, the criminal justice system, industrial management, and the Department of Agriculture. This was on a comparatively small scale, but it represented a significant widening of the reach of sociology, and was necessary for applied sociology to begin to develop. The origins of this expansion of applied sociological expertise needs to be studied field by field, but it is a considerable oversimplification to attach too much importance to the availability of funding.

The extent of the impact of external institutions upon the development of the discipline can easily be exaggerated. What difference did the existence of the foundations make? Although in some fields the existence of foundation support may have been a necessary condition for applied sociology being carried out—as in the case of Elton Mayo's industrial research and *An American Dilemma*—it was not a sufficient condition. Changes in the character of sociology between 1918 and 1940 from a more theoretical toward a more empirical discipline would have occurred without foundation intervention, and did so in fields like rural sociology and criminology where foundations were not the primary source of financial support. Foundations reflected at least as much as they determined changes that were under way in the subject, though the precise interplay is a complex one not yet fully explicated.

The shift of sociologists in the 1930s to research into population and rural society for the federal government and into the media and consumer behavior for clients in private industry may be represented as distortion of the internal intellectual logic of the discipline. It is, nonetheless, at least as plausible to argue that such trends reflected both internal differentiation of the field and the ability of leading figures to seize opportunities that were offered to them. Just as Ward, Giddings, and Park had been in the earlier generation, sociologists continued to be recruited from diverse backgrounds, Lynd, for example, from the ministry and Lazarsfeld from Austrian quantitative psychology with an admixture of socialism. The growth of media research that Lazarsfeld pioneered in the later 1930s reflected not only his own entrepreneurial talents, but a keen interest in current significant developments in American society. Sociology as a discipline changes over time not only in response to institutional support, but also to changes in contemporary society. The ship of sociology charts its course both according to what those on board decide to do and in response to changes in its environment. The development of applied sociology in the interwar period demonstrates the complexity of the interaction between the two.

References

Abrams, P. 1968. *The Origins of British Sociology, 1834–1914*. Chicago: University of Chicago Press.

American Sociological Association. 1989. "Future Organizational Trends of the ASA." *Footnotes* 17(6) (Sept.):1–5, 9.

Arnove, R. F. 1980. "Foundations and the Transfer of Knowledge." In *Philanthropy and Cultural Imperialism,* ed. Arnove 305–30.

———, ed. 1980. *Philanthropy and Cultural Imperialism*. Boston: G. K. Hall.

Bannister, R. C. 1988. *Sociology and Scientism: The American Quest for Objectivity 1880–1940*. Chapel Hill: University of North Carolina Press.

Brim, O. G. 1958. *Sociology and the Field of Education*. New York: Russell Sage Foundation for the American Sociological Association.

Bulmer, M. 1980. "The Early Institutional Establishment of Social Science Research: The Local Community Research Committee at the University of Chicago, 1923–30." *Minerva* 18:51–100.

———. 1983. "The Methodology of Early Social Indicators Research: William Fielding Ogburn and *Recent Social Trends,* 1933," with W. F. Ogburn, "A Note on Method: An Unpublished Memorandum on the Methodology of the President's Research Committee on Recent Social Trends, 1929–1933." *Social Indicators Research* 13:109–130.

———. 1984. *The Chicago School of Sociology: Institutionalization, Diver-*

sity and the Rise of Sociological Research. Chicago: University of Chicago Press.

———. 1991. "W. E. B. DuBois as a Social Investigator: *The Philadelphia Negro.*" In *Social Survey,* ed. M. Bulmer, K. Bales, and K. K. Sklar, 170–88.

Bulmer, M., K. Bales, and K. K. Sklar, eds. 1991. *The Social Survey in Historical Perspective, 1880–1940.* Cambridge: Cambridge University Press.

Bulmer, M., and J. Bulmer. 1981. "Philanthropy and Social Science in the 1920s: Beardsley Ruml and the Laura Spelman Rockefeller Memorial, 1922–1929." *Minerva* 19:347–407.

Bulmer, M., and D. Fisher. 1984. "Debate on the Interpretation of the Role of Foundations." *Sociology* 18:573–87.

Chambers, C. A. 1971. *Paul U. Kellogg and the SURVEY.* Minneapolis: University of Minnesota Press.

Coleman, J. 1972. *Policy Research in the Social Sciences.* Morristown, N.J.: General Learning Press.

Converse, J. M. 1987. *Survey Research in the United States: Roots and Emergence, 1890–1960.* Berkeley: University of California Press.

Coser, L. 1965. "Foundations as Gatekeepers of Contemporary Intellectual Life." In *Men of Ideas,* ed. L. Coser, 337–48. New York: Free Press.

———. 1977. *Masters of Sociological Thought: Ideas in Historical and Social Context.* New York: Harcourt Brace Jovanovich.

Deegan, M. J. 1988. *Jane Addams and the Men of the Chicago School, 1892–1918.* New Brunswick, N.J.: Transaction Books.

Diner, S. J. 1980. *A City and Its Universities: Public Policy in Chicago 1892–1919.* Chapel Hill: University of North Carolina Press.

DuBois, W. E. B. 1899. *The Philadelphia Negro.* Philadelphia: University of Pennsylvania.

Eaton, A., and S. M. Harrison. 1930. *A Bibliography of Social Surveys: Reports of Fact-Finding Studies Made as a Basis for Social Action, Arranged by Subjects and Localities.* New York: Russell Sage Foundation.

Fisher, D. 1980. "American Philanthropy and the Social Sciences in Britain, 1919–39: The Reproduction of a Conservative Ideology." *The Sociological Review* 28:277–315.

———. 1983. "The Role of Philanthropic Foundations in the Reproduction and Production of Hegemony." *Sociology* 17:206–33.

Frank, R. 1988. "'Interdisciplinary': The First Half Century." *Items* 42(3):73–78. New York: S.S.R.C.

Harrison, S. M. 1931. *The Social Survey.* New York: Russell Sage Foundation.

Hinkle, R. C., Jr., and G. Hinkle. 1954. *The Development of Modern Sociology: Its Nature and Growth in the United States.* New York: Random House.

Hull House. 1895. *Hull-House Maps and Papers, by Residents of Hull-House, A Social Settlement.* New York: Crowell.

Hutchins, R. M. 1930. "Address of Dedication (of the Social Science Research Building, University of Chicago)." In *The New Social Science*, ed. L. D. White, 1–4. Chicago: University of Chicago Press.

Jackson, W. A. 1985. "The Making of a Social Science Classic: Gunnar Myrdal's *An American Dilemma*." *Perspectives in American History*, New Series 2:221–67.

———. 1990. *Gunnar Myrdal and America's Social Conscience: Social engineering and Valid Liberalism, 1938–1987*. Chapel Hill: University of North Carolina Press.

Janowitz, M. 1970. "Sociological Models and Social Policy." In *Political Conflict: Essays in Political Sociology*, ed. M. Janowitz, 243–59.

———. 1975. "Sociological Theory and Social Control." *American Journal of Sociology* 81:82–108.

Johnson, G. B., and G. G. Johnson. 1980. *Research in Service to Society: The First Fifty Years of the Institute for Research in Social Science at the University of North Carolina*. Chapel Hill: University of North Carolina Press.

Karabel, Jerome. 1988. "Commentary on Bulmer and Sica." Commentary presented at conference on "Sociology and Institution-Building." Arizona, Nov. 16–17.

Karl, B. E. 1963. *Executive Reorganization and Reform in the New Deal: The Genesis of Administrative Management 1900–1939*. Chicago: University of Chicago Press.

———. 1969. "Presidential Planning and Social Science Research: Mr Hoover's Experts." *Perspectives in American History* 3:347–409.

———. 1974. *Charles E Merriam and the Study of Politics*. Chicago: University of Chicago Press.

———. 1983. *The Uneasy State: The United States from 1915 to 1945*. Chicago: University of Chicago Press.

Karl, B. E., and S. N. Katz. 1987. "Foundations and Ruling Class Elites." *Daedalus* 116(1):1–40.

Kohler, R. E. 1978. "A Policy for the Advancement of Science: The Rockefeller Foundation 1924–1929." *Minerva* 16:480–515.

———. 1987. "Science, Foundations and American Universities in the 1920s." *Osiris*, 2d ser., vol. 3:135–64.

Lagemann, E. C. 1987. "A Philanthropic Foundation at Work: Gunnar Myrdal's *An American Dilemma* and the Carnegie Corporation." *Minerva* 25 (4):441–70.

———. 1989. *History of the Carnegie Corporation of New York Since Its Foundation and Growth in the 1920's*. Middletown, Conn.: Wesleyan University Press.

Lazarsfeld, P. F. 1969. "An Episode in the History of Social Research: A Memoir." In *The Intellectual Migration: Europe and America, 1930–1960*, ed. D. Fleming and B. Bailyn, 270–337. Cambridge, Mass.: Harvard University Press.

Lazarsfeld, P. F., and J. G. Reitz. 1975. *Introduction to Applied Sociology*. New York: Elsevier.

Lazarsfeld, P. F., W. Sewell, and H. L. Wilensky, eds. 1967. *The Uses of Sociology.* New York: Basic Books.

Lynd, R. S. 1939. *Knowledge for What? The Place of Social Science in American Culture.* Princeton, NJ: Princeton University Press.

Lyons, G. M. 1969. *The Uneasy Partnership: Social Science and the Federal Government in the Twentieth Century.* New York: Russell Sage Foundation.

Miller, R. B. 1982. "The Social Sciences and the Politics of Science: The 1940's." *The American Sociologist* 17:205–09.

Myrdal, G., with R. Sterner and A. Rose. 1944. *An American Dilemma: The Negro Problem and Modern Democracy.* New York: Harper.

Oberschall, A. 1965. *Empirical Social Research in Germany, 1848–1914.* The Hague: Mouton.

Ogburn, W. F. 1930. "Folkways of a Scientific Sociology." *Studies in Quantitative and Cultural Sociology; Papers Presented to the Annual Meeting of the American Sociological Society.* Chicago: University of Chicago Press.

Ogburn, W. F., and A. Goldenweiser, eds. 1927. *The Social Sciences and Their Interrelations.* Boston: Houghton Mifflin.

Perry, H. S. 1982. *Psychiatrist of America: The Life of Harry Stack Sullivan.* Cambridge, Mass.: Belknap Press, Harvard University.

Rhoades, L. J. 1981. *A History of the American Sociological Association 1905–1980.* Washington, D.C.: American Sociological Association.

Recent Social Trends. 1933. *Recent Social Trends in the United States: Report of the President's Research Committee on Recent Social Trends.* New York: McGraw Hill.

Ross, D. 1979. "The Development of the Social Sciences." In *The Organization of Knowledge in Modern America, 1860–1920,* ed. A. Oleson and J. Voss, 107–38. Baltimore, Md.: Johns Hopkins University Press.

Rossi, P. and W. F. Whyte. 1983. "The Applied Side of Sociology." In *Applied Sociology,* ed. H. E. Freeman et al., 5–31. San Francisco: Jossey Bass.

Rule, J. 1978. *Insight and Social Betterment: A Preface to Applied Social Science.* New York: Oxford University Press.

Shils, E. 1948. *The Present State of American Sociology.* Glencoe, Il.: The Free Press.

———. 1980. "Tradition, Ecology and Institution in the History of Sociology." In *The Calling of Sociology and other Essays on the Pursuit of Learning,* E. Shils, 165–256. Chicago: University of Chicago Press.

Sokal, M. M., ed. 1987. *Psychological Testing and American Society, 1890–1930.* New Brunswick, N.J.: Rutgers University Press.

Stanfield, J. H. 1985. *Philanthropy and Jim Crow in American Social Science.* Westport, Conn.: Greenwood.

Stouffer, S. A. 1930. "An Experimental Comparison of Statistical and Case History Methods of Attitude Research." Ph.D. diss. University of Chicago.

Street, D., and A. Weinstein. 1975. "Problems and Prospects of Applied Sociology." *The American Sociologist* 10:65–72.

Szreter, R. 1980. "Institutionalising a New Specialism: Early Years of the

Journal of Educational Sociology." *British Journal of Sociology of Education.* 1(2):173–82.

Wheatley, S. C. 1988. *The Politics of Philanthropy: Abraham Flexner and Medical Education.* Madison, Wis.: University of Wisconsin Press.

Wiebe, R. 1975. *The Segmented Society: An Introduction to the Meaning of America.* New York: Oxford University Press.

10

The Rhetoric of Sociology and Its Audience

ALAN SICA

Theorizing and Generational Differences

Perhaps it has become a commonplace that a split exists between scholars educated just after World War II, inspired by the belief that sociology could help build or rebuild social institutions, and those coming later, who found sociology attractive because of its critical edge, its destructive, even deconstructive, capabilities. It seemed to the latter cohort to promise a distinct method for understanding what a philosopher has recently called "deconstructive living," a world of uncertain values, of a "groundlessness of our unities and 'firsts'" (Kolb 1986:193). For students in the United States twenty years ago, just such "a variety of essential differences and contradictions" (Gasché 1986:163), with the emphasis upon "essential," seemed everywhere in evidence, and most noticeably in all the major social institutions. Though no one here knew it, a young French academic was at the same time doing his best to outlaw most of what had been accepted since Kant as the standard norms of presentation in philosophy. That Derrida's work, long since passé in his native country but still the rage here, would have such irrevocable impact on the humanities was as unpredicted during the "troubles"—as the late 1960s were named by the Right—as the Bennington undergraduate novel, *Less Than Zero,* was unforeseen until it arrived. My point in this chapter will be, in some sense, to compare what it means to read *Less Than Zero* as an important youthful fictional accomplishment in 1982, and to recall what it meant to have read *This Side of Paradise,* a Princeton undergraduate novel, sixty-two years before. I say "in some sense" because I want to use these alarming explosions of fictional creativity as markers for institutional change, not because I am interested for the moment in enlarging the sociology of literature. Yet one need not be Leo Lowenthal to see that literature reflects (and then influences) cultural tone, and an important part of that influence is the form which language takes in trying to convince. What is today linguistically, and therefore theoretically, possible bears little relation to that earlier time when "institution building" seemed both empirically obvious as a socially successful activity and a meaningful concept as well.

We have been asked to write about how the social organization of the discipline affects sociology's potential impact on society, and to review the changing character of an aspect of sociology's organization since World War II and appraise its implications for its capacity to engage in institution building. We might pursue this in a number of ways, one of which could deal with the civic responsibilities or moral significance of sociology for society. We are also reminded that by so doing, we are showing recognition of Morris Janowitz's commitment to institution building by sociology. It may seem both puerile and pedantic to recite our assignment, but perhaps it is justified by the wish to go about the task precisely, as Janowitz himself might have done.

Lest this appear coy, let me return to my opening remark about generational differences and the perception of what is theoretically accurate and societally possible. Meeting Professor Janowitz for the first time several years ago and spending time with him, even in his much reduced physical state, was like opening a door to a large and carefully appointed room in sociology's mansion that up to that point was never known to exist for members of the next generation. If Gouldner's telling counterpoint of living "from" sociology or "for" it was ever embodied in a scholar, Janowitz seemed to be that person. At first I could not reconcile his keen intelligence and perpetual irony—which seemed much like the mindsets of Mills, Marcuse, or Gouldner, all critics of the field—with his almost boyish hope and insistence that sociology had a future and an irreplaceable role in the American life of the mind. Slowly, over some months, I began the long march between generational perceptions of what is and was important, what is and was theoretically meaningful.

One day, for instance, after listening to an abstract lecture by a European scholar about social interaction, Janowitz mumbled to me upon leaving the room, "Was all in Thomas and clearer." "W. I.?" I asked. He nodded. Another incident that gave me some pause was the evening when Edward Shils spoke to the Janowitz seminar on the history of sociology; the kindnesses and spartan regard that each held for the other let the youngsters know that much had passed between and before these elders to which the youngsters would never be party. It was soon after that Shils told me his manifold objections to "metatheory," arguing that if one hoped to make a difference in the field, skillful institutional analysis was the proper route. Metatheory should be left to philosophers. Yet, as one looks through new books that pile into academic bookshops nationwide, dozens of what Shils called "metas" arrive for every one that analyzes what could more or less still be understood as a "social institution." So when I was asked to write about institutions, it seemed that the past had returned, as Nietzsche and Eliade said it would. Once again I am forced to puzzle over the phrase "institution building," what social institutions are currently experiencing, and what, if anything, our field of study can say about these transactions that might be enlightening, or even helpful.

The Later Chicago School on "Institutions"

It seems reasonable, then, even necessary, to begin with Janowitz's own work. He was himself far from oblivious to problems of the kind I am broaching. Twenty years ago, in the era of Model Cities—from which his research benefited materially—he wrote about sociology's impact on institutions, not by way of its "scientific" prowess, but by its ability to shape public discourse:

> By the middle of the 1960s sociological categories had come to pervade popular and professional thinking about slum schools and education of the lower class. Militant demands for improving the effectiveness of inner city education have incorporated the rhetoric of sociology because of the realities of social class and race. Terms such as "cultural deprivation" and "deviant behavior" were no longer technical jargon but the language of political debate. (Janowitz 1969:1)

Thus Janowitz begins his *Institution Building in Urban Education* (1969), a product of a time in which sociologists of his stature could command substantial research money and were then paid careful heed when results were reported. His phrase "the rhetoric of sociology" is not, I believe, meant to be taken self-critically, ironically, or self-consciously. He simply means what he says, that sociology and social research, for a short time in American political history, had become capable of getting under people's skin by changing the language in which they thought, just as economics had done in the Depression and psychology continues to do today. There seemed to be little doubt in his mind at the time he wrote this short book that sociology's "rhetoric" was a good thing overall, and that identifying institutions and affecting their development was a major part of sociology's job, its public debt, to a polity that was generous in its support. This collection of related sentiments, which seems incredibly distant from those of our own day, is well represented in Janowitz's ingenuous discussion of what he calls 'people changing' institutions: "there has developed a body of research literature on 'people changing' institutions and a common language of discourse between social investigators and selected administrators. . . . It is clear, however, that the social and moral climate of mental hospitals or training schools can be altered to become more compatible with the standards of a humane society that stresses self-respect and dignity" (1969:3).

If it was true those twenty long years ago that such a common language existed between researchers and their clients, and that they shared a "moral vision" of humanitarian treatment for their charges, that very rhetorical situation is no longer with us, except perhaps as an underground memory that occasionally shows its head rather timidly. Janowitz's pungent skepticism about everyday life was not allowed into his programmatic prose, a characteristic that sets him off markedly from reflective researchers today.

Janowitz referred to the concept of institutions and the problem of their perpetuation and growth in many of his works, notably *The Reconstruction of Patriotism* (1983:12ff) and a famous article on social control (1975). However, the single work that reached further into the public mind than any of his others, and perhaps therefore did not receive the warmest reception from the fraternity he had worked so hard to help create, was *The Last Half-Century.* Since he begins the book with this unusual statement, "At present the conservation of the effective heritage of sociology is as important as the generation of new knowledge" (1978:xi), it seems prudent to recapture Janowitz's "effective heritage" itself, particularly with regard to what he called institution building. This occurs for the most part in 7 pages (1978:399–406). One sentence into his argument, Janowitz refers us, for fundamental definition of the concept, to Eisenstadt's introduction to the Weber volume in the Heritage of Sociology Series—for which the field will always be in Janowitz's debt. It may well seem odd that Eisenstadt chose *On Charisma and Institution Building* (1968) as the subtitle for the Weber volume, since the latter concept is not one that leaps from Weber's pages. Yet Eisenstadt is able, in his lengthy remarks, to posit an interesting set of conceptual problems to which Weber's work can conceivably be applied, or even viewed as partially solving. When Eisenstadt says that Weber's "most general concern, permeating all his work, was with what may be called, in the terminology of modern sociology, the processes of institution building, social transformation, and cultural creativity" (xvi), we are hearing Parsons's and Shils's voices more than Weber's own. Later comes an admission which seems to me more valuable for understanding Weber and whatever utility he might have for institutional analysis: "It is this continuous tension between what may be called the constrictive and the creative aspects of institutions and of social organization that is of central interest to Weber" (1968:xvii). It is indeed this tension (*Spannung*) that gives Weber's work its liveliness and continuing influence, and not so much his concern for building anything, either conceptual or institutional (see Sica 1988:65–66).

Eisenstadt holds that charisma is the dynamizing force within institutions that would otherwise drift into ossification. It is charisma that "contains strong tendencies toward the destruction and decomposition of institutions" (1968:xix). This tendency to "burst the limits" of accepted patterns seems to bother functionalists much more than it did Weber, who was at home with the fact that charisma "may arise from the darkest recesses of the human soul, from its utter depravity and irresponsibility of its most intensive antinomian tendencies" (1968:xx). This is certainly the way Weber understood genuine charisma, which shows no mercy, nor asks for any, in pursuing its unique project of social transformation. Yet Eisenstadt relies upon Shils's 1965 article, "Charisma, Order, and Status," to put the genie back into the bottle, for it is argued that "these charismatic 'connections' may . . . also become resident, in varying degrees of intensity, in institutions" (1968:xxvi). The idea that the explosive unpredictability and sheer excitement which attaches the run of humanity to charismatic personalities could become "resident" in an institution for any length of time seems related to a lion-tamer's hope that his charges will look ferocious in the ring even though they are fond of him and want his affection. Shils elaborates on this domestication of charisma:

> Society has a center. There is a central zone in the structure of society. This central zone impinges in various ways on those who live within the ecological domain in which the society exists. . . . The center, or the central zone, is a phenomenon of the realm of values and beliefs. It is the center of the order of symbols of values and beliefs, which govern the society. It is the center because it is the ultimate and irreducible; and it is felt to be such by many who cannot give explicit articulation to its irreducibility. (Quoted in Eisenstadt 1968:xxx)

The entire essay from which these excerpts come is a miraculous effort to geld the bull. Shils correctly outlines Weber's understanding of charisma, but then redraws it "more systematically than Weber was able to do" (Shils [1965] 1975:256) so that it all points toward the "Need for Order": "No one can doubt the grandeur of the historical-

philosophical vision in Weber's view of the uniqueness of modern society. . . . Yet it is too disjunctive in its conception. . . . It is too historicist" [1965] (1975:261).

There is much here to fight about, but fortunately I am most concerned for the moment with the question of institution building, not
the accuracy of functionalist Weber readings. Without going into the
detail necessary for a credible refutation, let me say that this is simply
an ideological, moral-ethical agenda, rather than something close to
an "objective" portrait of how charisma functions or what made up
social institutions in 1965, when the essay appeared. The idea that
there is some hegemonic center for values and beliefs, that it is irreducible, and that ordinary folk cannot readily identify it sounds sus-
piciously like high-church sneering. If these kinds of sentiments found
an audience twenty-four years ago, imagine how the following (appearing under the subhead "A Digression: Individual Variations in the
Need for Order") would play to academic listeners today, or even to
the remnants of the literate laity:

> The need for order is not equally great among all men. Many, of
> course, whose "antennae" are short, whose intelligence and imagi-
> nation either are limited or have not been aroused by a cultural tra-
> dition which exhibits events of central significance, do not have the
> need to "know" the cosmos or society as a whole or to be in contact
> with its "vital" or "animating" principle. For such persons, who are
> many in the world, the need for affection, for self-maintenance, for
> justice, for self-transcendence, can be gratified largely in personal
> primary groups with spouse and offspring and kinsmen, or in work-
> ing collectivities with colleagues and immediate subordinates. Much
> of the order they need, as well as the affection and rewards they
> desire, perhaps even most that is of value to them, is found in such
> circles of small radius. . . . Only idiots—idiots in a sense halfway
> between the classical Greek usage and present-day psychological
> usage—can, however, dispense entirely with cosmic and social or-
> der. Most people, occasionally and intermittently, feel the need to
> see themselves in a deeper, wider frame of things. Birth, death, mar-
> riage, transitions from one ordered condition to another—even
> when they are orders of narrow radius—cause faint or dormant sen-
> sibilities to open. . . . In no society can the problem of the larger
> order be avoided entirely. (Shils [1965] 1978:262)

The rhetorical dimension to this argument is overwhelming. One can
warm to it, in appreciation of the good sermon it wishes to be. It could
also be interpreted as condescending, factually wrong, or even a testament of faith by a social scientist writing a strong moral-ethical program in the language of social theory.

The person in the history of social thought most congenitally resistant to this tone, these suppositions, these theoretical outcomes—and
I include Marx in my figuring—is Weber. It is a credit to Shils's creativity and his heroic self-regard that he could so capsize Weber's intentions while pretending to help him reach safe harbor. It is not for a
moment true that Weber was too historicist to understand modern
society correctly, or that he misjudged the place of charisma—of the
Amt, Gentil, or *Erb* varieties—as it became routinized. The difference
between his concluding bleakness and Shils's "need for order" is that
the former looked at the data and found no plausible redemption,
whereas the latter still sees it as not only possible, but absolutely
necessary. It is a matter of two smart analysts examining similar phenomena and taking their rhetoric along opposed axiological paths.
Weber did not need salvation—from secular or sacred sources or
from their problems—and it is this hard-edged quality that sets him
apart from other theorists, and makes him so despicable to those
who wish to believe in something, whether it be order, religious dogma, progress, absolutist ethics, consensualism, or any other irrational
course.

I have made this detour into Shils via Eisenstadt and off the main
trunk of Janowitz because these men influenced each other profoundly; they shared information, beliefs, prejudices, and publishing
opportunities, and presented a picture of social life in a uniformly
powerful rhetoric. Let me say immediately that the substance of what
Janowitz has to say regarding institution building, of what Eisenstadt
claims is true for charismatic infusions into the rigidity of forms, of
what Shils argues regarding social order and its underlying value
scheme, reflects, in each case, large portions of good sense. Moreover,
and in the end most importantly, all three have their hearts in the right
place from the point of view of the left-liberal sociological ethics that
brought my generation into the fold, even if they would not see that
or admit it themselves. They are good men pursuing worthwhile
causes—or so they were when they first formed the ideas they kept
belaboring over the years. Yet when I, part theorist, part historian of
sociology, part citizen of a nation-state in enormous trouble, read their
works today, I wonder where they found these ideas, why they wrote
about them the way they did, and what difference it made in the intellectual and sociopolitical landscape around them over the last forty
years or so.

For example, why does it seem to Eisenstadt that social institutions
have "a double aspect. . . . their organizational exigencies on the one
hand, and their potential close relations to the realm of meaning on

the other" (xxxvii)? If this was true twenty years ago, does it hold now? Once again, we turn to Janowitz's last words on the subject.

Sidney Hook taught Janowitz (1983:xii) to avoid the "burden of both materialism and idealism" by instructing him, as an undergraduate, in the flexible doctrines of pragmatism. And from W. I. Thomas, he found something called "reason" as applied to social life. For instance, "the underlying question is to assess the prospects for reasoned direction for societal change" (399), which in many ways summarizes Janowitz's goals for sociology's role in the public sphere. It is no accident that the Thomas volume in Janowitz's "Heritage" series, an early number in the set put together by the general editor himself, offers soon after his fond introduction a chapter called "Rational Control in Social Life." In *The Polish Peasant,* from which this extract is taken, the same material is merely titled "Methodological Note." The memorable first paragraph reads:

> One of the most significant features of social evolution is the growing importance which a conscious and rational technique tends to assume in social life. We are less and less ready to let any social processes go on without our active interference and we feel more and more dissatisfied with any active interference based upon a mere whim of an individual or a social body, or upon preconceived philosophical, religious, or moral generalization.
>
> The marvelous results attained by a rational technique . . . .
> (Thomas and Znaniecki 1927, 1:1)

Consider for a moment how Foucault or any of the postmodernists or many feminists or Marxists might read this paragraph. Would it not be taken as a self-indictment of the hubris that has typified Western male society since the Renaissance? Would libertarians not find it offensive precisely for its trumpeting of control that comes from without and may well speak on behalf of that kind of social control most feared in a cultural atmosphere adumbrated by Huxley and then Orwell? Yet this was clearly not what Thomas meant in writing these lyrical passages, nor what Alfred Knopf understood by the intent of the book when he brought out a trade edition ten years after its very limited initial appearance. Once again we see the force that rhetoric has for both writer and audience. It seems entirely likely that Thomas meant nothing evil or manipulative by his words, and that for him, "reason" or "rational" in these contexts were virtually synonymous with "good" or "fair." The excruciating irony of a scholar calling for Taylorian control of social life—"Our success in controlling nature gives us confidence that we shall eventually be able to control the social world in the same measure" (1927:1)—who soon after publishing this document was himself pilloried by demonic government agents, fits perfectly with today's sentiment regarding *any* form of control, external or internal. I am sure the irony did not escape Thomas, but neither did it alter his theorizing in the way it would those who later experienced involuntary exile, such as Horkheimer and Adorno, Pollock and Kirchheimer, Marcuse and Neumann. It was not that these scholars were such devoted Hegelians that they accepted only dialectical interpretations of events. Rather, they felt first-hand what social control can mean when carried out by official thugs, something American theorists have been fortunate to escape ever since the sunny times and reasonable pages of William James or Josiah Royce.

In this context, it is worthwhile to quote Janowitz at length, since he is characteristically frank about what he thinks sociology has to offer those in charge of managing institutional growth:

> When I speak of institution building, I mean those conscious efforts to direct societal change and to search for more effective social control which are grounded in rationality and in turn are supported by social-science efforts. Two assumptions are immediately involved. First, conscious institution building does not assume a rationalistic view of man and society. The application of the scientific method . . . confirms the limits of rational economic and psychological man and denies the possibility and indeed the desirability of relying exclusively or mechanically on such models as the basis for institution building. The difficult and unending task is to identify the particular relevance of rationalistic models, for the limits of their applicability involve matters of judgment if not intuition.
>
> Second, the notion of institution building means that, with the growth of the division of labor and the separation of work from the community of residence and family, the elites and subelites recognize the need and desirability of enlarging citizen participation in decision making.
>
> Thus to consider institution building is to examine the actual and potential influence of scientific thought—especially social-scientific—on ongoing institutions. Conscious efforts at institution building include the fusion or, if you will, the balancing of scientific thought with the full range of disciplined creativity which draws on traditional and innovative humanistic enterprise. (1983:400–401)

If one recalls the socialist intellectuals who ran Austria between 1920 and 1932, several of whom have attained enduring intellectual prominence for their theoretical and practical writings, these sixty-five years after fascists ground their ideals under boots; or if one thinks of Woodrow Wilson's education, his utopian scheme for a united world, his gifted literacy; if one even takes in Winston Churchill or Adlai

Stevenson or Averell Harriman as members of an "elite" in charge of building this or that institution and of encouraging citizen participation in decision making—then, of course, Janowitz's remarks make perfect sense. However, if one instead scrutinizes what is now offered by way of leadership and also, more importantly, the nature of electronically cretinized masses and their typical response to the notion of civic or public activity in pursuit of some unprovincial ideal, then Janowitz's sentiments become the product not of experience circa 1975 when they were written, but instead the dreams of a young man just before the invention of McLuhan's Mechanical Bride. In fact, if W. I. Thomas's influence on Janowitz is given its full due, then many of his "domain assumptions" (Gouldner 1970) were invented by this one-time English and classics professor at around the time Small began sociology at Chicago. Out of about 1,300 scholars in the index of *The Last Half-Century,* Thomas is cited 16 times, more than anyone except Lasswell, Shils, or Weber. There is a late nineteenth century philosophical anthropology at work in Janowitz's imagination, even if his writing sounds mostly contemporary. It is just this strong vision, unapologetically given, that seems so hard for theorists of my generation to appreciate.

For instance, when Janowitz chides Horkheimer for having written *The Eclipse of Reason,* which, he claims, makes "the argument that organized social investigation of the real world undermines reason" (1978:401), one must wonder if he is responding to the title or the book's contents, which do not, it seems to me, make any such argument. Horkheimer's attack upon the degeneration of reason in the public sphere was first published in 1947, and it is in the Frankfurt School tradition that questions the direction of cultural and political movement and, as such, is even more relevant today than when it appeared, if in somewhat different form. Nonetheless, it is as if Janowitz, the careful scholar and wide reader, could no more accept the Frankfurt critique of our civilization than could Shils, because it partook of a depressing, un-American, so-called romantic view of things that did not jibe with certain key aspirations these theorists had for their society. This is something Shils has been saying for a long time, and he is sometimes very amusing when doing so, as in the introduction to one of his volumes of collected essays:

> In the fifties, the old dissatisfaction of American intellectuals with the state of their culture in society took a new form. It became a critique of "mass culture." This was not a phenomenon with which I had ever had much sympathy. Looking at television and reading comic strips had never appeared to me to be a worthwhile activity

for educated persons; I had given up baseball at the age of fifteen or sixteen and had never gone in for crime novels or burlesque shows, but I did find the condescending and bitter abuse by certain intellectuals of those who enjoyed these pastimes rather distasteful. It seemed to me unworthy for disappointed and broken-down Trotskyites and *Edelmarxisten,* mostly of the Frankfurt provenience, to take revenge on the working and middle classes for not having measured up to their unrealistic and uninvited expectations. (Shils, 1972:xi)

As highbrow humor, this is good stuff, but as intellectual history, it reads very strangely—at least, for those of my generation who began not by reading Dwight Macdonald ripping apart mass culture and the Great Books, but Adorno and Horkheimer on what rotten fruits had fallen from the tree of Enlightenment—for purely intellectual reasons. If one compares, say, the TV pabulum of the mid-1950s and the comic strips of that time with the programmed viciousness of both media today, Shils seems to have been dead wrong in his estimate of the importance these "pastimes" would assume in American cultural life. It makes more sense now to refer to them as the main feature of existence for many, particularly younger, people than mere accompaniments to an otherwise full life of social interaction and institution building.

That said, however, I must try to practice genuine hermeneutics and give Janowitz a chance to defuse his own liberal enthusiasm, even if he does it in somewhat muted and incidental form. He observes:

In the middle of the 1970s, there has emerged increased realism about the complexities, limitations, and subtleties involved in the application of social research to institution building. The self-image of the sociologist as philosopher-king continued to be held by only a minority of social researchers. . . . Most sociologists, however, believe that, besides the intellectual limits and defects of their discipline, there were "tough" and at points almost intractable institutional, professional, and political barriers that had to be dealt with. (1978:403–4)

He does not emphasize "intractable," but I certainly would. Nor does he show in the ensuing pages how these stupendous barriers to what he earlier called "prospects for the reasoned direction of social change" might be dealt with. What he does instead, which is most understandable given his ultimate political and intellectual values, is to warn against falling into what Lukács called the Grand Hotel Abyss inhabited by intellectuals who enjoy failure—their own and that of others. Mid-1970s sociology began to admit this "increased realism" into its post-Parsonsian celebration of American culture, but this "does not mean that the social scientist abandons this methodology and accepts a cynical outlook" (1978:406). Following this avuncular comment, Janowitz launches into a spirited attack upon what he calls "Hedonism and 'The Therapeutic Syndrome'." This fits well indeed with his sense of reality—he finds it odd, for instance, that in 1974 homosexuality was no longer officially designated a disease by physicians—but it would jar most of his younger colleagues and their semi-literate students today.

Institution-Building in "Pre-Postmodern" Culture

What seems apparent from Janowitz's analysis, at least with reference to the part dealing with institution building, is his blindness to the state of public culture at large. He comments frequently upon sociology's need to inform and educate elites and subelites, to inculcate them with certain liberal-democratic ideas that would have pleased, among others, the young Sidney Hook or the mature John Dewey. The colossal ignorance among American youth, not only pertaining to arcana like the classics of literature or history, but to anything in printed form, does not figure in Janowitz's analysis. He seems to believe that leaders may be persuaded to do right if social knowledge is presented to them forcefully enough and in terms that fit their schemes of reality. Who, precisely, are these idealized leaders, loaded down with the sort of exact information that sociology seems seldom able to provide, going to lead, and where? In this way, oddly enough, Janowitz's macroanalysis lacks a dimension to a thorough understanding of contemporary life that is also apparent in Russell Jacoby's celebrated polemic, *The Last Intellectuals,* even though the latter is written from an approximately Frankfurt-Marxist point of view and is hostile to most of those thinkers for whom Janowitz has high regard.

Because I find Janowitz's intellectualism and his dedication to the sociological task utterly admirable, I am prompted to dig still deeper into the origins of his approach, full of sharp, instructive remarks, but so at odds with the way I see the same social world. If nothing else, this becomes a small exercise in both the sociology of intellectuals and the sociology of sociology itself. In hunting for significant leads, one notices that very early in his detailed introduction to the Thomas volume in the Heritage series (1966:xi), Janowitz once again relies upon Shils, this time Shils's famous monograph, "The Calling of Sociology," that served as epilogue to the compendium published in 1961, *Theo-*

ries of Society (Parsons et al.). For many years this book displayed the authoritative lineage of functionalist (and to some extent, nonfunctionalist) social thought. Shils's long meditation, played out against one of Weber's favorite themes, and written nearly thirty years ago, has become an intriguing historical document from the point of view of sociology's rhetoric, and also as a key to this perplexing concept of institution building with which both he and Janowitz seem quite comfortable. It deserves our close attention.[1]

It is hard to say what influence Shils's lengthy statement had on either the teachers or students of social theory during the sixties, when the book was selling fastest. Today one hears that even at the finest universities, undergraduates who major in sociology are no longer required or expected to read the classical trinity—Marx, Durkheim, Weber—because "they are too hard." If that is the case, perhaps it is unlikely that even then many readers ever understood Shils's complex formulation very well. But surely Janowitz did, which is our immediate concern. Shils wishes to advance a highly contentious and sparsely documented history of sociology in a tone of relieved victory over an uncertain, prescientific, politically messy birth and adolescence. With "the theory of action"—never explicitly attached to the names of Parsons and Shils—sociology and its theoretical structure have come of age and can begin to forget the days when it struggled against intellectual confusion, sociopolitical discomfort, and academic revilement. This is the kind of document that plays havoc with historians' labors later on. Unless one knew that in a widely read book the year before, Mills had mercilessly ravaged the very theory that Shils here celebrates as a finished triumph for sociological thought, one's perception of the field circa 1960 would be contrary to what may well become the official or consensually approved version; that is, Mills's version. Shils's rhetoric is built of the same masonry that found itself being used in defense of creationism just after the publication of Darwin's worldshaking book. This is not to equate Shils's substance with that of the creationists, but only to point out that the serenity and stratospheric remove his prose so skillfully evokes has nothing at all to do with the impending explosion and implosion that the social sciences faced within the decade. For Shils, the major quandaries seem solved, the outlines of theory are clearly drawn; even the fathers of the discipline, often taken as holy and unsurpassable, became warmups for the real

1. I will quote from the original, not the "revised and enlarged version" that is the centerpiece of his third volume of essays (Shils 1980:3–92), since the first has surely been read by more sociologists.

game that came to be called "the theory of action."[2] Shils writes in
the early part of his essay: "*The Structure of Social Action* was the
turning point. It was this work that brought the greatest of the partial
traditions into a measure of unity" (1961:1406). He is sincere, one
hopes, yet quite wrong from any extra-Parsonsian point of view. As
many observers, including even its author, have admitted, the book
was virtually unread after publication. Its plates were unceremon-
iously destroyed during World War II and converted to matériel—
with the consent of distinguished sociologists who were privately
asked by the publisher if the book merited preservation—and only in
the late sixties did the paperback edition begin to have much of a
readership, largely, one suspects, because of the infamy brought to it
by Mills and many others.

I am not arguing for a view that would consider Parsons's first book
either a poor or unimportant one. It was his best and most essential,
regarding his own vision and in its contribution to the theoretical education of American sociologists. My point of difference with Shils is
his apodictic tone regarding the lasting value of structural functionalism and its obvious superiority to other forms of theorizing, most
notably Marxism and its offshoots on one hand, phenomenology and
other "idealisms" on the other. And part of this alleged superiority is
the use of "institution" in the special way Parsons used it,[3] which also,
and perhaps because of him, evolved into unexamined dogma in the
field at large. There is in Shils (and also in Parsons, though less clearly
because of his awful writing) a sentiment of certainty, even majesty,
which makes the field out to be intellectually rock-solid and eminently
powerful as a tool for political and cultural analysis—of the Parsonsian variety, of course—in much the same way that Janowitz thought

2. This is almost precisely what Alexander (1987) has tried to do in his rewriting of
theoretical history since the Second World War, so that Parsons's "dominance" of the
field after 1945—which, one might well argue, existed mainly within a small radius of
Cambridge, Massachusetts—is presented not as an ideologically sustained suggestion,
but as demonstrated fact. What Shils did to Parsons's adversaries in 1961, Alexander
continues today, though with somewhat less elegance and "celebralism," to coin a word.
(See also Smelser 1988, for a related strategy.)

3. One of Parsons's many psychologistic definitions: "In a social system, roles vary
in the degree of their institutionalization. By institutionalization we mean the integration of the complementary role-expectation and sanction patterns with a generalized
value system *common* to the members of the more inclusive collectivity, of which the
system of complementary role-actions may be a part" (from *Toward a General Theory
of Action* (1951), reprinted in Leon Mayhew, ed., *Talcott Parsons on Institutions and
Social Evolution* (1982), 117). It is just this sort of cant that undid Parsons's ambitions
for a unified theory of social action (and social life at large), especially when it came
into the hands of readers like Mills, Sorokin, Bierstedt, and many others.

it could contribute to institution building. It is very hard from today's vantage point to understand whether this rhetorical stance was calculated posturing or actually reflected theoretical and empirical beliefs—or perhaps took in a bit of both. The importance of this stylistic phenomenon lies in its impact upon sociologists at large, that is, on those who read, understood, and believed what Shils was offering by way of disciplinary history. His history is an uplifting and interesting one that mostly reflects what went on at Chicago and Harvard, long after both schools had lost whatever dominance they may have shared. Yet, for all this uncertainty as to the "objective" basis of Shils's account, there is much in "The Calling of Sociology" to ponder, both as well-crafted ideological statement circa 1960 and as a cautionary tale for today.

The sheer artfulness of Shils's phrases is hard to resist. For example, "So, for many years, sociology lived its life, despised and scarcely tolerated by publicists, amateurs, and professors of philosophy, economists, and students of literature." Early sociologists, taken up with defense of their methods, "spent much time in the assertion of methodological principles that received neither reinforcement nor guidance from a matrix of experience. Even in pragmatic America, the country of legendary theorylessness . . ." (1961:1407). It is pleasant to mock and poke fun along with a talented writer, as in the case, for instance, of Mencken's immortal attack on the cultural emptiness of the American South (which, it is not often remembered, he wholly withdrew a few years after he made it). Even when Shils is making free with factual detail and giving vent to political and moral opinion dressed as reliable history, it is intellectually intriguing to follow his moves—so much so that, as with any accomplished stylist, one might forget to keep up that guard that is necessary in confronting just this sort of discourse.

After some pages of background about sociology's European and American past, Shils turns abruptly to his principal concern under the subhead "Intellectual Discipline and Moral Sentiment," which could, I think, be taken as a summary description of everything he wrote. From little other than deeply held personal values comes this:

> Modern society, especially in its latest phase, is characteristically a consensual society; it is a society in which personal attachments play a greater part than in most societies in the past, in which the individual person is appreciated, in which there is concern for his well-being—not just in a veterinary sense, but as a moral personality. The humanitarianism of the present age, which extends beyond the boundaries of national societies; the growing acknowledgments as

well as demand for the moral equality of races; the welfare policies
and dreams of states; the very desire to please; the greater concern
for the claims of the living than for the claims of the dead—all of
these features of contemporary Western, and increasingly of the
modern sector of non-Western, societies disclose a concern with the
happiness of the individual human being and an appreciation of
the moral dignity of his interior life. (1961: 1410)

This verges on poetry, and shares with it a noticeable imprecision
about the way the social world works, while partaking of its ability
to stimulate enthusiasm for the conditions of life as experienced, at
least in its most desirable forms. With hindsight it almost sounds like
a segment from a talk John Kennedy could have given to an audience
of intellectuals just before being elected. There is throughout Shils's
essay, and in much of his other work on these topics, a unique merging
of insistent analytic precision with heartfelt, almost poignant moralism that seems only a little bit embarrassed at its own intensity and
lack of self-protection or wariness. Shils reminds me of Carlyle, Ma-
cauley, and Bagehot (not to mention Leo Strauss on persecution and
the art of writing (1988)) in his completely unfashionable appeal to
what the young Marx called "moral rationality."

He continues in the same vein:

> Sociology in its development runs closely parallel to this deep and
> broad flow of the river of modern life. From a distant and almost
> police-like concern with the "condition of the poor," from a concern
> with numbers as clues to national wealth and power, from a desire
> to "unmask" and discredit the hopes and fantasies of the race, soci-
> ology has advanced to a fundamental orientation—incipiently pres-
> ent in the classics, and now tentatively elaborated in the prevailing
> direction of sociological theory [i.e., Parsons]—that appreciates not
> just the animality or mechanical properties of man, but his cognitive,
> moral, and appreciative humanity. This has corresponded to the de-
> velopments, in these categories, throughout the morally and intellec-
> tually sensitive sections of the human race. Sociology is a part of this
> growth in humanity. (1961:1410–11)

There are any number of similarly extraordinary, almost fantastic
dream-wishes throughout the essay. Within four years of the essay's
publication, the United States was in the midst of the worst bout of
civil disobedience, political violence, race war, and general "legitimation crisis" that it had faced in a century. Does this mean that the
Parsons's/Shils's "general sociological theory"/"theory of action" need
not concern itself with analyzing contemporary life with any measure
of accuracy, or is it simply evidence of wishful myopia, as when Par-

sons lectured at a university then under open siege by its students, saying calmly and with the noise of violence audible from outside the hall, "There is a growing tendency toward consensus in the nation today"? If it is true that social theory speaks only for and to "the morally and intellectually sensitive sections of the human race," then the life of its writers becomes much easier, almost Oxbridge-like in its static isolation from the bustle of London and the worrisome struggles that make up most contemporary survival. Passages like those just quoted are like a rippling brook that lulls the weary hiker into a rejuvenating sleep, if only for a few moments. As such, they probably serve a good purpose. But if they are taken, as they were I think meant to be, as either an accurate portrayal of sociology's history or its prospects at the beginning of the "new frontier," then they slip from the category of social theory and institutional analysis into that of inspirational literature for the sophisticated.

Mixed with a good deal of such preachment are some very sharp observations that one did not find at the time in other theorists' work. After considering sociology's peculiar relationship to science, Shils points out an avenue of thought that until the very recent past, when it was first appropriated by young scholars, had not been in the least noticed by his colleagues.

> In purely cognitive respects, sociology could be a science like any other science, and it might well become such. Sociology is not, however, a purely cognitive undertaking. It is also a moral relationship between the human beings studied and the student of the human beings. . . . The communication of the results of research is an opinion-affecting action. . . . [This] raises a question about the appropriate forms of sociological discourse about living persons and about contemporaneous events.
>
> The logical structure of a sociological proposition might not be affected by these observations. Sociology is not only science: it is rhetoric at the same time, directed to an open situation. The rhetoric of sociology, in a very serious sense, does, however, require more circumspection than it has yet been accorded. (1961:1413)

One of the blessings of learning as wide and deep as Shils's is the ability to put entire enterprises into a perspective that more limited viewpoints cannot manage. Since he wrote this work, and especially in the last few years, the question of rhetoric in sociology and the role that it plays in the "moral relationship" between researcher and those researched has at last begun to be written about at length (see Brown 1987; Edmondson 1984; Green 1988; Sica 1986). It is not as yet a standard concern for sociologists, but it will become so as the wisdom

of Shils and later writers begins to be felt regarding the specific use of
language in communicating sociological versions of truth. When most
sociologists and their theorists begin seriously to understand that
being "scientific" does not relieve them of the responsibility to tend
their rhetorical performances carefully, much of the current malaise
that surrounds sociology will disappear. It is reasonable and probably
necessary that natural scientists cannot make themselves understood
to outsiders, so they are exempt from worrying too much about language, especially that put in verbal rather than numerical form. So
long as they have their army of eager and well-paid popularizers, their
discoveries will not get lost from public view and appreciation. We are
not, of course, in that situation at all, as Shils recognized long ago:

> It is of a piece with that phase and outlook of sociology that caused
> it to be designated as an "oppositional science." As an orientation
> more sympathetic, or at least more open, to the constitution of so-
> ciety comes to the fore, this factor will diminish. It is legitimate,
> moreover, to expect the rhetoric and mood of sociology to become
> more compassionate and less impelled by the bitterness of a disap-
> pointed rationalism in its contemplation of the poor human race.
> This too will aid in the diminution of the extraneous sources of
> strain. (1961:1425)

Shils is more concerned here with getting the chip off of sociology's
shoulder than I am, but his point about rhetorical smoothing is nevertheless correct. "Proof," which nowadays almost always takes numerical form, is not effective—even when intellectually possible—regarding sociologically interesting or important matters. It is the power of
rhetoric, the *apparent* reasonableness of arguments, that either per-
suades readers and listeners or fails to change them. I do not mean
here to subscribe to Habermas's theory of communication, but more
to the ancient tradition, such as that of Cicero who himself was not
above twisting the "objective" details of a case in order to score a
rhetorical point.

Sociological Rhetoric and the Public Sphere

Philosophy took the so-called "linguistic turn" some time ago and has
been trying ever since to evaluate its meaning. (Sociology wisely
watches from the sidelines to see what becomes of the humanities due
to this experiment.) When Gadamer claims in his major work, *Truth
and Method* (1975), that it is not we who speak language, but language that "speaks" us, and when Wittgenstein demonstrated the vir-

tual impossibility of proving anything beyond common sense when using language, then those who had for so long thought they understood and accepted Marx's eleventh thesis on Feuerbach became nonplussed. Has "interpreting" the world become in fact the only way of "changing" it? Is language that powerful, and are the more dramatic forms of social change so outmoded by McLuhan's world that words alone are left? Recently a starlet playing in a film about gang rape explained that her character insisted on a court trial where she could "tell the story," because only in language is there power of the kind she wished to exercise. This unusual screen presence took a literature degree from Yale and presumably came upon the theories of Paul de Man, Harold Bloom, or Geoffrey Hartman, whose distinct but penetrating notions of language have made their works truly important even for social theorists. The argument is similarly made that during Reagan's regime, life worsened for many people by any "objective" measure, but that his elderly reassurance created an atmosphere of comforting hope—the ubiquitous misuse of the word "hopefully" is part of this—which is more tolerable and politically acceptable than the fact-filled realism Carter offered his constituency. Words have always been more powerful than anything else in human life, but sociology does not seem lately to have thought very carefully about what its own word use and conceptual display might mean to an audience desperate for remedies but impatient of complexity and imprecision. "Facts," no matter how elegantly presented, do not "speak" for themselves.

Shils knew all of this some time ago, though he drew different conclusions from the growth of "mass culture" in the fifties than I am drawing from mass cretinization and vulgarization in the eighties. Shils's remarks in "The Calling" about social theory's utility to the inevitable process of human "self-interpretation" read now almost like a prayer. When he writes, "To be technological means to be manipulative; it means treating the events to be controlled as having no affinity with the manipulator, as being incapable of exercising rational judgment or of possessing or discriminating valid empirical knowledge" (1961:1419), one might confuse him with Marcuse, Illich, or Ellul. He speaks warmly of "intellectual, moral, and aesthetic creativity" as necessary elements of theorizing, as well as an ideal precondition for those "collective transformations" that the social order regularly achieves. He summarizes, "Thus, sociological theory is not just a theory like any other theory; it is a social relationship between the theorist and the subject matter of his theory. It is a relationship formed by the sense of affinity" (1961:1420). Of what does this "affinity" consist? Though Shils does not pursue this point—in fact, he seems overall to put forth his observations as if they reflect readily observable reality—it seems to me that affinity means, on one vital level, some common linguistic bond or sensibility. If there is truly a "mutuality inherent in the theory of action"—that is, between theorist and theorized—does not this mutuality reside for the most part in fundamental evaluations of action, probable and virtual, that are concretizations of intent? Is not intent always expressible as ideals, if one insists on their being made public? Is there any longer a "vocabulary of motive" worthy of the name?

Professional worriers have been sounding the alarum about mathematical, geographical, and scientific ignorance in the youth of today's most developed countries. I do not find these pronouncements very important. If a British youth believes that Czechoslovakia neighbors Indonesia, or an American adolescent cannot dispense with her calculator to tally the restaurant bill, these deficiencies can be corrected rapidly enough by an infusion of money into teaching, as was done when Sputnik struck. But the language that no longer means anything exact, the phrases that begin to make up public dialogue—"hopefully," "in hindsight," "at that point in time," "to the best of my recollection," and all the other perversions of speech that now make up entire dictionaries of official slang—these are more detrimental to the prospects for Janowitz's or Shils's humanitarian programs for institution building than sheer ignorance. When I asked students what the bumper-sticker, "Shit Happens," means, they grin and are unsure. I wonder to them if there is some literary or musical referent to the phrase, some advertising gambit, some connection to anything recognizably interesting or culturally meaningful. "No . . . it just means (shrug) 'shit happens' and you can't do anything about it." Where in Shils's theorizing about "collective transformation"—about the "consensual relationship" that he sees coming along nicely in those "morally and intellectually sensitive sections of the human race" who can appreciate "the moral dignity of the interior life"—does one slip in some theoretical recognition for the apparently widespread sentiment that "Shit Happens"?

Let me not be misunderstood. Any word can come into acceptability or fall out quickly enough—consider "fag" for both cigarette and homosexual, now both temporarily banned from public usage. Language is always enriched and renewed. But the question of what is in "good taste" is not at issue here. In the past—one might check the OED for a kind of documentation—words came into usage and went out, but the level of literacy itself did not decline. "Children's litera-

ture" is no longer comprehended by children—e.g., *Treasure Island,
Robinson Crusoe, Call of the Wild, Arabian Nights,* and so on—because there is too much wordplay and too many sentiments associated
with words that are no longer readily experienced or expressed, particularly among youth. If the Romantic, Victorian, and Edwardian
eras bent over double to cultivate sensibility and taste, drilling this
into their children through appropriate literature, our culture has
gone equally far in the other direction. Certain tendencies, then, and
their theoretical consequences, seem almost too clear: institution
building can be reduced in large part to verbal or linguistic or expressive rearrangements and the action they call up, and when the publicly
known intellectual stock of what is available for such "collective
transformation" falls below a certain threshold, building becomes
jeopardized. Witnessing the progressive and confused falling apart of
institutions, of the language required to keep them going, becomes an
important task of the intellectual (e.g., Bloom, Hirsch, and Jacoby).
Our truck of bricks has been hijacked, so we end with the plaint,
"What institutions? What building?"

The temptation to continue in hermeneutic dialogue with Shils is
strong. His texts, thick with acuity, are directed, for the most part, by
a moral vision that is unequaled among today's theorists, for whom, I
would imagine, his display of axiological fire and positioning seem
discomforting and almost gauche. It is hard, apparently, to be a serious scientist and think in moral terms at the same time. If our century
has taught us nothing else about instrumental versus humanitarian
knowledge, this at least has been learned.

Let us give more attention to Shils, knowing it is impossible to do
justice to his ideas here. Consider, in view of the antilinguistic condition of contemporary social life just outlined, a few other remarks that
Shils fixed deliberately into his "Calling of Sociology" (1961):

> Man's existence as a moral and rational being is a fact of a different
> order from his existence as a biological entity. Our perception of
> these properties in him is possible only through organs involving our
> own moral and rational powers. These qualities that we perceive in
> man call to the like qualities in ourselves and demand the recognition of an affinity that has ethical and political implications. . . .
>
> The numerous investigations into industrial society . . . are conducted in a radically iconoclastic mood. This iconoclasm is not
> merely the realistic dissipation of erroneous view; it is almost always
> directed against authority. There is often an overtone to the effect
> that those in authority have acted wrongly, out of incompetence,
> blindness, or disregard for the common good.

The result is an outlook that radically distrusts the inherited order of society. It is an outlook that has much to recommend it on the moral side and many intellectual achievements to its credit. It is nonetheless defective intellectually. (1421–22)

Writing of this kind suggests a comparison between Bing Crosby singing "White Christmas" and numerous popular "artists" today who practice belligerence, vulgarity, hostility, meanness, and intolerance—while promoting the same in their young audiences. Shils could argue seriously that "general sociological theory is a turning away from this preoccupation with presentness," a presentness that he characterized as "more decently integrated" than ever before, including "more mutual awareness, more perception of others, more imaginative sympathy about the states of mind and motivation of others, more fellow feeling," and, lest we not forget, "the still small, but nonetheless real and growing respect for the rights of Negroes, African and American; the increased responsiveness to the human claims of women and children" (1961:1429). It was not only from sophomoric spite that Harvard undergraduates who studied under Parsons in the early sixties—as noted by his teaching assistant (Mayhew 1982:55)—called his American society course "Every day in every way American society is getting better and better." What Shils and his friend shared was a desire for a nicer social environment, but saying does not make it so unless the sayer has an audience prone to discipleship.

The Limits and Opportunities for Sociological Rhetoric

The idea that sociology must contend with its own rhetoric, internally and externally, implies that there is a broader audience for sociological books than just the discipline itself. In the memorable past social science at large tried to speak to governing elites, the educated laity who care about such matters, and even those general masses who normally do not respond to serious books, but on occasion can be dragged into class, as it were—as for such works as *Lonely Crowd, White Collar, Organization Man, Habits of the Heart,* and a very few others. Most sociology books brought out today by highly regarded publishers are sold to libraries, and read only by other sociologists, mostly young ones trying to find their place in the academy. It is ironic that a mainstay of serious bookshops is that the biggest spenders are impoverished graduate students, not their affluent professors. Of course there are exceptions—some sociology books sell many thousands of copies, especially if adopted for classroom use—but by and large a serious book of social research or theory can expect a sale of fewer than 2,000 copies in cloth, oftentimes many fewer. When one considers the figures used to measure television audiences or film attendance, such numbers are enough to bring on pronounced skepticism regarding the "influence" sociological works might have on extradisciplinary debate. Yet sociological vocabulary and imagery, even its understated politics, have entered popular discourse over the last several decades, often via journalists.

All of this skirts the principal issue. Whether or not 50,000 people actually buy a sociological best-seller is in a sense insignificant. After all, many of these sales are through book clubs and other mass marketing devices, and the usual "laws" of commodity overconsumption apply. The real question is how many read the work, understand what they have read, and then use this knowledge to some meaningful end in their lives and the lives of those with whom they deal day to day. Naturally, social scientists at large surely hope that the literate laity, shrinking though it certainly is relative to the pretelevision period of twentieth-century life, pay more attention to the printed word and take it more to heart than most of today's college readers. There is scarcely any way of "measuring" these kinds of questions, except post facto, when it might be inferred, for instance, that perceptible changes in behavior may have somehow been connected to reading Phil Slater's *The Pursuit of Loneliness* or Paul Starr's book on American medicine.

If it is now acceptable, even laudable, for literary critics to write only for ultrasophisticates or for physicists to do the same, then surely some segment of sociology's army should be allowed to write at full bore in hope of speaking only to colleagues who have already accumulated very substantial knowledge in a given area. But others, and perhaps the vast majority, ought to tend carefully to their rhetoric so that what they have discovered about social life can quickly and easily enter public discussion, either on its own power in printed form, or bastardized through electronic means. To do this it is almost certain that some claims to rigorous science must be relaxed. If it is discovered, for instance, that the likely long-term consequence of poorly funded daycare is not good for children or their parents, this needs to be broadcast with haste and in the most persuasive manner. Scientific regimens can be saved for unread appendices in such studies, where they rightfully belong. The point is to communicate sociological findings brilliantly, even irresistibly, so that readers who are anxious for clarification of their dilemmas can turn once again with some relief to explanations provided by sociologists, and are not left to the cold embrace of television for answers to their questions.

The extraordinary German intellectual historian, Hans Blumenberg, whose life has been spent analyzing how we conceive of modernity and the scientific perceptions which condition its peculiar qualities, has recently begun also thinking about matters that pertain to my argument. In a new anthology, with the inviting title *After Philosophy: End or Transformation?* (1987), Blumenberg's chapter is "An Anthropological Approach to the Contemporary Significance of Rhetoric." It would repay close study in the context of my remarks about Shils's and Janowitz's use of language, but for the moment I will borrow only his conclusion:

> What remains as the subject matter of anthropology [or sociology] is a "human nature" that has never been "nature" and never will be. The fact that it makes its appearance in metaphorical disguise—as animal and as machine, as sedimentary layers and as stream of consciousness, in contrast to and in competition with a god—does not warrant our expecting that at the end of all creeds and all moralizing it will lie before us revealed. Man comprehends himself only by way of what he is not. It is not only his situation that is potentially metaphorical; his constitution itself already is. . . . Self-persuasion underlies all rhetoric. (1987:456)

These phrases and this way of conceptualizing are foreign to American sociology, especially its sociology of itself, even though they make good sense when applied to our rhetorical situation. One can certainly spend virtuous scholarly time writing an institutional history of the field, as has just been done for English professors (Graff 1987), and there is a great deal of useful material as well in works like Lepenies's *Between Literature and Science: The Rise of Sociology* (1988) and Bannister's *Sociology and Scientism: The American Quest for Objectivity, 1880–1940* (1987). Even so, perhaps more urgently needed and to the point are difficult-to-classify works of philosophy and literary criticism, such as Blumenberg's just mentioned, or Samuel Weber's *Institution and Interpretation* (1987), where what figures centrally are motifs and denials and rhetorical inventions rather than names, dates, locations, or ambitions neatly chronicled in the time-worn tones of court history.

Social theory and societal analysis are both species of language unusually used; that being the case, those who are concerned about their development must be as alert to their linguistic nuances as they are to the manners and talk of those social actors they are trying to interpret. The alternative is to keep pretending our field is a science and that its theory will someday be reducible to model or formula. While this charade is played out, the societies needing to be understood will continue moving into that postmodern, postverbal, post-everything realm where science will be able only to witness stochastic processes, where, in fact, the stochastic and aleatory will become the norm and the predictable a fluke—even more than is now the case. For analysis of that condition—what we might call "institution exploding"—nonscientific interpretations of convincing narrative form will do most good. Our scientific pretensions and wishes will be humbled, but the utility to ourselves and our keepers will more than compensate for this bitter loss.

References

Alexander, Jeffrey C. 1987. *Twenty Lectures: Sociological Theory Since World War II.* New York: Columbia University Press.

Bannister, Robert C. 1987. *Sociology and Scientism: The American Quest for Objectivity, 1880–1940.* Chapel Hill: University of North Carolina Press.

Blumenberg, Hans. 1987. "An Anthropological Approach to the Contemporary Significance of Rhetoric." In *After Philosophy: End or Transformation?* ed. Kenneth Baynes, et al., 429–48. Cambridge, Mass.: MIT Press.

Brown, Richard Harvey. 1987. *Society as Text: Essays on Rhetoric, Reason, and Reality.* Chicago: University of Chicago Press.

Edmondson, Ricca. 1984. *Rhetoric in Sociology.* London: Macmillan Press.

Eisenstadt, S. N., ed. 1968. *Max Weber on Charisma and Institution Building.* Chicago: University of Chicago Press.

Ellis, Bret E. 1982. *Less Than Zero.* New York: Simon and Schuster.

Gadamer, Hans-Georg. 1975. *Truth and Method.* New York: Seabury Press.

Gasché, Rodolphe. 1986. *The Tain of the Mirror: Derrida and the Philosophy of Reflection.* Cambridge: Harvard University Press.

Gouldner, Alvin. 1970. *The Coming Crisis of Western Sociology.* New York: Basic Books.

Graff, Gerald. 1987. *Professing Literature: An Institutional History.* Chicago: University of Chicago Press.

Green, Bryan S. 1988. *Literary Methods and Sociological Theory: Case Studies in Simmel and Weber.* Chicago: University of Chicago Press.

Horkheimer, Max. [1947] 1974. *The Eclipse of Reason.* New York: Seabury Press.

Jacoby, Russell. 1987. *The Last Intellectuals.* New York: Basic Books.

Janowitz, Morris. 1966. *W. I. Thomas on Social Organization and Social Personality.* Chicago: University of Chicago Press.

———. 1969. *Institution Building in Urban Education.* New York: Russell Sage Foundation.

———. 1975. "Social Theory and Social Control." *American Journal of Sociology* 81:(1)82–108.

———. 1978. *The Last Half-Century: Societal Change and Politics in America.* Chicago: University of Chicago Press.

————. 1983. *The Reconstruction of Patriotism*. Chicago: University of Chicago Press.

Kolb, David. 1986. *The Critique of Pure Modernity: Hegel, Heidegger, and After*. Chicago: University of Chicago Press.

Lepenies, Wolf. 1988. *Between Literature and Science: The Rise of Sociology*, trans. R. J. Hollingdale. Cambridge: Cambridge University Press.

Mayhew, Leon, ed. 1982. *Talcott Parsons on Institutions and Social Evolution*. Chicago: University of Chicago Press.

Shils, Edward. 1961. "The Calling of Sociology." In *Theories of Society: Foundations of Modern Social Theory*, ed. Talcott Parsons et al., 1405–48. New York: Free Press.

————. [1965] 1975. "Charisma, Order, and Status." *American Sociological Review* 30. Reissued in *Center and Periphery: Essays in Macrosociology*, 1975:256–75. Chicago: University of Chicago Press.

————. 1972. *The Intellectuals and the Powers and Other Essays*. Chicago: University of Chicago Press.

————. 1980. *The Calling of Sociology and Other Essays on the Pursuit of Learning*. Chicago: University of Chicago Press.

Sica, Alan. 1986. "Hermeneutics and Axiology: The Ethical Content of Interpretation." In *Sociological Theory in Transition*, ed. M. Wardell and S. Turner, 142–57. Boston: Allen & Unwin.

————. 1988. *Weber, Irrationality, and Social Order*. Berkeley: University of California Press.

Slater, Phil. 1970. *The Pursuit of Loneliness: American Culture at the Breaking Point*. Boston: Beacon.

Smelser, Neil, ed. 1988. "Introduction" *Handbook of Sociology*. Beverly Hills: Sage.

Starr, Paul. 1982. *The Social Transformation of American Medicine*. New York: Basic Books.

Strauss, Leo. 1988. *Persecution and the Art of Writing*. Chicago: University of Chicago Press.

Thomas, W. I., and Florian Znaniecki. 1927. *The Polish Peasant in Europe and America*. 2 vols. New York: Alfred Knopf.

Weber, Samuel. 1987. *Institution and Interpretation*. Minneapolis: University of Minnesota Press.

11

From Education to Expertise: Sociology as a "Profession"

WILLIAM BUXTON AND STEPHEN P. TURNER

The earliest exponents of "sociology" in the United States used the term to mean both "systematic knowledge of society" and "systematic reform teachings." Only in the 1890s did they feel a strong need to distinguish between the two. The first large body of empirical research on "sociological" topics was performed by bureaus of labor statistics, agencies created by the state to collect data and opinions on matters relating to the life of the laboring classes. This research was specifically understood to be an instrument of reform: the bureaus were a political concession to labor, and most of their research, which involved the first large-scale voluntary questionnaire studies undertaken in the United States, was designed to demonstrate the factual validity of the reform arguments made by the labor movement and to publicize these facts to the citizenry at large. The advocates of "social science" who formed the American Social Science Association believed that the teaching of "social science" was the main aim of social science, and the main means of reform.[1] The founder of American sociology, Lester F. Ward, wrote his systematic treatise as a demonstration of the possibility of constructing a teachable scientific doctrine of reform (Foskett 1949).

We would find these self-conceptions oddly inverted today: for us, "sociology" is a body of knowledge that, incidentally, is taught; for them, it was a public teaching that, incidentally, was a body of knowledge. They thought of this body of knowledge as "scientific," but they had in mind no special theory of science. To the extent that, for example, Ward discusses the topic of the epistemic status of social science at all, it is primarily the distinction between rational and religious or traditional, or more simply between the contrast of the

---

1. L. L. Bernard and Jessie Bernard provide the classic discussion of the edifying model and its internal conflicts as embodied in the American Social Science Association ([1943]:1965:545–607).

self-conscious, or thought-through, with the unreflective or preju-
diced.

In this chapter, our concern will be with the transformation of this
idea and its variants to the present conception of sociology as contained in such phrases as "policy science" and "knowledge utilization." The transition took place over many years and remnants of the
older model were present within sociology, and to an even greater
extent in the public image of sociology, at the beginnings of the post-
World War II era. We will concentrate on the background to the attempt, during the early postwar years, to construct a new conceptual
model of the place of sociology in relation to the state and public life,[2]
and examine in some detail the Harvard background to Talcott Parsons's conception of sociology as a "profession"—it is a ghost that
haunts present sociology, which has largely failed to become a legitimate profession and has, in addition, lost most of its older audience.
One might treat this topic entirely as a history of ideals, unrealized
ideals, for most of the thinking that went into the creation of a new
role for sociology went unactualized, or only partly actualized. The
model proved far more difficult to institutionalize and finance than
their advocates expected. But Parsons's model had some interesting
organizational successes, and gained significant support from foundations. Moreover, the model contributed an essential element to the
larger model of sociology that had emerged by Parsons's illuminating
report on the profession of 1959, on the eve of the great expansion of
sociology. The successes were impermanent nevertheless. To understand the reasons for this, one needs to understand the weaknesses
that were there from the start, and to understand them one needs to
understand what problems the model initially solved.

Edifying Sociology: The Original American Sociology and Its Audiences

The older kind of sociology promoted careers in which the tasks of
edification, the means of propagating the results of research, the
means by which the research was supported, and the theory of educ-

2. Parsons and some of the other sociologists of the era sought to integrate their
conception of the social role of the man of knowledge (to take a phrase of the title of
Florian Znaniecki's work on the subject) into their general conception of modern society. The reflexive aspect of these conceptions is perhaps the best developed feature of
the previous literature on the issue. Studies such as Alvin Gouldner's *The Coming Crisis
of Western Sociology* have, however, concentrated on the supposed "legitimating" functions of sociological theorizing in relation to the public at large. There is a sense, as we
shall see, that this was precisely the audience that they rejected. Our aim will be to

ability went together. The careers are illustrative. Ward was a government scientist, a protégé of one of the great political talents in the history of science, John Wesley Powell, whose greatest achievement was to fashion a politically popular and useful geological survey (Turner 1987). Ward began his career as an edifying reformer by serving as the editor of a freethinking journal called *The Iconoclast*. Ward had trouble finding an audience, but he was read in reformist circles and was a member of a coterie of government scientists in Washington that was itself oriented to the public and the public uses of science rather than to disciplinary or academic science. Franklin H. Giddings, a member of the next generation of sociologists, the son of a congregational minister, was a working journalist before his economic writings in the pubic press and his work for the Massachusetts Bureau of Labor Statistics and in the Cooperative Movement led to an academic position. Throughout his life as an academic, Giddings wrote as a journalist, contributing frequent editorials to the *Independent,* many of which were small gems of sociological reasoning. He also served on boards of settlement houses and related agencies, gave talks at New York public gatherings, and, during the First World War, served as a propagandist by giving a series of lectures in the South. Giddings even had a political career, serving on the New York School Board and entertaining aspirations for the position of mayor. E. A. Ross, one of the other founders of the American Sociological Society, wrote almost exclusively for "popular audiences." One of the first Chicago Ph.D.'s in sociology, Charles A. Ellwood, had himself been introduced to the idea of social science by reading R. T. Ely's Chautauqua volume; throughout his life he was a success with the heirs to this audience, including Protestant ministers, as an opponent of fundamentalism. Ellwood's books were on several occasions "book of the month" selections or alternates for major book clubs, and several of them were translated into many languages (1923, 1923a, 1929, 1938).

In each of these cases the writers were bound to the nonacademic public in crucial and direct ways. The common trait is this: in each case, most or all of the financial support of the activities came from the audiences for the activities. Reform-minded citizens supported and attended lectures and bought the books written by sociologists. Before the emergence of a textbook market in the twenties, if writers such as Giddings, Ross, or Ellwood could not communicate to a nonacademic public, they would not have been able to publish their books. This closely dependent relationship with their audience was clearly under-

---

examine the audiences they sought to put in the place of the public, and the tasks they sought to substitute for public "legitimation."

stood and accepted by the early sociologists themselves. In his editorial preface in the first volume of the *American Journal of Sociology (AJS)*, Albion Small described the demand for sociology and the purposes it was to serve in terms that derived from his mentor, Ely. An "undisciplined social self-consciousness" in the larger public, articulated in "popular philosophies of human association," had been produced by the increasing social interaction of the age (1895:2). A social "movement" that was a counterpart to these philosophies, "fostered by reflection on contemporary social conditions" (1895:2), had emerged. These "popular attempts to explain present forms of society, and to get favorably placed for effecting change in social conditions," not "schools," were the primal and continuing source for sociology.

> It is a very callow sociologist who imagines that he and his colaborers are inventing the subject matter of a new science. They are trying to perfect means of answering obtrusive questions which the ordinary man is proposing every hour. They are not creating but representing popular curiosity. Life is so much more real to the people than to the schools that the people are no sooner possessed of some of the tools of thought, and some means of observation, than they proceed to grapple with more vital questions than the scholars had raised. Hence social philosophies, popular in source, partial in content, but potent in political effect, get vogue before scholars know the terms of the conditions which these rule of thumb philosophies claim to explain. The doctrines of professional sociologists are attempts to substitute revised second thought for the hasty first thoughts composing the popular sociologies in which busy men outside the schools utter their impressions. (1895:6)

Popular intellectualizing about society, produced by the press of changed social circumstances, thus creates "a strenuous demand for authentic social philosophy" that constitutes "a summons to unique forms of service" for the academic sociologist.

The relationship between sociology and its public, in short, was defined in the first instance by the actions and intellectual needs of this public. Moreover, the verdict of men of affairs with respect to the value of its "revised second thought" of sociologists is the ultimate source of "authority" in the relevant sense, the sense of possessing power to produce practical effects in social action. To have this power, sociology needed to sustain the interest of this public by speaking its language, responding to the problems the public articulated first.[3] This

3. The *American Journal of Sociology* was conceived as a means to respond to this summons by contributing to the synthetic task implied by these conditions. It would also "attempt to translate sociology into the language of ordinary life. . . . It is not supposed essential to the scientific or even the technical character of thought that it be

conception was embodied in the way "empirical research" in early sociology was financed. In the case of the survey movement and the rural surveys done by university-based rural sociologists, the work was done largely through the donation of time and money by persons in the community in which the survey was being performed, and the persons participating in the survey both as questioners and respondents were the primary audience for the survey results. The creation of appropriate exhibitions and the recruitment of competent local professionals for help in the survey and advice as to what sorts of inquiries would be most useful or meaningful were major features of the survey movement.

The idea of a community survey is given as an exercise in Small and Vincent's Chautauqua textbook of 1894. The point of such a study is for the members of the community themselves to come to appreciate the character of their social relations. In rural sociology this was developed in special ways that involved the voluntary help of school children, who would produce a map for a county fair that would visually display the bonds between town and country, precisely the lesson the rural sociologists wished to teach *as a means* of beginning the improvement of rural life through the "socialization"—by which they meant bringing into the social life of the community—of the poor "hoe-farmer" and his family (Galpin 1920:315–55).

There were often additional sources of funds for research of this kind. *The Polish Peasant,* for example, was financed by a woman with reformist aims who wished to publicize the problems of Polish immigrants. The Russell Sage Foundation contributed heavily to community surveys. Yet these were cases where the audience for the survey and the financial sponsors overlapped. Mrs. Ethel Dummer, W. I. Thomas's angel, was a person like the person she hoped the books would enlighten on the question of Polish immigration. "Defining the situation" was understood by her as a means of reform, and a better means than the methods of traditional charity, which had in this case proven inadequate.[4] The Russell Sage leadership was composed of reform-

made up of abstractly formulated principles. On the contrary the aim of science should be to show the meaning of familiar things, not to construct for itself a kingdom for itself in which, if familiar things are admitted, they are obscured under an impenetrable disguise of artificial expression. If sociology is to be of any influence among practical men, it must be able to put its wisdom about things that interest ordinary men in a form which men of affairs will see to be true to life. That form will frequently be the one in which not theorists but men of affairs themselves view the facts concerned. These men are then the most authoritative sociologists" (1895:13–14).

4. Mrs. Dummer, a Chicago philanthropist, also underwrote Thomas's research on the "unadjusted girl" during the 1920s and supported activities of the American Sociology Society.

minded civic leaders, the top crust of the class of persons who the social surveys, such as the Pittsburgh survey, were intended to stir community action. The practice in performing these surveys was to rely on the local knowledge of members of the professional classes in the expectation that they would be affected by the survey and support the reforms it suggested. The state Bureaus of Labor Statistics of the late nineteenth century, which were the precursors to the social survey movement, provided material for the labor leaders and reformist audience that supported them politically in the state legislatures.

Such relationships were not without their constraints, some of which were hard to bear. Writers such as Ward found it difficult to find an audience for, or get much of a living out of, his sociology, and did paleobotanical work for money even after his formal retirement from the Geological Survey. Veblen's books were all published under a commonly used device by which the author guaranteed a minimum of sales: only one of his books passed the minimum. At the academic salaries of the day, these were difficult burdens. Textbook writing was a financially viable compromise, and especially in the twenties and thirties it was the primary publication outlet for sociologists. Nevertheless, this was also a form supported by its audiences (albeit the captive audiences of students in the classes that were assigned the texts), which had its own constraints, namely, the constraints of the demands of the professorial audience that selected the textbooks for use, selections themselves constrained by considerations of what the student market could bear.

These constraints were felt acutely by social scientists, many of whom, by the twenties, did not bow to them as cheerfully as Small had done. The reasons for this are not hard to discover. The ideal of sociology as a pure science had entered into the self-conception of sociologists with Giddings and his students, who did not, in fact, abandon the older task and the older audiences (and who in several cases, such as Howard Odum, were extremely effective in dealing with the larger public), but rather drew increasingly sharp lines between scientific (meaning for them quantitative) knowledge and other kinds of writing. The 1922 report of the American Political Science Association that led to the creation of the Social Science Research Council had listed five needs: time for research, clerical support for research, funds for "field work," "adequate provision . . . for the publication of results of scientific research of a type that do not possess immediate commercial value" (i.e., publication subsidies), and the education of university authorities and the public in "the necessities of political science" (Social Science Research Council 1933:1). From this point on, sociology came to be dominated by researchers whose publications and the routine research work that went into the publications were heavily subsidized, freeing them from the demands of reformer audiences.

This produced a social division that turned brutal in the late twenties and thirties. Many sociologists had retained a wider audience. Ellwood, Sorokin, and Harry Elmer Barnes were each successful "public intellectuals," to use Jacoby's term (1987), and had been as or more successful at it than his own favorite example, C. Wright Mills, ever became. They lost their struggle for the profession. The sociologists who were subsidized and wrote primarily for the narrow audience of professional sociologists wound up dominating professional sociology, and the public intellectuals, including each of these three, died as professional outcasts. But they saw that the freedom from the constraints of the older kind of relation with the public carried an intellectual and moral price—dependence on the foundations and on the networks of favor-granting and information that enabled them to gain subsidies—and they were unwilling to pay this price.[5]

The Rockefeller Era

The standard image of the history of American sociology reduces these changes in audience to incidents in the story of the "professionalization" of the discipline; the sociologists who lost are stigmatized as inadequately professional. The image is misleading, especially with respect to the lessons of the past for the present dilemmas of academic sociology. The continuities between the early edifying era to the present are important. In the first place, the public audience was a significant concern for many sociologists until well into the post–World War II period, and the authors who were involved with such organizations as the Social Science Research Council in its first decade did not aban-

---

5. Barnes left the academic world and became a newspaper columnist, until he was fired for his antiwar views at the beginning of World War II, and made a living from his books, which poured forth at a great rate on a variety of subjects. Ellwood wrote a series of articles denouncing the SSRC-funded versions of sociology as "Emasculated Sociologies" (1933) and a book attacking the philosophical premises of quantitative sociology designed to bring back the Wardian edifying sociology that SSRC sociology had supplanted. His *A History of Social Philosophy* (1938), a book club selection, concluded with a discussion of the underlying contrast between the Wardian and Sumnerian views of the possibilities of social telesis. Sorokin, who was on good terms with Ellwood, also successfully published with conventional publishing houses for the larger public. His poor relations with his peers in the discipline are legendary.

don it entirely; nor did they intend to abandon it, as the effort that went into such works as *Recent Social Trends* indicated. Two of the more prominent "edifying" ideas (of social research as a mirror for society[6] and of the need to replace ordinary ways of political and social thinking with more "scientific" modes of thought) also had a central role in the post–World War II period.[7] Only after the War was a campaign mounted against "popular" sociological writing, notably by sociologists who were foundation officials and who were concerned that too much credit was given by universities to sociologists who wrote textbooks and popular works. In the second place, the transition to a "professional" audience was itself in large part made possible by the existence of alternative means of financial support. Support, of course, was not given without strings: the demands of audiences were replaced by the demands of grantors.

In the interwar years, the subsidies that replaced the hard work of selling books and lecturing to paying audiences and summer schools derived almost entirely from Rockefeller sources, channeled through the Institute of Social and Religious Research (ISRR) in the case of Lynd and such statistically oriented sociologists as Luther Fry. The

6. The idea of sociological research as a mirror to hold to society for the purpose of edification did not disappear in the twenties. Ogburn's *Recent Social Trends* is an example of this genre on a national scale, as was *An American Dilemma*. Yet from the work of the ISRR on, one can identify some shifts in the intended audience for sociological writing. Some of the shifts are consequences of incremental developments of methods. The dissertations by F. A. Ross on school attendance (1924) and T. J. Woofter on Negro migration (1920), which introduced multivariate correlations, partialling, and the familiar multivariate regression equation, were simply not readable, at least in their statistical portions, by the untrained. Partialling became the staple of the "sociological" side of the Institute for Social and Religious Research, though the publications of the ISRR were designed to minimize the technicalities in their presentation. This kind of work could not have been supported by a wide public audience.

7. George Lundberg's famous tract, *Can Science Save Us?* was published in 1946. Even at this date, the argument for a "natural science of society" is utilitarian: "the best hope for man in his present social predicament lies in a type of social science strictly comparable to the natural sciences" (1946:35). The problem, he believed, is in the persistence of "prescientific folkways" in our modes of public social discussion and the fact that as yet "we have about such questions very little positive knowledge—verifiable generalizations—of the type that we have in the other sciences and by virtue of which they perform their marvels" (1946:7). This fact has decisive bearing on the ideal of edification: "whether education will help solve our social problems depends on the validity of what we teach. There is no doubt that much of what we teach on social subjects is worse that useless, because it consists merely of transmitting the errors, prejudices, and speculations of bygone generations. Unless knowledge is constantly tested and replenished through scientific research, education may be an enemy rather than an aid to social amelioration" (1946:7).

Social Science Research Council was the source in the case of Ogburn, Rice, Lynd, and others. Park and the Chicago School depended primarily on the Local Community Research Committee of the University of Chicago (Bulmer 1984:129–50). The sums invested in the subsidization of the work of these scholars were staggering, and it is perhaps useful to bear some of these cruder realities of finance in mind. That the transition to a professional style of empirical sociology could not have taken place without this financial support is perhaps obvious: to subsidize the efforts of research workers, particularly the persons who performed the calculations of partial and multiple regression by machine, the data collectors, or the field researchers, took professional rather than volunteer help, and this cost a great deal of money, as did the subsidization of the publication of books that the general public would not buy.

Sociologists gained this support because the persons who financed social science, in this case the Rockefeller officials, saw the social sciences as an instrument for other purposes: as useful or potentially useful. What took place in the interwar years was a long and fitful process of mutual testing and social invention in which the social sciences devised various projects and administrative devices that were presented to the foundations for their support, and the foundations selectively financed proposals and evolved new expectations based on the successes and failures of past efforts. Social scientists did not know how to satisfy the vague ideas of the foundation leadership, but they did know that some progress could be made in certain established directions, such as statistical practice, and that statistical analysis could be performed on trends or phenomena publicly regarded as problematic: the labor statisticians had taken up virtually all the same problems in the nineteenth century, and they could be taken up again with the new methods of partialling and multiple regression. Many of the changes that took place in this period were incremental changes of this sort, and were increases in scale, rather than intellectual innovations.

Despite their desire to make the social sciences "realistic," the Rockefeller officials had no interest in the "scientistic" ambitions that informed the enterprise that developed. In the early thirties they cut back drastically on funding. Many products of SSRC subsidization, such as F. Stuart Chapin's *Social Science Abstracts,* ceased to exist. The SSRC itself began to look for other ideas that would raise funds, and found Rockefeller support for the professionalization of public administration. Conventional scientistic statistical sociology had no other place to go for funding that could fully replace what the Rockefeller philanthropic efforts had provided, and over the next ten years they struggled to conceive an appropriate role. The models of funding that were eventually developed owed something both to the experience of the flush years of the late twenties and the efforts of the lean years of the late thirties. Most notable in this regard was Paul Lazarsfeld. Although he never considered himself to be a sociologist, he developed a model of social, psychologically oriented survey research that served as proprietary research for business interests.[8]

In what follows we will be concerned with a model of much broader influence, namely, that of "professional formation" developed at Harvard in the 1930s under the rubric of the "industrial hazards project." The interest of this model is in its effects: it was later refined and systematized by Talcott Parsons (another nonsociologist), and became the basis for the ideal image of the social role of the sociologist, especially in relation to the public, to financial sponsors, and to other professions.[9] As with Lazarsfeld's model of the professional survey researcher, the solution had its origins outside of sociology in the efforts of the Harvard professional schools to address the problems of the professions in dealing with a changing industrial order. In spite of its arcane origins, the idea behind Parsons's model of sociology as a profession spread or was independently arrived at and supported by others. It became a major plank in the program for sociology established in the postwar period.

The Henderson Model: Social Science as a Helper to the Professions

From 1924 to 1929, the Laura Spelman Rockefeller Memorial dispensed some $21 million for social-scientific research. The Bulmers

8. The Bureau of Applied Scientific Research had itself shifted to government support by the sixties, but the model of the relation of the researcher to the sponsor was similar. The relation was contractual, the aims negotiated with the sponsor. In each case the sponsor ordinarily had an interest in the collection of the data or its analysis that was at variance with its use as "pure science." In some sense the proprietary research model survives in the work of Lazarsfeld students such as Rossi, especially in evaluation research.

9. The Lazarsfeld model was to use a survey project in two ways: to produce a proprietary document for the business or agency that paid for the research (and was typically overcharged), and to write an academic study using the same material (together with material added to the surveys for academic purposes that the overcharging made possible). Some variation of this practice is characteristic of survey research even to the present day: when government agencies commission survey work, their aims and the reason the money is spent are systematically at variance with the aims of the sociologist who wishes to produce an academic study. The academic survey researcher re-

estimated this amount to be the equivalent of $112 million in 1980 dollars (Bulmer and Bulmer 1981:385–86). In 1930, in the twilight of the era of its most generous support for the social sciences, the Rockefeller Foundation approved a grant of $875,000 to Harvard University in support, over a seven-year period, of "a comprehensive program in industrial hazards" (Rockefeller Foundation 1930). The project was centered in the work of Elton Mayo on the "personnel problems of industry" and in that of Lawrence J. Henderson and his collaborators on "the nature and consequences of fatigue." The grant was to be administered by a newly formed "Committee on Industrial Physiology," consisting of Mayo, Henderson, biologist William Morton Wheeler, Wallace Donham, and David Edsall (deans of the business and medical schools respectively). Edsall initially served as chair, after having negotiated intensively with foundation officials to have the proposal approved.[10]

Even by the heady standards of social-scientific support established by the LSRM in the previous decade, the grant was exceedingly generous.[11] Moreover, the terms of the grant allowed for a good deal of discretion and flexibility in its deployment. Not only could the budgets of Mayo and Henderson be increased as the Committee saw fit, but the available balance of the grant (around $25,000 to $35,000 a year) could be considered as a "fluid research fund" and allocated to "such projects within the general program as may promise most important results" (Rockefeller Foundation 1930:3). Rockefeller officials and committee members had reached an understanding that this portion of the grant would be used to support Henry Murray's work in psychopathology, McFie Campbell's research on psychiatry (both as they related to Mayo's study), and for Ph.D. students in engineering working with Philip and Cecil Drinker in the area of industrial hygiene (Pearce 1929:2).[12]

---

solves the conflict by producing both kinds of results. There are, of course, other models. A classic paper by Merton and Lerner discusses the issues of sociology as a policy science in a way that parallels Parsons's discussions but focuses more directly on the practical dilemmas of the empirical researcher, who, especially in government positions, is liable to become a "bureaucratic technician" (1951).

10. Having been an active member of the Rockefeller Foundation Board, Edsall had an intimate understanding of both the criteria and the tacit procedures used for assessing proposals.

11. The $875,000 allotted to Harvard represented about one-third of the entire amount given to the social sciences in 1930 ($2,617,000) (Rockefeller Foundation 1931:1–4).

12. This fund would eventually be used to support Douglass V. Brown's research in medical economics, Lloyd Warner's study of Newburyport, and a race relations study

Given that none of its central participants were directly linked to recognized social science disciplines, why was the Industrial Hazards Project supported by the Rockefeller Foundation under the purview of its newly formed social science division?[13] Examined against the backdrop of Foundation policy at the beginning of the 1930s, their enthusiasm for the Harvard proposal can be easily understood. In some sense, it was to the Harvard group's *advantage* that its work was *not* connected to recognizable fields of social science. From the early days of Rockefeller intervention in the social sciences, including such enterprises as the Chicago Local Community Research Committee and the SSRC itself, the aim of Rockefeller officials was to break down the boundaries between the social scientific disciplines as institutionalized in American universities. By encouraging the pursuit of knowledge for its own sake—largely through individual scholarly initiative—the disciplines were an obstacle to the engaged and problem-oriented but "realistic" research the Rockefeller officials favored. While the Foundation had been, and was still willing to, support so-called basic social scientific research, this support was instrumental, aimed at increasing the "realism" of the academic social sciences. The Rockefeller strategists, however, never lost sight of their firmly held creed that the "advancement of knowledge" was not "an end in itself" but a means "to promote the well-being of mankind throughout the world."[14]

With the formation of a new social science division in 1929 (under the direction of Edmund E. Day), Rockefeller social science funding went into a period of transition in emphasis, though not fundamental change. The earlier concern to build up the foundations of social scientific inquiry was displaced by "direct support of specific research

---

of Natchez, Mississippi. This somewhat broad interpretation of industrial hazards continually placed the Committee at loggerheads with the officers of the Rockefeller Foundation, who felt that research of this kind had little bearing on industrial hazards.

13. The amount allocated to the Harvard Industrial Hazards Project was almost equal to the *total* amount ($888,000) given to five institutions for "general social science research" in 1930 (Rockefeller Foundation 1931:1). Consistent with this distribution of support, E. E. Day, director of the Social Division, expressed to Mayo his conviction "that the program constitutes one of the best prospects we have in the general field of the social sciences in this country," and he looked for "large accomplishments during the ten-year period for which the new grant provides support (Day to Mayo 1930:1).

14. These were the original words (likely penned by Frederick W. Gates) used to state the purpose of the Foundation when it obtained a charter from the state of New York in 1913 (Collier and Horowitz 1976:64–65). They have served as a continuous point of reference for policy matters throughout the life of the Foundation.

projects and programs" relevant to problems of social control.[15] The only such "recognized field of inquiry" to receive support in 1930 was "the field of hazards of economic enterprise, particularly as these relate to . . . issues of general economic stability" (Rockefeller Foundation 1930).

By virtue of its inherently practical orientation, the Industrial Hazards Project accorded well with the Foundation's interest in "the processes by which the results of research are given practical effectiveness" (Rockefeller Foundation 1931a:1). Moreover, with its concern for the problems of industrial life, the scope of the industrial hazards project was consistent with the Rockefeller Foundation's longstanding interest in the area of industrial relations (Geiger 1986). Yet the project was not approved solely because it accorded with Foundation priorities. Elton Mayo's work had been continuously supported by various Rockefeller entities since 1923, and had been almost uniformly praised by Foundation officials. Thus, his ongoing research undoubtedly provided some of the impetus for the formation of a wide-scale program in industrial hazards, rather than the other way around. This work, among all the projects that Rockefeller support had made possible during the twenties, most closely fit the original premises of Rockefeller social science support.[16] Mayo's work came to the attention of Donham and some of his colleagues, who were able to make arrangements for Mayo to come to Harvard in 1926.[17] His interests in industrial psychology fit with a number of initiatives already underway at Harvard. Upon becoming Dean of the Business School in 1919, Wallace Donham began to actively transform its approach to teaching and research by putting particular emphasis upon

15. Kohler describes how the scope for the social sciences had come to be defined by the end of the 1920s: "To increase the body of knowledge which, in the hands of competent technicians, may be expected in time to result in substantial control. To enlarge the general stock of ideas which should be in possession of all intelligent members of civilized society. To spread appreciation of the appropriateness and value of scientific methods in the solution of modern social problems" (1976:511). Issues of control became paramount in the 1930s, in all likelihood because of the deepening depression.

16. The grant to the industrial hazards project amounted to almost 90 percent of the total funding ($980,000) in the field of industrial hazards and economic stabilization for 1930. Mayo's work in the Industrial Research Department of the University of Pennsylvania received support, beginning in 1923, from John D. Rockefeller Jr.'s personal fund "as a matter of special interest." It received yearly extensions until 1926, when support for Mayo's work was taken over by the LSRM (Bulmer and Bulmer 1981:383).

17. Donham was able to convince President Lowell to approve the appointment of Elton Mayo as Professor of Industrial Sociology in conjunction with a joint fundamental study of human relations in industry (Cruikshank 1987:63).

the "case method," [18] whereby students would learn from simulated experiences with real business situations. He also came to the view that capitalism was in a crisis (see Donham 1931), which demanded better knowledge of the relations at the workplace. While Edsall had a nominal interest in workers' health and safety,[19] his standpoint in relation to occupational health was that of the corporate manager. "Hazards of industry" were not only of concern because they damage health. As Edsall affirmed in a press release, they could cause industry "very grave financial loss" and threaten its stability (Edsall 1929:1). Edsall's concern with the threat to the stability of industry posed by industrial illness was in accord with the notions of Mayo and Donham about how psychological states affected worker morale and productivity.[20]

In the midtwenties, Donham and Mayo began to realize the relevance of medical and physiological research to their efforts, and drew in a biologist and Harvard doyen, L. J. Henderson, to explore matters of common concern. Henderson was enthusiastic about Mayo's proposed work in the area of "human problems of administration," and established the fatigue laboratory at the school (as well as moving his office there) so that he could work more closely with him, in what proved to be an "important, happy, and mutually stimulating association" (Donham quoted in Cannon 1945). As Mayo began to merge his efforts with those of Henderson, Donham, Edsall, and others, he came to see their work as providing the nucleus for a major research initiative in the area of industrial relations. Along similar lines, Donham attested that the part of the business school in the project represented an extension of Mayo's work. Nevertheless, Mayo's efforts required the support of both a greater "physiological background," provided by Henderson and the medical school, as well as "industrial and social background," to be provided through the Business School (Donham to Edsall 1929:2).

The Industrial Hazards Project was an effort to demonstrate how a "collaborate [sic] attack" (Mayo 1930) of this kind could be put into

18. This had been originally developed by Harvard law professor Christopher Columbus Langdell in 1870. Having been impressed by the method during his time as a law student at Harvard, Donham sought to adapt it to the Business School curriculum.

19. He had played a significant role in the formation of the Department of Industrial Hygiene in 1919 and in the founding of the School of Public Health in 1922, where he served as dean (in addition to his Medical School deanship).

20. Mayo had observed that fatigue, as manifested in "morbid preoccupations," was attributable to imbalances between a worker's expenditure of energy and the demands of his work situation (Mayo 1929:5).

practice. Their commitment to this approach was strengthened when it was realized that the Foundation would be supportive of collective research. As Edsall reported to Mayo, upon learning (in a conversation with Edsall) of the collective approach that the Harvard group had in mind, E. E. Day "seemed very much interested in the large general scheme." Edsall went on to suggest that Day would look much more favorably upon the work of Mayo and Henderson if their contributions were "building stones in the general scheme" rather than "individual things." Accordingly, Edsall had given Day the "picture . . . of a large scheme, into which your [Mayo's] work and Henderson's fitted" (Edsall to Mayo 1929a). In the proposal he submitted to the Rockefeller Foundation the following September, Edsall took great pains to stress how the various Harvard ventures fit into a shared "general scheme." As he described his strategy in the proposal to Stanley Cobb (in an effort to explain to Cobb why he and his collaborators had not been included in the application): "I of course have to . . . stress those [areas] that I think that R.F. people will take an interest in. It has been the most difficult job I ever undertook anyway to prepare that memo. in such form as to make things hold together as an intelligent general scheme that they would think rational" (Edsall to Cobb 1929b).

Edsall's efforts were successful. Following his visit to Harvard in October of 1929, Foundation officer Raymond Pearce maintained that the "combination of work under Drinker, Mayo and Henderson properly represents as wise and complete an approach to the solution of industrial hazards as could be worked out" (Pearce, 1929:2). Similar sentiments were revealed in the Foundation resolution to allocate funding for the project: "The general program, dealing as it does with all phases of industrial hazards, is essentially unique and gives promise of highly significant contributions in a field in which scientific contributions are greatly to be desired. Liberal support of the program seems desirable until the work has passed well beyond its present experimental stages" (Rockefeller Foundation 1930:3).

The diffusion of knowledge into realms of life where it could be acted upon by professionals was an established Rockefeller method. Its earlier successes in reforming the medical profession and medical training were always present in the minds of Rockefeller officials. Supporting "social technology—or social engineering" as practiced in "schools of professional training," that is, as they embodied the "well-recognized divisions of business, law, public administration and social work," continued this idea.

Social science could have the practical effects that the Rockefeller officials wanted it to have through "professional" schools that "seek to translate the findings of the social sciences into practical techniques" and "bridge the gap between scientific research and the situations of practical life," thus helping to bring about "changes in our social institutions and social practices." In particular, these schools were thought to be of "great importance in training those who later control our economic, political and social affairs" (Rockefeller Foundation 1931a:1). The conditions at Harvard were especially favorable for training of this kind, because so many professional schools and academic departments could be potentially involved (Rockefeller Foundation 1930:1). In particular, the integration of the project's work with the Business School meant that it could potentially influence the training of future corporate leaders. Moreover, through extension activities operating through a variety of channels, business practitioners could be influenced directly.[21]

While the industrial hazards project was funded by the division of social sciences, conventional social scientific research, as it had developed in American universities, was largely absent from the project. The core of the project was Mayo's work on applied industrial psychology, supplemented by the Fatigue Lab's physiological research and insights from medicine. However, these on their own were insufficient to address the broader problems of how labor management could be brought to bear on human adjustment in industry. This task, according to Donham, "required not only Mayo's expertise in philosophy, but an economic and sociological background" (Donham to Edsall, 1929:2). But the conventional social sciences were largely dismissed by Henderson and his colleagues. "Unlike the Departments of Economics, Government, and Social Science," Henderson claimed, "we make every effort to base our work on experimental investigations and upon what is the equivalent of the clinical experience of physicians, but that, on the other hand, we aim to include that minimum of carefully constructed and cautiously limited theoretical analysis that appears to be necessary whenever men are taught by a method that is not simply apprenticeship" (Henderson 1938a:4). Henderson believed that the goal of social science education should be "the formation of social scientists, like the best physicians, skillful in both theory and practice" (1938:1). To this end, Henderson organized two courses

21. Mayo's teaching and research became the basis for a series of weekend workshops for business executives, organized and directed by Business School professor Philip Cabot, beginning in January 1935. Recruited "from the high but not the highest," the intent was to "influence those executives who would soon have greater responsibilities (Cruikshank 1987:163).

that were offered under the auspices of the Department of Sociology (of which he was an outside "member") in which those involved with the various professional initiatives were encouraged to participate. One of these, the Pareto Seminar, was first offered in 1931–32. Henderson was attracted to Pareto's conception of "residues" (sentiments or values) and "derivations" (beliefs functioning as ideologies). From the standpoint of the framework provided by clinical medicine, it would be possible to diagnose these forms of nonlogical action, thereby contributing to society's equilibrating processes.[22] According to Henderson, the professional practitioner was to act in relation to the social order in the same manner way that a physician dealt with illness. The human organism was believed to have natural healing processes that, if left to themselves, would restore the body to a state of equilibrium. In some circumstances, interventions would be needed to assist these natural healing processes. His Paretan-inspired conceptual scheme allowed one to make a diagnosis (as a prelude to intervention).[23]

Another course, Sociology 23, "Methods and Results of Certain Sociological Methods," was taught beginning in 1936–37. In this course Henderson undertook to apply the Paretan-derived schema to concrete reality. Known informally as "concrete sociology," the course consisted of a series of lectures given by persons with concrete experience of the real world. More specifically, as he later explained, "the plan of Sociology 23 contemplates the professional formation in the use of theory of all sorts of men,—social scientists of every kind as well as men of affairs" (1938:5). At the beginning of the course, Henderson outlined a conceptual framework that was supposed to provide an orientation to the concrete cases that were examined. Henderson eventually hoped to publish the introduction and the lectures, along with an appendix on various "residues" in history, as a text-

22. Although the Paretan language was distinctive, the underlying ideas themselves were not particularly original; nor was the idea that knowledge of equilibrating processes was the key to constructing an applied role for the social scientist. Giddings, for instance, had developed virtually the same line of argument in his discussion of "social telesis" (Giddings 1924:169).

23. As a recent article puts it: "Henderson's ideal of management, like Mayo's, consisted in discovering the informal organization of small work groups in the plants and redirecting their functional sentiments toward goals harmonious with the formal organization of the manager. The skilled administrator for Henderson was a kind of Hippocratic clinician who could patiently assist the natural tendencies of the social organism to restore its condition of spontaneous cooperation" (Cross and Albury 1987:182).

book of concrete sociology. The reception of this idea by publishers was lukewarm, and the project never saw print.

The failure of Henderson to find a publisher was symptomatic. Although the aim of the program was, in a sense, to edify, the audience to be edified was small, and an audience of professionals. The Cabot weekends or the case study method helped to secure reciprocity with this special audience. However, the "reciprocity" could not, realistically, include the financial support of this audience: this was necessarily subsidized edification. The conditions for such a relation between experts and the limited audience of "professionals" thus included substantial financial support. The new model was subsidized, specialized edification for audiences that would not be impressed with what Brinton described as the "preacher's tricks" (1939) of the older kind of edifying sociologist. From this we may derive a working definition of "expertise": it is edification in which the hearers are not the primary payers. The SSRC sociologists of the twenties and thirties had subsidies, but they had failed to do what Henderson did: establish a reciprocal bond with a valued audience. The successful "expert" must find a valued audience *and* secure subsidies, direct or indirect: the subsidies are needed because the audiences cannot support the "expert" through lecture fees, royalties, or similar means.

Despite Henderson's ambition and substantial Rockefeller support, the work of the industrial hazards project did not have the immediate impact upon professional and academic practice envisaged by its proponents.[24] By extension, the goals of the project (mirroring Rockefeller Foundation concerns) to bring about social control and understanding in the public sphere by way of influencing professional schools and professional training were not realized. This failure was rooted in the insularity of the project. While it pointed the way towards greater cooperation among like-minded professionals, it offered little sense of how these insights could be expressed organizationally so that foundation and state support could be routinized. Moreover, it failed to provide an ongoing basis for the mediation of its ideas to the professional strata and to the general public, with a view to generating social control. What the project lacked was a theory of how the practice of professionals could be socially organized. It fell to Henderson's most influential protégé, Talcott Parsons, to translate the thought and activities of the Industrial Hazards Project into a full-scale program of social-scientific *institutionalization*.

24. The response by publishers to "Concrete Sociology" was lukewarm, and it never saw the light of day. While its rigor was respected, it was felt to be too austere to have any sort of general appeal.

Parsons as a Henderson Protégé

Parsons not only participated in the Pareto Seminar and presented case studies in Sociology 23, but was invited by Henderson to discuss the work of Pareto with him at length, after Henderson had read a draft of *Structure of Social Action*.[25] That Henderson regarded the *Structure* as legitimating his own efforts is evident in a statement he sent to Rockefeller Foundation Director Raymond Fosdick:

> the learned study of Talcott Parsons shows that there is a clearly marked convergence of the conclusions of theorists from Hobbes to Marshall, Durkheim, Max Weber, and Pareto, upon a certain set of abstractions, concepts, or variables which seem to be adequate for the construction of a simple, modest frame of thought that can be acquired without great difficulty and used to good purpose.

He went on to say that "My introductory lectures for Sociology 23 are intended to expound this conceptual scheme. I know that it can work because I have seen it work effectively for some forty persons" (1938:4).

In developing this scheme, Parsons was indebted to Henderson.[26] In one of the papers that he presented to Sociology 23 (Parsons 1938), Parsons observed that "a profession has not only a tradition and skills, it has a 'function.' Its members perform services which are called for, having a relation to practical problems confronting other individuals in the society. Thus a function in turn implies a 'situation' to which the function is oriented. The medical function may be defined . . . as the maintenance and restoration of 'health.'" Hence, medical practice may be oriented to "the restoration of health by dealing with a given disturbance of . . . equilibrium." Along the same lines, "the sick person may be regarded as one who is out of adjustment with his normal routine of functioning" (1938:8–9).[27] Parson's conception of the relationship between the medical practitioner and the well-being of patients was virtually identical to that of Mayo and Henderson. From

25. The manuscript was referred to Henderson for critical comment, according to Parsons, "in connection with my appointment status" (Parsons, 1970:832).

26. His notion of the social system, as he later acknowledged, was influenced by Henderson's work on Pareto (Parsons [1951] 1964:vii).

27. It is evident that the meaning of function for Parsons was purposeful activity. By virtue of consistent action along these lines, the equilibrium of the social system was to be maintained. This conception is seriously at odds with the commonplace view that Parsons viewed society as a self-equilibrating organism, whose functioning was automatic. His standpoint was not that of the passive biologist, but rather the activist medical practitioner, whose interventions would ensure the health of the social system.

this foundation, Parsons began to develop an account of how institutionalized social control could be developed. Fundamental to the process of institutionalization was the "modern half" of the pattern variables (disinterestedness, universalism, functional specificity, and affective neutrality). They not only defined the patterns that controlled social action, but also served as guidelines to professional practice. In effect, by virtue of performing according to these patterns, the professions would also be contributing to the exercise of social control.[28]

Parsons's Model: The "National Morale" Phase

Wartime circumstances provided the impetus for the consolidation of this approach. Parsons was active in a number of different ventures whose intent was to contribute to the war effort.[29] He used the Henderson/Mayo schema as the basis for expanding the diagnostic skills of social analysis. The industrial morale that had been the concern of the industrial hazards researchers became embodied in "national morale"—the focal point for the initial work of Parsons and his circle of Harvard colleagues. As part of the Harvard chapter of "American Defense," a committee concerned with issues of national morale was formed. Parsons became involved in the group during the summer of 1940 upon hearing a radio address by the Chairman for Massachusetts of the national committee, Harvard President James B. Conant. He agreed to serve as the vice-chairman of the Committee on National Morale, whose members included Gordon Allport, Carl Friedrich, Edward Hartshorne, and Henry Murray. Parsons described the mandate of the group as

> doing intellectual work which might be useful for clarification of thinking and policy on problems in the field of national morale, interpreted broadly as the morale of any country involved in the present crisis. We decided that this could best be done in the form of discussion groups which would survey the field, one nation at a time, . . . and attempt in the end to formulate the results in rather comprehensive memoranda, the material of which could be put to various uses. (1941)

28. For a more detailed account of the pattern variables and their significance for Parsons's theory of professionalization, see Buxton 1985.

29. These included the National Morale Committee of American Defense—Harvard Group, The Civil Affairs Training Program, and the Enemy Branch of the Foreign Economic Administration.

After initiating discussion groups on Germany and Japan, the committee hoped to turn its attention to France and the United States.

In exploring what factors made for morale, or conversely, the conditions that placed morale in jeopardy, Parsons elaborated the Hippocratic standpoint developed by Henderson. This was particularly evident in his reflections on how a propaganda policy could be most effectively developed and implemented (Parsons [1942] 1964). He noted that "it would be surprising if the fundamental structural and functional aspects of it [institutionalization] should be confined to the one relatively narrow functional sphere of medical practice" ([1942]1964:160). On this basis, he likened the social system to a functioning organism, whose natural tendencies to heal itself could be assisted by professional intervention. In this case, the role of the Hippocratic clinician was to be played by a form of "social psychotherapy":

> Just as deliberate psychotherapy in the medical relationship is in a sense simply an extension of functional elements inherent in the structure of the role of physician, so, on the social level, the propaganda of reinforcement would be simply an extension of many of the automatic but latent functions of existing institutional patterns. ([1942] 1964:173)

In the same way that "conscious psychotherapy takes advantage of the patterning of the physician's role" to control the patient, Parsons argued, "influence on the social structure might be exerted by deliberately working 'along with' existing control mechanisms" ([1942]1964:171).

The role of the physician was taken to be the appropriate model for the application of propaganda, for "to treat propaganda policy as a kind of 'social psychotherapy' is to act directly in accordance with the essential nature of the social system" ([1942]1964:174). By affirming the presence of shared cultural norms, in a manner akin to a psychiatrist, the social scientist could thereby help integrate dissonant tendencies into the social order. It was for this reason that the proposed propaganda agency, under the tutelage of social scientists, was to be modeled upon psychotherapy ([1942]1964:174).

Parsons understood very well that this kind of propaganda was directly descended from the edifying efforts of traditional social science in the United States, for he emphasized that "the social sciences . . . have been particularly important in the diagnosis of the situation of society, the meanings of various phases of its history and of tendencies to change" ([1942]1964:165). The relationship to this traditional public was conceived in a way that inverted Small's formulation: the public was now a patient to be treated therapeutically. The role of helping the professional propagandist also provided an answer to one of the puzzles about sociology as a profession: the "functionally specific" contribution of the sociologist to the division of labor in the social sciences could include the giving of advice to propaganda agencies on the subject of sociology's special knowledge, namely, the value-orientations and norms that serve the essential well-being of the social system. Propaganda agencies were only one of the potential audiences Parsons envisioned for sociology, however, for he thought that this knowledge would be useful to other policy makers and "professionals."

These goals of sociology were to be realized in collaboration with anthropology and social psychology. The division of labor coalesced within the Committee on National Morale. The problem of morale was considered to be global, demanding a comparative analysis of how individual motivations intersected with social institutions. Given the need to determine the factors making for national morale in each particular country, the appeal of cultural anthropology was obvious. Moreover, Parsons's concern that the Committee help build national morale led him to draw on social psychology—in its applied psychotherapeutic form—for its insights into how social control could be more effectively exercised. Wartime exigencies, in this sense, provided an opportunity to use sociological analysis in such a way as to redefine the situation in terms of a more realistic and less distorted version of the liberal democratic view. What "we can 'do' about it" is, "with the backing of the defense group, to state our views and contribute our bit to getting across an acceptable definition of the situation" (1941a). Parsons's views on morale, propaganda, and social control complemented the activities of other members of the Committee on National Morale during its early years. In addition to offering a seminar in "morale research," Gordon Allport and Harry Murray produced a volume entitled *Worksheets in Morale* (Allport 1968:396). Allport also collaborated on a long article surveying the contributions of social psychology to the war effort, particularly in relation to the building of morale (Allport and Veltfort 1943). Edward Hartshorne wrote on the role of youth culture in National Socialism (1941). The Committee members did not limit their efforts to academic publication per se, but rather engaged in what Parsons described to President Conant as "a set of activities and plans in the field of the application of some aspects of social science to the war situation." The aim was to bring to bear "our own sociological knowledge of and approach to the social situation in those countries in order to clarify some of the principal factors which must underlie any intelligent practical policy." Such a "broad understanding of the 'state of the social system'" was "of great importance in such practical fields as propaganda policy, the rather general orientation of foreign policy, and perhaps most of all, the problems of post-war settlement" (1942a). As Parsons stressed to Conant, "this initiative has already born at least indirect fruit." His junior colleague and co-director of the Committee on National Morale, Edward Hartshorne, had in September 1941 joined the Psychology Division within the Office of the Coordinator of Information. As part of a shift towards the use of "comparative sociology" to provide a "general background analysis of different countries," the Psychology Division enlisted the expertise of the Harvard group on two occasions. "These two studies," according to Parsons, "have already gone far to demonstrate the possible fruitfulness of sociological and other social science techniques in an applied field in which they have not previously been utilized to any significant extent." He optimistically noted the interest of the Coordinator's Office in work of this kind (1942a).

Closely related to this initiative, in the fall of 1941, Parsons had been approached by Dr. Bartholomew Landheer of the Netherlands Information Bureau in New York. He proposed to Parsons that "a series of sociological studies of the social situation in some of the occupied countries of Europe be initiated." Subsequently, a meeting was held, attended by a group of sociologists and representatives of governments in exile from occupied countries (Netherlands, Poland, Czechoslovakia, and France). It was agreed that a study of the pre-occupation social structures of the four countries would be undertaken, to be followed by an investigation of the "social effects of military occupation." The Coordinator's office, Parsons noted, was also very interested in these proposed studies.

Parsons did not view this as mere application or as consulting work. He emphasized to Conant that it was urgent that these initiatives be integrated into the academic structure of Harvard. While faculty and students could take part in such activities on an informal basis, "if . . . funds and official status were available a very much higher order of accomplishment would clearly be possible." Parsons thought that the Rockefeller Foundation could possibly grant funding for the Occupied Countries study, if official university status for the project could be arranged, and raised the question with Conant of whether "there might not be a possibility of attempting to get a foundation grant to promote studies of this sort more generally at Harvard."

It should be clear that I am thinking of this whole problem in terms of the potential development and usefulness of some of the newer work which centers in parts of the fields of sociology, anthropology, and psychology, as distinguished from much of the traditional work done in such fields as economics and government. In addition to its potentiality of immediate usefulness in relation to the war the situation I have outlined would seem to present a favorable opportunity for promoting the development and recognition of this type of work. If an experiment along these lines were successful it might have far-reaching ramifications in academic social science. I think Harvard has here an opportunity to do some pioneering work which might well have great importance for the future of the social sciences both here and in the country at large. (1942a)

Despite Parsons's concerted efforts, the Rockefeller Foundation ultimately declined to support the kind of university-based research initiative that he had proposed. Nevertheless, support from a different quarter suddenly materialized. Harvard was chosen as one of the sites for the Civic Affairs Training Program, which was to begin operation in 1943. Its purpose was to prepare officers "for military government service in occupied territory," through the provision of instruction in military government policies and practice, the teaching of foreign languages, instruction about "certain foreign peoples," and training about how to use one's skills and knowledge effectively in foreign countries (Hyneman 1944:342).

Parsons was selected as one of the instructors in the program at Harvard, which had been designated to focus on China and the Mediterranean. According to Parsons, the training program held out the prospect for undertaking research projects along the lines he had been advocating. "Once in something like that," he confided to his former student, Kingsley Davis, "the chances for further opportunities opening up are very much better than they are in attempting to do anything from the outside" (1943b). While Parsons's task as an instructor was to impart material of relevance to the task of military administrators, he used the program as an opportunity to further refine the "comparative analysis of institutional structure," which he held to be "of great importance in fields like general foreign policy and propaganda," and "central to any proposal to administer foreign areas with a minimum of friction with the local populations" (1943a). More generally, Parsons saw the "Army program in area and language work" as providing "a great boost to the field of comparative institutions in the future." The responsibility of training "for highly practical purposes . . . ought to go quite a long way toward giving some parts of sociology a far more mature attitude and standing" (1943c).

In addition to administering and contributing to the Army training program, Parsons continued his involvement in issues related to the morale problem in Germany. In particular, he turned his attention to how German society could be transformed into a liberal democracy in the postwar period. With his emphasis upon situations as the basis for attitudes and actions, Parsons contended that one could not simply induce desired social transformations by changing the character structures of the individual members of German society. Parsons encountered this position at a "Conference on Germany After the War," where the "psychoanalytically oriented psychiatrists" in attendance suggested that if "psychiatrically oriented 'teams'" would "educate German parents to change their ways, so as to produce nonauthoritarian personalities in their children," German society would be transformed (1969:63). Consistent with his views on how the emergent social order would develop, he suggested that the most effective way to transcend National Socialism was through a "dynamic change in institutions . . . those patterns which define the essentials of the legitimately expected behavior of persons insofar as they perform *structurally important roles* in the social system" ([1945] 1964:239). A stable institutional structure would, in turn, ensure "the interlocking of so many motivational elements in support of the same goals and standards" (240).

The implied interdependence between character structure and institutions meant that "any permanent and far-reaching change in the orientation of the German people probably cannot rest on a change of character structure alone, but must also involve institutional change; otherwise institutional conditions would continue to breed the same type of character structure in new generations" (238). In effect, Parsons's recommendations for the postwar treatment of Germany drew on the insights yielded by the fusion of institutional sociology, psychotherapy, and cultural anthropology that he and his co-workers at Harvard had established.

The wartime experience of cooperation between the three fields set the stage for the formation of the Department of Social Relations in the postwar period. Parsons's strategy was complex. First, he established a functionally specific place for sociology in the division of labor in the social sciences, as exemplified in his advice on reconstruction in postwar Germany: on such matters as the systemic relations between institutional, characterological, and cultural aspects of a situation in which intervention was needed, sociology could say something distinctive about the institutional level and the interrelations between levels. Second, Parsons established a set of scholarly relationships, which mimicked the older Henderson network, between scholars in the area of social relations, and he worked to define the cognitive problems of these disciplines in relation to one another. Third, he connected this work to purposes that promised permanent subsidization. Area studies, from which the Russian Research Center benefited, proved to be one of the major funding success stories of the next twenty years, with the SSRC administering major programs, the Ford Foundation contributing massive amounts of money, and, ultimately, the federal government supporting the work. Area studies is, indeed, the archetypical domain of the "expert": virtually every expert is subsidized, and the audience is small, but highly valued—persons who must make decisions relating to the national interest. Parsons had a considerable role in the governance of the Russian Research Center, and his conceptual scheme was influential among the scholars who worked in it (see Moore [1954]1966:181). This was precisely the relationship Parsons believed should hold between pure theory and the intellectualizations of specific professional domains.

In the postwar period, the foundations proved to be highly receptive to this model. The Russell Sage Foundation trustees "declared their faith in 'experimentation and demonstration designed to bring about a closer and more effective relationship between the professions concerned with social welfare, health, and related fields, and those engaged in advancing knowledge of human behavior,'" and secured funds from the Carnegie Corporation and Ford Foundation to advance those aims (Lansing 1956:43). The "Gaither report" commissioned for the new Ford Foundation concluded that support under the heading of "Individual Behavior and Human Relations" should be directed toward "increasing the use of the knowledge of human behavior in medicine, education, law, and other professions, and by planners, administrators, and policy makers in government, business, and community affairs" (Gaither 1949:91).[30]

---

30. The continuities with the older conception are still evident in this document, however. One of the other areas of interest was the study of the causes of "man's beliefs, needs, and emotional attitudes" so that "this knowledge may be used by the individual for insight and rational conduct," a characteristic "edifying" activity involving a wide public audience. The emphasis of the report, however, is on the difficulty of foundations in applying social science knowledge "in efforts to deal with social problems" that result from the lack of "well-recognized professions with established fields of expert jurisdiction to which laymen are accustomed to defer" (Gaither 1949:114). The examples of past successful uses of "foundation aid" to deal with this lack included "the development of professional standards in such fields as medicine, education, public welfare and social service, library work, city management, psychiatry and clinical psychology, and personnel administration." Support served to "raise their standards of performance, improve their operating techniques, and increase their ability to use the resources of all types of research" (1949:115).

Funding of this kind and, later, federal funding enabled sociologists to establish themselves in medical schools. This bond with the professions, which was alien to the SSRC mode of scientization of the social sciences as practiced in the late twenties and early thirties, was the source of a great deal of federal funding for sociology in the fifties and sixties. The sales pitch was that subsidizing sociology was an indirect subsidy to the causes that sociologists served as experts. Medical sociology research, sociologists in medical schools (and basic sociology, especially methodology, that served medical social research indirectly) could thus be made the beneficiary of the desire to improve professional practice.

The Program Realized

If we leap ahead to Parsons's 1959 report on the discipline, one can see that Parsons described the professionalization of sociology in terms that were virtually identical to those that he had used in the thirties. He reiterated the key idea that the audience of sociology was not the public directly, but professionals, stressing that "it is of the highest importance to the development of sociology that its relation to a whole series of applied functions be *mediated* through the professional schools which train practitioners in these functions and which form centers for 'action research' aimed at yielding directly practical results" (1959:557).

One can also see through this text how many problems remained with the program of the professionalization of the discipline. The successes he reported were substantial: "within the last generation sociology has risen substantially in relative prestige" (1959:553). Parsons attributed this to the professionalization of the discipline in general, and specifically to the increasing differentiation of sociology from "non-scientific aspects of the general culture, such as philosophy, religion, literature and the arts" (which is to say, differentiation from activities with a large public audience that reciprocally supports them); the differentiation of sociology as a science from "practice" and the emergence of a "proper relation" to applied fields; the differentiation of sociology from other fields in the social sciences; and the "extent to which the canons of scientific adequacy and objectivity have come to be established as the working code of the profession" (1959:547).

The phrasing barely conceals an anxiety that is expressed elsewhere in the report. The anxiety is that, after all, the basis of sociology's success continues to be the concerns of the old edifying sociologists (the concern with the solution of the traditional social problems, and with what Parsons considers the "ideological" aspects of sociology), and that the successes of sociology with the wider public[31] continue to overshadow the achievements of "professional" sociology. Parsons conceded that the strengthening of sociology's position in the university and "in the world of practical affairs" corresponded temporally to an increased importance of sociology as contributor "to our society's ideological 'definition of the situation'" (1959:553). He sensed, as did Mills in *The Sociological Imagination,* published the same year, that sociology was becoming fashionable, and said that "perhaps we may say that, ideologically, a 'sociological era' has begun to emerge, following an 'economic' and, more recently, a 'psychological one'" (1959:553). He grasped that some sociological writers had successfully tapped into the "broad ideological preoccupation" with what he called "the conformity problem," and he understood that the popularity of the discipline as an undergraduate major had little to do with, and was perhaps inimical to, its "technical" pretensions (1959:554).

The vocabulary Parsons uses in discussing these issues is what Mary Douglas calls the language of purity and danger. "The emergence of sociology into a central position in the focus of ideological preoccupation means that it must serve as a primary guardian of the scientific tradition, counteracting the many tendencies to introduce biases and distortions" (Parsons 1959:555). Parsons was also practical enough to recognize that the confusion between sociology and social reform, which he treats as a problem of incomplete differentiation (1959:548), not only continued to be an essential condition for the success of sociology but was taking on ever more threatening implications as a result of its potential for breaking down the achievements of professionalism (1959:555). Keeping the interest of undergraduate students, he saw, depended on making some concessions to their unfortunately confused expectations and "ideological" concerns. The concessions he had in mind were, however, designed to separate the activity of teaching undergraduates from the profession by creating more rigid lines between types of careers in academic sociology (1959:554)—a strategy long discussed in SSRC circles.[32]

---

31. Such as those of David Riesman, whose *The Lonely Crowd* was a major publishing success in the fifties.

32. Donald Young was especially adamant that deans should not reward textbook authors, and he preferred a scientist model of propaganda for the social sciences, in which popularizers would promote and explain the achievements of researchers, thus helping to make a case to the public for funding (1948). Such a work was in fact subsidized.

Today, when these pressures, and the undergraduate audience that produced them, have largely disappeared, we may more calmly begin to reflect on the coherence of the strategy of treating sociology as a "profession," and on the idea of the "mediation" of sociology's contributions through the professional schools. It is evident today that, despite Parsons's brave talk of 1959, the idea that sociologists had taken a permanent place in the medical schools "in an organizational status parallel to that of physiologists, biochemists, biophysicists, bacteriologists, and so on" (1959:556) was in error. Sociology is in retreat in the Schools of Medicine and Public Health in which it briefly flourished, and the role of sociology in Mental Health, the area of the first and most successful inroads, is under assault even by the patients. However, sociologists are increasingly to be found in schools of business, but this is because organizational studies has increasingly become simply an alternative and largely autonomous specialization within management studies. We may take these two cases as alternative outcomes of a similar process.

Medical sociology was the product of grants; the "experts" it produced needed to establish a stable relationship with an audience of professional practitioners. This never happened, at least to the extent that was originally envisioned, and, as a consequence, funding ultimately diminished. The reasons physicians never took sociology seriously are many, but one that is of general significance in connection with the "professional" model is this: the methodologies and explanatory paradigms that proved so successful in establishing a domain for sociology in medicine, for example, by showing that certain medical outcomes were statistically associated with "social" variables, proved to be poorly adapted to the policy problems they revealed. The research paradigm of demonstrating a statistical relationship between some social attribute or socially distributed condition and some undesirable outcome, such as infant mortality, rarely pointed unambiguously to solutions. The solutions tried by well-meaning physicians and public health officials possessing this knowledge rarely were very effective: not only were the correlations between policy-mandated inputs and demonstrable outcomes often very low, but the character of the failures raised questions about the validity of the implicit causal reasoning that had motivated the policies. In most cases, there was a great deal of redundancy or overdetermination built into the "social problems" that policies sought to eliminate: eliminating one "cause" simply meant that a different "cause" would produce the same outcome. Sociologists never overcame this deficiency or successfully adapted their methods to the practical demands of the audience, and it is unclear how they could have done so—in any case, the bond between the "experts" who were created by the grants to medical sociologists and their putative audience never gelled.

Other cases are somewhat different. Sociological ideas and methods of various kinds have entered the thinking of teachers of management, and sociology has influenced the legal profession, from the "sociological jurisprudence" of the turn of the century to the critical legal studies movement of the present. The lawyers and management thinkers who were inspired by sociology kept the audiences that these ideas gained them; the kind of continuing dependence characteristic of the relation between medicine and biochemistry was not established.

The edifying impulse has not entirely disappeared in American academic sociology. But the "public" audiences that formerly supported sociologists by buying books and attending lectures, such as the Chautauqua reading groups and liberal Protestants, have changed or disappeared. The older themes of the edifiers are now subject to programs of the welfare state that produce interested "professionals" of a different kind. A few books reach a wider public—but none of them reach a public as large as the one Riesman reached in the fifties or the potboilers of Father Greeley reach today. The themes of the works that do succeed, such as Bellah's *Habits of the Heart* or the work of William J. Wilson, are the evergreen themes of race and poverty—Myrdal's topic—and the ills of American individualism, which are the same themes, with minor variations, that Riesman and Lynd took up, and that had been stressed by Giddings and Ely, veteran of the cooperative movement, and by C. J. Galpin, seeker of rural community. But the trained incapacities of disciplinary sociologists to communicate to wider audiences means that successes of this kind will become less frequent, and much less relevant to the "mainstream" of the discipline. In any case, the demand for literature of this type is not sufficient to sustain an academic discipline.

Despite the endless and intermittently successful attempt to link the "behavioral sciences" to such causes as national security, the most consistent support for the creation of a professional sociology has historically come from persons who shared the social concerns of the edifiers. The primary backers of the incorporation of the social sciences into the National Science Foundation, from Harley Kilgore to Hubert Humphrey (England 1982:54, 271), were liberal reformers.[33]

---

33. Ironically, the exception to this was Nixon, who, as vice-president, supported expansion of the social sciences in the NSF.

So there is a sense in which professional sociology was established using the moral capital that edifying sociology had accumulated. This capital is now gone, and the path to recouping it is closed; the great venture of the creation of a professional sociology was a failure, except in the realm of conventional disciplinary politics. One aim of the "professional" model was to find a way to sustain a scientific sociology, to provide it with a secure base from which to make claims for subsidies. To the extent that mainstream sociology has "succeeded" without securing this alternative base, its successes are Pyrrhic.

"Success" is obviously not an unproblematic concept. Even so, some simple reflections on the readership and patronage of sociology will suffice to show how serious the constraints on any "solution" to the problems of the discipline are, and how fragile the "institutionalization" of the discipline has been. Albion Small's journal never did what he hoped it would: despite a content that emphasized reform authors and Christian Socialists, it remained a publication with a small and also narrow readership. Odum's *Social Forces,* made possible by the massive Rockefeller support of his institute, did better with respect to the narrowness of its audience in the twenties, when it served as a sociology journal and as a journal of opinion for and about the south, earning the approbation of such literary figures as Mencken and coming under attack by the fundamentalist ministers of North Carolina. From this point on, subsidies were essential. Even the most famous literary successes of sociology, *Middletown* and *The Lonely Crowd,* were supported by John D. Rockefeller, Jr. and the Carnegie Corporation, respectively. The necessity for direct publication subsidies waned with the academic revolution of the fifties and sixties and the consequent expansion of library sales, which constituted an indirect subsidy for books that would not have been publishable had they been dependent on individual purchasers. Nevertheless, the increased costs of publication, the flood of published works, and the reduced ability of libraries to acquire have diminished this indirect subsidy. In a simple way, this underlines the dependence of sociology, as presently constituted, on patronage. The alternatives to this dependence are few.

A return to the public of an Ellwood is not feasible: the public of socially concerned liberal Protestants is no longer there, or is no longer capable of supporting the kinds of books Ellwood wrote. The conditions under which sociology must operate as an academic discipline in a modern university preclude this. The gap between what is accepted in the university as scholarship and what is accepted by the modern equivalents of Small's "men of affairs" is sufficiently large that few sociologists can successfully satisfy both[34] and, in addition, satisfy the expectations and needs of increasingly disencultured undergraduate and graduate students.

Manuscript Sources

Quoted material from archival sources has been published with permission of the Rockefeller Archive Center, the Francis A. Countway Library of Medicine, the Baker Library, and the Harvard University Archives.

BL   Manuscripts Department, Baker Library, Harvard Business School, Boston, Massachusetts. (Faculty Papers of Lawrence J. Henderson).

HUA   Harvard University Archives, Cambridge, Massachusetts. (Faculty Papers of Talcott Parsons; School of Overseas Administration Collection).

FCL   Francis A. Countway Library of Medicine, Boston, Massachusetts. (Harvard Medical School Deans' Subject File, 1899–1953, Rockefeller Gift for Industrial Physiology).

RAC   Rockefeller Archive Center, Pocantico Hills, New York. (Rockefeller Foundation Collection).

References

Allport, Gordon W. 1968. *The Person in Psychology: Selected Essays*. Boston: Beacon.
Allport, Gordon W., and Helene R. Veltfort. 1943. "The Uses of Psychology in Wartime." *Journal of Social Psychology* (S.P.S.S.I. Bulletin) 18:165–233.
Bellah, Robert, et al. 1985. *Habits of the Heart: Individualism and Commitment in American Life*. Berkeley: University of California Press.
Bernard, L. L., and Jesse Bernard. [1943]1965. *Origins of American Sociology: The Social Science Movement in the United States*. New York: Russell and Russell.
Brinton, Crane. 1939. "What's the Matter with Sociology?" *Saturday Review of Literature*, May 6.
Bulmer, Martin. 1984. *The Chicago School of Sociology: Institutionalization, Diversity, and the Rise of Sociological Research*. Chicago: University of Chicago Press.

34. The early generations of American sociologists, most visibly the generation of Odum and Ogburn, had a partial solution to this problem. They did not attempt to write "sociology" for a broader public, and divided their lives in ways that allowed them to be academic sociologists as well as reformers, public figures, and institution builders.

Bulmer, Martin, and Joan Bulmer, 1981. "Philanthropy and Social Science in the 1920's: Beardsley Ruml and the Laura Spelman Rockefeller Memorial, 1922–29." *Minerva* 19:347–407.

Buxton, William J. 1985. *Talcott Parsons and the Capitalist Nation-State.* Toronto: University of Toronto Press.

Cannon, Walter B. 1945. "Lawrence Joseph Henderson 1878–1942." *National Academy of Sciences Biographical Memoir* 23:31–58.

Collier, Peter, and David Horowitz. 1976. *The Rockefellers: An American Dynasty.* New York: Holt, Rinehart, and Winston.

Cross, Stephen J., and William Albury. 1987. "Walter B. Cannon, L. J. Henderson, and the Organic Analogy." *OSIRIS,* 2d ser., 3:165–92.

Cruikshank, Jeffrey. 1987. *A Delicate Experiment: The Harvard Business School 1908–45.* Boston: Graduate School of Business Administration, Harvard University.

Day, Edmund E. 1930. Letter to Elton Mayo. 14 May, RG 1.1, Series 200, Box 34, File 4069, RAC.

Donham, Wallace. 1929. Letter to David Edsall. 20 August. Deans' Subject File, Industrial Physiology, FCL.

———. 1931. *Business Adrift.* New York: Whittlesey House, McGraw-Hill.

Edsall, David. 1929. "Statement" (for Mr. Lamb of the [Harvard] University publicity bureau). Deans' Subject File, Industrial Physiology, FCL.

———. 1929a. Letter to Elton Mayo. 22 April. FCL.

———. 1929b. Letter to Stanley Cobb. 26 August. FCL.

Ellwood, C. A. 1923. *Christianity and Social Science: A Challenge to the Church.* New York: Macmillan.

———. 1923a. *The Reconstruction of Religion: A Sociological View.* New York: Macmillan.

———. 1929. *Man's Social Destiny in the Light of Science.* Nashville: Cokesbury.

———. 1933. "Emasculated Sociologies." *Social Science* 8:109–14.

———. 1938. *A History of Social Philosophy.* New York: Prentice-Hall.

England, J. Merton. 1982. *A Patron for Pure Science: The National Science Foundation's Formative Years, 1945–57.* Washington: National Science Foundation.

Foskett, John M. 1949. "The Frame of Reference of Ward's Dynamic Sociology." *Washington State University Research Studies* 17:35–40.

Gaither, H. Rowan. 1949. *Report of the Study for the Ford Foundation on Policy and Program.* Detroit: Ford Foundation.

Galpin, C. J. 1920. *Rural Life.* New York: Century.

Geiger, Roger L. 1986. *To Advance Knowledge: The Growth of American Research Universities, 1900–1940.* New York: Oxford University Press.

Giddings, Franklin H. 1922. *Studies in the Theory of Human Society.* New York: Macmillan.

Gouldner, Alvin. 1970. *The Coming Crisis of Western Sociology.* New York: Basic Books.

Hartshorne, Edward Y. 1941. "German Youth and the Nazi Dream of Victory." New York: America in a World of War, Pamphlet No. 12.

Henderson, Lawrence J. 1938. Statement to Rockefeller Foundation. Henderson Papers, Box 19, File 22, BL.

———. 1938a. "Draft—Committee on Industrial Physiology." Henderson Papers, Box 19, File 22, BL.

Hyneman, Charles. 1944. "The Army's Civil Affairs Training Program." *American Political Science Review* 38:342–53.

Jacoby, Russell. 1987. *The Last Intellectuals: American Culture in the Age of Academe.* New York: Basic Books.

Kohler, Robert E. 1976. "A Policy for the Advancement of Science: The Rockefeller Foundation, 1924–29." *Minerva* 16:480–515.

Lansing, Al. 1956. "He Built a Bridge from Science to Everyday Life." *Saturday Review* 39:42–43.

Lundberg, George. 1946. *Can Science Save Us?* New York: Longmans, Green.

Lynd, Robert S., and Helen Merrell Lynd. 1929. *Middletown: A Study in American Culture.* New York: Harcourt, Brace.

Mayo, Elton. 1929. "The Human Factor in Industry." Deans' Subject File, Industrial Physiology, FCL.

———. 1930. Letter to E. E. Day. 5 May. 200s, Harvard University, Industrial Hazards, 1929–30, RG 1.1, 200, Box 342, File 4069. RAC.

Merton, Robert K., and Daniel Lerner. 1951. "Social Scientists and Research Policy." In *The Policy Sciences,* ed. Daniel Lerner and Harold D. Lasswell, 282–307. Stanford: Stanford University Press.

Mills, C. Wright. 1959. *The Sociological Imagination.* New York: Oxford University Press.

Moore, Barrington. [1954] 1966. *Terror and Progress—USSR.* New York: Harper and Row.

Myrdal, Gunnar (with the assistance of Richard Sterner and Arnold Rose). *An American Dilemma: The Negro Problem and Modern Democracy.* New York: Harper.

Ogburn, William, ed. 1933. *Recent Social Trends in the United States: Report of the President's Committee on Social Trends.* New York: McGraw-Hill.

Ouchi, William G. 1981. *Theory Z: How American Business Can Meet the Japanese Challenge.* Reading, Mass.: Addison-Wesley.

Parsons, Talcott. [1937] 1968. *The Structure of Social Action.* New York: Free Press.

———. 1938. "A Sociological Study of Medical Practice." Paper Presented at Sociology 23 Seminar. Sociology 23 Lectures. Box 23, Lawrence J. Henderson Papers, BL.

———. 1941. Report of the Committee on National Morale. Parsons Papers, Correspondence and Related Papers ca. 1930–59, Box 3, HUA.

———. 1941a. Letter to Edward Hartshorne. 29 August. Parsons Papers, Correspondence and Related Papers ca. 1930–59, Box 3, HUA.

———. [1942] 1964. "Propaganda and Social Control." In *Essays in Sociological Theory,* rev. ed., 142–76. New York: Free Press.

————. 1942a. Letter to James Conant. 8 February. Parsons Papers, Correspondence and Related Papers, 1923–40, Box 15, HUA.

————. 1943a. Memorandum on a Possible Sociological Contribution to the Proposed Training for Military Administration. School of Overseas Administration, Box 2, HUA.

————. 1943b. Letter to Kingsley Davis. 21 January. Parsons Papers, Correspondence and Related Papers ca. 1930–59, Box 16, HUA.

————. 1943c. Letter to Marion Levy. 15 September. Parsons Papers, Correspondence and Related Papers ca. 1930–59, Box 13, HUA.

————. [1945] 1964. "The Problem of Controlled Institutional Change." In *Essays in Sociological Theory,* rev. ed., 238–74. New York: Free Press.

————. [1951] 1964. *The Social System.* New York: Free Press. Repub., paperback ed.

————. 1959. "Some Problems Confronting Sociology as a Profession." *American Sociological Review* 24:547–59.

————. 1969. *Politics and Social Structure.* New York: Free Press.

————. 1970. "On Building Social Systems Theory: A Personal History." *Daedalus* 99, 4:826–81.

Pearce, Richard M. 1929. Officer's Diary. 18–19 November. Visit to Harvard with Edward E. Day. 18–19 November. RG 12.1, Box 52, RAC.

Riesman, David, et al. 1950. *The Lonely Crowd.* New Haven: Yale University Press.

Rockefeller Foundation. 1930. Trustee Minute of 16 April. 200S, Harvard University, Industrial Hazards, 1929–30. RG 1.1, Series 200, Box 342, File 4069, RAC.

————. 1931. Memorandum of 22 July entitled "The Social Sciences in 1930." RG 3, Series 910, Box 2, File 12, RAC.

————. 1931a. Memorandum of 31 July entitled "Continuation of Limited Program in Support of Schools of Social Technology." In "Social Sciences—Program and Policy, August 10, 1931." RG 3, Series 910, Box 2, File 12, RAC.

Ross, Frank A. 1924. *School Attendance in 1920.* Washington, D.C.: Government Printing Office.

Small, Albion. 1895. "The Era of Sociology." *American Journal of Sociology* 1:1–15.

Small, Albion, and George Vincent. 1894. *An Introduction to the Study of Society.* New York: American Book Company.

Social Science Research Council. 1933. *Decennial Report: 1923–1933.* New York: Social Science Research Council.

Turner, Stephen. 1987. "The Survey in Nineteenth-Century American Geology: The Evolution of a Form of Patronage." *Minerva,* 25(3):282–330.

Woofter, Thomas Jackson, Jr. 1920. *Negro Migration: Changes in Rural Organization and Population of the Cotton Belt.* New York: W. D. Gray.

Young, Donald. 1948. "Limiting Factors in the Development of the Social Sciences." *Proceedings of the American Philosophical Society* 92:325–35.

Index

AAUP. *See* American Association of University Professors (AAUP)
Abrams, Philip, 166, 317
Adams, Samuel, 70
Addams, Jane, 141n, 325–26
Administration: in birth of departments, 278; contract research, 252–58; studies, 144, 182–83
Administrative Science Quarterly, 182n, 183
Adolescent Society (Coleman), 188
Adorno, Theodor, 155n, 355, 357
Affirmative action laws, 117
African studies, 142n
After Philosophy: End or Transformation? (Blumenberg), 370
Aging, studies of, 23, 120–21
AIDS, 126
Air Force, U.S., 240
AJS. See American Journal of Sociology (AJS)
Alavi, Hamsa, 181
Albury, William, 389n
Alexander, Jeffrey C., 48, 49, 156, 173, 360n
Alfred P. Sloan Foundation, 84
Allport, Gordon, 392, 394
American Anthropological Association, 149n
American Association for the Advancement of Science (AAAS), 128
American Association of University Professors (AAUP), 241, 247
American Dilemma, An (Myrdal), 10, 320–21, 331, 335, 337, 339, 340, 380n
American Economic Review, 230
American Economics Association, 141n
American Journal of Sociology (AJS), 65, 69, 376; early audience for, 376n; interdisciplinary citation patterns,

143nn, 144–47; number of articles, 230; research methodology in, 308
American Political Science Association, 141n, 378
American politics, study of, 175, 176
American Social Science Association, 373
American Society of Criminology, 307
American Sociological Association (ASA), 5, 6, 23, 307, 322, 375; and education in sociology, 129, 130, 133–34; and employment of sociologists, 117–21, 125; lobbying for research funding by, 126; membership, 99, 199, 319–20; other social sciences, relationship with, 141n, 146n, 168n, 175; Peace and War Section, 64–65, 68, 79, 85–86; on policy-making role of sociology, 33; Task Group on Graduate Education, 133–34
American Sociological Review (ASR), 65–66; interdisciplinary citation patterns, 143nn, 144–47; number of articles, 230; research methodology in, 308
American Sociological Society. *See* American Sociological Association (ASA)
American Sociologist, The, 117
American Soldier, The (Stouffer et al.), 18, 69, 71, 242, 312n, 320–21, 327
American Statistical Association, 322
Anderson, D., 303
Andreski, Stanislav, 63, 76
Angell, Robert, 76, 79
Anthropology, 327, 328, 337, 370; American values in, 47; departments of sociology and, 148, 277–79, 281–82; division of labor between sociology and, 26, 138–41, 148–58, 169, 180–81, 184, 270n; education in, contrasted with sociology education, 22, 186–88; GRE scores in, 21–22, 112,